International Economics
A European Focus

We work with leading authors to develop the strongest
educational materials in business and economics,
bringing cutting-edge thinking and best learning practice
to a global market.

Under a range of well-known imprints, including
Financial Times Prentice Hall, we craft high quality print
and electronic publications which help readers to
understand and apply their content, whether studying
or at work.

To find out more about the complete range of our
publishing please visit us on the World Wide Web at:
www.pearsoned.co.uk

International Economics

A European Focus

Barbara Ingham

Reader in Economics
University of Salford

 Prentice Hall
FINANCIAL TIMES

An imprint of **Pearson Education**
Harlow, England • London • New York • Boston • San Francisco • Toronto • Sydney • Singapore • Hong Kong
Tokyo • Seoul • Taipei • New Delhi • Cape Town • Madrid • Mexico City • Amsterdam • Munich • Paris • Milan

Pearson Education Limited

Edinburgh Gate
Harlow
Essex CM20 2JE
England

and Associated Companies throughout the world

Visit us on the World Wide Web at:
www.pearsoned.co.uk

———————————

First published 2004

© Pearson Education Limited 2004

ISBN 0 273 65507 8

British Library Cataloguing-in-Publication Data
A catalogue record for this book is available from the British Library

10 9 8 7 6 5 4 3 2 1
08 07 06 05 04

Typeset in 10/13 pt Century Book by 68
Printed by Ashford Colour Press Ltd., Gosport

The publisher's policy is to use paper manufactured from sustainable forests.

Contents

Contents

Part 2 International monetary economics

Part 3 The global economy

Foreword

This book will be a most important asset for all undergraduate students of economics and many business studies students. It is fully up to date (the discussions of strategic trade policy and ethical trade in Chapter 4, of ethical trade in Chapter 5 and of e-commerce in Chapter 15 are particularly good), without being daunting. Its four greatest virtues are its friendly and lucid approach to the student, its firm grasp of developing-country and globalisation issues, its political/historical perspective and its use of up-to-the-minute case studies. These virtues put together add up to an innovative, approachable and exciting textbook which sets itself ambitious goals and most impressively achieves them.

Paul Mosley
Professor of Economics
The University of Sheffield

Preface

Massive changes took place in the world economy in the last quarter of the twentieth century. The speed with which markets in goods, services and finance were liberalised had no historical precedent. Added to this was the rapid collapse of the Soviet empire and the growth of the new technologies which were to fuel globalisation. All this was set against the background of a world economy in which trade relative to world output was growing faster than ever before. Of course, the challenges to the world economy have also become increasingly apparent: the political implications of the growth of multinationals, environmental degradation, barriers to the free movement of people, financial crises in emerging markets, 'failing' states and international terrorism.

Changes in the international economy require appropriate changes in the subject matter of international economics. I have tried in this textbook to reflect recent developments in the world economy without in any way compromising the central components of an international economics course, which must remain rooted in classical analysis and the doctrine of comparative advantage.

The aim of the book

International economics texts customarily divide the subject into the 'trade' aspects, and the 'monetary' aspects of the subject.

Part I of this book covers material on trade theory and policy. It is centred on the proposition that by participating in international trade, countries can increase the efficiency with which they utilise resources and can reap dynamic benefits such as scale economies. International trade presents challenges as well as opportunities and these are explored. Readers are introduced to the analytical tools which will enable them to examine and discuss many different issues in the international economy.

Part II explores the basics of international monetary economics. It covers balance of payments accounting, the foreign exchange market, the exchange rate and economic policy. A further chapter is devoted to capital flows and financial crises.

Part III focuses on the institutions of the global economy, with chapters on the European Union, Europe's transition economies, and international institutions such as the IMF, the World Bank and the United Nations. There is a final chapter which covers some of the emerging issues in the international economy: electronic commerce, the digital divide, intellectual property rights, money laundering, and biotechnology and trade.

Particular strengths of the book are:

- *The European focus.* One of the main reasons for writing this text was to offer a 'European' perspective on the international economy. Although there is no shortage of quality texts on international economics, the more popular ones are written by US authors and understandably offer a view of the world economy heavily influenced by the world's most powerful nation. This text focuses instead on the world economy from the standpoint of Europe. There is also a long tradition of European economic thought which the text aims to highlight and acknowledge.
- A marked emphasis throughout on the *dynamics of trade*, which are often neglected. A chapter on trade and growth deals with the advantages of trade liberalisation and 'openness' to the world economy. Factor movements, particularly labour migration, are given special emphasis.
- A comprehensive treatment of trade policy, including the *political economy of trade protection*, social objectives, 'fair trade', and the role of the WTO.
- Clear and simple models of exchange rate determination, which are subsequently modified to reflect the *real world of foreign exchange markets*. A detailed discussion of different exchange rate regimes, including the *currency board system*.
- Explanations of first-, second-, and third-generation models of currency crises, together with a discussion of the potential role of 'early warning systems' and 'safety zones'.
- Full discussion of the principles of *economic management in the euro area*, the Stability and Growth Pact, the role of the European Central Bank, and the costs and benefits of the single currency.
- In-depth treatment of the external consequences of reform in Europe's *transition economies*, focusing on exchange rates, currency and capital markets, and EU enlargement.
- A strong emphasis on the *political and international relations* context in which trade takes place. Discussions of the role of the IMF in the world system of trade and payments. Explanation of the World Bank's comprehensive development framework, and the work of the UN *on human rights and human development*.

Who should use this book?

The book is aimed primarily at undergraduate students taking Level 2 or Level 3 courses in international economics, for which the prerequisite is an introductory course in micro- and macro-economics. As well as students specialising in economics, the book is likely to be of interest to students on business studies, management and social science programmes. Those intending to pursue postgraduate studies in international economics or international business should also find some useful foundation material, and there is a selection of recent research-based articles in the bibliography at the end of the book which has been drawn up specifically with their needs in mind. Finally, I hope that the general reader with an interest in current international issues will also find the material stimulating and rewarding.

Distinctive features

- *Clear style.* The material is presented in an accessible way with a strong narrative quality. Economic analysis is sound, without over-reliance on theoretical formalism. There is an introduction and list of objectives at the beginning of each chapter, plus chapter summaries, key concepts and questions for discussion at the end of each chapter.

- *Case studies.* Most of the chapters contain case studies, suitable for seminars, class discussions or individual reflection. A commentary is provided for each case study, linked to the appropriate material within the text.

- *Research-based learning.* The material has been extensively 'class tested'. It incorporates, wherever possible, the latest research findings. Reference is made, in particular, to World Bank and IMF-sponsored research, which is readily accessible on the internet.

- *Geometric appendix.* An optional appendix, Appendix A, introduces students to the offer curve, the box diagram and the contract curve. The text sets out clearly the reasons why geometric techniques are important as a pedagogic device in the pure theory of trade.

- *Web material.* Appendix B draws the student's attention to the wide range of statistical research and other useful materials available via the internet. There is a list of appropriate sites, together with guidance on accessing them.

- *Website.* The textbook is supported by its own website at **www.booksites. net/ingham,** which is regularly updated.

Acknowledgements

Among the many individuals and institutions to whom I owe a debt, I would like to mention a long-standing colleague, Dr E.W. Brasslof, and his work in international economics with Sidney J. Wells. The issues which they explored in an earlier international economics text, in particular the role of classical political economy, the significance of location decisions and the centrality of European integration after 1945, remain highly relevant to the discipline. I also owe a deep debt to Hla Myint, whose lectures and writings on classical trade theory were the inspiration for a continuing interest in the dynamics of trade.

I am grateful to the following for permission to reproduce copyright material:

Figure 2.2 adapted from 'Productivity and export ratios for sales of textiles and motor vehicles – US and UK workers', *Economic Journal*, Dec. 1951 and Sept. 1962 (MacDougall, G. D. A., 1951 and 1962); Table 3.1 from 'International trade theory: the evidence', pp. 1339–95 (Leamer, E. and Levinsohn, J., 1995), Figure 3.2 adapted from 'West German trade 1985' (Leamer, E., 1995), and Figure 4.4 adapted from 'Political economy of trade policy' (Rodrick, D., 1995), reprinted from Grossman, G. M., and Rogoff, K. (eds) *Handbook of International Economics*, Vol. 3, © 1995 with permission from Elsevier; Table 4.1 from *Tariffs Pre-and-Post Uruguay Round (Industrial Countries)*, republished with permission of the World Trade Organization; Table 6.1 adapted from *Economic Development and Cultural Change*, pp. 523–43, University of Chicago Press (Dollar, D., 1992) and Figure 7.1 from *Journal of Political Economy*, 102(2), 95–371 (Taylor, A. M. and Williamson, J. G., 1994), reprinted by the publisher The University of Chicago Press; Tables 7.1, 8.1, 8.2, 8.3, 8.4, 8.5, 8.6, 8.7, 13.1 and Figure 8.3 from UK Government statistics, various years: Crown Copyright material is produced with the permission of the Controller of HMSO and the Queen's Printer for Scotland; Table 8.10 from *Geographical Breakdown of Euro Area Trade in Goods (2001 Euro billions)*, Table 8.11 from *Financial Account of the Euro Area January–July (2001 Euro billions)*, Table 8.12 from *Net International Investment Position of the Euro Area (Euro billions – ECU billions in 1997)*, Table 9.4 from *Effective Exchange Rate of the Euro*, Table 12.1 from 'Central Banks in the Euro Area, the United Kingdom, the United States and Japan', *ECB Monthly Bulletin*, Nov. 2002, Table 12.2 from *ECB Annual Report* (2001), Table 12.3 from *Fiscal Positions in the Euro Area (2000–2001)*, and Table 12.4 from *Unemployment in the Euro Area (ECB Statistics)*, Figure 7.2 from *Euro Area Merger & Acquisition Investment Abroad (1998–2002)*, Figure 9.2 from *Repo Turnover Relative to Foreign Exchange Swaps in the Euro Area (1998–2001)*, Figure 9.5 from *Effective Exchange Rates of the Euro, the Dollar, and the Japanese Yen*, Figure 9.6 from *Financial Flows Between US and the Euro Area, (1995–2002)*, republished with permission of the European Central

Bank; Figure 11.1 adapted from *Global Development Finance, 1999*, World Bank; Table 13.2 and Table 13.3 adapted from *Escaping the Under-Reform Trap, International Monetary Fund Staff Papers*, Vol. 48 (Special Edition), pp. 88–108 (Aslund, A., Boon, P., and Johnson, S., 2001), Figure 7.3 from *FDI Flows in Central and Eastern Europe*, Figure 13.2 adapted from *What Moves Capital to Transition Economies*, Vol. 48 (Special Edition), pp. 109–45 (Garibaldi, P. *et al.* 2001) Washington DC: International Monetary Fund; Tables 13.4, 13.5, 13.6, 14.4, 15.1, 15.3, and Figures 15.1, 15.2 and 15.3 from *Human Development Report 2001* (UNDP, 2001), Oxford University Press; and Figure 15.4 adapted from *Biotechnology: The Making of a Global Controversy*, Cambridge University Press (Bauer, M. W. and Gaskell, G., 2002). I am grateful to WIPO for permission to reproduce 'An anti-piracy program for Africa's music industry' published in *WIPO Magazine* July–September 2002, p. 10; this document originally provided by the World Intellectual Property Organization (WIPO), the owner of the copyright. The Secretariat of WIPO assumes no liability or responsibility with regard to the transformation or translation of this data.

I am also grateful to the Financial Times Limited for permission to reprint the following material:

Case Study 3.1 In the industry biosphere, only the strong survive, © *Financial Times*, 7 August 2002; Case Study 3.2 Questions raised about the Cisco club, © *Financial Times*, 7 October 2002; Case Study 4.1 Brazil warns US on free trade pact, © *Financial Times*, 7 August 2002; Case Study 4.2 Clouds over US wheat farmers, © *Financial Times*, 26 September 2002; Case Study 5.1 A good deal on trade, © *Financial Times*, 29 July 2002; Case Study 6.1 Waiting patiently for the single regional market, © *Financial Times*, 6 September 2002; Case Study 7.1 Investment going east boosts EU integration drive, © *Financial Times*, 31 October 2002; Case Study 7.2 Central and eastern Europeans already sampling life in EU, © *Financial Times*, 24 July 2002; Figure 7.4 European migrants (% by region), 2000, © *Financial Times*, 24 July 2002; Figure 7.5 Migrant labour in selected European economies, © *Financial Times*, 24 July 2002; Case Study 9.1 Dollar falls (Market Report), © *Financial Times*, 10 November 2002; Case Study 9.2 A difficult week for the US, © *Financial Times*, 16 October 2002; Table 9.7 New international bond issues, © *Financial Times*, 7 November 2002; Case Study 10.1 Weak dollar hits Hyundai figures, © *Financial Times*, 15 November 2002; Case Study 10.2 Zimbabwe tightens exchange controls amid economic gloom, © *Financial Times*, 15 November 2002; Case Study 11.1 Spanish investors worry about exposure to Brazil, © *Financial Times*, 29 July 2002; Case Study 12.1 City warns EU over single financial market, © *Financial Times*, 25 November 2002; Case Study 12.2 Economists rake over coals of ejection from ERM, © *Financial Times*, 16 September 2002; Case Study 12.3 Single currency 'boosts eurozone trade', © *Financial Times*, 9 September 2002; Case Study 12.4 Spain sets eurozone example with second balanced budget, © *Financial Times*, 26 September 2002; Case Study 12.5 Structural problems run deep, © *Financial Times*, 25 November 2002; Case Study 13.1 Viewpoint (Irina Kryachuk), © *Financial Times*, 10 November 1999; Case Study 13.2 Foreigners remain on the sidelines despite market's strong performance, © *Financial Times*,

16 September 2002; Case Study 13.3 Poland seeks more EU compensation, © *Financial Times*, 27 September 2002; Case Study 14.1 IMF's favourite sons could spell trouble for their parents, © *Financial Times*, 16 August 2002; Case Study 14.2 Debt relief plan missing targets says IMF study, © *Financial Times*, 6 September 2002; and Case Study 15.2 Netherlands acts against re-sold Aids drugs, © *Financial Times*, 3 October 2002.

In some instances we have been unable to trace the owners of copyright material, and we would appreciate any information that would enable us to do so.

Chapter 1

Introduction and overview

Why international economics?

International Economics is the application of economic theory to situations in which countries are closely connected, through the exchange of goods and services, or through some other type of economic relationship, such as that between a creditor country and a debtor country. International economics is concerned with the interrelationships and interdependencies between national economies.

Paul Samuelson, Nobel prizewinner and one of the foremost economists in the world today, has written that no complete understanding of any modern economy is possible without a thorough grounding in international economics. International economics illuminates the interaction between domestic economic events, and important changes in the world economy. Samuelson himself has made important theoretical contributions to the pure theory of trade. He joins a long line of distinguished economists, going back to Adam Smith, the founder of modern economics, who believed that the international economy is where economics begins.

Does the international economy call for any special economic theory? Or can it be treated using the general principles of economics? Writing in the 1930s, the economist Gottfried Haberler stated that international economics requires only the application of general economic theory.

> It is the individual economic subject who buys and sells, pays and is paid, grants and receives loans, and, in short, carries on the activities which, taken as a whole, constitute international trade. It is not, for example, Germany and England, but individuals or firms located in Germany and England who carry on trade with one another.
>
> *The Theory of International Trade* (1936)

An important feature which distinguishes 'national' from 'international' transactions is factor mobility. The classical economists Adam Smith and David Ricardo, writing in the late eighteenth and early nineteenth centuries, believed that although labour and capital moved freely within countries, from one region to another and from one occupation to another, factors of production between different countries were highly immobile. If factors are immobile internationally then international exchange will follow different economic 'laws' from purely domestic transactions.

Of course the classical writers did not believe that capital and labour were completely immobile between countries. Factor mobility as a distinguishing feature of international economics is very much a matter of degree. Adam Smith recognised the significance and far-reaching effects of labour emigration. And in today's international environment factor mobility between countries is often very great. Labour, capital, managerial skills and technology move freely between countries, often through the medium of the multinational company.

Factor mobility is not the only feature which distinguishes 'international' economics. A striking characteristic of international exchange in everyday life is that it usually involves a foreign currency transaction. Goods, services and assets are priced in the currency of their country of origin. To make exchange possible prices are translated into the currency of the trading partner. Rates of exchange between different currencies alter on a daily, even on an hourly, basis. This is a source of change in the relative prices of goods and services internationally which is not experienced within the domestic economy.

Each of the twelve euro area countries today mints a different euro coin. Though the faces of euros are identical regardless of where they are minted, the reverse carries a national image from the country which mints the coin. Because euros exchange on a one-to-one basis, consumers and firms within the euro area are quite indifferent as to whether they receive a German-minted euro, or a French-minted euro, or any other euro, in exchange for goods and services. Euros are acceptable on a one-to-one basis for transactions within the euro area irrespective of where they are minted. But when US goods, services and assets are bought by European residents, euros must be converted into dollars, with all the price and risk elements that this implies. Where the relative values of currencies can change, it is a matter of great significance that one country's currency differs from another.

In addition to separate currencies, each country may have its own financial markets, and set of interest rates, to reconcile the demand for money in the economy with the supply of money as determined by the monetary authorities. As a further complication, differences in interest rates between countries mean different regimes of *monetary management*. This may lead to massive flows of financial capital between countries in response to interest rate differentials. Countries may also have different approaches to government taxation and spending. Different fiscal regimes can affect the level and direction of international transactions. A country which decides to raise revenue by taxing imports, for example, significantly alters its economic relationship with its trading partners.

Finally, international economics may be distinguished by the close connection it has with political science. Traditionally, economics as a discipline has been concerned with individual choice, how the consumer allocates income between competing wants, or how producers allocate resources between competing end uses. Political economy, on the other hand, is about the values and choices a society makes, and the various influences upon those choices.

From its beginnings, international economics had a strong element of political economy. The classical writers, Smith and Ricardo, whose theories are central to international economics, believed themselves to be operating in the sphere of political economy: the art of persuading the government of the day of the benefits of free trade against the sectional interests of the landowning classes. In the present day, powerful multinational companies put great effort into persuading governments to deliver the type of international environment which they believe is necessary for their enterprises to flourish. This fusion of economic analysis with economic policy, and with foreign policy and international relations, is very much a distinguishing feature of international economics. In practice, the nation state has always transcended the individual sum of its parts – those millions of choices made by individual producers and consumers.

Why a European focus?

Most international economics textbooks which have been published since the 1960s originate in the United States, and focus on the place of the US in the international economy. These texts are almost without exception authoritative and stimulating, and some, such as Charles Kindleberger's *International Economics*, are classics in their own right. But none have a significant European dimension, and this can be a drawback because Europe is much more than a collection of individual countries. Despite very real differences in nationality, derived from divergent historical experiences, European economies have a shared inheritance which has contributed to their distinctive role in the world economy.

Classical liberalism which forms the basis of the economists' doctrine of free trade, dominated the international scene before 1914. The pure theory of trade, which is central to Part 1 of this book, was spearheaded by the major European thinkers: Jevons in England, Menger in Austria and Walras in Switzerland. Many of the significant contributions in international economics have been part of the European intellectual mainstream: the Heckscher–Ohlin factor proportions model, Haberler's opportunity cost exposition of comparative advantage, Burenstam–Linder's demand-based trade model, Gustav Cassel's purchasing-power parity theory.

Historically, too, Europe has a cohesion within the world economy. For the past two hundred years the countries of Europe have been economically interdependent and interrelated. Events in one country are quickly reflected in neighbouring states. After 1945 Europe split into the 'social democracies' of the west and the 'people's democracies' of the east, but the experience of Europe's transition economies since 1989, when the Berlin Wall came down, would tend to suggest that the divisions between the two halves of Europe have not run deep. There are no irreconcilable economic differences. All of the countries of central and eastern Europe now aspire to membership of the European Union and the euro area. European economic integration has been a long process which began with the European Coal and Steel Community in 1950 and culminated in the launch of the euro in 1999. The evolution of the

EU single market and the establishment of the euro provide compelling reasons for highlighting Europe's role within the international economy in the twenty-first century.

Overview

The text is divided into three parts:

Part 1   Trade theory and policy
Part 2   International monetary economics
Part 3   The global economy.

Part 1, which comprises Chapters 2 to 7, covers the theory of trade, developments in the theory of trade, 'old' and 'new' arguments for trade protection, international trade policy, the WTO, the dynamics of trade and growth and international factor mobility.

Part 2, which comprises Chapters 8 to 11, deals with the balance of payments of the UK and the euro area, foreign exchange markets, exchange rates and economic policy, capital flows and financial crises.

Part 3 consists of Chapters 12 to 15. Chapters 12 and 13 focus on Europe, both the EU and Europe's transition economies. Chapter 14 deals with international institutions: the IMF, the World Bank and the United Nations. Chapter 15 looks at new issues in the international economy, including electronic commerce, intellectual property protection, money laundering, biotechnology and trade.

There are separate appendices on the geometry of trade (Appendix A) and on the use of internet sources (Appendix B).

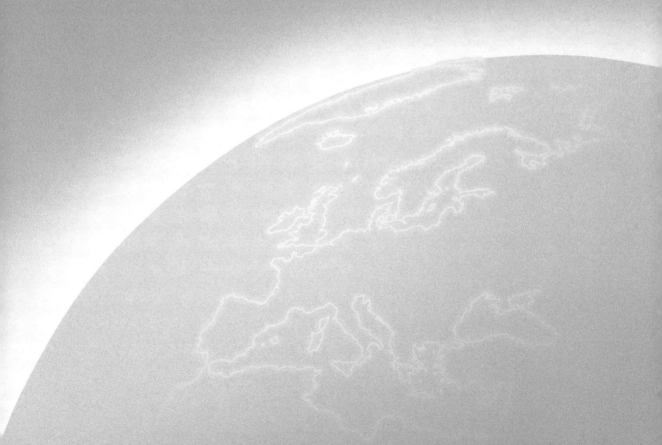

Part 1

Trade theory and policy

Chapter 2

The theory of trade

Introduction

The theory of trade has a central place in economic analysis, and underpins the doctrine of free trade. Free trade doctrines have a long and fascinating history in Europe. In 1846 Britain repealed the Corn Laws, an historic event which marked the start of the era of free international trade, and lasted until the great depression of the 1870s. The Corn Laws were the duties on imports of grain, which had been in force in England since the middle of the fifteenth century. Other European countries had similar taxes: France, Sweden, Bavaria, Belgium and Holland.

The reasoning behind the Corn Laws was as follows. Grain, chiefly wheat, is a staple foodstuff, especially important in the diets of labouring people. But its price varies greatly from year to year, depending on the size and quality of harvests. Duties on imports were levied on a sliding scale in order to stabilise the price of wheat. When the domestic price was high because of a poor harvest, duties were lowered to permit imports. When the domestic price was low because of a bumper harvest, import duties were raised.

In the decades leading up to the repeal of the Corn Laws in Britain, the system had fallen into disrepute. In fact the sliding scale of duties was tending to increase rather than reduce fluctuations in the price of wheat. When the domestic price was high, traders tended to withhold supply to raise the price even further. They anticipated that import duties would soon be lowered, which was in fact what tended to happen. Then, when duties fell, traders began to import large quantities of grain. As supply rapidly increased, and prices fell dramatically, import duties were quickly increased. The net effect was to amplify market fluctuations through speculation, making a vulnerable market even more unstable, much to the detriment of consumers.

The Corn Laws had another important effect. They benefited agricultural interests at the expense of the newly emerging manufacturing sectors. High prices of grain, maintained through restricting foreign supply, increased the value of land. Landowners, understandably, came to constitute an important pressure group for the maintenance of the Corn Laws. Against these landed interests were ranged the burgeoning manufacturing classes. In Britain, the opposition to the Corn Laws centred on Manchester, the home of the textile industry. The 'free traders' as they were called, believed that lower grain prices were needed so that the labouring classes in industrial areas would have access to cheap foodstuffs. Led by Cobden, formerly a manufacturer, the free traders argued for the opening-up of British markets to cheap grain imports from overseas. Manufacturers were also anxious that free trade principles should be reciprocated in other countries, so that foreign markets would be opened up to exports of cheap manufactured goods from Britain.

In Britain free trade principles eventually triumphed. In the twentieth century, with the important exception of the period 1918 to 1939, free trade principles also came to dominate the world economy. In this chapter we explore the economic principles which underpinned the doctrine of free trade, a doctrine which is arguably one of the most robust of any in present-day economics. Chapter 2 starts with the mercantilist thinking which pre-dates the free trade era, and passes on to the writings of Adam Smith and David Ricardo, which formed the basis of the case for free trade. These principles were reinterpreted in terms of modern economics by the economist Haberler in the 1930s.

Finally, a word of warning – the theory of comparative cost, on which everything in this chapter rests, is deceptively simple! In 1996, the world-famous US economist Paul Krugman came to Manchester, UK, to give a paper to mark the 150 years which had elapsed since the repeal of the Corn Laws. He entitled his address 'Ricardo's Difficult Idea: Why Intellectuals Don't Understand Comparative Advantage'. In it he made clear that intelligent people who read, and even those who write about world trade, often fail to grasp the idea of comparative advantage. The aim of this chapter is to ensure that you fully understand the basis of the theory of trade.

Objectives

When you have completed this chapter, you should be able to:

- outline the key features which distinguish *mercantilist* economic thinking;
- show how Adam Smith's theory of *absolute advantage*, in the book *Wealth of Nations*, broke with the mercantilist tradition;
- define *absolute* and *comparative advantage* and show how they constitute a *basis for trade*;
- understand the theory of comparative advantage when it is stated in terms of the modern concept of *opportunity cost*;
- describe how *factor endowments* may constitute an explanation of the basis of trade;
- know the results of *formal testing* of the *Ricardian* and *Heckscher–Ohlin* models of trade;
- relate your knowledge of the theory of trade to *real world trade patterns* in the nineteenth and early twentieth centuries.

Mercantilism

The theory of trade is part of the classical liberal tradition of economic thought. Classical liberalism is often described as the dominant ideology of capitalism. It is associated with the industrialisation of western Europe, a process which began in the eighteenth century.

Mercantilist economic thinking is a philosophy of political economy which pre-dates classical liberalism. It was characteristic of economic thinking in Europe from the late Middle Ages through to the sixteenth and seventeenth centuries.

It is important to understand the key principles of mercantilist thinking because mercantilist ideas lingered on in international trade even when they had been largely discredited in the domestic context. Indeed in the present day there are many who are still wedded to certain mercantilist philosophies in the international economy, and advocate protectionist policies in foreign trade which might be described as 'neo-mercantilist'.

Mercantilism emerged in the period between 1300 and 1500, when Europe was experiencing an acute shortage of gold and silver bullion for use as money in domestic and international transactions. Trade was growing but the money supply could not keep pace. To ensure sufficient bullion to meet the rising needs of commerce, monarchs and their advisers discouraged imports of goods since an excess of imports over exports required the export of gold and silver in payment for imports. By the same token, every effort was made to expand exports of goods, since exports would draw in gold and silver from abroad and thus increase the domestic money supply. Of course, since one country's exports are another's imports, this could never be a recipe for harmonious international relations. All countries could not enjoy the benefits of an export surplus!

The following features characterised the mercantilist system as it operated in Europe in the centuries before the rise of free trade:

● Extensive *regulation of imports and exports*. Some imports were prohibited altogether, others were subjected to high rates of import duty. In England the Navigation Acts of 1651 and 1660 aimed to exclude foreign ships from both the import and export trade. Even the export of raw materials (wool, for example) from England was restricted in order to keep input prices low and make the finished product (textiles) more profitable in foreign and domestic markets.

● *Trade monopolies* flourished. Governments permitted one merchant (or a group of merchants acting together) to operate in domestic and foreign markets. This meant that merchants could sell goods abroad at high prices because there was no price competition among sellers. Merchant capitalists with monopoly power dominated economic activity in England, France, Spain, Belgium and Holland.

● *Smuggling* flourished. Large profits could be made by traders who were willing to import or export prohibited goods. Smuggling of bullion was especially profitable. Most of the gold from South America flowed into Spain. In Spain there were severe penalties, including death, for merchants who smuggled bullion out of the country. Nevertheless, large quantities of Spanish bullion found its way into all parts of Europe.

● There were significant incentives for European governments to establish *colonial empires.* England France, Holland, Belgium and Spain established colonies. Colonies enabled the metropolitan country to control trade with weaker countries. The colony was required to provide cheap raw materials for manufacturers in the metropolitan countries. Colonies also provided protected markets for a home country's manufactured exports.

Even when bullion supplies to Europe increased in the mid-sixteenth century, mercantilist restrictions on international commerce remained. This was because it was widely believed that tariffs were a good way to increase domestic output and employment, and to boost the power of the monarch. Tariffs were a source of revenue for the monarch out of which the army and navy and huge state bureaucracies could be paid. Import restrictions, it was believed, stimulated domestic manufacturing by keeping out foreign competition. To this end there were in place wide-ranging domestic regulations covering manufacturing and commerce. These included patents and monopoly rights, statutes governing apprenticeships, maximum wage rates, and tax exemptions and subsidies.

From the seventeenth century onwards, however, it became increasingly apparent that regulations imposed on domestic output and employment, together with restrictions on international trade, were hindering the growth of enterprise. Writers such as Dudley North (1641–91) argued that economies would flourish only if restrictive laws which bestowed special privileges were removed. By the beginning of the eighteenth century there was a growing recognition, even in mercantilist writings, that emerging capitalists needed greater freedom to pursue profitable investment opportunities. This was the background against which Adam Smith published the path-breaking book *Wealth of Nations* in 1776, which is universally regarded as the foundation of modern market economics, and is the starting point for the theory of trade.

Adam Smith and absolute advantage

Adam Smith was a Scotsman, born in 1723, the son of a Scottish Judge Advocate and Comptroller of Customs. He became Professor of Logic and then of Moral Philosophy in the University of Glasgow. This was followed by travels in France as tutor to the young Duke of Buccleuch, with a final appointment as Commissioner of Customs, which he held until his death in 1790. Smith can justifiably be described as the first professional economist! He was also thoroughly familiar with the practicalities of trade and tariffs.

Smith's *Wealth of Nations* has been described as the most profound intellectual achievement of classical liberalism. It was conceived as an attack on what Smith called the mercantile system. The basis of Smith's criticism of mercantilism was that it enabled certain merchants to enrich themselves by exploiting monopoly concessions and other 'extraordinary privileges'. Such activities did not enhance the material welfare of society. Regulations governing foreign trade, such as bounties, monopoly grants and restrictive trade treaties, though they secured a large stock of bullion and a favourable trade balance, and may have enriched individual merchants, nevertheless conferred no general benefit on society.

What Smith favoured was a free market where hard work, enterprise and thrift would be rewarded. In a free market, without state regulation, monopoly and privilege, entrepreneurs would be encouraged to behave in a competitive, efficient and dynamic manner. In pursuing profit they would contribute to the wider social interest. They would be rewarded for doing things which added to the welfare of society, not for actions that diminished the common good.

Specialisation and exchange

Adam Smith observed that the division of labour increases productivity and wealth. As individuals specialise in certain activities they become more skilful and productive. But they also become more dependent on others for their needs. Specialisation therefore implies exchange 'where every man may purchase whatever part of the produce of other men's talents he has occasion for' (*Wealth of Nations*, book I).

Specialisation and exchange enable everyone in a community to benefit by purchasing goods and services from low-cost sources of supply. According to Smith, it is 'the maxim of every prudent master of a family, never to attempt to make at home what it will cost him more to make than to buy'. Smith then extended this principle into the sphere of foreign trade: 'What is prudence in the conduct of every private family, can scarce be folly in that of a great kingdom.' If commodities could be purchased abroad more cheaply than they could be made at home, then it would be foolish to put obstacles in the way of importing them. Such restrictions could only impede the welfare of the whole community.

The critique of mercantilism, together with the case for free trade, is contained in books III and IV of *Wealth of Nations*. There are three powerful ideas to bear in mind in the remainder of this chapter:

- *A nation's wealth depends on its productive capacity.* Gold and silver do not of themselves constitute a nation's wealth. Gold and silver can be 'wasted' on luxury spending. But if gold and silver are used to purchase materials and tools, or to employ labour, then productive capacity and future wealth is assured.
- *Laissez-faire is the best way to increase productive capacity.* Governments should remove restrictions and privileges to permit the expansion of industry and trade. Once freed from the burden of the state, social harmony and economic progress will triumph.
- *International trade is mutually beneficial for all trading countries.* Every country benefits from being able to export those commodities which it produces efficiently, and being able to import those commodities which it produces inefficiently. There are no 'losers' from free trade. All are 'gainers'.

Absolute advantage

Smith claimed that a country should specialise in, and export, commodities in which it had an absolute advantage. An absolute advantage existed when the country could produce a commodity with less labour per unit produced than could its trading partner. By the same reasoning, it should import commodities in which it had an absolute disadvantage. An absolute disadvantage existed when the country could produce a commodity only with more labour per unit produced than could its trading partner.

Table 2.1 is a simple arithmetical example of the principle of absolute advantage. The countries in the table (the UK and the US) are not, of course, the ones familiar to Smith, nor are the commodities (wheat and cloth) the ones which feature in *Wealth of Nations*, but the principle is universal. To simplify matters, we will continue to use these two commodities and countries whenever we are dealing with the two-country, two-commodity case.

Table 2.1 indicates that the UK has an absolute advantage in cloth production and an absolute disadvantage in wheat production. The US has an absolute advantage in wheat production and an absolute disadvantage in cloth production. Both countries will gain if the UK specialises in cloth and exports it to the US, and the US specialises in wheat and exports it to the UK. In modern terminology, trade is a positive sum game. Everyone gains from specialisation and exchange, though we may note from the outset that there is no reason to expect everyone to gain equally.

Labour theory of value

The classical economists, of whom Smith was the first, regarded labour as the sole source of value. The quantity of labour embodied in a commodity measured the value of that commodity.

The arithmetical example of Table 2.1 is consistent with a labour theory of value, since the exchange value of each commodity is determined by the amount of labour time (output per unit of labour) necessary for its production. The classical writers operated with a labour theory of value. Although Smith had not developed a price-related demand schedule in the modern sense he did recognise that demand for a commodity needed to be taken into consideration. Producers in search of profit would not continue to produce commodities for which there was no market. Market demand was needed if producers were to cover their costs of production. Market demand would determine what commodities were to be exchanged and the relative amounts to be produced.

Table 2.1 Absolute advantage (arithmetical example)

Output per unit of labour	UK	US
Production of wheat	5	20
Production of cloth	10	6

Smith also recognised that workers differed in aptitudes and abilities. The lazy and unskilled worker would be less productive than the industrious and skilled worker. It is labour, as opposed to the labourer, which is the measuring rod in the labour theory of value. Labour, Smith claimed, was alone 'the ultimate and real standard by which the value of all commodities can at all times and places be estimated and compared' (*Wealth of Nations*, book I).

Political economy

Adam Smith's demonstration of the gains from specialisation and exchange, based on the principle of absolute advantage, constituted an immensely powerful argument for free trade. At the time of publication of *Wealth of Nations*, Britain was already the most advanced capitalist country in the world economy. We can imagine even today how appealing Smith's book was to the newly emerging manufacturing interests in Britain who wished to be freed from state regulation, to import raw materials and to sell goods abroad. Its sentiments also appealed to the labouring poor, who stood to gain from the opening-up of British markets to imports of cheap grain from overseas.

Smith, and other classical economists, regarded themselves as operating in the sphere of political economy. They were in the business of persuading governments what they ought to do. They were concerned with normative, as opposed to positive, economics. The normative implication of Smith's (and later of Ricardo's) economics was free trade.

The philosophy of economic liberalism, of which the free trade doctrine is a key element, took strong root in Britain in the early nineteenth century. The repeal of the Corn Laws, which came at the end of decades of pressure from industrialists, consolidated Britain's lead in the world economy. Economic liberalism was much slower to gain acceptance elsewhere in Europe. In continental Europe protectionism had a firmer grip. The ideas of Friedrich List, the German nationalist economist who died in 1849, had a loyal following. List believed that protectionism was an important defence for Germany against the rapidly growing political and economic power of Britain.

David Ricardo and comparative advantage

Born in 1772, David Ricardo was of Dutch parentage. His family was Jewish and settled in England where his father followed the profession of stockbroker. The younger Ricardo also made his fortune in stockbroking, and then retired from business to embark upon his intellectual journey. His most important work, *The Principles of Political Economy and Taxation*, was first published in 1817 and contained, in addition to his theory of international trade, work on the theory of value, wages, profit and rent, a theory of accumulation, and a theory of economic development. It is a complete account of the workings of an economic system, much more rigorous and less philosophic than *Wealth of Nations*. The contribution of David Ricardo was to demonstrate that even though a country may be absolutely more efficient than another in the production of all tradeable goods, nevertheless trade will be mutually advantageous.

Absolute advantage explains a certain proportion of trade taking place in the world economy in the eighteenth and early nineteenth centuries. Britain probably had an absolute advantage in manufactured goods in the early stages of industrialisation and an absolute disadvantage in the production of commodities like sugar and tobacco, which required specific climatic conditions. Sugar, tobacco, raw cotton and tea were significant commodities in Britain's import bill.

But suppose a country has an absolute advantage over its trading partner in respect of *all* commodities. Is there any basis for mutually advantageous trade? Adam Smith thought not. If the trading partner had no absolute advantage, then there would be no opportunity to trade.

Consider Table 2.2. The US has an absolute advantage in the production of both wheat and cloth. By 1860, this was a distinct probability. The US was an agricultural economy capable of producing large quantities of low-cost wheat, as the margin of cultivation was extended westwards. But due to high rates of investment, productivity levels were also rising in certain types of manufactured cotton goods. Productivity levels could well have outstripped those in the UK.

Based on Smith's principle of absolute advantage, Table 2.2 suggests that there is no basis for trade between the UK and the US. The US is absolutely more efficient in the production both of wheat and cloth. But, looking again at Table 2.2, it is clear that the US is relatively more efficient in the production of wheat (four times more efficient than the UK) than it is in the production of cloth, where it is three times more efficient than the UK. The US has a comparative advantage in wheat production. The UK, comparatively speaking, is more efficient in cloth production than wheat.

Ricardo was the first of the classical economists to recognise that it is relative rather than absolute values which are fundamental to the operation of a market economy. This insight was critical to the further development of the theory of trade.

Consider again Table 2.2. The US has a fixed quantity of labour available to produce wheat or cloth. One unit of labour can produce 20 units of wheat or 6 units of cloth. Assume that trade takes place and the US sends 20 units of wheat to the UK. To produce 20 units of wheat the US has sacrificed 6 units of cloth. But the US will be able to obtain 8 units of cloth from the UK in exchange for 20 units of wheat, because within the UK 20 units of wheat trade for 8 units of cloth. In the UK, 1 unit of labour can produce 5 units of wheat or 2 of cloth. Assume now that trade takes place and the UK sends 2 units of cloth to the US. To produce 2 units of cloth, the

Table 2.2 Comparative advantage (arithmetical example)

Output per unit of labour	UK	US
Production of wheat	5	20
Production of cloth	2	6

> **Box 2.1 Ricardo's analysis of comparative cost**
>
> Ricardo's analysis of comparative cost constituted such a powerful case for free trade because it demonstrated that benefits accrue to trade even if one economy is more efficient than another in the production of a wide range of goods. As the world economy expanded in the nineteenth century, leading economies emerged which were indeed more efficient than others over a wide range of output. But this did not destroy the basis of trade. On the contrary, economists argued even more strongly for free trade. Economists have extended and refined Ricardo's analysis over the past two hundred years, but they have not changed the essential argument for free trade based on the principle of comparative advantage.

UK has sacrificed 5 units of wheat. But the UK will be able to obtain 6.6 units of wheat from the US in exchange for cloth because within the US 2 units of cloth trade for 6.6 units of wheat.

Recognition of the principle that it will be beneficial for a country to specialise in the commodity in which it has a comparative advantage, and export it to another country in exchange for a commodity in which it has a comparative disadvantage, is fundamental to the doctrine of free trade. In drawing attention to the principle of comparative cost, Ricardo showed enormous insight. Although absolute advantage provides a basis for trade, it is likely, in practice, to apply to a fairly limited range of goods: trade in foodstuffs and raw materials between tropical and temperate zones, for example. Comparative advantage, on the other hand, can apply whenever there are productivity differences between countries, in respect of two or more commodities.

Opportunity cost and the pure theory of trade

So far in this chapter, the free trade doctrine has been discussed in terms of a labour theory of value in which the value of a commodity is determined by the amount of labour time used in its production. Following on from Smith and Ricardo, economists in the nineteenth century subsequently modified and finally abandoned the labour theory of value. It was replaced with the familiar economics 'tool-box' of the present day, in which the value of a commodity is related to its market price, which depends not only on supply and cost conditions, but also on demand.

Neo-classical trade theory

The economists who later overturned the labour theory of value were from continental Europe as well as from Britain. Jean Baptiste Say (1767–1832) was French. Though a firm disciple of Smith, he was the first economist to break away entirely from the labour theory of value. He is generally credited as developing the forerunner of formal equilibrium analysis. Of the three 'founders' of the marginal utility school in the late nineteenth century, Jevons was from England, Menger from Austria (Vienna) and Walras from Switzerland (Lausanne).

The 'neo-classical' thinkers, led by Jevons, Menger and Walras, developed theories of an economic system based on large numbers of producers and consumers. Given a competitive market economy, prices would guide consumers and bring about the most efficient allocation of resources in order to maximise society's income. Neo-classical economists also made great use of mathematical and geometric exposition in order to show functional relationships between important variables such as price and quantity demanded. The use of mathematics ensured greater rigour in the development of their theories.

This is the context in which economists have developed the pure theory of trade. The pure theory of trade treats international trade within the framework of neo-classical theory. It carries through to the present day Adam Smith's belief in the invisible hand of the market, competition and the benefits of laissez-faire policy in relation to international exchange. The pure theory abandons the labour theory of value. Instead it is based on rigorous analysis of consumer and producer behaviour.

The pure theory of trade can be developed through a system of equations and this is the most exact way of presenting it. In this chapter, however, we rely on a simple geometric exposition instead of on equations. The more advanced geometric analysis which is necessary to demonstrate the principles of general equilibrium analysis can be found in Appendix A: The geometry of trade.

Opportunity cost

The doctrine of free trade holds good even if we discard the labour theory of value. The Austrian economist Gottfried Haberler first demonstrated this in the 1930s, utilising the concept of 'opportunity cost'. If the concept of the 'indifference curve' is also introduced into the analysis, it becomes possible for the first time to demonstrate the gains in real income from trade. What follows here is a simplified form of the pure theory of trade based on Haberler's *Theory of International Trade* (1933).

Assume two countries, the US and UK, and two commodities, wheat and cloth. The purpose of the analysis is to demonstrate that the UK gains from specialising in the production of cloth in which it has a comparative advantage, and exporting it to the US in exchange for wheat in which it has a comparative disadvantage. The gains from trade come about because the domestic opportunity cost of cloth in terms of wheat differs from the international opportunity cost of cloth and wheat.

Figure 2.1 shows the UK (country A). The axis Oy represents units of wheat. The axis Ox represents units of cloth. If all resources available in the UK are devoted to producing cloth, On' units of cloth will be produced. If all the resources available in the UK are devoted to producing wheat, On units of wheat will be produced. Any point on the curve nn' represents a combination of wheat and cloth production. nn' is the production possibility frontier for country A. Assuming all resources are

Figure 2.1 The gains from trade

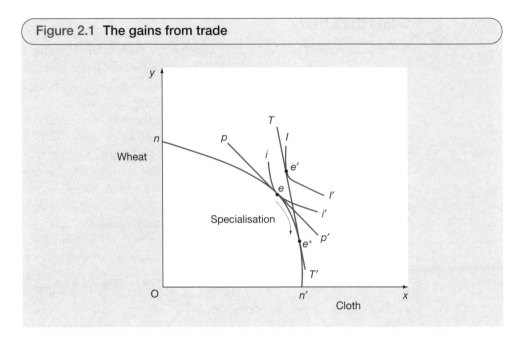

fully employed, country A will be producing at some point on the production possibility curve where both wheat and cloth are produced.

Where on the production possibility curve will country A be located? To answer this question we need information

● on the *preferences of consumers* in country A for wheat relative to cloth, and
● on the *relative prices* of wheat and cloth.

Remember, at this stage we have not introduced the possibility of foreign trade. Information on relative prices is therefore represented by the *domestic price schedule*. Information on preferences is represented by the *community's indifference curve*.

The indifference curve ii' in Figure 2.1 shows the two goods, wheat and cloth, and the combinations of wheat and cloth that are equally acceptable to consumers in country A. The price schedule pp' shows the relative prices of wheat and cloth, the rate at which they can be traded one for another in country A. In effect, the slope of pp' is the domestic opportunity cost.

The 'no foreign trade' or 'autarky' equilibrium is at e. Here the marginal rate of transformation in production (the slope of nn') is equal to the marginal rate of substitution in consumption (the slope of ii') and is equal to the domestic opportunity cost (the slope of pp'). At e, country A produces Ow of wheat, and Oc of cloth. This equilibrium represents the most efficient use of resources for both producers and consumers and yields the maximum level of real income in country A.

Gains from trade

We now open up country A to foreign trade. To simplify matters, the analysis uses a partial equilibrium approach, showing the effects of trade on country A only. If we were to introduce country B, as in a general equilibrium approach, more sophisticated geometric tools would be needed. (See Appendix A.)

We know that foreign trade is beneficial if the domestic opportunity cost is different from the international opportunity cost of wheat and cloth. A line TT' is constructed to represent the international terms of trade, i.e. the rate at which wheat trades (exchanges) for cloth in the international economy. Because it differs from the domestic opportunity cost it is constructed with a different slope to pp'. TT' also indicates how much cloth country A will produce when it is opened up to trade. It must be tangential to nn' because after trade, country A must still be somewhere on its production possibility curve, producing both wheat and cloth. The location is indicated by the new post-trade equilibrium $e*$. Country A has moved along the production possibility curve to $e*$, where it is producing more cloth and less wheat. It has specialised in cloth at the expense of wheat because it is assumed to have a comparative advantage in cloth.

Exports of cloth trade at the more favourable international opportunity cost represented by TT'. TT' is determined by supply and demand conditions for wheat and cloth in country A and country B. To arrive at the post-trade equilibrium for country A, move out along TT' until a point of tangency is reached with a higher indifference curve II', at e'. At this point, country A's marginal rate of substitution in consumption (slope of II') is equal to the marginal rate of transformation in production (slope of nn'), and is equal to the relative prices of wheat and cloth in international markets (slope of TT'). II' represents a higher level of real income for country A. Foreign trade, which has led to specialisation and exchange, results in a higher level of real income at the new post-trade equilibrium e'.

Factor endowments

What is the source or basis of comparative advantage? Eli Heckscher (1919) and Bertil Ohlin (1933) were the two Swedish economists who provided an answer to this question. The answer itself, and the theoretical structure that underpins it, has turned out to be very influential in international economics.

Why are there differences in comparative advantage? Why do domestic opportunity costs differ from international opportunity costs? According to Heckscher and Ohlin it was because of differences in relative factor endowments between nations. Countries like the United States and Canada were relatively abundant in fertile land. Other countries, such as the UK, were relatively abundant in labour. The UK could produce cotton textiles relatively cheaply because large amounts of cheap labour were used in the production process. Wheat was cheap in the US relative to cloth because fertile land was abundant in the US relative to labour. Cotton goods were cheap in the UK relative to wheat because labour was relatively abundant in the UK.

- Countries have a *comparative advantage* in commodities which use more of their *relatively abundant factor of production.* A labour-abundant country will export labour-intensive goods. A capital-abundant country will export capital-intensive goods.
- Countries have a *comparative disadvantage* in commodities which use more of their *relatively scarce factor of production.* A labour-scarce country will import labour-intensive goods. A capital-scarce country will import capital-intensive goods.

The Heckscher–Ohlin theory tells us that questions about a country's *pattern of trade* – which goods and services it exports and which goods and services it imports – can be answered in terms of factor endowments. It will become clear later in this chapter that the appeal of the Heckscher–Ohlin explanation of comparative advantage does not lie in its power to explain real world trade patterns. As an explanatory model its present-day relevance is very limited. If it ever applied anywhere, it was probably only in the period 1850–75 when reductions in transport costs opened up vast areas of cheap, fertile land, and made available exports of land-intensive agricultural products from North and South America and Australia.

If the Heckscher–Ohlin model has serious limitations in an *empirical* sense, why is it still important in international economics? The answer is that it is a trade model which has important *theoretical* qualities. Many of these qualities it shares with the Ricardian approach to comparative cost. But there are key differences. An important difference is that the Heckscher–Ohlin model abandons the classical labour theory of value, and enables several factors of production to be incorporated into the analysis.

Comparing the Ricardian and Heckscher–Ohlin trade models

The economist Jagdish Bhagwati suggested in 1961 a useful schema for comparing the Ricardian and Heckscher–Ohlin models. This schema also plays a role in the 'testing' of the Ricardian and Heckscher–Ohlin (H–O) models.

Schema for evaluating Ricardian and Heckscher–Ohlin trade models (following Bhagwati)

Assumptions
Predictions
Empirical evidence
Normative implications
'Fruitfulness' in terms of further work

The assumptions and predictions of the two trade models

Table 2.3 shows that the Ricardian and H–O models hold the majority of their assumptions in common.

Both the Ricardian and H–O trade models assume perfect competition, so that the prices of goods entering into international trade perfectly reflect productivity differences (Ricardo) or factor endowments (H–O). There are no monopolistic tendencies which

Table 2.3 Summary of assumptions of Ricardian and Heckscher–Ohlin trade models

Ricardian	Heckscher–Ohlin
1 Perfect competition in factor and product markets	Perfect competition in factor and product markets
2 Constant costs (linear homogeneous product function)	Constant cost (linear homogeneous product function)
3 Zero transport costs	Zero transport costs
4 Labour perfectly mobile domestically but immobile internationally	Labour perfectly mobile domestically but immobile internationally
5 Labour theory of value: costs are determined by amount of labour utilised	Several factors of production. Commodities display different factor intensities
6 Different production functions for the same commodity in different countries	The same production function for the same commodity in different countries

Assumptions 1, 2, 3, 4 are the same for both models. Assumptions 5 and 6 differ between the two models.

might undermine the relationship between labour productivity and the price of goods (Ricardo), or factor endowments/factor intensities and the price of goods (H–O).

Both models also assume that costs of production are constant with respect to scale of output. Again, this is necessary to maintain a clear relationship between price and productivity (Ricardo) and price and factor endowments (H–O). There are no economies of scale to complicate the issue.

In both models transport costs are zero. This assumption is highly unrealistic but necessary, again to ensure that international price ratios reflect productivity differentials (Ricardo) or relative factor endowments (H–O), rather than such things as location, distance and other costs of moving goods across national boundaries.

Finally, if factors of production could move between countries, then factor mobility would rule out differences in the prices of goods and factors of production which give rise to trade. It is only because factors of production are immobile internationally that trade in goods and services becomes possible. None of the above assumptions could be regarded as realistic, but in this, as in other areas of economics, they are necessary to the logical development of the model.

The final two categories of assumptions differ between the models, and highlight the difference in approach between the classical model of Ricardo, and the later H–O model which sits more easily in the neo-classical tradition.

First, the Ricardian model assumes only one factor of production, labour. The costs of traded commodities are determined by the amount of labour utilised in production. The H–O model, on the other hand, has several factors of production. The relative prices of traded commodities are determined by the different factor intensities that they display.

Second, in the Ricardian model the relationship between labour inputs and output for the same commodity differs in the two trading countries. In other words, production functions for the same commodity differ internationally in the Ricardian model.

In the H–O model production functions are the same for both countries when producing the same commodity. In producing commodity x, country A and country B both face the same production function. It is the factor intensities which differ between commodities x and y, and factor endowments which differ between countries A and B.

Following Bhagwati's schema and comparing the Ricardian and H–O trade theories, there are important differences in assumptions which may lead to differences in predictions about likely trade patterns.

If Ricardian theory is selected, then a country's exports and imports – the pattern of trade – are determined by productivity differences. A country will export those commodities in which its labour productivity is comparatively high, and import those commodities in which its labour productivity is comparatively low.

If H–O theory is followed, then a country's pattern of trade is determined by relative factor endowments. A country will export commodities which embody its relatively abundant factor, and will import commodities which embody its relatively scarce factor.

Empirical evidence has been kinder to the predictions of the Ricardian model than to the H–O model. The H–O model does not stand up very well to the test of real-world evidence. Why? Reservations about the real-world relevance of the H–O trade model have long been voiced by economists, and they seem to centre on the fact that trading nations usually have very similar factor endowments. The bulk of world trade is between countries which have similarly structured economies. More than this, the trade which takes place between these countries tends to be in commodities which have very similar factor requirements.

Normative implications and further work

There is no difference between the H–O and Ricardian models so far as their normative, i.e. policy, implications are concerned. Both approaches strongly support a policy of free trade. Trade is a positive sum game. All gain by participating in international exchange.

The H–O model is superior to the Ricardian model, however, in that it can be used to tell us something about how the gains from trade will be distributed. There are, potentially, four factors of production in the H–O model and the prices of these factors (rents on land, wages for labour, interest payments on capital and profits for enterprise) are the rewards accruing to the factors, i.e. their real income. The H–O model enables the economist to reach a general equilibrium solution which indicates how the invisible hand of the market determines what exports should be produced, how they are to be produced and how the gains from trade are distributed among the different factors of production in the trading countries.

It is the ability of the H–O model to provide a general equilibrium solution which explains why it occupies a central place in the pure theory of trade, and why economists have found it so useful in stimulating further theoretical work.

Testing the Ricardian and Heckscher–Ohlin models

The Ricardian model

The Ricardian model, in which trade patterns depend on productivity differences, comes out well from empirical investigation. The earliest tests were carried out by G. D. A. MacDougall, and published in the *Economic Journal* of December 1951 and September 1952.

MacDougall inferred from the Ricardian model that, in comparing US and UK patterns of trade, the ratio of US exports to UK exports would be relatively high in commodities where the ratio of productivity of US workers to UK workers was also relatively high. So, in taking a cross-section of industries, MacDougall found that in industries like textiles where US productivity was *very close* to UK productivity, the volume of US exports was very close to the volume of UK exports. In industries such as car production, where US productivity was much greater than UK productivity, US exports were much greater in volume than UK exports. This result broadly confirms the Ricardian model in which productivity differences (comparative costs) determine trade patterns.

Figure 2.2 illustrates the results of MacDougall's empirical work. It uses the methodology of correlation, a statistical indication of the relationship between two variables. Positive correlation yields an upward-sloping pattern as the two variables

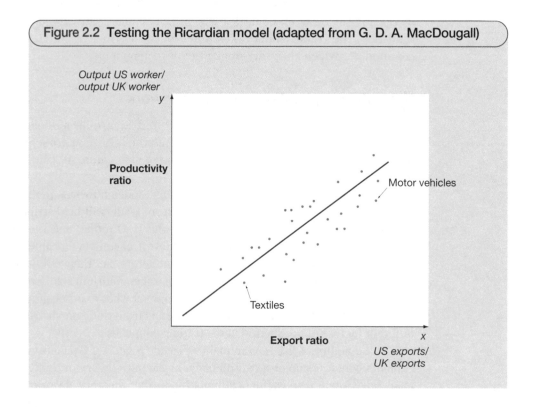

Figure 2.2 Testing the Ricardian model (adapted from G. D. A. MacDougall)

x and y are plotted. Negative correlation is indicated by a downward-sloping pattern as the variables x and y are plotted.

In MacDougall's test of Ricardian theory, productivity ratios are measured on the y axis and export ratios on the x axis. Productivity ratios and export ratios are correlated for a range of manufactured goods. There is a clear positive relationship between productivity ratios and export ratios across the commodities, ranging from textiles (low US productivity and low US exports) to motor vehicles (high US productivity and high US exports).

The Heckscher–Ohlin model

The most famous test of the Heckscher–Ohlin model is that carried out by the US statistician Wassily Leontief which was published in 1953. It used what was then a pioneering methodology. The methodology was that of *input–output analysis*. It was to win Leontief the Nobel Prize in 1973.

Essentially input–output analysis involves representing the output of any product in terms of its input requirements. A simplified example might relate to cotton textiles, which require a certain quantity of fuel (electricity), raw materials (raw cotton), capital equipment (machinery for spinning and weaving) and labour (to produce the final output). Extended to the economy as a whole, it is possible to represent all transactions in the economy in a 'snapshot' form, at a particular point in time. The aim is to highlight the interrelationships in the economy, as the output of one sector (say, textile machinery from the capital goods sector) is used as input in other sectors. In an economy such as the Soviet Union before liberalisation, planners could use input–output analysis to avoid bottlenecks, particularly for critical inputs such as energy and raw materials.

It is important to know something about the history of Leontief's work, because here is an example of a methodology in search of something to test, rather than the other way around! For an economy the number of calculations required to produce a comprehensive input–output table is vast. It is no coincidence that Leontief's work coincided with the development of computers in the US in the late 1940s, because one of the first uses of the technology was the construction of an input–output table for the US economy for the year 1947.

Having constructed the input–output table, Leontief considered its possible uses. Testing the Heckscher–Ohlin model was just one of these potential uses. It enabled Leontief to compare the factor intensity of US exports with the factor intensity of US import-competing goods. Ideally, Leontief would have wished to look at the factor intensity of actual imports, rather than the factor intensity of US goods which replaced imports. This was not possible because data in the input–output table relate only to the US. However, Leontief was quite justified in using import replacements because of assumption 6 in Table 2.3, i.e. that the same commodity has the same production function in different countries. This means that if, say, cotton textiles are relatively labour-intensive in the US, they are also relatively labour-intensive in the UK. If motor vehicles are relatively capital-intensive in the US, they are relatively capital-intensive in the UK.

The Leontief paradox

When Leontief had completed his calculations it emerged that the US exported relatively labour-intensive goods and imported relatively capital-intensive goods – as measured, in the latter case, by the factor requirements of import-competing goods. The results were regarded as paradoxical because, by the end of World War II, the US economy was generally regarded as the most capital-abundant country in the world economy, a position which it has maintained ever since.

Leontief himself re-did the calculations using an input–output table for a later year, but the results were largely the same and it must be admitted that although more refined data and better methods of testing the H–O model have emerged over the past forty years, and even though other countries and even trade blocs have featured in observations and testing, the results for the H–O model have been, at best, mixed.

Faced with the poor empirical performance of the H–O model, the economist has two choices: either

- *reject the H–O explanation of differences in comparative advantage*, and pursue instead alternative explanations of trade patterns such as the ones discussed in the next chapter; or
- accept that the H–O explanation of differences in comparative advantage may still be valid and look for *reasons for the paradox* which are consistent with an underlying H–O framework.

Because the H–O model is such a powerful *theoretical* construct in neo-classical analysis, economists seem reluctant to abandon it altogether! The following reasons for the paradox have been advanced in various research papers, by economists who believe that the H–O explanation of trade patterns is fundamentally correct, despite its poor empirical showing.

Reasons for the Leontief paradox

- *Natural resources are neglected.* This was one of the earliest explanations of the paradox, and one which initially was favoured by Leontief himself. By concentrating on labour and capital, the test had neglected to take into account the relatively *abundant natural resources* of the US. On closer investigation, exports may have been natural-resource-intensive rather than capital-intensive.
- *Exports are skill-intensive.* Labour is not a homogeneous commodity. The US has a relatively skilled labour force. Labour-intensive exports may have embodied relatively large amounts of the *abundant skilled labour* in the US economy.
- *Factor reversals* occur. US import-competing goods may be produced in a capital-intensive way in the US, even though actual imports are labour-intensive. Although such factor reversals are ruled out by assumption in the H–O model, they remain a distinct real-world possibility, depending on the *relative prices of factors of production.*
- *Trade policy* is responsible for the paradox. The H–O model assumes perfect competition and free trade, but the US has very powerful labour unions which

lobby for *protection against labour-intensive imports*. This means that entrepreneurs in profit-maximising import-competing industries are able to use relatively capital-intensive techniques, even though actual imports may be relatively
labour-intensive.

Although all four of these 'solutions' to the paradox feature strongly in later
empirical research, it appears that economists are no nearer a satisfactory resolution of the paradox. Results have been inconclusive.

The influence of the free trade doctrine

From its early beginnings in the writings of Smith and Ricardo, the pure theory of
trade emerged as part of the marginalist revolution led by Jevons in England, Menger
in Austria and Walras in Switzerland. It was reinforced in the writings of the important 'second generation' of neo-classical thinkers, those whom Haberler acknowledged in his 1933 book: Marshall in England (his paper 'Pure Theory of Foreign
Trade' (1879)); Wieser and Böhm-Bawerk of the Austrian School; and Pareto from
Lausanne.

Smith and Ricardo operated in the sphere of political economy, the art of persuading governments and sectional interests of the mutual benefits of free trade. Political
economy was very much an English phenomenon. Even Marshall, trained as a math-
ematician and fully at home with formal analysis, was anxious to root his enquiries
in economic reality. The continental European writers, though no less committed to
competitive markets, were more technical in their approach, more mathematical and
formalist.

It is also apparent that free trade doctrines were slower to gain a hold on governments in continental Europe than they were in Britain. Britain was the first country
to adopt a policy of free trade, ushering in an era of freer trade in the international
economy which lasted from 1850 to 1875. Between 1840 and 1880, Britain reduced
tariffs by 20 per cent.

It is not clear, however, how much of the free trade movement in Britain was due
to the persuasive powers of economists. Economic historians have argued that the
reductions in tariffs in Britain were not due to free-trade doctrines, but rather to the
fact that government revenues were rising for other reasons, and there was no need
to tax imports in order to balance the budget. In particular, income taxes in Britain
were coming to represent an increasing proportion of government revenue, helped
by rising national income.

France liberalised trade policy after 1860, but this was largely through reciprocal bilateral trade treaties with most favoured nations (MFNs). Often these
treaties had a political rather than an economic purpose. When France concluded
a trade treaty with Prussia, the aim was to exclude Austria-Hungary rather than
to embrace wholeheartedly a free-trade doctrine. The south German states too
were protectionist, great supporters of their *Zollverein*, the free-trade area which

maintained a high *common external tariff*. The *Zollverein* was not reformed until 1866.

The United States was also slow to convert to free-trade principles. Import duties were increased every year until 1865. Sectional interests continued to lobby successfully for protectionism through to the 1880s. As late as 1880, the import duty on steel in the USA was 100 per cent. Wool had a 35 per cent tariff.

The world depression in output and employment from 1873 onwards resulted in renewed pressure for protection. W. Cunningham, the contemporary historian, remarked of Britain that, 'the Science of Political Economy speaks with far less authority and receives far less respectful attention than it did some years ago' (*The Rise and Decline of the Free Trade Movement*, 1904). Nevertheless, Britain just about held on to free-trade principles, and in 1906 the Conservative Party lost an election fought on protectionist principles. Significant opposition had come from the skilled artisan classes, fearing higher food prices.

In Germany, under the influence of the depression of the 1870s, Bismarck introduced a new German tariff, which was further increased in 1890. In France imports of US wheat were the cause of popular agitation. Rates on a number of agricultural products were raised in the 1890s. By 1892 French tariffs on agricultural products averaged 25 per cent.

The USA had always been more protectionist than Europe and raised tariffs (the McKinley tariff) in 1890. At that point in time the average US tariff was 57 per cent. Interestingly the US tariff was justified by the need to protect US workers from the cheap-labour goods of Europe.

The Depression of 1929 signalled further decisive rounds of protectionist policies. Both nominal tariff levels and trade restrictions, such as *quotas*, were raised in order to forestall massive price declines. Italy imposed quotas on French exports of wines and perfumes. France retaliated with quotas on Italian fruit and vegetables. In the US tariffs were raised to help farmers and were later extended to non-agricultural products. Barter agreements on a bilateral basis began to feature in international trade. Hungary started to exchange foodstuffs for Czechoslovakian coal. By 1935 world trade had fallen to one-third of its 1929 level. European nations such as Britain, with significant colonial links, tried to ride out the storm by entering into preferential trading agreements with colonies and dominions. Germany entered into bilateral clearing arrangements through the banks with countries such as Yugoslavia and Romania. By 1938, more than half of Germany's foreign trade was being carried out through bank-based bilateral clearing arrangements.

The experience of the 1930s is a salutary lesson when economists contemplate the triumph of ideas represented in the free trade doctrine. The new liberal economic order which was constructed by the allies at Bretton Woods in 1944 marked the re-emergence and triumph of an intellectual tradition which had faltered in the 1890s and had collapsed altogether by 1939. In Chapter 5 we learn about the painstaking reconstruction of a free trade agenda, beginning with the ill-fated ITO, later GATT, and the successive rounds of item-by-item trade negotiations under GATT which culminated in the Uruguay Round of trade negotiations and the setting-up of the World Trade Organisation. The theory which has underpinned the doctrine of free trade over the last two centuries can truly be described as *robust* in surviving, among other things, the political and social dislocation of two world wars and economic slumps in two world depressions.

Summary

- The theory of trade is the basis of the doctrine of free trade. Free trade principles emerged in Britain as a protest against the effects of the Corn Laws.

- Mercantilist economic thinking was characteristic of Europe up to the seventeenth century. It featured wide-ranging domestic regulations and restrictions on imports and exports.

- Adam Smith, the founder of modern economics, presented a critique of mercantilism, together with the case for free trade based on the principles of absolute advantage.

- David Ricardo recognised that it is relative or comparative advantages which lead to mutually beneficial trade. Comparative advantage applies whenever there are productivity differences between countries.

- Modern economics replaces the classical labour theory of value with the concept of opportunity cost. This enables the economist to develop the pure theory of trade within the framework of neo-classical theory.

- Heckscher and Ohlin believed that the source of comparative advantage is differences in relative factor endowments between countries. Countries export commodities which embody the relatively abundant factor, and import commodities which embody the relatively scarce factor.

- The Ricardian and H–O models have most assumptions in common, but have two important categories of assumptions that differ. These relate to the number of factors of production, and the properties of the production functions.

- The Ricardian model performs better in empirical investigation than the H–O model. Various explanations have been put forward for the Leontief paradox.

- The theory of trade which underpins the doctrine of free trade is very robust. It has survived and triumphed over many vicissitudes in the world economy.

Key concepts

- Corn Laws
- Mercantilism
- Labour theory of value
- Absolute advantage
- Comparative advantage
- Opportunity cost
- Leontief paradox

Questions for discussion

1 'We can best understand Adam Smith's views on trade if we regard them as a reaction to mercantilism.' Explain.

2 Why were the ideas of Smith and Ricardo so devastating to mercantilist thinking?

3 Explain how differences in comparative advantage permit 'gains from trade'.

4 Why does the Heckscher–Ohlin model still occupy a central place in international economics?

5 Why do India and the US both export rice, when their factor endowments appear to be so different?

6 'While few economists believe the Ricardian model is an adequate explanation of trade, nevertheless predictions are supported by empirical evidence' (Paul Krugman). Discuss.

7 What explanations can be offered for the Leontief paradox? Do you find them convincing?

8 Why do economists claim that free trade is preferable to restricted trade? Are they right?

Suggested reading

Bhagwati, J. (1964) 'The pure theory of international trade: A survey', *Economic Journal*, March.

Foreman-Peck, J. (1983) *A History of the World Economy: International Economic Relations Since 1850*, Brighton: Wheatsheaf.

Grossman, G. M. and Rogoff, K. (1995) *Handbook of International Economics*, vol. 3, Amsterdam: Elsevier Science.

Haberler, G. (1936) *The Theory of International Trade*, revised English translation, London: Hodge & Co. Ltd.

Jones, R. W. and Kenen, P. B. (1984) *Handbook of International Economics*, vol. 1, Amsterdam: Elsevier Science.

Jones, R. W. and Kenen, P. B. (1985) *Handbook of International Economics*, vol. 2, Amsterdam: Elsevier Science.

List, F. (1856) *National System of Political Economy*, trans. G. A. Matile, Philadelphia: J. B. Lippincott & Co.

Smith, A. (1776) *An Inquiry into the Nature and Causes of the Wealth of Nations*, London; references to E. Cannan (ed.) edition (1937), with new preface by George J. Stigler, Chicago: University of Chicago Press.

Sraffa, P. (ed.) (1951) *The Works and Correspondence of David Ricardo*, Cambridge University Press, vol. 1, *On the Principles of Political Economy and Taxation*, Ch. VII.

Chapter 3

Developments in the theory of trade

Introduction

In recent years there have been important developments in the theory of trade. In the view of some economists these developments have amounted to a 'revolution' in trade theory.

Since the emergence of the classical theory of trade, the character of international trade has changed dramatically. If we look at Britain's trade in the nineteenth century, it was clearly based on capital and skills giving a comparative advantage in favour of manufactured goods. Imports consisted mainly of raw materials and foodstuffs. By the 1970s the picture had changed. Britain's exports were still predominantly those of manufactured goods, but now so too were Britain's imports. Indeed the largest part of all international trade today is between countries with similar factor endowments. The same categories of goods and services appear on both the import and the export side of a country's balance of trade.

The transformation which has come about in real-world trade patterns calls for explanation. The analysis needs to move away from simple comparative advantage, based on productivity differences or factor endowments, towards a more complex analysis based on the advantages which occur within firms. These are:

● access to markets
● access to technology
● scale economies, and
● organisational advantages.

The celebrated international economist Paul Krugman has been a leading figure in this revolution in trade theory. He has pointed out that the type of market structure which gives rise to such advantages within firms is unlikely to be that of perfect competition.

A good deal of trade now seems to arise because of the advantages of large-scale production, the advantages of cumulative experience, and transitory advantages resulting from innovation. In industries where these factors are important, we are not going to see the kind of atomistic competition between small firms that is necessary for 'perfect' competition.   (Krugman, 1995)

Does this mean that we should be concerned about the way these firms operate in international trade? Are they somehow misbehaving? Not according to Krugman. What is happening is that we have relaxed the assumptions of perfect competition on which the pure theory of trade is based. To capture real-world trade patterns we need to take into account a complex set of factors. We need to focus less on the endowments of nations, and more on the behaviour of firms in different market situations.

Objectives

When you have completed this chapter, you should be able to:

- understand the circumstances in which changes in *technology* can provide a basis for trade;
- discuss the effects of *demand* on the pattern of trade;
- comment on the place of the *monopolistic firm* in foreign trade;
- define *increasing returns* and explain how they help explain why firms locate in particular areas;
- explain *geographical clusters* of activity;
- describe a *gravity trade model*.

Technology and trade

Can differences in the technological competitiveness of countries explain their pattern of trade? Since the early 1960s economists have become increasingly convinced that the answer to this question is yes, and that technology can be an important basis for trade.

Product cycle theory

Some countries tend to innovate. They produce and export newly invented goods. Other countries are imitators. They produce and export goods which are well known in the international economy. Why is there this difference between countries? The answer was provided by Raymond Vernon in the theory he set out in 1966. The theory relies on the concept of the product cycle.

The life of a product can be divided into three stages:

Stage 1: *new product*
Stage 2: *mature product*
Stage 3: *standard product*.

The new product at stage 1 is developed in an innovative and technologically advanced country. The product tends to economise on the scarce factor of production. In a country like the UK, for example, it is likely to economise on labour and natural resources. The new product is also likely to appeal to the higher income band, because the technologically superior country tends to be relatively wealthy. Sales of the new product are directed at the domestic market at stage 1 in the product cycle and no foreign trade takes place.

Very soon the product begins to mature. This ushers in stage 2. The production process becomes standardised and scale economies can be realised. At this point, exports start, probably directed at other high-income countries. It is possible too that the firm(s) responsible for this product decide in stage 2 to start production abroad. They might begin to locate production in export markets in order to economise on transport costs and perhaps to exploit relatively abundant and hence cheaper factors of production.

Finally, in stage 3, the product becomes standardised in the world economy. It is now well known and accepted by consumers worldwide. The production process is also within the capabilities of a wide range of countries which tend to imitate rather than innovate. By this stage it is probable that the technologically superior country has moved on to other new products. It is likely to be *importing* from other countries the standardised product which first launched the product cycle.

Empirical evidence

There is support for the product cycle in empirical research. The research is not all-embracing, as are, for example, the tests of the Heckscher–Ohlin and Ricardian models (Chapter 2). Rather, *particular aspects* of the product cycle are highlighted by individual pieces of research.

- Industrialised countries, like the US, Japan and the regions of Europe, tend to *export the majority of newly invented goods*. Developing countries tend to export older, established products.
- *Research and development* is critical to the emergence of new products. There is a strong correlation between export performance and spending on research and development of new products.
- An industry's *exports* tend to be *higher*, as a percentage of total sales, for *newer products*. Imports are generally a higher proportion of industry sales for older products. The year(s) in which products are introduced can be significant, therefore, in explaining the import/export mix for these products.
- *Technological leapfrogging* is a distinct possibility. A country which starts out as technologically inferior to its trading partner may eventually surpass it. This happens when new technologies appear which may not be profitable for leading countries. For example, they might be labour-intensive technologies, whereas the leading country is labour-scarce. Such technologies might instead be taken up by labour-abundant lagging countries.

Are we measuring technology?

Technology is better captured by a dynamic rather than a static framework. This raises the question as to whether we can separate out something called technology when testing the product cycle and similar explanations of trade patterns. Technology-based theories have identified an important set of variables that help to explain trade patterns. The technology variables all relate to the 'newness' of products and processes. However, in a dynamic context, they are tied in to the ability of a firm to develop and exploit new opportunities. It is difficult to distinguish evidence which supports technology as such from evidence which supports dynamic gains through technologically related processes, such as the long-run accumulation of knowledge and the development of human skills.

Dynamic comparative advantage?

The product cycle suggests that trade patterns may be important dynamic phenomena because they are the result of long-run, self-reinforcing processes. The key is the accumulation of knowledge, and the interactions between market opportunities and international competition. The pattern of global specialisation appears to be a dynamic process. It may be that it is best interpreted using dynamic tools (growth theory, for example) rather than the tools of static analysis (i.e. the pure theory of trade) (see Chapter 6).

Patterns of demand

The Swedish economist Staffan Burenstam Linder was the first economist of modern times to stress the importance of demand as opposed to supply conditions in determining the pattern of trade.

In his 1961 book, Burenstam Linder argued that the importance of differences in factor proportions in determining trade and the location of production had been overestimated. However, he retained the factor proportions approach to explain trade in primary products. The pattern of trade in primary products is determined by natural resources. A country abundantly supplied with natural resources has a comparative advantage in the exploitation of those resources.

Manufactured goods are a different matter altogether. Here, according to Burenstam Linder, domestic demand is the key explanatory variable. A firm is encouraged to produce a particular commodity because it perceives a significant domestic market. It could even be that the entrepreneur has personal experience of a gap in the market on which future investment can be based. As the firm grows, the trade horizon of the firm is gradually lifted.

> Only after what has probably been a considerable period of producing for the domestic market will the entrepreneur become aware of the profit opportunities offered by producing for foreign countries. The export market will not be entered until then. However,

once this stage is reached, there is nothing to prevent exports taking up a larger, and even a substantially larger, share of total sales than that absorbed by the home market.

(S. Burenstam Linder, 1961)

The implication of the Burenstam Linder model is that international trade in manufactured goods will be much stronger between countries with similar per capita income levels. This is because the per capita income level of a country will yield a particular pattern of tastes. The model leads one to expect that the most rapid rate of growth of trade in manufactured goods would indeed be between developed countries, which have similar per capita income levels. Nevertheless, as Burenstam Linder points out, demand for luxury cars in poor countries is consistent with the model. Such demand is not extensive enough to permit domestic production. Certain consumers in the poor country with tastes or per capita incomes out of line with the majority cannot meet their needs from domestic production and must import certain varieties of goods from richer countries.

The Burenstam Linder trade model was not expressed in formal terms. Instead it had a narrative: a compelling story about which goods enter into a country's trade, and with whom the goods are traded. Tests of the model have tended to follow the hypothesis that differences in per capita income will lower the intensity of trade. This is, of course, the opposite of the Heckscher–Ohlin model which implies that countries with different per capita incomes are likely to have different resource endowments and offer a different basket of goods to their trading partners.

The results of testing the Linder model on the basis of similarities in per capita income levels have been rather mixed. It seems that trade may be very intensive between countries with similar levels of per capita income, but that result can often be explained simply by the fact that the countries are near neighbours and hence have lower transport costs, or that they are members of the same trade bloc, both of which are responsible for the growth of trade between them. So it can be very difficult to disentangle the effects of a single variable (in this case demand) on the pattern of trade.

Imperfect competition

In 1979, Paul Krugman published an article which spearheaded the new theories of trade. The pure theory of trade assumes all markets are perfectly competitive. If this assumption is relaxed, it is possible to widen significantly the explanations we can offer for real-world trade patterns.

The analysis which follows in this section is an abbreviated version of the Krugman model. Readers who wish to take the economic theory further can consult Krugman (1979) and Helpman and Krugman (1985).

The monopolistic firm in foreign trade

In the real world, most firms have a degree of monopoly power. They are not price-takers as the pure theory of trade suggests. They have some influence over the price of their products. Monopoly power often derives from scale economies. As the firm increases output, unit costs decline. This favours larger firms, and larger firms tend to acquire monopoly power. So a theory based on a monopolistic market structure, in which the firm enjoys economies of scale, accords to a significant degree with the realities of the world economy.

Figure 3.1 shows the firm in a *monopolistic situation*. It faces a downward-sloping demand curve *dd'*, and a downward-sloping marginal revenue curve *mr mr'*, indicating that to increase sales the firm would need to lower prices. The analysis also relaxes the Heckscher–Ohlin assumption of constant costs. The firm is assumed to enjoy economies of scale, hence the average cost curve *ac ac'* and the marginal cost curve *mc mc'* slope downwards.

The profit-maximising firm is in equilibrium where marginal revenue equals marginal cost, producing O*q* output which is sold at price O*p*. At this point the firm enjoys monopoly profits equivalent to the shaded area under the demand curve, and above the average cost curve.

The role of international trade is to increase the size of the market for a product. Increasing the size of the market enables goods to be produced at lower unit costs. But the firms engaged in international trade are earning monopoly profits, partly at least in consequence of the existence of scale economies. Monopoly profits, we know, tend to attract new firms into an industry. How do firms keep out competitors? One strategy they use is product differentiation. Firms try to differentiate products in order to maintain customer loyalty. The end result is that consumers have a wider range of choice of products, though firms can still enjoy economies of

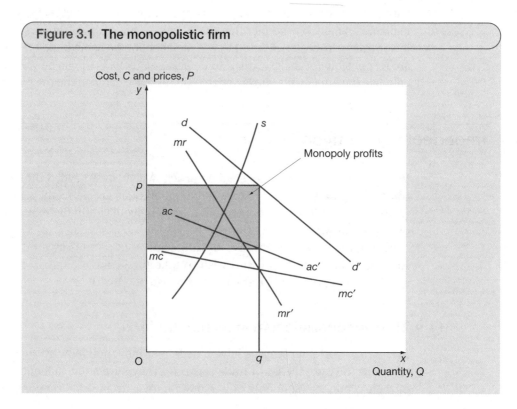

Figure 3.1 The monopolistic firm

scale (and consumers lower prices) because of the larger markets made available through foreign trade.

The results of the model for international trade can be summarised as follows:

● Trade *enlarges the size of the market* for firms and enables scale economies to be realised.
● The *range of goods available* to consumers in both countries rises.
● The trade between the two countries is likely to be in *similar but differentiated goods*.

At first sight we would expect this model to be well supported by empirical evidence. After all, in the real world, scale economies are very important. Trade in the real world is largely the exchange of similar goods, and this is the prediction of this model.

Economists have concluded, however, that though imperfect competition models represent a step in the right direction, they do not help a great deal in explaining real world trade. Leamer and Levinsohn (1995) report empirical work on the monopolistic competition model, which shows that the US and Japan engage in much less trade than is predicted by the model, whereas European Union countries engage in much more trade than is predicted by the model. Clearly some important variables explaining trade between the US and Japan, and within the EU, are omitted in imperfect competition models: such things as distance or membership of a trade bloc, for example. This is not to say that economies of scale and product differentiation are unimportant in international trade, rather that the imperfect competition model which uses these concepts is probably not the best way of linking up trade theory with the evidence which is available.

Increasing returns

Increasing returns tend to encourage monopoly. Increasing returns within firms (economies of scale) are the result of such things as specialisation of labour, or better use of large indivisible factors of production. Falling unit costs encourage monopolistic tendencies in a firm. Decreasing costs suggest that firms should grow. As individual firms come to dominate the market, it becomes necessary for the economist to use models of imperfect competition to predict their behaviour. Of course firms must always be aware that high monopoly profits will attract new entrants to the industry, hence the widespread use of product differentiation to secure customer loyalty.

Increasing returns may also be external to a firm. They can accrue to an industry, or to a group of industries which comprises many firms. If increasing returns are external to a firm, it is still possible to use a competitive model to predict a firm's behaviour.

Increasing returns which are external to a firm can help explain why firms locate in particular areas. They are critical for the emergence of 'growth poles' – commercial centres with an ever-increasing, self-reinforcing momentum of growth. Firms choose to locate where there are other firms because of the existence of increasing returns.

Once a growth pole becomes established, circular processes come into play which keep it going and push it forward.

What are the most important sources of those increasing returns which are external to a firm?

- *Infrastructural investment*, in transport, power, administration and so on, entails high fixed costs. Simultaneous expansion of many firms shares out high fixed costs. Without enough potential users, the investment will probably never take place. But if it does take place, it will reduce costs for existing firms and attract new firms to that location.
- *Labour market* benefits, in the form of insurance or '*risk-pooling*' effects. Workers have greater security from unemployment when large numbers of employers are in the same location. Migrants, in particular, will be attracted to regions where there are large diversified labour markets. Similarly, employers may also favour locating in proximity to other employers, relieving them of some of the costs of lay-offs. They may also have the advantages of a pooled market for highly specialised skills.
- *Complementarities of demand* reduce the risk of not finding a market. Firms sell their products to other firms as well as to consumers. When large numbers of diversified firms are located on the same site, there is increased knowledge of different products and increased possibilities for face-to-face contact. Risks of not finding a market are reduced and the incentive to invest increases.
- *Contracting out* is an important aspect of modern business. Specialised suppliers of services are able to locate within growth poles. This is important in relation to specialised high-technology industries. Again the possibility of face-to-face contact increases the attraction of a particular location.
- *Knowledge spillovers* come about through the informal exchange of information at a personal level. When people and firms congregate spatially, there is much greater scope for knowledge spillovers than for people working in spatially isolated firms. A likely outcome from knowledge spillovers is that unit costs fall in individual firms as the industry as a whole accumulates knowledge.

All these economies are external to the firm. No doubt the reader can think of others. They are external to the firm because (unlike the cases in the previous section) there are no advantages in being a large firm. Unit costs are the same for both small and large firms. Advantages accrue to being part of an industry, or group of industries, in a single location. Indeed increasing returns which are external to a firm tend to suggest that typically it will be many small and medium-sized *competitive* firms which locate in a growth pole.

What is the likely impact of increasing returns on the pattern of trade? The answer is that increasing returns tend to lock countries in, for better or for worse, to their existing patterns of trade. A country starts out with a comparative advantage in the production of particular goods, let us say household durables like vacuum cleaners, washing machines and refrigerators. Increasing returns encourage many producers and their suppliers to locate in a particular region. Increasing returns drive down costs in many of these firms. So far so good. But then the locational advantages which have led to lower unit costs encourage firms to continue in business long after comparative advantage, possibly based on technological change, has switched to other firms and even to other countries. Increasing returns will have locked a country into a pattern of trade which runs counter to broader considerations of comparative advantage. Producing outdated consumer durables offers very few long-term dynamic benefits for an economy.

Spatial concentration and trade

Increasing returns and cumulative processes are pervasive and give an often decisive role to historical accident.

(Krugman, 1995)

One of the 'classics' of international economics is Bertil Ohlin's *Interregional and International Trade* (1933). The clue is in the title. There should really be no qualitative difference between interregional trade flows and international trade. As Ohlin said, 'the theory of international trade is only a part of a general localisation theory'. One 'location' will trade with another. If we can find out where economic activity takes place, and why it is there rather than somewhere else, then we have the basis for a theory of international trade.

Until comparatively recently, international economics has been remarkably uninterested in where economic activity takes place. Most international economics textbooks still offer no sustained treatment of the geographic concentration of economic activity. This is in spite of many real-world examples:

● Silicon Valley in California;
● High technology and biotechnology in Cambridge, UK;
● Aerospace and engineering in Toulouse in France.

Modelling self-reinforcing spatial concentration is very difficult for economists. There is interaction of increasing returns, demand and transport costs, and that is only the beginning. Consider, for example, what the Swedish economist Myrdal wrote in 1957. Myrdal, as a development economist, was one of the few leaders in the discipline who was interested in spatial issues. In his book, *Economic Theory and the Underdeveloped Regions*, he wrote,

Commercial centres are, of course, usually located in places where reasonably good natural conditions for the construction of a port exist, and centres for heavy industry are most often located, not too far away from coal and iron resources . . .

But within broad limits the power of attraction of a centre has its origin mainly in historical accident . . . Thereafter the ever-increasing internal and external economies – interpreted in the widest sense of the word to include, for instance, a working population trained in various crafts, easy communication, the feeling of growth and elbow room, and the spirit of new enterprise – [are] fortified and sustained by their continuous growth at the expense of other localities and regions.

(Myrdal, 1957)

Internal and external economies are difficult enough to measure but variables like 'the spirit of enterprise' and 'the feeling of elbow room' are virtually impossible to capture in any systematic way. This does not mean that they are unimportant, and it does not, of course, excuse economists for neglecting them.

The US manufacturing belt

Paul Krugman has written about the US manufacturing belt as a good example of industrial concentration through the interaction of increasing returns, transportation costs and demand.

The stylised story runs as follows. In the early history of the US no strong geographical concentration could take place. Agriculture dominated the economy. There were few scale economies in manufacturing and transport costs were high. As the country began its industrial transition, manufacturing arose in areas of the highest population. Through time, even though new land and new resources became available elsewhere in the west, the initial advantages of the manufacturing belt which was located in the north-east and the eastern part of the midwest, remained intact. As late as 1957, the manufacturing belt contained 64 per cent of US employment. The manufacturing belt persisted even after the centre of gravity of agricultural and mineral production moved away. The manufacturing belt continued to manufacture everything which did not need to be close to the consumer or close to specific natural resources. This is the circularity that tends to keep a manufacturing core in existence once it is established.

CASE STUDY 3.1

In the industry biosphere, only the strongest survive

Clusters is a term given to geographical areas in which a large number of companies working in the same industry or sector have concentrated. They are a common feature of active and healthy economies. Examples include Silicon Valley in California, the high-technology and biotechnology concerns around Cambridge in the UK, and the aerospace and engineering companies around Toulouse in France.

Companies in a cluster are locked together in a kind of interdependence, like organisms in a biosphere. They compete for market share, employees and resources. They also rely on each other. Acting together, they generate skills and knowledge of their particular sector that form a kind of critical mass on which all the members can draw. Clusters often begin with a single company: Silicon Valley's technology cluster famously began with Hewlett-Packard. These successful companies generate talented managers and entrepreneurs, who in time leave to set up new concerns. As these grow, skilled employees begin to migrate between businesses, seeking the best opportunities.

As clusters grow, they begin to interact with the communities within which they are situated. Local universities become involved in providing specialist training and technical research. The keeping-up of the skills base is particularly important; many clusters decline because the skills base has disappeared. The Cambridge cluster in particular has prospered through its relationship with the university.

Clusters can be exciting places. The atmosphere, in the early stages at least, often encourages entrepreneurship and risk. Casualties are often high but employees and managers from failed companies are usually reabsorbed into the industry. Takeovers tend to be more common than bankruptcies, largely as a result of intense competition. There are really only two ways to survive in a cluster environment long-term: to grow continuously into the biggest fish in the pond, or to develop self-dependent systems and move out, relocating to a region where competition will be less vigorous. The former strategy was adopted by Larry Ellison at Oracle, who saw early on that the only way to win in Silicon Valley was to become big. The latter path was pursued by Bill Gates and Paul Allen at Microsoft; they preferred independence and moved to the Pacific north-west.

Clusters are often favoured by politicians and economic planners, who see opportunities for overall prosperity. But working in a cluster is not for the faint-hearted. They offer little security and few safety nets. As in a biosphere, only the strong survive.

Source: Morgen Witzel, *Financial Times*, 7 August 2002. Reprinted with permission.

Comment on case study 3.1

The geographical concentration of firms is referred to as a cluster. Generally, a cluster is regarded as a positive sign, indicating a healthy and vibrant economy.

Although the firms in a cluster are competitive, together they generate increasing returns which lower costs for all firms. The contrast is with economies of scale which are internal to a firm. These tend to encourage firms to grow to a large size and exercise monopoly power. Increasing returns which are external to a firm are consistent with very competitive market structures.

Increasing returns which are external to a firm take many forms. Skills and knowledge move between businesses. Firms interact with the communities in which they are located. Local universities often play a key role in high-technology clusters, by providing specialist research and training.

Surviving in the cluster long-term may mean growing into the largest and most powerful company, a tactic adopted by Oracle in Silicon Valley. Alternatively, there is Microsoft, which took an independent line by moving out of Silicon Valley to the Pacific north-west.

CASE STUDY 3.2

Questions raised about the Cisco club

Even by the clubby standards of Silicon Valley, Cisco Systems' board stands out. Eight of the 12 directors are closely linked to Stanford University, from which the company was in effect spun out. Ten of them work almost within throwing distance of each other.

These close ties have prompted concern among some corporate governance experts, who suggest the composition of the board is more appropriate for a start-up than one of the world's largest technology groups.

Cisco's is by no means the only Silicon Valley board with strong local ties – six of the nine directors at Oracle, the software group, are executives of the company or Stanford professors.

But the collapse of Enron and WorldCom, coupled with Silicon Valley's dramatic reversal of fortunes, have increased investor concerns about corporate governance issues. Some say Cisco should take steps to resolve any questions about the independence of its board.

'It's very hard as an outsider to know what the level of conflict would be. But there is certainly a perception of conflict and you would think any organisation would want to avoid that perception,' says Tom McLane, vice-chairman of the Directorship Search Group, a corporate governance consultancy.

Cisco insists its shareholders are well served by its board of Valley insiders, all of whom have enough understanding of the technology and the industry to challenge management. Steven West, the lone director who no longer lives or works in Silicon Valley, is a 20-year veteran of the technology industry.

Moreover, the company notes its board conforms to new listing requirements expected to be adopted later this year.

Joseph Grundfest, a professor of law and business at Stanford University and a former securities and exchange commissioner during the Reagan administration, says he personally knows several Cisco directors and is satisfied the majority of board members are independent.

'You can't push these people around,' says Mr Grundfest, who is also an Oracle director. Cisco's board comprises three company insiders – John Chambers, president and chief executive, Larry Carter, chief financial officer, and John Morgridge, chairman – two tech sector venture capitalists, five officials at tech companies that buy Cisco products and two Stanford faculty members.

New listing requirements proposed by the New York Stock

Exchange and Nasdaq, where Cisco is quoted, state that the majority of a company's board must be independent of management and without material relationships to the company.

Cisco says its outside board members are independent because the relationships between Cisco and the directors' companies or institutions are not financially significant enough to be 'material'.

But Beth Young, director of special projects at the Corporate Library, a corporate governance lobby group, says investors should be concerned about the nature of relationships among a group of directors who move in the same circles.

Source: Scott Morrison, *Financial Times*, 7 October 2002. Reprinted with permission.

Comment on case study 3.2

There is a downside to geographical concentration and the local links developed by many high-tech companies with prominent universities.

Cisco Systems in Silicon Valley has close links with Stanford University through eight of its twelve directors. Another Silicon Valley company, Oracle, has six out of nine directors who have links with Stanford University. Some Oracle directors are professors at Stanford University. Directors and managers who move in the same circles and work in

universities which buy Cisco and Oracle products, raise issues of conflict of interest.

Economists usually see the positive side of geographical concentration, the skills and knowledge which move between businesses and the communities in which they are located. Shareholders may have a different take on this. The collapse of Enron raised huge issues of corporate governance. Boards of directors made up of company insiders have come under increasing scrutiny in the USA.

Gravity trade models

Gravity trade models incorporate distance into patterns of international trade. Typically, a gravity model is a log-linear relationship in which trade between two countries is expressed as a function of:

- two countries' income levels;
- two countries' populations;
- the distance between two countries.

More sophisticated gravity models include tariffs and transport costs, and what are termed dummy variables, to account for languages and culture in adjacent countries, tastes and preferences.

Algebraically, the model is expressed as follows:

$$X_{ij} = \alpha Y_i^{\beta 1} N_i^{\beta 2} Y_j^{\beta 3} N_j^{\beta 4} D_{ij}^{\beta 5} A_{ij}^{\beta 6} \pi_k P_{ijk}$$

where

X_{ij} is the value of trade flowing from country i to country j;
Y_i and Y_j are the gross domestic products (GDPs) of countries i and j;
N_i and N_j, the populations of countries i and j;
D_{ij}, the distance between countries i and j;
A_{ij} is a dummy variable representing geographical adjacency of i and j;
P_{ijk} is a dummy variable representing preferences between countries i and j.

Gravity trade models are something of a paradox in international economics. In empirical terms they are very successful. Countries close together trade more than countries which are far apart, other things being equal. The effect of distance on trade flows is highly significant (Figure 3.2).

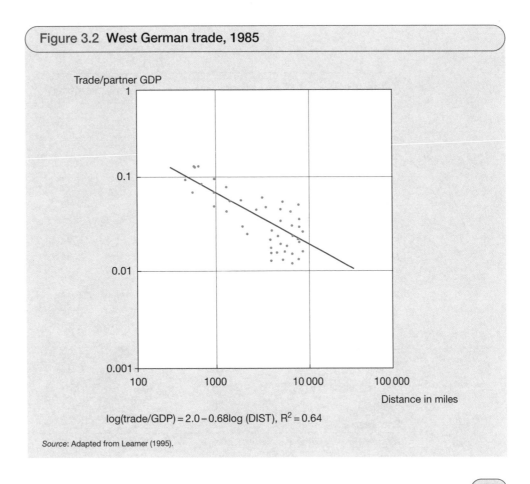

Figure 3.2 **West German trade, 1985**

log(trade/GDP) = 2.0 − 0.68log (DIST), R^2 = 0.64

Source: Adapted from Leamer (1995).

A scatter diagram (Figure 3.2) illustrates the relationship between distance and trade. On the horizontal axis is measured distance to the centre of the trade partner's country. On the vertical axis is total trade (imports and exports) scaled by the partner GDP. Both scales are logarithmic. The figure shows the clear relationship between distance and trade, based on the empirical results of a large number of studies.

The paradox arises because although gravity models are empirically robust, they have little interest for economists because their theoretical underpinnings are unclear. Gravity models are concerned with total trade between a pair of countries, whereas international economics is more concerned with the trade which a country carries out with the rest of the world. The choice of bilateral trading partners is not of great concern to economists, and is one reason for their lack of interest in gravity models.

Interestingly, the effect of distance on trade is not diminishing through time. Comparing 1970 and 1985, for many commodities the adjacency share had increased (see Table 3.1).

To conclude, gravity models have their uses in economics, when researchers are trying to model the trade flows within countries. They can be used for a wide variety of tasks. Interest in regional trading blocs, for instance, has generated a number of new gravity models. But the models are descriptive rather than theoretical. They indicate what is happening in the international economy but do not tell us why.

Table 3.1 **Percentage of trade between adjacent countries (OECD countries)**

	1970	1985	Ratio
Total	30.6	27.6	0.9
Wood	32.7	42.4	1.3
Paper and paper products	35.9	37.7	1.05
Transport equipment	41.1	36.8	0.9
Glass and glass products	37.1	34.4	0.93
Metal scrap	31.8	33.2	1.04
Rubber products	34.1	31.9	0.94
Industrial chemicals	27.9	27.8	1.0
Textiles	30.3	25.3	0.84
Beverage	26.9	23.2	0.86
Petroleum refineries	18.2	22.9	1.26
Tobacco	22.2	20.0	0.9
Electric machinery	25.2	18.9	0.75
Leather	26.5	16.9	0.64
Footwear	17.7	16.4	0.93

Source: Adapted from Leamer and Levinsohn (1995).

Summary

- Trade theory has undergone something of a revolution in recent years. There is much more emphasis on the behaviour of firms in imperfect competition and the effect this has on trade.

- Since the 1960s the importance of technological competitiveness has been recognised. The product cycle follows trade from a new product, through to a mature product, and finally a standard product. Some countries tend to specialise in newly invented products, others in products which are well known in the international economy.

- There is some support for the product cycle in empirical evidence. However, it is difficult to measure technology and it is best captured by a dynamic rather than a static framework of analysis.

- Demand conditions, as opposed to supply conditions, can be important in determining the pattern of trade. International trade in manufactured goods will be much stronger between countries with similar per capita income levels.

- The pure theory of trade assumes perfectly competitive markets. If we assume instead that firms are in monopolistic situations, this widens the explanations of real-world trade patterns to encompass scale economies and product differentiation.

- Increasing returns which are external to a firm mean that there are no advantages to being a large firm. Typically many competitive firms will locate in a growth pole. They may lock into patterns of trade inconsistent with comparative advantage. Modelling spatial concentration is very difficult for economists.

- Gravity trade models incorporate distance into patterns of international trade. Gravity models perform well in empirical testing but they have little interest for economists, who regard them as descriptive rather than theoretical.

Key concepts

- Product cycle
- Burenstam Linder model
- Monopoly profits
- Increasing returns
- Spatial concentration
- Clusters
- Gravity trade models

Questions for discussion

1 What is a product cycle? Which items in international trade are at present undergoing a product cycle?

2 How important are demand conditions in determining patterns of trade?

3 How does the Burenstam Linder model explain trade between Europe and the US?

4 What are the implications of the Burenstam Linder model for developing countries?

5 Give examples of
– increasing returns which are internal to a firm;
– external economies resulting from the interaction of firms' decisions.

6 How useful are gravity trade models?

7 Do you agree that developments in the theory of trade amount to a revolution in trade theory?

8 To what extent are the various developments in trade theory complementary? Conflicting?

Suggested reading

Burenstam Linder, S. (1961) *An Essay on Trade and Transformation*, Stockholm: Almqvist and Wiksell.

Grossman, G. M. and Rogoff, K. (1995) *Handbook of International Economics*, vol. 3, Amsterdam: Elsevier Science.

Helpman, E. and Krugman, P. (1985) *Market Structure and Foreign Trade: Increasing Returns, Imperfect Competition, and the International Economy*, Cambridge, MA: MIT Press.

Jones, R. W. and Kenen, P. B. (1984) *Handbook of International Economics*, vol. 1, Amsterdam: Elsevier Science.

Jones, R. W. and Kenen, P. B. (1985) *Handbook of International Economics*, vol. 2, Amsterdam: Elsevier Science.

Krugman, P. (1979) 'Increasing returns, monopolistic competition, and international trade', *Journal of International Economics*, vol. 9, no. 4, pp. 469–79.

Krugman, P. (1995) *Strategic Trade Policy and the New International Economics*, Cambridge, MA: MIT Press.

Leamer, E. (1995) 'International trade theory: the evidence', in E. Leamer and J. Levinsohn, eds, *Handbook of International Economics*, vol. 3, pp. 1339–95, Amsterdam: Elsevier Science.

Markusen, J. R. and Wigle, R. M. (1990) 'Explaining the volume of North South trade', *Economic Journal*, vol. 100, pp. 1206–15.

Myrdal, G. (1957) *Economic Theory and the Underdeveloped Regions*, London: Gerald Duckworth.

Ohlin, B. (1967) *Interregional and International Trade*, rev. edn, Cambridge, MA: Harvard University Press.

Vernon, R. (1966) 'International investment and international trade in the product cycle', *Quarterly Journal of Economics*, vol. 80, pp. 190–207.

Chapter 4

Theory of trade protection

Introduction

One of the most important issues in international economics is that of free trade versus protection. The traditional literature on trade makes clear that trade restrictions impose efficiency costs on an economy. They can also constrain growth. Yet not everyone, not even every economist, agrees that there should be no trade protection.

This chapter begins by describing different types of protectionism. It is necessary to look at the different types of protectionism because governments face many policy choices in relation to protectionism. It is not simply a matter of choosing between free trade and protection. For example, a government might be called upon to decide whether it is 'better' to assist industries by tariff protection or whether production subsidies are to be preferred. Economists will often have advice to offer on the 'best', i.e. least distorting, form of protection. To appreciate this advice, we need to know the different forms of protection available to the policy-maker.

Suppose the economist's advice is to support free trade but that this advice is routinely ignored. It could be because the government is responding to interest groups and wider political considerations. Jagdish Bhagwati, a distinguished trade economist, provided in his book *Protectionism* (1988) an account of the interest groups and ideologies which are often ranged for and against free trade in the modern world economy. These are the interest groups which can be highly influential in thinking on protectionism. Export interests, for example, may push for highly privileged positions in foreign markets. The government will be expected to bargain on their behalf, using arguments which stress bilateral links and the need for reciprocity in trading arrangements. Economists will also need to recognise that people who disagree with free-trade principles are not always acting out of self-interest. Social concerns about the redistributive effects of trade may also be important. So declining sectors are more likely to receive protection than booming sectors, not only because of self-interested lobbying by employers and workers in problem areas, but also because voters are known to be willing to bear the costs of protecting declining industries, at least in the short run.

Suppose then that governments, having considered all the arguments, introduce protectionist measures. It does not always mean that the government's economics education is flawed. But to rule out this possibility, economists need to present a clear and coherent theoretical framework for understanding issues in trade policy.

> **The intellectual quality of an argument may not always be decisive but, other things being equal, it can make a great deal of difference. No matter how powerful the interests behind a policy may be, they will have substantial difficulty if their policy cannot be backed by a convincing theory.** (Krugman, 1995)

This chapter provides the theoretical framework for an analysis and evaluation of trade policy. It will become apparent that the economic analysis of trade policy has changed substantially in recent years. The 'old' arguments for protection, which were based on the perfect competition model, have given way to 'new' and more persuasive arguments. The 'old' arguments were not intended to make deep inroads into the traditional case for open markets. The 'optimum tariff' argument for protection, for example, is intended to be very much an exception to the free-trade rule: a special case which is notable as much for its theoretical beauty as for its real-world relevance. But the 'new' arguments for protection, which abandon the competitive model, are an altogether different matter. They are far more sophisticated and wide-ranging. This new thinking provides policy-makers, *if they so wish*, with a strong economic rationale for an active protectionist trade policy.

Again, to quote Paul Krugman,

> **The idealised theoretical model on which the classical case for free trade is based will not serve us anymore. The world is more complex than that, and there is no question that the complexities do open, in principle, the possibility of a successful activist trade policy.**

Does this mean that 'anything goes' in relation to trade policy? Probably not. There is still the problem of identifying just those firms, people and sectors which need some help. Even when they have been identified, there is the problem of predicting outcomes. A subsidy to export firms, for example, might result in higher profits and expanded output and employment. But the subsidy could equally well find its way directly into the pockets of the firm's directors and shareholders, with minimal impact on output and employment. Trade theory rarely indicates which of these two outcomes is the more likely in practice.

Finally, as we will see in the next chapter, governments do not make trade policy in a vacuum. However strong the arguments for protection, trade policy must be conducted within the rules of the international institutions, particularly of the WTO.

Tariffs and non-tariff barriers

Countries use a variety of measures which come under the broad heading of 'trade protection'. The measures listed in this section may not be exhaustive, but it contains the major instruments of trade policy.

Tariffs, or customs duties

A tariff is a tax imposed on the import or export of a good or service that crosses a national boundary. Tariffs can take a number of forms. A specific tariff is imposed as a fixed amount per unit of import or export: for example, £1 per bottle of wine, or £10 per ton of coal imported. Tariffs which are specific are easy to collect. They depend only on the number of items or the volume of a product. The disadvantage is that they do not reflect the value of imports or exports. An *ad valorem* tariff relates to the total value of a commodity imported or exported, say 10 per cent of its monetary value. For example, an item valued at £100 could have 10 per cent, that is £10, levied as an import or export duty. The value of an item is usually determined by an invoice or bill of lading. Finally, compound tariffs are a combination of specific and *ad valorem* tariffs.

Successive rounds of GATT negotiations, culminating in the Uruguay Round and the establishment of the WTO, have had a dramatic effect in lowering tariffs worldwide. Average customs duties in the world economy are now very low. But there are still 'tariff peaks' on so-called sensitive products. For industrialised countries, tariffs of 15 per cent and above are generally recognised as tariff peaks.

Another tariff-related concept in trade policy is 'tariff escalation'. Tariffs can be applied at a low rate on raw materials, rising on semi-processed goods, and being highest of all on finished products. Tariff escalation operates in the interests of domestic manufacturing. Raw materials are allowed in with low or zero rates of protection. Intermediate goods attract some protection, with the highest rates being reserved for the final goods. The effect is to concentrate protection on the final stages of manufacturing. It has the effect of discouraging value-added processing in the countries from which the raw materials originate. Processed goods which are intended for export cannot compete once a tariff is imposed. The result is to keep the raw materials exporter out of the market for manufactured goods.

Non-tariff barriers

As tariffs have declined in importance in the real world, non-tariff barriers have increased. They are now the main obstacles to free trade in the international economy.

Import quotas limit the number of units of a good or service that can enter an economy. They can be imposed unilaterally (by one country) or multilaterally (by a number of countries) and are imposed by the importing country to reduce supplies of foreign products. Examples of import quotas can be found on a variety of products in the world economy: coal, chemicals, iron and steel, fertilisers and plastic materials. Import quotas are the most significant trade barrier in the world today.

Export quotas are imposed by an exporting country for one of two reasons. Either there is a wish to manipulate the world price by restricting supply – OPEC oil exporters, for example – or quotas are imposed to prevent exports of 'strategic' goods: for example, military hardware, strategic raw materials such as uranium or technologically sensitive material such as certain types of computer software.

Import and export quotas, like tariffs, are fairly transparent. It is straightforward enough to learn of their existence, and their trade restricting intent is clear. Usually it is possible to work out their effects on trade.

There are two other NTB's (non-tariff barriers) which are less transparent: VER's (voluntary export restraints) and subsidies.

- *Voluntary export restraints* are quotas imposed by the exporting country. The word 'voluntary' is a misnomer because the true situation is one in which the exporter agrees to curtail exports in order to forestall other trade restrictions. In 1981, for example, Japan imposed a VER on her exports of cars to the US. Had Japan not set up a VER, the US would have put a quota on imports of Japanese cars. The most famous VER of all was the multinational MFA (multifibre arrangement). This limited exports of textiles from newly-industrialising countries to the US and Europe. The Uruguay Round generally reduced VERs, and abolished altogether the multifibre arrangement.
- An export *subsidy* is a government payment to a firm which sells its products abroad. It can be specific (a fixed sum) or ad valorem (a proportion of the value of goods and services exported). Subsidies affect income distribution and distort markets. Producers receive large benefits at the expense of the taxpayers who fund the subsidy, and consumers who bear the burden of higher prices. One of the best-known subsidy schemes is the CAP (Common Agricultural Policy) of the European Union.

Other policies in restraint of trade

Not all policies which turn out in practice to have protectionist effects are designed to be in restraint of trade. They may have objectives such as health and safety, and their protective effects may be unintended. Or health and safety might disguise an intention to operate in restraint of trade. Barriers to trade related to health and safety issues are non-transparent and are difficult to remove.

Other trade barriers which seem to be increasing in importance in the world economy are government procurement and marketing and packaging standards.

● *Government procurement.* Governments purchase many of the goods and services necessary for education, defence, health, infrastructure and so on. The GPA (Government Procurement Agreement) was negotiated under GATT. It extends free trade principles of non-discrimination and transparency to government procurement. Measures which go against GPA include preferential prices, offsets (such as domestic content requirements) and lack of competitive tendering. All of these measures discriminate in favour of domestic firms.
● *Marketing and packaging standards* can also discriminate against imports. The requirement, for example, that soft drinks be supplied in returnable, i.e. glass, bottles discriminates against imports in favour of domestic suppliers. Similarly, *customs procedures* can be turned into barriers which place great burdens on potential foreign suppliers attempting to enter domestic markets. In the 1980s, France had customs regulations which effectively restricted the paperwork for high-tech imports to a handful of overworked regional customs houses.

Table 4.1 Tariffs pre- and post-Uruguay Round (industrialised countries)

Product category	Import value from all sources (billions US$)	Average tariff % pre-Uruguay	Average tariff % post-Uruguay
All industrial products	736.9	6.3	3.9
Textiles and clothing	66.4	15.5	12.1
Metals	69.4	3.7	1.5
Wood	40.6	3.5	1.1
Non-electrical machinery	118.1	4.8	2.0
Chemicals	61.0	6.7	3.9
Transport equipment	96.3	7.5	5.8
Manufactured articles	76.1	5.5	2.4
Developing economies' products	465.8	7.6	5.0
Natural resources-based products	80.2	3.2	2.1

Source: WTO.

In their analysis of trade policy, economists tend to overlook the huge variety of protectionist measures which can be taken by governments. The tariff is the basis of the analysis. This plays down the fact that post-Uruguay Round tariffs in developed countries are low. They average less than 4 per cent (Table 4.1). Tariffs are relatively insignificant in the modern world economy, at least in an empirical sense.

Exchange and capital controls as barriers to trade

Exchange controls refer to the restrictions placed on access to foreign exchange and the uses to which it can be put.

A small number of countries in the world economy still maintain dual or multiple exchange rates. There may be one rate for imports and another for exports. Different types of imports, 'necessities' and 'luxuries' may attract different rates. There may also be one rate for trade and another for capital account transactions.

Capital controls refer to restrictions placed on the free movement of financial capital between countries. Nearly two-thirds of countries in the world economy have foreign exchange restrictions associated with the capital account.

Sometimes there is outright prohibition of capital movements, or central banks might discourage lending overseas by the commercial banks. Taxes can be imposed on short-term capital flows in order to discourage speculative movements. Dual or multiple exchange rates can be used to restrict capital flows.

Table 4.2 lists some of the more common exchange and capital controls.

Table 4.2 Exchange and capital controls

Exchange rates	Dual exchange rate structure
	Multiple exchange rate structure
	Taxes on foreign exchange
Controls on payments	Advance payments on imports required
	Documents for foreign exchange required
	Guarantees required for export proceeds
	Letters of credit required for exports
Controls on direct foreign investment	Controls on outward direct investment
	Controls on inward direct investment
Controls on real estate transactions	Restrictions on purchase abroad by residents
	Restrictions on purchase locally by non-residents
	Restrictions on sale locally by non-residents
Controls on investors	Limits on portfolio invested abroad
	Limits (minimum) on portfolio invested locally
	Currency-matching regulations on assets and liabilities

Why do we regard exchange and capital controls as barriers to trade? It is because these controls have the effect of increasing the transactions costs associated with foreign trade. They also tend to encourage unproductive 'rent-seeking' behaviour on the part of importers and exporters.

'Rent-seeking' behaviour

Anne Krueger (1974) pointed out that in many developing economies government restrictions are all-pervasive, particularly in international trade. Where there are exchange and capital controls, they are likely to give rise to economic rents in a variety of forms, i.e. economic surpluses accruing to factors of production, over and above the minimum sum necessary to keep them in their present use.

Let us take a firm which is anxious to get foreign exchange to finance imports, or a firm which is trying to persuade a government to relax its capital controls in order that the firm may hedge the risks involved in foreign trade. First, the firm will probably need to locate in the capital city, in order to gain access to officials. There is a cost involved in this new location. It may not be the best place to locate from an economic point of view. To improve the chances of getting foreign exchange, or to lobby for a relaxation of capital controls, the firm may decide to employ the relative of an official, even though he or she may not the best person for the job. This is another cost. There may also be need to resort to bribery, corruption, black markets and smuggling which impose further economic costs. This is competitive behaviour, but the competition is for licences and preferment. The restrictions on exchange and capital have given rise to economic rents, and competing for these rents has imposed additional costs on the economy.

Exchange and capital costs also tend to reduce the volume of trade. It becomes very expensive to finance foreign trade. More particularly, it becomes difficult and expensive to hedge against the risks involved in foreign trade. The end result is likely to be a decline in the volume of trade, as the cost of financing trade increases, and as it becomes more difficult to accommodate the risks involved in foreign exchange transactions.

Welfare effects of a tariff

So far in this chapter we have noted that there are many ways in which barriers to international trade can be constructed. The tariff is only one of them. Nevertheless, the theory of the tariff is essential as a first step in considering the traditional arguments for protection. In the standard analysis of the welfare effects of a tariff, economists have organised their discussion of protection around the 'dead-weight' welfare losses arising out of distorted production and consumption decisions.

In Figure 4.1, DD represents the domestic demand for commodity Z, SS represents domestic supply. Ow is the world price. At this price, domestic supply is Os', domestic demand is Od', and the shortfall between domestic demand and domestic supply, $s'd'$, is made up by imports. In an attempt to protect the domestic industry, the government

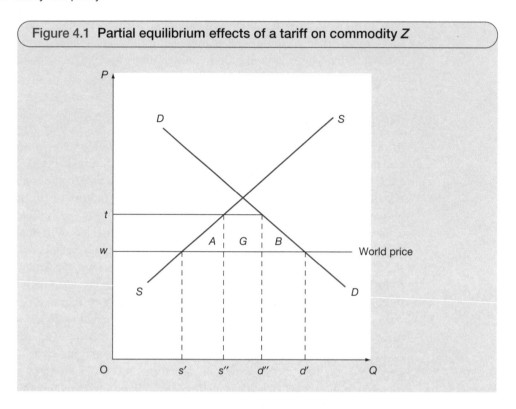

Figure 4.1 Partial equilibrium effects of a tariff on commodity Z

imposes a tariff which raises price to Ot. This reduces domestic demand to Od'' and increases domestic supply to Os'', with consequent reduction of imports to $s''d''$.

The focus of attention is on the two triangles A and B, and the rectangle G.

Consumer surplus

Consumer surplus is the area between the price line and the demand curve. This is the amount which consumers would have been willing to pay for commodity Z, over and above what they end up paying. Consumer surplus is an approximation to what being able to buy commodity Z is worth to consumers, in excess of what they actually pay. A tariff cuts consumer surplus. With a new price line, the area under the demand curve representing consumer surplus is reduced.

Producer surplus

Producer surplus is the area between the price line and the supply curve. The supply curve is the producer's marginal cost curve. The area lying above the marginal cost curve and below the price line represents 'economic rent', the difference between total revenues and total cost. The imposition of a tariff increases this area; hence producers gain from a tariff. The greater the cost to consumers of importing commodity Z, the more willing they are to buy it from domestic suppliers. Domestic suppliers benefit from higher prices and increased sales as a consequence of the tariff.

Net national loss from the tariff

We can now estimate the net national loss from the tariff.

- Area B represents a loss to consumers. They have to cut their total consumption of commodity Z. What consumers lose in area B is a 'dead-weight' loss in the sense that nobody else gains from this. The reduction in consumer surplus is a loss of efficiency caused by the tariff. It is often referred to as the *consumption effect* of the tariff.
- Area A is the welfare loss which accrues when consumers move from imports to more expensive domestic production. The extra cost of shifting to more expensive home production is termed the *production effect*. Area A is a 'dead-weight loss' in the sense that consumers lose out but no-one else gains.
- The government's tariff revenue is equivalent to wt (the height of the tariff) times the volume of imports, $s''d''$. On Figure 4.1, it is equivalent to the rectangle G.

A and B represent loss to consumers, over and above the gains to producers, and the gain to the government in terms of tariff revenue.

Does the loss to consumers, A plus B, comprise the net national loss from a tariff? The answer is yes, providing two assumptions are made:

- The gains/losses of different groups are valued in the same way. Consumers' losses can be exactly offset, pound for pound, by producers' gains and the gains in government revenue. This assumption involves a serious value judgement of how important the different groups are in terms of their gains and losses.
- The importing country is a price-taker. The world price of commodity Z is given. The importing country cannot affect the world price by taking any actions to limit supply.

This standard analysis of a tariff identifies A and B as the welfare losses associated with protection. The analysis tends to imply that the costs of protection are rather small, in comparison say, to total national income. Are the welfare effects of a tariff insignificant?

There are a number of reasons why we should *not* conclude, on the basis of this analysis, that the welfare losses of a tariff are relatively unimportant.

- Figure 4.1 illustrates a *partial equilibrium approach*. It focuses only on supply and demand in a single market, that for commodity Z. But there are relationships between markets, and many repercussions of tariffs. The welfare effects need to be measured by means of a more complex general equilibrium analysis, which takes account of all potential linkages, before a valid conclusion can be reached.
- Even though the *net national loss* may be small relative to national income, the *cost of the tariff to consumers* is *heavy*. The tariff redistributes income. Producers gain, and so does anyone who benefits from increases in government revenue. But consumers lose out.
- There are costs to tariffs which this analysis does not recognise. In the previous section we noted that protection encourages firms to *compete for economic rents*

(producers' surplus) in very wasteful ways. Firms locate in places which give them access to governments. Entrepreneurs try to influence policy-makers; perhaps they resort to bribery and corruption. Rent-seeking behaviour may be highly competitive but it does not improve economic efficiency.

● Economic rents may cushion producers and *discourage them from seeking those technological improvements* which would reduce their costs. In the long run, therefore, the true losses from a tariff may be much greater than the standard short-run analysis suggests.

'Old' arguments for protection

In the classical theory of trade, two exceptions to free trade were recognised quite early on: the optimum tariff argument and the infant industry argument. But they were recognised as exceptional arguments. Economists who advocated protection as a general rule – for example Hamilton in the United States and List in Germany – had only a limited impact on attitudes towards protectionism.

In the 1930s protectionist ideas revived. The case for protection resurfaced as the 'optimum tariff' theory. There was also a new interest in promoting industrialisation through tariff protection, a policy developed in the main by European scholars.

In this section we consider the two traditional arguments for protection which have received serious attention from economists: the optimum tariff and the infant industry arguments for protection.

The optimum tariff

If country A provides a large share of the market for one or more of its imports, it may be able to exercise monopsony buying power. There is still a dead-weight loss to country A in terms of economic efficiency, but this is offset by the gains to country A from forcing the supplier of its imports (country B) to pay part of the tariff.

Consider Figure 4.2. JJ' represents demands for imports of commodity Z in country A. The foreign supply curve for Z is represented by FF'. The foreign supply curve slopes upwards, instead of being horizontal at a given world price. The initial free trade equilibrium is at e, where Of is imported at price Op.

Country A then imposes a tariff on Z. This raises the price paid by consumers in Country A to Om but lowers the price of Z received by country B to On. There is a welfare loss in country A, as consumers decide to buy less of Z now that the price has risen.

But this loss in A is more than offset by gains in A as the foreign supplier is obliged to sell at a lower price in country A. In effect, the foreign supplier, country B, is paying the major part of the tariff. The dead-weight loss, b, is heavily outweighed by the gain of V by country A.

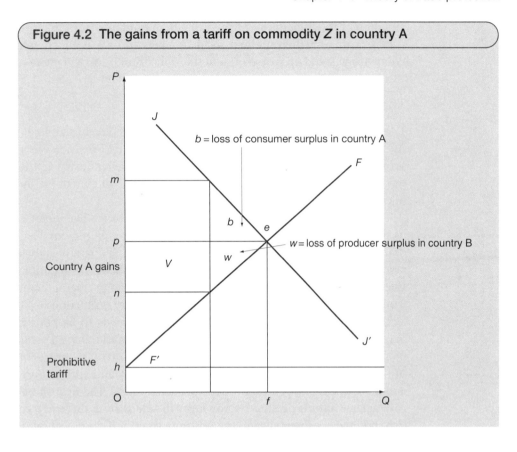

Figure 4.2 The gains from a tariff on commodity *Z* in country A

The tariff has succeeded in increasing welfare in Country A, *but* there are limits to the power of country A to achieve these welfare gains. Essentially the tariff must not be so high as to make the market unprofitable for foreign suppliers. If a tariff drives prices down below the supplier's marginal cost curve, i.e. below the supply curve, say at O*h*, then foreign suppliers will withdraw from the market. The *optimum* tariff for country A therefore lies somewhere between the free-trade position (no tariff) and the prohibitive tariff.

Though the optimum tariff may increase welfare in country A, its trading partner(s) lose out. Welfare equivalent to area *V* has been transferred from country B to country A. This is not a net welfare loss as *V* represents a *transfer* from B to A. But country B has also lost producer surplus equal to *w*, because imports are now discouraged by a tariff. The loss to world welfare is, therefore, represented by the two triangles, *b* and *w*.

Retaliation

Country B has lost out from the imposition of a tariff by country A, and may retaliate with a tariff of its own. This is why the optimum tariff is often described as a 'beggar-my-neighbour' policy, which is likely to provoke retaliation and result in a wider violation of the principles of free trade. If an optimum tariff policy by country A triggers a tariff war, then the end result is likely to be a reduced volume of trade. All countries will end up worse off and the gains from trade will evaporate.

The infant industry

The infant industry argument for protection is deceptively simple. It was first used by Alexander Hamilton in the USA (1790), and later by Friedrich List (1841) to support protection for German manufacturing against British industry. In the 1940s and 1950s the argument was revived to support economic development via industrialisation, in newly independent developing countries.

The idea is to introduce a tariff on a temporary basis. The infant industry can grow up behind this tariff wall. As the infant industry gains experience ('learning by doing') its costs will fall. Eventually it will have a comparative advantage and will be able to compete in the international economy without the need for tariff protection. Everyone will gain, so the argument goes. In the long run, all countries will benefit from the falling costs encouraged by infant industry protection.

The argument for infant industry protection needs to be constructed with great care if it is to have validity in terms of orthodox market-based economics. The argument cannot be allowed to depend on the realisation of the firm's internal economies of scale. This is because a firm should be able to anticipate future cost reductions and allow for them in present investment decisions. The firm should be able to borrow against future profits. Borrowing will tide it over the early years when losses may be made. If capital markets are imperfect and do not allow the smoothing of gains and losses, the government may need to intervene by underwriting loans, but not by imposing tariffs which distort international markets.

However, suppose future benefits are external to the firm, and cannot be reaped by the individual firm. For example, the firm may be training a specialised labour force, which will benefit all firms within the industry. Workers often leave the firm which trained them to go and work for competitors. Or new knowledge may be acquired which cannot be kept secret but must be shared with all firms in the industry. In these cases, social benefit may outweigh private benefit. Even here, however, the preferable policy for the infant industry is a direct subsidy rather than a tariff. A subsidy can be used to compensate firms in the industry directly for the training of labour. Or a subsidy could be aimed towards the 'learning process' involved in new production methods. It should be noted, however, that subsidies are rarely carefully thought out and targeted. Rather than stimulating an infant industry, they often go to line the pockets of directors and shareholders. Private profitability may be enhanced, but costs, employment and output will be unaffected.

Non-economic arguments

'Optimum tariff' and 'infant industry' are two of the traditional arguments for protection, which have recognisable economic foundations. There are, in addition, traditional non-economic arguments which have held sway from time to time.

● Distribution of income. A tariff might be justified on the grounds that it favours what would otherwise be a disadvantaged group. It might be workers in a particular industry, people living in certain regions, farmers, the poor and so on. Economists respond by pointing out that the distribution of income can be managed better by taxes and transfer payments. Tariffs distort markets and may well reduce the volume of trade and national income. Then everyone, including the disadvantaged groups, loses out.

● Security and defence. Even the free trader Adam Smith was prepared to sanction the Navigation Acts which imposed tariffs on the use of foreign ships and shipping services. The idea was to maintain a navy for use in war. The national defence argument for protection was a key justification among mercantilist thinkers. In more recent times, in the 1950s and 1960s, the US imposed restrictions on oil imports on the grounds that a thriving domestic oil industry was a strategic necessity.

External economies and research and development

An external economy is a benefit from an economic activity which accrues to individuals and/or firms other than those engaging in the economic activity. External economies, under certain assumptions, can be used to justify trade protection. New thinking about trade policy builds on externalities and the traditional infant industry argument for protection. In this case the focus is high-technology production. The exports come from the US, Japan and Europe, and from some of the newly industrialising countries like Korea.

In high-technology production, 'learning-by-doing' has important external effects. Krugman (1984) has argued that import protection may be an effective form of export promotion, where there are significant dynamic benefits from learning by doing.

The Krugman model differs from the traditional infant industry argument in two important respects:

● *Oligopoly* rather than perfect competition is the underlying market structure.
● A key role is assigned to *research and development*. High-technology industries are the ones in which research and development expenditure plays a prominent role.

Modelling the behaviour of oligopolistic firms, to incorporate both spending on research and development and the existence of tariffs, is a complex exercise, far more difficult than the traditional infant industry approach which is based on the behaviour of a competitive firm. The sequence envisaged by Krugman runs as follows:

● The government in country A imposes a tariff on imports of a high-technology product, let us say computer chips.
● This raises the output of computer chips in country A and, assuming scale economies, reduces costs in country A.
● Higher profits associated with lower costs can finance increased spending on research and development.

● Research and development reinforces the initial reduction in costs associated with the imposition of a tariff. Lower costs through research and development enable country A to replace country B in the sales of computer chips in *all* world markets.

Baldwin and Krugman have concluded from research they carried out in the 1980s that it was government intervention in international trade which enabled countries like Japan, France and Korea to establish an international presence in high-technology industries such as the production of computer chips. Japan, for example, initially lost out from the tariff. Japanese consumers paid higher prices and obtained less consumer surplus in the computer chip market than they would have received under free trade. In the long run, Japanese trade policy was 'successful' in the sense that it enabled an internationally competitive industry to emerge.

Krugman's study of the international trade in computer chips reinforced his belief that governments could engage in what he and other economists have termed 'strategic trade policy'. A strategic trade policy is one which aims to alter how firms behave. It has two distinguishing features:

● Strategic trade policy is based on the business choices made by firms. It is the study of trade policy under the assumption of imperfect competition. The firm in perfect competition is a 'price-taker', and does not make active business decisions.
● Strategic trade policy incorporates important business decisions outside the traditional price/quantity dimension. These decisions relate to such things as scale economies, spending on research and development, 'learning by doing' and inter-firm rivalries.

There are various ways in which governments can intervene to influence business decisions, using import protection as a means to promote exports. An initial *tariff on imports* is one possibility. Such intervention has the disadvantage of attracting censure and sanctions within the WTO. International agreements do not, however, rule out intervention on the side of research and development. Trade intervention in the form of research and development subsidies is an attractive option for governments, especially if they wish to focus on the type of export production which confers important externalities. In the US the government has provided research and development subsidies to high-technology sectors via university research. Stanford University has had a major impact on the whole of Silicon Valley. Publicly funded defence research can also offer subsidised support to export industries. More directly, the government can underwrite bank lending to high-technology industries. If external economies are allowed to come into play, then quite modest initial interventions can have a very significant long-term impact.

◯ Does 'anything go?'

The new thinking about trade makes one thing clear, the idealised theoretical, model on which the case for free trade is based will not serve us anymore ... But this does not mean that anything goes.
(Paul Krugman, 1984)

What are the qualifications which economists need to bear in mind when assessing strategic trade policy?

- It is difficult to *identify* and *measure* externalities. Policy is complicated because the policy-maker needs to assess the scale of *future* benefits. Assessing likely future spillovers has a large element of guesswork.
- It is often difficult to *predict the outcome of interventions.* An export subsidy might raise profits and encourage more research and development spending. But it is just as likely that the subsidy will be pocketed by directors and shareholders and have no beneficial spillovers.
- Is the government any better at '*picking winners*' than the world at large? How are potential winners to be identified? Are they located in small firms or large firms? Old firms or new firms? Is subsidised research and development always effective in stimulating innovations?
- What about the impact of strategic trade policy on *international agreements*? How does it fit in with the philosophy of the WTO? Is it likely to provoke retaliation abroad and reduce the volume of trade?
- Exports may be better promoted by a *favourable broad-based economic environment*, rather than specific targeting. Education, in the widest sense, creates a fertile environment for innovation and entrepreneurship. Sound macro-economic management may be more beneficial in the long run to export promotion than specific tariffs or subsidies directed at particular industries and sectors.
- Government policy will always be susceptible to *self-serving claims* and special pleading by pressure groups seeking protection. Strategic trade policy runs the risk of sliding into corruption and rent-seeking behaviour, which injures taxpayers and consumers worldwide, and destroys political credibility.

Imperfect competition and the transfer of monopoly profit

'Newer' analytical approaches to protection relax the assumption of perfect competition. The analysis in this section relies on insights first provided by James Brander and Barbara Spencer (1981).

In perfect competition, profit is the normal return to entrepreneurship. But perfect competition does not provide a realistic description of the circumstances in which most firms operate. Most industries have only a small number of firms. Prices exceed marginal cost and profits are generally above the normal return to scarce factors of production. The profit which is earned over and above what the entrepreneurial factor could earn in other activities is described as 'monopoly profit' or 'economic rent'. Trade policy can be used to secure more monopoly profit or economic rent for a country.

We can assume to begin with that firm N, located in country B, is the only supplier of commodity Z to country A. It is a monopoly firm. Therefore, country A relies on a monopoly firm for commodity Z.

DD' is country A's demand for firm N's product. The foreign firm is a monopoly, and country A, therefore, yields a downward-sloping demand curve. Assume that the

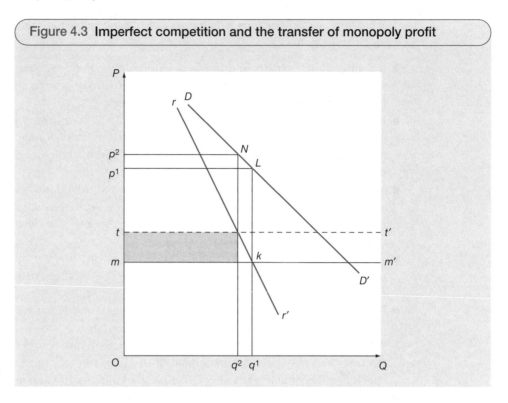

Figure 4.3 **Imperfect competition and the transfer of monopoly profit**

marginal cost curve mm' is constant. Firm N will maximise profits where the marginal revenue (rr') equals marginal cost, producing Oq^1 output which is sold at Op^1 price. Monopoly profit (or economic rent) is represented by the rectangle mp^1kL.

The home country now wishes to extract some of this monopoly profit for its own benefit. Country A imposes a tariff equal to mt. To firm N, this is simply another cost associated with selling commodity Z in country A. Quantity produced falls to q^2 and price rises to p^2. The shaded area (tariff × quantity demanded) is the tariff revenue. It has been extracted from the monopoly profit of the foreign supplier.

If the transfer of profit is greater than the loss of consumer surplus, then there is a welfare gain in country A. Of course, world welfare is reduced because of the fall in trade. Again we are in a situation of 'beggar-my-neighbour' policies, where gains are achieved at the expense of trading partners, and invite retaliatory measures that leave everyone worse off compared with free trade.

Barriers to entry

There are a number of points which can be made in relation to this analysis. One of the most important concerns market entry. Monopoly profits will not persist indefinitely in an industry. New firms will enter the market, attracted by large profit opportunities. The implication is that the Brander–Spencer analysis may apply only to 'natural' monopolies where the opportunities for the entry of new firms are very restricted. Natural monopolies have limited real-world relevance.

◯ Other problems

It will be very difficult for a government to identify industries or sectors which are earning monopoly profits. Does the entrepreneurial factor receive a high reward simply because it has monopoly power, or is it because its managers are of a higher quality and are more skilful and enterprising? Do certain industries and sectors appear to earn high rates of return because we are concentrating on the successes rather than counting the failures? It is not easy to measure economic rent. There are no easy ways of isolating it from high returns which are due to other reasons.

Political economy of trade policy

> Perhaps no other area of economics displays such a gap between what policy makers practice and what economists preach as does international trade. The superiority of free trade is one of the profession's most cherished beliefs, yet international trade is rarely free.
> (Dani Rodrik, 'Political Economy of Trade Policy', 1995)

Barriers to trade in the world economy are far more widespread than can be justified by economic analysis. As we have seen in the previous sections, the optimum tariff and infant industry arguments for protection have to be heavily qualified in order to make them acceptable in terms of economic analysis. Even the 'newer' theories associated with imperfect competition, research and development and innovation have to be heavily qualified in the light of real-world applications. And even where some intervention is justifiable in terms of economic analysis, more often than not non-trade intervention such as subsidies can be shown to lead to fewer distortions than tariffs and quotas on foreign trade. Yet trade barriers persist.

We also notice that trade protection benefits only a small number of import-competing firms and workers. The majority of consumers frequently lose out. And yet policy-makers sooner or later will be seeking re-election. Is it in the interests of politicians to favour small groups when they are hoping for re-election and re-appointment to important jobs?

If there is a bias towards protectionism in economic policy, does it mean that the policy-makers are economically and politically naïve? Have they failed to understand the economic case for free trade? Are they unaware of the impact of their decisions on the majority of voters? It is, of course, always possible that the answer to these questions is yes! But economists always give the policy-makers (and their civil service advisers) the benefit of the doubt. To understand real-world trade policies, we need to abandon the idea of 'national' interests and 'national' preferences. What we have in reality are the preferences of individuals, and the preferences of policy-makers, which somehow come together to determine trade policy. In effect we need a political economy model of trade policy.

Rodrik has provided a schema of what such a model should contain (Figure 4.4). Box A represents individual preferences. This part of the model explains the consequences of trade policy for individuals. Individuals derive their income from different

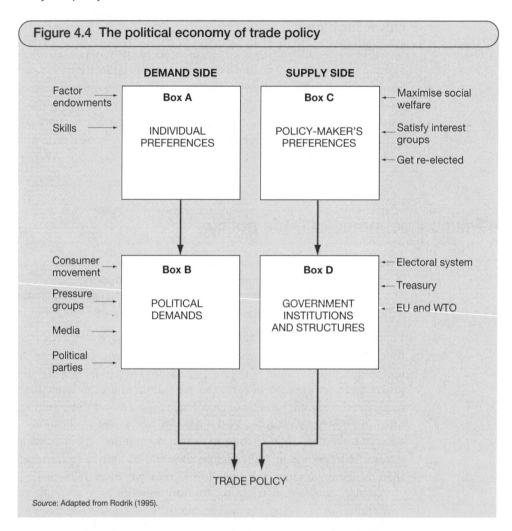

Figure 4.4 The political economy of trade policy

DEMAND SIDE   SUPPLY SIDE

Factor endowments → | **Box A** — INDIVIDUAL PREFERENCES |

Skills → | |

| **Box C** — POLICY-MAKER'S PREFERENCES | ← Maximise social welfare

← Satisfy interest groups

← Get re-elected

Consumer movement → | **Box B** — POLITICAL DEMANDS |

Pressure groups → | |

Media → | |

Political parties → | |

| **Box D** — GOVERNMENT INSTITUTIONS AND STRUCTURES | ← Electoral system

← Treasury

← EU and WTO

TRADE POLICY

Source: Adapted from Rodrik (1995).

factors of production and sectors. Using a Heckscher–Ohlin model, for example, one can determine individual preferences for or against trade policy on the basis of the individual's factor endowments or skills.

Box B models how individual preferences are channelled though interest groups. The interest group may be a political party. Or it could be a 'grass-roots' movement based on anti-globalisation, third-world development or the environment. It could also be a consumer group. Very few economists are happy modelling this part of trade policy because they know very little about political organisations and the ways in which they operate by lobbying politicians through public relations, and so on. For that reason this part of the model is often ignored or taken as a 'given' by economists. This is a pity since it can critically influence trade policy outcomes.

Box A plus box B represents the 'demand side' of trade policy and is the one on which economists usually concentrate. But there is also a critical 'supply side'. Box C represents the preferences of politicians. Again this is an area where economists are often left high and dry. Does the politician wish to favour a particular group? Has he or she been sponsored by a pressure group? Are their preferences directed by wider social interests?

Box D models the institutional structure of government. It deals with the answer to the questions of who actually decides on trade policy. How does the executive reconcile the conflicting demands? How are trade policies linked to other policies? How does the executive reconcile trade budgetary and trade policy objectives? A full 'supply-side' treatment would also require box D to model the electoral system (first-past-the-post or proportional representation), other countries' institutional structures, the structures of international institutions such as the WTO and the EU, and so on.

Clearly it is difficult, if not impossible, to produce a trade policy model which can take account of all the 'political economy' forces which, in practice, determine trade policy.

Self-interest and the prisoner's dilemma

"The concepts of 'self-interest' and the 'prisoner's dilemma' shed light on some of the gaps we have identified in the political economy of trade policy."

⬭ Economic self-interest

Sometimes it is difficult to know where economic self-interest lies. For example, it might be thought that anyone in the UK who spent a large proportion of their income on cheap fashion clothing would favour the lowering of tariffs on imports to the UK from Asian countries, if this would bring them lower prices. But economic analysis tells us that this is not necessarily the case. People who spend a large proportion of their income on a commodity do not necessarily stand to gain from free trade in that commodity. Everything depends on what *factor services* that person supplies in their own economy.

This insight derives from the Heckscher–Ohlin model (Chapter 2) or, to be more precise, from an important extension of the Heckscher–Ohlin model called the Stolper–Samuelson theorem. It was first set out in 1941 by Wolfgang Stolper and Paul Samuelson. Trade in goods can be shown, under certain assumptions, to substitute for trade in factors of production. Trade leads to an increase in the price of the abundant factor (which had a relatively low price in the pre-trade situation), and a fall in the price of the scarce factor (which had a relatively high price in the pre-trade situation). Assuming full employment before and after trade, the Stolper–Samuelson theorem says that with free trade, the increase in the price of the abundant factor, and the fall in the price of the scarce factor, leads to a rise in the real income of those who own the abundant factor, and a fall in the real income of those who own the scarce factor.

Let us go back now to consider the case of the person in the UK who spends a large proportion of his/her income on cheap fashion clothing, say from China. Should they favour the relaxation of trade controls? The answer may well be no. We assume China's clothing is a relatively labour-intensive product. If that is the case, the UK worker will favour protection. Imports use the UK's relatively scarce factor of production. Those who own the scarce factor in the UK, i.e. workers, will see with free trade a fall in their real incomes. However, those who own capital, the abundant factor in the UK, may see things differently. Capital is the abundant factor. With free trade, the real income of those who own the abundant factor will rise.

This insight has an important implication for the political economy of trade policy. In the UK, there are more voters who are 'workers' than voters who are 'capitalists'. With a 'one-person-one-vote' system, free trade should be doomed. But the gainers (capitalists) can always compensate the losers (workers) by offering higher wages. If what the capitalists gain from free trade is greater than the compensation they need to pay in the form of higher wages to their workers, then free trade is likely to be the favoured outcome. In many real-world situations, however, the gains to the capitalists will not be sufficient to compensate those who lose from a policy of free trade.

What triggers group action?

Although trade models can help identify economic self-interest, we need a different approach to explain how individual self-interest is then transformed into group action – those interest groups which lobby for trade protection.

Some of the insights offered by economists on this point include the following:

● Individuals are more likely to lobby for protection as a group when their *income declines*. Industries which are suffering catastrophic falls in *profits* and *employment* will lobby for protection. In these circumstances, both workers and capitalists may join together to pressurise policy-makers.
● Individuals will lobby for protection as a group if they are faced with rising *uncertainty*. There is a tendency for groups to lobby for protection to reduce the variability of prices and incomes. This is why commodity stabilisation schemes are supported by many primary producers.
● Interest groups are more likely to lobby for *tariffs and quotas* than for direct subsidies. Tariffs and quotas often bring greater welfare losses to the nation, but the general public is unaware of this, believing that the foreigner pays. The group lobbying for protection plays on the public's lack of knowledge. The self-interest framework also indicates that governments are more likely to agree to tariffs and quotas. Subsidies are very transparent and have to be financed through taxation or borrowing. Public opinion, therefore, may be very hostile to any subsidies which appear in the government's current expenditure statistics.

The prisoner's dilemma

It is possible to translate economic self-interest at the level of the nation into game-theory terms. With protection, we could be dealing with a situation in which the government in country A, and the government in country B, acting in their own self-interest, choose to protect. Yet both country A and country B would be better off if neither engaged in trade protection. By acting unilaterally and invoking trade protection, both countries fail to achieve the best possible outcome. This is the familiar situation of the prisoner's dilemma.

Consider the example of the prisoner's dilemma in Figure 4.5. Country A and country B each gain welfare equivalent to £500 billion if they adopt free trade (segment I).

Now suppose country A adopts protection, but country B does not. Country A gains £500 billion but country B loses out and gains only £50 billion (segment III). Country A gains at the expense of country B because the terms of trade turn in country A's favour, and the free trade country, country B, bears the cost. Similarly, if country B adopts protection and country A stays with free trade, country B gains £500 billion, but country A gains only £50 billion (segment II). If both countries opt for protection (segment IV), each gains £100 billion.

The prisoner's dilemma scenario shows that both countries will 'defect' from free trade, i.e. engage in protection, because this is the highest welfare that can be achieved irrespective of the strategy followed by the other country. If any country goes for free trade, while its trading partner protects, the gain would be less than

Figure 4.5 The prisoner's dilemma in trade policy

	COUNTRY B	
	Co-operation (free trade)	Defection (protection)
COUNTRY A — Co-operation (free trade)	**I** £500 billion, £500 billion	**II** £50 billion, £500 billion
COUNTRY A — Defection (protection)	**III** £500 billion, £50 billion	**IV** £100 billion, £100 billion

£100 billion, i.e. £50 billion. So both countries opt for protection, and gain only £100 billion each. They would be much better off under free trade!

Income distribution and social objectives

Voters and policy-makers do have broader social concerns where foreign trade is concerned. In this final section of Chapter 4, the focus is on using trade policy to affect the distribution of income.

Max Corden (1974) introduced the concept of a 'conservative social welfare function' to explain trade policy which is determined by social values in relation to a nation's income distribution. A conservative social welfare function seeks to avoid any significant absolute reductions in the real incomes of any section of the community. So temporary protection is often given to industries which are being seriously affected by an unexpected upturn in imports. The aim is to prevent workers in that industry suffering a significant fall in income. Corden argued that social objectives always assign heavy weights to decreases in income. Given changes in income brought about by trade changes, up or down, of equal magnitude, the tendency will always be to take the decreases more seriously and introduce measures to prevent significant shifts in income away from workers.

Other economists have taken Corden's ideas a stage further, arguing that trade policy does not attempt only to restore the status quo, but rather that it often tries to increase the standard of living of the least well-off workers. Research in the US in the 1980s indicated that it was precisely those industries with a high proportion of workers on low wages that had the highest levels of protection. The industries in question included textiles, clothing, toys, furniture and jewellery.

There is no doubt that trade policy can be used to redistribute income in a society: either to restore the status quo or to favour particular groups or interests. But there is a huge gap in our understanding. Why should trade policy be the favoured means of redistributing income when there are other, more efficient means of achieving that objective, namely through taxation and spending?

> Saying that trade policy exists because it serves to transfer income to favoured groups is a bit like saying Sir Edmund Hillary climbed Mt. Everest because he wanted to get some mountain air. There was surely an easier way of accomplishing that objective.
>
> (Dani Rodrik, 1995)

The preference of political systems to use trade interventions for distributional purposes is widely known. Almost all governments use, or have used, trade policies for that purpose. But why should they favour protection over other redistributive policies, when they face an upsurge in imports? Unfortunately, none of the explanations put forward by economists to date as to the preferences of governments for trade policies over other policies is particularly convincing. Rodrik has called for economists to change their priorities and address this question in a more focused way.

Fair trade

Economists tend to assume that economic agents, producers and consumers are motivated by self-interest. But this is not always the case. Individuals can and do take ethical positions and often gain satisfaction from belonging to socially driven organisations. Trade policy may endorse views about socially responsible trade which are held by the general public.

A significant proportion of the public believes that trade policy should take into account poverty in the developing world and wider environmental issues. The 'fair trade' movement, which is widely supported in Europe, is an interesting example of socially responsible trade. Fair trade products are available in NGO-run shops and mainstream retailers in developed countries, and have spread from tea and coffee to cover imports of ground nuts, chocolate, bananas, mangoes and honey.

None of these products is produced in significant quantities in developed countries, so the objective must be to influence income distribution and the environment in producer countries. Local co-operatives are supported, and encouraged to market the crop themselves. The co-operative guarantees that the crops are grown in a sustainable way, and ensures that revenues are distributed to farmers on a 'fair' basis. In production, the emphasis is on locally sourced inputs. Organic methods are employed which make as little use as possible of imported chemicals, fertilisers and pesticides.

Partnerships between NGOs, governments, businesses and civil society could be expected to reinforce consumers' views about 'socially responsible' trade, translating them into trade policy. Trade policy could be explained, therefore, by the government's attitude to the welfare of certain disadvantaged groups within the international economy, reflecting the ethical concerns of their own consumers.

CASE STUDY 4.1

Brazil warns US on free trade pact

Paul O'Neill, US treasury secretary, yesterday left Brazil having been given the clear message that in spite of the regional economic crisis it will not accept a Free Trade Agreement for the Americas (FTAA) unless the US cuts trade barriers and opens its market.

President Fernando Henrique Cardoso said publicly that their talks had been 'constructive' and that he awaited 'effective support from the United States'.

But privately, it emerged yesterday, Mr Cardoso made clear his country's disappointment with US trade protectionism. Brazil is interested in an FTAA only in exchange for 'access to markets', the president told Mr O'Neill.

Mr Cardoso's message came as President George W. Bush yesterday put his signature to the trade promotion authority (TPA) bill. This 'fast-track' authority allows him to negotiate trade agreements without the threat that they will be picked apart by congressional amendments.

Armed with fast-track authority, the administration hopes to relaunch FTAA negotiations as a policy initiative towards Latin America. Talks are set to conclude by 2005.

'With the approval of the TPA by Congress, President Bush now has a crucial instrument to conclude the FTAA, increasing the flow of merchandise and ideas between our citizens and improving the economic conditions in the entire hemisphere,' says Mr O'Neill.

The Brazilian government, eager to obtain US support for its negotiations on aid from the International Monetary Fund to help stem its sliding currency, treated Mr O'Neill's visit with diplomatic courtesy.

The stand-off Mr O'Neill triggered last week when he questioned Brazil's ability to manage foreign aid was put aside after

his strong statements of support this week. 'Brazil has the right economic policies in place to maintain stability so that the economy can continue to grow' Mr O'Neill said. 'We also support the current negotiations of Brazilian authorities with the IMF.'

US barriers on steel imports and a renewal this year of massive farm subsidies have hit the growth prospects of Brazil's most competitive industries, angering business and politicians. The TPA approved by Congress last week, Brazil argues, restricts negotiations on a series of 'sensitive' agricultural exports.

'FTAA negotiations were never going to be easy but with the wave of [US] protectionism, we know they will be even more difficult,' said Celso Lafer, foreign minister.

Brazil's opposition candidates in October's presidential elections have also expressed serious concerns about FTAA. The leftwing Workers' Party, which leads opinion polls ahead of October's presidential elections, says that if US protectionism persists, 'FTAA will not be a free trade agreement but an economic annexation of the continent'.

Source: Raymond Colitt, *Financial Times*, 7 August 2002. Reprinted with permission.

Comment on case study 4.1

The US is interested in concluding a free trade agreement for the Americas (FTAA). Negotiations are expected to be concluded by 2005. The US president has been given extra 'fast-track' powers (TPA) to negotiate the trade agreement without having to go back to the Congress. In Congress, politicians seeking to satisfy special interest groups would have been likely to have put forward many amendments to a free trade pact, delaying its implementation and reducing its effectiveness.

Brazil, which would be a key signatory to a Latin American free trade agreement, is sceptical about

US intentions. Brazil's most competitive industries are agriculture and steel. Both face increasing US protectionism. Farm subsidies in the US have increased and steel imports are subject to higher tariffs. Brazil's left-wing government, following election in October 2002, is unlikely to support the FTAA unless increased access to US markets is on offer, with a lowering of trade barriers. The TPA (Trade Promotion Authority Bill) which gives the US president his 'fast-track' authority, is unlikely to help, as it exempts certain 'sensitive' products from the trade negotiations.

CASE STUDY 4.2

Clouds over US wheat farmers

Relief has finally come to the parched, wheat-growing plains of the American Midwest. In the last two weeks, rain has returned

after the most severe summer drought in living memory.

Some farmers say it was worse than the great 'Dust Bowl'

drought of the 1930s, which decimated livestock and forced thousands of people off farming land.

But while the return of rain is being welcomed by farmers, who are in the midst of planting next year's wheat crop, clouds of a different variety are gathering over US wheat growers.

The reintroduction of federal farm subsidies, and a recent near-doubling in the price of wheat to around $4 a bushel because of the drought, could spark a significant increase in US wheat acreage in the next six months as farmers attempt to cash in on more favourable prices by planting more wheat.

Yet this comes as US wheat growers are facing increased competition in the global export market from new entrants such as Russia and countries in central and eastern Europe. Russia is not only expected to surpass the US in wheat production this year, but will export wheat for the first time.

'It's going to be tough. You're going to end up with a considerable increase in world wheat supplies unless we have another drought or some other act of nature hurting production. It's setting the stage for a rather large wheat crop for the next two years,' says Brenda Tucker at Chicago-based Ag Research Company.

In Kansas, the largest wheat producing state in the US, prices were already heading higher as summer started because of a lack of rainfall as early as spring.

Prices started to rocket as the drought began and spread to Canada, also a big wheat producer. Pricing support came from the futures markets, where commodity funds seeking to diversify away from equities pumped cash into wheat futures on the Chicago Board of Trade and elsewhere.

December wheat futures on the Kansas City Board of Trade – the largest grain exchange after the Chicago Board of Trade – rose 40 per cent from $2.95 in May to $4.87 in early September.

Ms Tucker says the reintroduction of farm subsidies, under a new farm bill signed by President Bush, is likely to result in a sharp increase in US wheat acreage. The subsidy available to growers of wheat is 54 cents a bushel, a considerable incentive to switch from other crops.

'I talk to farmers who produce from South Dakota to Louisiana and Texas who're telling me they are planting wheat for the first time in 10 years because they are looking at the profitability of doing so,' she says.

Source: Jeremy Grant, Financial Times, 26 September 2002. Reprinted with permission.

Comment on case study 4.2

The American midwest is where the US grows wheat, and massive prairies supply a large proportion of US needs for grain, as well as contributing to the balance of payments through exports. Wheat crops are dependent on the weather. In the 1930s, the drought which brought the great 'Dust Bowl' caused widespread hardship to farming families. In 2002, there was a similar drought which led to a near-doubling of the price of wheat.

President Bush reintroduced subsidies for wheat farmers. Together with the rise in the price of wheat, these encouraged farmers to plant more wheat. The subsidies provide a considerable incentive for farmers to switch to wheat from other crops. This means there could be a substantial increase in supply, and fall in price, in the future. Adding to this problem is competition from farmers in central and eastern Europe. In 2002, Russian wheat production exceeded that of the US and was a Russian export crop for the first time.

Summary

● Many measures come under the heading of trade protection. They include tariffs, quotas, VERs and subsidies. Other policies such as government procurement, marketing and packaging standards, and health and safety regulations may also operate in restraint of trade.

69

● Exchange and capital controls can also reduce the volume of trade. The cost of trading increases and it becomes difficult and expensive to hedge against risk.

● Although tariffs are declining in real-world importance, the tariff forms the basis of the standard analysis of the welfare losses of protection. The standard analysis identifies dead-weight losses of consumers as the welfare losses of protection. They are not unimportant, even though the net national loss may be small relative to national income.

● The 'old' arguments for protection are those of the optimum tariff and the infant industry. There are also traditional non-economic arguments which focus on income distribution, and security and defence.

● New thinking about trade policy focuses on externalities. The context is oligopoly rather than perfect competition, and a key role is assigned to research and development. Governments can engage in strategic trade policy to promote exports via import protection.

● If the assumption of perfect competition is dropped, as in the Brander–Spencer approach, the home country can extract monopoly profit from a foreign supplier via a tariff.

● There may be a bias towards protectionism in economic policy. This does not mean that policy-makers are ignorant of free trade theories. What is needed is a political economy model of trade policy, which includes individual and policy-makers' preferences, political demands, and government institutions and structures.

● Economic self-interest and the prisoner's dilemma can shed light on some aspects of the political economy of trade policy. Voters and policy-makers may also have broader social concerns about income distribution and fair trade.

Key concepts

- Specific, ad valorem, and compound tariffs
- Non-tariff barriers
- Voluntary export restraints
- Subsidies
- Exchange and capital controls
- Rent-seeking
- Producer and consumer surplus

- Optimum tariff
- Infant industry
- Strategic trade policy
- Political economy model of trade policy
- Prisoner's dilemma
- Conservative social welfare function
- Fair trade

Questions for discussion

1 Explain the different methods used by governments to restrict the volume of imports into domestic markets.

2 Can protectionism ever be a valid economic policy?

3 Show how the gains and losses from a tariff can be measured using the concepts of producer and consumer surplus.

4 Why does government revenue increase with a tariff but not with an export subsidy? Why might a government choose an export subsidy in preference to a tariff?

5 Explain what is meant by strategic trade policy. Does it undermine the case for free trade?

6 Is the doctrine of free trade undermined by the existence of imperfect competition in the world economy?

7 What practical guidelines could you offer a government which is intending to pursue a strategic trade policy?

8 Can free trade ever be fair trade?

9 Do people who spend a large proportion of their income on food stand to gain from the removal of protection on agricultural products?

10 Define an 'infant industry'. Do any industries in the UK fulfil the necessary conditions for protection as an infant industry?

Suggested reading

Baldwin, R. E. (1987) 'The political economy of trade policy', *Journal of Economic Perspectives*, vol. 3, no. 4, pp. 119–35.

Brander, J. and Spencer, B. (1981) 'Tariffs and the extraction of foreign monopoly rents under potential entry', *Canadian Journal of Economics*, vol. 14, no. 3, pp. 371–89.

Corden, W. M. (1974) *Trade Policy and Economic Welfare*, Oxford: Clarendon Press.

Krueger, A. (1974) 'The Political Economy of the Rent-Seeking Society', *American Economic Review*, vol. 64, pp. 291–303.

Krugman, P. R. (1984) *Import Protection and Export Promotion: International Competition in the Presence of Oligopoly and Economies of Scale, Monopolistic Competition and International Trade*, Oxford: Clarendon Press.

Krugman, P. (1995) *Strategic Trade Policy and the New International Economics*, Cambridge, MA: MIT Press.

Rodrik, D. (1995) 'Political Economy of Trade Policy', *Handbook of International Economics*, vol. 3, ch. 28, Amsterdam: Elsevier Science.

Stolper, W. F., and Samuelson, P. A. (1941) 'Protection and Real Wages', *Review of Economic Studies*.

Chapter 5

International trade policy

Introduction

International trade in the twenty-first century does not correspond to the textbook model, in which finished goods are produced in one country to be transported by air, sea or land for sale in another country. More than one-third of all international trade today takes the form of intra-firm exchanges. Frequently a firm manufactures components in one country, assembles them in a second country, to be sold as finished goods in a third country or even to be re-exported back for sale in the country of origin.

In addition to this there are now powerful trade blocs in the world economy: for example, the European Union (EU) and the North American Free Trade Agreement (NAFTA). Where trade blocs with a common external tariff exist, it may be the case that an outside firm wishing to sell goods or services in a country belonging to a trade bloc may be obliged to invest in that country to overcome trade barriers. Japanese car plants have located in Europe, for example, in order to bypass the trade restrictions imposed by the EU on cars imported from non-EU countries. Only in 1999 did the EU finally lift its 'voluntary' agreement with Japan limiting exports of Japanese cars into the EU.

It is also the case that in the past two decades there has been a huge increase in the exposure of all firms to global competition. Markets have been liberalised and there has also been a revolution in telecommunications which has integrated the world's financial operations. Technology now ensures that market information and technical know-how crosses national boundaries at great speed.

In today's world firms can gain or lose their competitive edge in international markets very quickly. Jagdish Bhagwati, Professor of Economics at Colombia University in the US, has argued that trade based on comparative advantage is increasingly volatile and precarious. When firms in many countries can access similar technology and can borrow at the same rates of interest, the margins of comparative advantage can be very small. Slight shifts in cost can cause firms to move quickly from one country to another to maintain their international competitiveness. Bhagwati has termed this phenomenon 'kaleidoscopic comparative advantage'.

Changes in the framework of international trade have had two important conse-quences for trade policy:

- Firms have realised that comparative advantage is volatile and precarious. They are therefore very keen to ensure that their rivals do not engage in what they see as unfair trade. They put pressure on governments and on institutions like the World Trade Organisation (WTO) to harmonise policies in trading countries so that all have the advantages and disadvantages of a single trading framework.
- With international competitiveness so unstable, workers have come to feel increas-ingly insecure. The problem of job insecurity may apply equally to skilled, unskilled and professional and white-collar workers. As firms indicate their intention to move production overseas there is pressure on governments by firms and their employees to introduce regulatory frameworks which can safeguard workers' rights.

Chapter 5 is concerned with international trade policy. It is based on the fact that interest groups like trade unions, environmentalists, farmers' representatives and firms lobby governments to invoke protectionist measures. National governments do not, however, have complete freedom to impose trade barriers, even if they wished to do so. Membership of a trade bloc such as the EU constrains freedom of action. So too does membership of international institutions like the WTO.

The trade policy of nation states, their bargaining power in relation to trade mat-ters, and any likely retaliation from other countries form the subject matter of this chapter. The context is the WTO (and its predecessor GATT). The WTO has the over-riding responsibility to uphold the principles of free trade in the world economy because there is often a conflict between the principles of multilateral free trade and the commercial considerations of individual countries.

Chapter 5 looks at the role of the WTO in resolving the fundamental problem of how to reconcile the benefits of free trade with the demands of countries, firms, workers and consumers for protection from the effects of international competition. The chap-ter also shows how issues such as the environment, health and safety, and competition from low-wage economies have come to greater prominence over the past two decades. Nevertheless the underlying problem is unchanged. The WTO is required to promote the benefits of free trade and cross-border investment, while at the same time addressing the valid concerns of individuals about the costs of globalisation.

Objectives

When you have completed this chapter, you should be able to:

- explain why some countries are more *protectionist* than others, and why protectionist tendencies may vary over time in the world economy;
- discuss the ways in which the *WTO system* differs from that of its predecessor GATT;
- understand why *environmentalists* often appear to be dissatisfied with the WTO;
- outline the dilemmas facing the WTO with respect to food-safety issues;

- discuss whether a country is justified in keeping out goods and services from *low-wage countries*;
- define a *trade bloc* and explain what is meant by trade creation and trade diversion;
- appreciate the WTO's attitude towards the *trade policy of the EU* and, correspondingly, the EU's response to criticisms from the WTO.

Economic theory versus international political economy

In Chapter 4, we learned how economists over the years have offered many explanations for trade restrictions. Economists tend to regard protectionism as irrational or short-sighted. Under 'old protectionism' economists recognised two exceptions to the 'free trade is best' rule. They were:

- the *optimum-tariff* which under certain assumptions could improve a large country's terms of trade, and
- the use of trade barriers to shift the problem of *unemployment* to trading partners, although, under certain circumstances, this could provoke retaliation.

Writers in the tradition of old protectionism were also very much concerned with the process of trade bargaining which took place between nation states. Mercantilists, in particular, wrote extensively on the practical determinants of bargaining strength. Adam Smith, though a proponent of free trade, considered that a nation might do well to impose tariffs in order to force its trading partner to remove its own tariffs. Keynes himself, generally regarded as supporting free trade, nevertheless advocated, in the 1930s, a neo-mercantilist position, believing that if full employment were not achieved, then a tariff might help bring about a net increase in production.

Other supposed benefits of trade restrictions have received attention from economists arguing in the tradition of 'new protectionism'. In the modern world economy trade restrictions are often the result of *rent-seeking* behaviour on the part of interest groups. Politicians tend to 'reward' privileged groups such as powerful trade unionists or rich entrepreneurs for their support, by imposing restrictions on import-competing goods. Or, trade barriers may be used by governments to give a competitive advantage to monopolistic and oligopolistic firms ('strategic trade policy'), thereby promoting the activities of these firms in overseas markets.

Although the literature on new protectionism can be adapted to explain trade policy, as nation states jostle for economic advantage in international markets, that has not been the main objective of the theory. Indeed it is sometimes difficult to use economic theory at all, either 'old' or 'new' versions, to explain why some countries are more protectionist than others, or why protectionist tendencies in the world economy may vary over time. For this reason economists can choose to look elsewhere for clues, possibly in the literature of international political economy.

International political economy offers a number of generalisations about trade relations and bargaining strategies between nation states. All of them are plausible, and most of them are supported by respectable real-world empirical evidence.

- It is *large*, well-developed nation states that tend to favour economic openness. Such states tend to benefit the most from free trade. They are less likely to suffer from fluctuations in external markets. In consequence they are unlikely to be protectionist, other things being equal.
- Nation states that are predominantly *agrarian* tend to favour protectionism. When an economy shifts decisively from agriculture to industry, usually it will lower its tariffs.
- Countries that pioneer new *technologies* have an incentive to lower trade barriers. Often these innovations are concentrated in a *lead* economy. As new technologies diffuse through the world, *follower* countries often raise their trade barriers in order to compete for lead economy status behind a tariff wall.
- Nation states that are suffering from *external shocks*, such as war, depression and lack of public confidence, tend to favour trade restrictions. Economic downswings tend to favour protection, upswings tend to favour free trade.
- Nation states with strong *pressure groups*, possibly articulated through an effective legislature, can provide a strong push towards, or pull away from, protectionist tendencies, depending on the circumstances. Factors such as the quality of political leadership are also important in this context.

International political economy helps to explain why many developing countries have been very late converts to the doctrine of free trade. Most are, or have been, important producers of primary products: foodstuffs and raw materials. Since the mid-1990s, however, agricultural products have also been incorporated into the rules of the international trading system. Protectionist policies for agricultural products within developed countries, such as the EU's CAP, have been subjected to successive rounds of tariff reduction. This has had the effect of enabling non-EU members to access the European market for agricultural products. In principle this should bring about important long-term benefits to developing countries.

In the last decade, more than fifty developing countries have unilaterally lowered their own trade barriers as part of a comprehensive move towards liberalisation of markets. Sub-Saharan Africa remains the exception, maintaining many trade restrictions, particularly export taxes. Sub-Saharan Africa also has many other barriers associated with civil strife and dislocation. In consequence, it is a world region which is declining in importance in international trade.

From GATT to the WTO

Towards the end of World War II, forty-four nations met under the leadership of the Allied Powers to draw up plans for the post-war international system of trade and payments. The world economy was to be organised around three cornerstones: the

International Monetary Fund (IMF), the International Bank for Reconstruction and Development (IBRD or World Bank) and the International Trade Organisation (ITO). Of these three the ITO never came into existence, much to the disappointment of Keynes, because the US Senate refused to ratify its charter. In fact, even in Europe there was very little support for the ITO. Public opinion in the UK had moved against multilateralism and only a handful of members of parliament offered unqualified support for the ITO. In the US the business community opposed the ITO believing that the US export surplus was under attack from potential trading partners. US business argued that it would be subject to more trade discrimination with the ITO than without.

The place of the proposed ITO was taken by the General Agreement on Tariffs and Trade (GATT) which came into being in 1947. Its objective was to prevent a return to the protectionist measures which had so damaged world trade during the 1930s. Member countries of GATT, under the leadership of the US, were to meet from time to time to jointly negotiate on matters of trade policy. The successive negotiations were termed rounds. Altogether there were eight rounds of negotiations between 1947 and 1995. The aim was to reduce barriers to trade by removing tariffs, quotas, taxes, subsidies and administrative procedures which could operate in restraint of trade. Aside from the rounds of trade negotiations, GATT also fulfilled a watchdog role, monitoring the day-to-day trading policies of member countries.

Given its provisional basis (legally GATT was never more than a series of international agreements to negotiate on matters of trade policy), its achievements were quite remarkable. Little by little, in successive rounds of trade negotiations, multilateral trade principles were extended through the reduction of tariffs and the phasing out of quantitative restrictions. GATT also succeeded, through its panel of experts, in resolving a number of trade disputes between members.

The final round of GATT negotiations was the Uruguay Round of Multilateral Trade Negotiations. This is generally agreed to have been the most comprehensive and ambitious of all the GATT rounds. It lasted for seven years. The Final Act, which embodied the results of these negotiations, was signed in April 1995 in Marrakesh, Morocco. The Final Act is a very complex document, but it is possible to summarise its main provisions.

● The *multifibre arrangement* (MFA), which had protected member countries' textiles and clothing from foreign competition, was to be phased out.
● *Agriculture*, which had effectively been excluded from previous GATT rounds was to be brought within the provisions of GATT, leading to progressive *liberalisation of trade* in agricultural products.
● Rules were established to cover *intellectual property rights*. In seven areas it was permissible to *enforce protection*: copyright, trademarks, geographical indications, industrial design, patents, design of integrated circuits and the protection of undisclosed information.
● The GATT provisions were for the first time extended to cover *services*. The service sector is a large and growing part of world trade, covering such things as tourism, banking, shipping, telecommunications, insurance and software

development. The General Agreement on Trade in Services (GATS) aimed for a *gradual liberalisation* of trade in services.

● On industrial goods, *voluntary export restraints* (VERs) were to be *phased out*. These had come to be the favourite protectionist instrument in the US and the EU, affecting commodities like electrical appliances and cars. Countries such as Japan had been obliged to abide by quotas for their exports of cars and electrical goods to the US and the EU. The word 'voluntary' was somewhat misleading.

Developing countries

The Uruguay Round of GATT negotiations was also the first GATT round which actively promoted the participation of developing countries. It was the first to take seriously the contribution of developing countries to international trade. In previous rounds when negotiations reached critical points, developing countries were excluded from the debates. The Uruguay Round was different. In part this was a reflection of the growing importance through trade and capital flows of developing countries in the world economy. This can be seen both on the *demand* side (bigger export markets in the developing world for developed countries) and the *supply* side (increased competition in developed countries from third-world imports). On the *export* side over 40 per cent of US exports, 47 per cent of EU exports, and 48 per cent of Japanese exports now go to developing or transition countries. Asia and Latin America are the world's fastest-growing markets. On the *import* side, the main fear has been that cheap labour in the developing world will force wages down in developed countries. Economists continue to point out, however, that in rich countries higher wages are justified by higher productivity due to higher standards of education, more efficient management and superior infrastructure. The expectation is that when developing countries' productivity catches up, their wages will also rise.

The WTO

GATT was established on a provisional basis, which in the end was to last for half a century. Although GATT had permanent headquarters in Geneva, legally it was never more than an international agreement to negotiate jointly on matters of trade policy. The final act of the Uruguay Round established a formal organisation called the WTO to replace GATT. This is generally considered to be the most important achievement of the Uruguay Round.

The WTO is a permanent body with its headquarters in Geneva. Decision-making comes about via a Ministerial Conference of representatives from all its member countries. The Ministerial Conference must meet at least once every two years. The first of these conferences was held in Singapore in December 1996, the fifth in Mexico in 2003.

The WTO framework is superior compared with its GATT predecessor because:

- It is a single undertaking with a *unified* legal basis. GATT was merely a series of multilateral trading agreements.
- Under the WTO there are clear *surveillance mechanisms* to oversee trade policy. There are annual reviews of international trade and reviews of members' own trade policies. This represents a considerable strengthening of policing procedures as compared with GATT.
- There are provisions for the WTO to *consult* with the IMF and the World Bank. This should bring a greater degree of co-ordination in the international economy as compared with the GATT system.

A further advantage claimed for the WTO is that its membership of countries is clear from the outset. Because WTO supports a rule-based trading system, all those who join the WTO must agree to abide by the provisions of the Final Act of the Uruguay Round. Under GATT, countries could join at various intervals from 1947 onwards. They could make use of what were termed 'provisional accession protocols' which allowed them to ignore GATT obligations and avoid GATT discipline. The same is not true of the WTO. All countries within the WTO agree to abide by the rules. For example, the WTO code obliges governments to treat foreigners and nationals equally when awarding government contracts. If domestic regulations clearly favour local firms over foreign firms, then this will not find favour with the WTO.

WTO and the environment

As long ago as 1971 GATT had established a Working Group on Environmental Measures and International Trade but the group did not meet for over twenty years. The Final Act of the Uruguay Round established a new Committee on Trade and the Environment (CTE) to operate within the WTO.

At present there are twenty multilateral environmental agreements in the world economy that have trade provisions. These provisions are discussed within the CTE. The most important are:

- the *Basel Convention* which controls the transport of hazardous waste across international borders;
- the *Convention on International Trade in Endangered Species* which restricts international trade in certain animals from the wild;
- the *Montreal Protocol* which applies restrictions on the production and export of CFCs in order to protect the ozone layer.

The CTE holds discussions once or twice a year on the multilateral environmental agreements, referring any problems to the dispute settlement mechanisms of the WTO. It is generally agreed, however, that progress by the CTE in addressing issues relevant to the environment has been slow. The CTE was asked to prepare a report for the first WTO Ministerial Conference, held in Singapore in December 1996. However, its 46-page report was criticised as having very little analysis and virtually no recommendations for specific actions. The basic problem is political. The WTO, like its predecessor GATT, makes decisions by consensus among its member countries. There is no consensus on trade/environment issues. If decisions cannot be reached by consensus, there are provisions for reaching decisions by votes, but anything contentious requires a three-quarters or even unanimous vote among member countries. This is difficult to achieve. The effect of environmental measures on the trade prospects of developing countries received specific attention at the Fourth Ministerial Conference of the WTO at Doha, Qatar, in November 2001. In the light of the Doha Declaration the CTE is expected to reflect in the future on the implications of environmental issues for the trade prospects of developing countries.

What then are the environmental issues on which it is difficult to reach agreement in the WTO? The issues divide into three types: domestic pollution, transborder pollution and global pollution.

Domestic pollution

Consider the case where pollution is domestic in nature and does not spill over national boundaries. Countries differ in their beliefs as to whether a lack of concern for the domestic environment constitutes 'unfair trade'. Richer countries tend to have higher environmental standards than poorer ones. Poorer countries operating in the same industry or sector may therefore have what some would regard as an unfair trade advantage. In 1995 Senator Boren in the US introduced legislation into Congress to prevent imports of carbon and steel alloys from countries with low environmental standards. He argued that the US spends 250 per cent more on environmental controls than its competitors and there was 'an unfair advantage employed by other nations exploiting the environment and public health for economic gain'. Of course competitors would not agree with this diagnosis of 'unfair trade'. They would reply that environmental diversity between countries is quite legitimate and should not interfere with free-trade principles. It is quite acceptable for different countries to *value* their domestic environment differently. In any case a rich country can afford to spend more on its own environment. Forcing poor countries to spend a high proportion of their income on pollution abatement will further drive down their standard of living.

Transborder pollution

What about pollution that spills over national boundaries? This is what economists term transborder pollution and it gives rise to transborder externalities, which are even more complex than those which arise with purely domestic pollution. Does a country being damaged by pollution from another have a right to ban imports from that country? Would Canada be justified in keeping out imports from the US on the grounds that US acid rain spills across the border into

Canada? Most economists, and the WTO, would argue that trade policy is a rather blunt instrument to tackle the specific environment problem of transborder pollution. Losses to Canada from reduced trade are likely to be much greater than the gains to Canada from less acid rain.

Global pollution

There is the argument that the WTO through the CTE could support trade sanctions to reduce global pollution problems. Problems such as ozone layer depletion and global warming can only be solved by international actions. But countries which choose to ignore agreements to reduce global pollution can free ride, i.e. they can get all the benefits of low global pollution levels while bearing none of the costs. The argument is that the WTO, via the CTE, could develop rules permitting the use of trade sanctions against free riders. To many people this makes political and economic sense but it would represent a departure for the WTO from a fifty-year tradition of steadfastly upholding free trade. The environmental argument would then have won out against the trade arguments.

Social issues and the WTO

The basic idea behind the call for 'social clauses' in international trade agreements is that lower labour standards in a country might confer an unfair competitive advantage relative to trading partners with higher labour standards. Lower labour standards would typically include not only lower *real wages* but also such undesirable features as child labour, legislation against collective bargaining by trade unions, and lax health and safety provisions. All of these, it is argued, could be responsible for 'cheap' labour leading to an 'unfair' competitive advantage. Usually the complaint about 'unfair' trade is made by major developed countries, in relation to imports from developing countries, which are said to be produced under exploitative labour conditions.

The fear of unfair competitive advantages conferred by low labour standards was present from the very beginning in GATT. Indeed the charter of the ITO (the institution that never came into being) stated that 'members recognize that unfair labour conditions, particularly in production for export create difficulties in international trade and accordingly each member shall take whatever action may be appropriate and feasible to eliminate such conditions within its territory'.

Although GATT itself never got to grips with the question of labour standards, the issue was raised again by the US and France at the end of the Uruguay Round. It was their intention that the WTO should discuss minimum labour standards, which would include freedom of association, collective bargaining, prohibition of forced labour and elimination of exploitative child labour. US Secretary of State Warren Christopher stated in 1996 that a discussion of trade and labour standards in the WTO was a US priority. However, Australia, Japan and South-East Asian countries are on record as being opposed to discussion of such issues within the WTO.

Economists and labour standards

Where do economists stand on the question of labour standards? First it is necessary to dispose of the type of argument associated with the late James Goldsmith who wrote the French best-seller *The Trap* in 1994. Goldsmith stated simply that competition from low-wage countries was a bad thing for developed countries like France. But economists have been quick to point out that low wages in themselves do not constitute an argument against free trade. The Ricardian theory of comparative advantage shows that trade can be mutually beneficial, regardless of differences in wage rates. If the productivity of French workers is higher than that of Indian workers we would expect French wages to be higher than Indian wages. French goods would still be able to compete internationally.

The demand that the charter of the WTO should include 'social clauses' that would allow restrictions to be placed on imports of products from countries without minimum labour standards is, however, supported by some economists. The Harvard economist Dani Rodrik supports the idea of social clauses, because he believes that globalisation has upset the balance of power between employers and employees. His arguments do not contradict comparative advantage. As an economist, Rodrik accepts that imports from low-wage countries are not necessarily a bad thing, but he argues that globalisation has made it easier for firms to shift production overseas. This has led to greater job insecurity, and has encouraged employers to stifle trade unions and reduce fringe benefits for workers. Workers are right to regard this as 'unfair trade'. Unless the problem is addressed, support for free trade among the population at large will diminish rapidly. Globalisation requires a higher degree of *social insurance* to make good the losses for those groups who are adversely affected by free trade. But governments are finding it harder and harder to raise the taxes necessary to finance increased welfare benefits. In any case, much of any increase in social spending goes not to workers but to pensioners, who gain from lower import prices but do not have jobs to lose. Rodrik has argued strongly that the WTO should be prepared to look at the broader effects of trade on labour markets if the social costs of globalisation are to be reduced. Those who oppose Rodrik point out that the WTO is not the correct international body to deal with problems of labour standards. The WTO should concentrate, they say, on preserving and promoting the benefits of free trade. Labour standards should be discussed in the International Labour Organisation (ILO).

The reason why social clauses are not discussed within the ILO at the present time is that the ILO has no enforcement mechanism. All it can do is try and persuade countries to adopt particular labour standards. The WTO, on the other hand, can use trade sanctions as a means of enforcement. That is why the pressure for social clauses is being felt in the WTO rather than the ILO. There is an obvious danger that protectionist interests will triumph. It would be far better to seek ways of enhancing the enforcement capabilities of the ILO, rather than including social clauses in the WTO.

Market access

The WTO, like its GATT predecessor, has agreed procedures for reducing or removing tariffs and non-tariff barriers in order to promote free trade. After eight GATT rounds of tariff reductions, average customs duties had fallen to a very low level. In the Uruguay Round, participants negotiated further cuts on a product-by-product basis. Nevertheless, there are still tariffs which restrict trade, especially tariffs in developed country markets on exports of non-agricultural products from developing countries. The WTO refers to 'tariff peaks' of 15 per cent and above on *sensitive* products. One such product is steel on which the US imposed tariffs in March 2002 in order to stave off bankruptcy in the US steel industry and force rationalisation and consolidation.

The WTO intends to reduce 'tariff peaks'. Following on from the Fifth Ministerial Conference in Mexico in 2003. They are scheduled to be phased out by 1 January 2005. Also to be subject to negotiation is 'tariff escalation' in which import duties are applied to semi-processed products rather than to raw materials, with even higher tariffs applied to finished products. The effect of tariff escalation is to protect domestic processing industries and discourage the development of processing activities in countries where the raw materials originate. Developing countries embarking on large-scale industrialisation are particularly affected by tariff escalation in developed country markets.

Anti-monopoly policy

A further aspect of market access is the promotion of competition. The EU has taken a lead in the WTO in linking free trade principles to anti-monopoly policy. In the area of telecommunications British Telecom was ruled against in the European Court of Justice for preventing private companies in the UK from receiving and forwarding international calls. The European Commission also required France to abolish the exclusive rights of the national telecommunications agency to supply telephone equipment.

The European Commission has put pressure on the WTO to focus on competition policy as a way of increasing multilateral trade. In 1996 the Commission forwarded a proposal for consideration at the First Ministerial Conference of the WTO in Singapore. It urged that a working group be established to consider a variety of issues including the establishment of a body of principles for competition policy, and the formulation of a disputes resolution mechanism to deal with violations of competitive principles.

Although the WTO Ministerial Conference in December 1996 accepted that a working group should be established to deal with the relationship between trade and competition, the conference declaration did not commit the WTO to going beyond existing provisions on matters relating to competition policy. One problem is that US anti-trust (i.e. anti-monopoly) legislation concerns itself only with the effects of monopoly on US consumers. It looks to see whether the monopoly raises domestic prices or reduces domestic output to consumers. It is not concerned with the way US businesses operate in foreign markets.

CASE STUDY 5.1

A good deal on trade

The deal reached in the US Congress late on Friday to give George W. Bush the 'fast track' authority needed to negotiate international trade agreements is an important victory for the president and his administration. It is also excellent news for the US, its trade partners and the global economy.

For Mr Bush, the breakthrough's significance goes beyond trade. Thrust on to the defensive by corporate scandals and financial market turmoil, he explicitly made swift passage of the bill central to a broader agenda of actions intended to bolster confidence in his economic stewardship. He can now plausibly claim to have gone some way to regaining the initiative.

The deal was secured only after intensive last-minute lobbying by the White House. Thankfully, Mr Bush refrained from further concessions to protectionist interests, to which he had shamelessly pandered in a misguided effort to win their support for the bill. It is nonetheless regrettable that, despite high popularity ratings, he did not show more backbone much earlier. It is to be hoped he will now conclude that politi-cal capital is there to be spent, not hoarded.

Internationally, the fast track agreement should allay fears that the US is retreating into trade unilateralism. The deal cannot undo all the damage to US international relations caused by its higher steel tariffs and the sharply increased agricultural subsidies provided for in its new farm bill. But it does signal US willingness to remain engaged and empowers its negotiators to pursue a more aggressive agenda. That should only benefit the Doha round of world trade talks.

Indeed, the US is already showing increased activism, notably by urging deep cuts in worldwide farm trade barriers as a priority for the round. That has not pleased the European Union and Japan. They have responded by calling the proposal hypocritical, because it requires relatively small reductions in US trade-distorting measures.

It is true the plan is designed, first and foremost, to serve US interests. But its overall goals are commendable. Furthermore, despite the farm bill, average US farm tariffs and spending are far lower than those in the EU and Japan. Brussels' recent agricultural reform plans would not change that because they would merely redirect – not reduce – existing subsidies.

By seeking to blame US double standards for its failure to tackle its own bloated and wasteful spending, the EU is fooling nobody – least of all the developing countries whose interests it claims to champion in the World Trade Organisation. Unless their demands for improved agricultural market access are met, the round will not succeed.

However, Washington is deluding itself if it thinks it can get its way without abandoning protectionist policies in return. Other WTO members will, rightly, be pressing it to lower barriers in areas including government procurement, textiles tariffs, shipping, financial services and anti-dumping policy.

All such barriers have stubborn defenders among producers and in Congress. Only if the Bush administration possesses the skill, courage and determination to overcome those obstacles will the hopes raised by the fast track deal be fulfilled.

Source: Financial Times, 29 July 2002. Reprinted with permission.

Comment on case study 5.1

The Bush administration has been criticised by some WTO member countries for the concessions it has made to protectionist interests in the US. In March 2002, for example, tariffs were raised on steel imports to protect US steel producers from bankruptcy. Even more contentious are the proposals in the farm bill now before Congress for increased agricultural subsidies for US farmers.

Congress has now given George W. Bush enhanced powers to negotiate trade agreements within the WTO, with the effect of reducing protectionism in the world economy. This should go some way towards appeasing important critics of the US, particularly the EU.

But is the EU itself operating double standards? After all its own record of protection for EU agriculture may not stand up to close scrutiny. The subsidies for EU farmers which should have been reduced have simply been redirected.

Nevertheless, Bush clearly has a fight ahead with WTO members. They are pressing Washington to abandon certain protectionist policies such as those relating to government procurement, financial services and shipping. These policies are strongly supported by special interest groups in the US and in Congress. The Bush administration will need a great deal of skill to negotiate a path between these conflicting interests.

Trade blocs and the WTO

The WTO is expected to uphold and promote the principles of free trade. How should it deal with trade blocs which promote free trade between member countries, but maintain trade barriers against non-members?

Regional trade blocs are growing in importance in the world economy. The longest-standing and most successful trade bloc is the EU. It has been joined by two other major trading blocs. The first, the North American Free Trade Agreement (NAFTA) (1993), includes the US, Canada and Mexico. The second, the Asia Pacific Economic Co-operation Forum (APEC) centres on Japan. According to the WTO, 109 regional trade agreements were notified to GATT between 1948 and 1994, of which one-third were signed between 1990 and 1994.

Economic theory and trade blocs

In deciding how to deal with trade blocs the WTO gets no clear help from economic theory. The first economist to address this question was Jacob Viner in the 1950s. He pointed out that when two countries reduce the trade barriers between them, then that 'creates' trade and raises real incomes, through specialisation and exchange. But if at the same time they decide to maintain trade barriers against a third country, this 'diverts' trade away from the third country which is a possible low-cost source of supply. It means a loss of real income in the first two countries. Trade creation and trade diversion are both consequences of trade blocs. The benefits of trade creation need to be weighed against the costs of trade diversion to assess the net gains or net losses from a trade bloc.

GATT had a presumption against trade blocs, enshrined in the principle of 'non-discrimination'. Member countries were not permitted to discriminate between one trading partner and another. If a country cut its tariffs on trade with one country, it had to do likewise for all countries. GATT, supported by the US over a very long period, saw the growth of trade blocs as being unhelpful to free trade.

In 1982 William Brock, then the US chief trade negotiator, decided to change the US's direction and pursue a trade agreement with Canada. Today's NAFTA is the consequence of that decision.

Paul Krugman has argued in support of trade blocs. He points out that much of international trade is based on geographical proximity anyway. Countries tend to trade with their near neighbours. If trade blocs are regional in character they will include near neighbours. In this sense, he argues, there are few opportunities for harmful trade diversion and many more opportunities for beneficial trade creation.

Arguments like those of Krugman have encouraged the WTO to look upon trade blocs in a more favourable light. Nevertheless trade blocs do contradict the goal of free trade on a multilateral basis. How can the WTO ensure that trade blocs which exist now, and those which may be brought into being in the future, become more liberal in their policies towards non-members? In its own report (1995) the WTO suggests three ways in which trade blocs can be made as non-discriminatory as possible.

● Countries forming trade blocs should be required to cut their tariffs against outsiders to the lowest level of any member of the trade bloc. This would be an extension of the principle of 'most-favoured-nation' (MFN) to countries which are not members of a trade bloc.
● Countries forming a trade bloc should be obliged to notify the WTO well in advance so that the WTO can study the agreements.
● The WTO should monitor existing trade blocs very closely.

These three changes will come into effect in the near future, but only if the WTO's member states agree.

The EU and the WTO

The WTO has surveillance mechanisms in place to oversee members' trade policies. Central to these mechanisms are the regular Trade Policy Reviews (TPR) in which member countries' trade and related policies are examined and evaluated. In 2000 the WTO reported on EU trade policies and noted that:

● The EU has been slow to relax quotas on industrial products over the past decade. Only twelve of the fifty-two product categories restricted in 1990 have been subsequently liberated.

- Anti-dumping measures are also restricting imports from a number of sources. These measures apply particularly to imports into the EU of iron and steel, electronic products and chemicals. In addition, state subsidies are undermining competitiveness in parts of the manufacturing sectors of EU member countries.
- In the agricultural sector the Common Agricultural Policy (CAP), which offers support to EU farmers, still discourages imports despite the CAP reform agreed in 1999. At the EU border high tariffs apply, estimated at 17 per cent.
- The EU maintains numerous preferential bilateral trade agreements from which the majority of WTO members are excluded. For example, among developing countries, preference is given only to African, Caribbean and Pacific countries (ACP). Most-favoured-nation treatment applies only to imports from Australia, Canada, Hong Kong, China, Japan, Republic of Korea, New Zealand, Singapore and the United States.
- The WTO also noted numerous 'food scares' at EU level which were likely to affect market access for exporters of foodstuffs to the EU. This is a consequence of the EU's food-safety policy.

Health and safety

This latter point, and others relating to standards of health and safety, do illustrate a deeper problem which is emerging in the WTO. National health and safety regulations have been growing in importance. The difficulty is deciding whether the regulations have a genuine purpose – for example, the health and safety of consumers – or whether they are simply a device to protect home producers from foreign competition. The EU decided some time ago that chickens slaughtered in the US do not meet EU safety standards. The US complained that although the US clean chickens in a different way from EU farmers, arguably the final product is just as safe to consume. Chickens were being kept out of EU markets in order to support EU chicken farmers. Indeed, the US Food and Drug Administration (FDA) goes further in claiming that the EU is not strict enough as far as many goods are concerned. EU drugs are required to satisfy a second set of FDA testing procedures before they can be imported into the US.

How many domestic regulations are justified and how many are intended solely to keep out foreign competition? If a country believes another's national regulations are just a cloak for trade protection, it can take its case to the WTO. If a guilty party fails to abide by the WTO ruling, the country that has taken the case can demand compensation or impose trade sanctions. In one well-publicised case, the EU did not comply with WTO rulings on imports of hormone-treated beef. In consequence retaliation was authorised by the WTO against EU exports in 1999.

EU's attitude to the WTO

Relations between the EU and the WTO have never been easy, but they deteriorated markedly during and following on from the Seattle Ministerial Conference. The EU Council has called for greater transparency in the WTO, and fuller participation of

WTO members in decision-making. The EU strongly supports the new comprehensive round of trade negotiations about to follow on from the Doha Ministerial Conference in November 2001. The EU is also looking for barriers to be lowered in areas which the US is committed to defend: namely, government procurement and international investment.

Reflecting the wider concerns expressed at Seattle, the EU Council has frequently called upon the WTO to address trade issues relating to labour standards, the environment and sustainable development. These are the issues which are likely in any case to dominate the WTO agenda over the next decade.

Summary

- There are various reasons why some countries may be more protectionist than others, or why protectionist tendencies in the world economy may vary over time. It is necessary to consider factors such as the role of special interest groups, the size of a country, whether the country is predominantly agrarian, the role of new technologies, and external shocks such as wars and depression.

- GATT, which came into being in 1947, aimed to prevent a return to the protectionist measures which had damaged world trade during the 1930s. It took the place of the ITO, the body favoured by Keynes which was unacceptable to the US Senate.

- The Uruguay Round of Multilateral Trade Negotiations, the final round under GATT, established the WTO in 1995. It is a unified institution with clear surveillance mechanisms and consultation procedures with the IMF and World Bank.

- The WTO has a Committee on Trade and the Environment. Consensus on environmental issues is difficult to achieve within the WTO.

- Another issue on which it is difficult to achieve a consensus in the WTO is labour standards. Usually it is developed countries who complain that developing countries produce exports with exploitative labour conditions. The economist Rodrik has argued that the WTO should be prepared to look at the effects of trade on labour markets, if the social costs of globalisation are to be reduced.

- For its future agenda the WTO aims to phase out 'tariff peaks' on sensitive products. It is also under pressure from the EU to strengthen its anti-monopoly policy.

- The WTO has suggested ways in which trade blocs can be made non-discriminatory. They should extend the MFN principle, and permit the WTO to study their agreements.

- The EU and the WTO do not have a harmonious relationship. The WTO has criticised EU trade policies, especially the CAP. It also notes numerous 'food scares' in the EU which illustrate a deeper problem of trade restrictions masquerading as health and safety provisions.

Key concepts

- International Trade Organisation (ITO)
- General Agreement on Tariffs and Trade (GATT)
- Uruguay Round
- World Trade Organisation (WTO)
- Committee on Trade and the Environment (CTE)

- Social clauses
- Labour standards
- Market access
- Tariff peaks
- Most-favoured-nation (MFN)
- Trade diversion
- Trade creation

Questions for discussion

1 What factors explain the considerable variation in trade restrictions between the different countries in the world economy?

2 Can 'free trade' ever be 'fair trade'? Discuss with particular reference to current issues within the WTO.

3 Do you think that a knowledge of economics is helpful when evaluating the role of the WTO in trade policy? Justify your answer.

4 Argue the case for and against a country restricting imports because of the environmental damage caused by their manufacture abroad.

5 Should international trade agreements set minimum labour standards for firms operating in low-income countries?

6 Are *developing* countries benefiting from trade policy changes under the WTO?

7 Is the US the only economy which can significantly influence international trade negotiations through the power of its own trade policy?

Team project on the WTO

Prepare a report and a presentation, with the title 'Reforming the WTO'. This should contain the recommendations of the team on the way forward for the WTO. The WTO has a website '**www.wto.org**' which may be a good place to begin.

Guidelines

Report writing is not difficult, but you need to follow some simple rules. Start by deciding what information you need. Bear in mind whom you are writing for and their level of knowledge. For example, does the audience have any acquaintance with trade theory and policy? You can use books, journals, newspapers and web-based sources. You might decide that it is appropriate to talk to certain people about the WTO and get their opinions on the best way forward. Having collected information, decide as a team what your approach will be and which are the points that you will wish to emphasise.

Suggested structure of the report:

- State briefly what the report is about.
- Tell the reader/audience about the present situation in the WTO. Where are we now?
- Explain why the situation needs to change. Why can we not leave things as they are?
- Set out some options for reform.
- Make a choice of a reform package. Justify your choice.
- Anticipate some objections to your choice and deal with them fairly.

Suggested reading

Bhagwati, J. (1997) 'The Global Age: From a Sceptical South to a Fearful North', *The World Economy*, vol. 20, no. 3.

Goldsmith, J. (1994) 'The new utopia: GATT and global free trade, reproduced from *La Piège* (*The Trap*), New York: Carroll and Graf.

Gordon, M. S. (1949) 'The character and significance of the general commitments that nations will make under the ITO Charter', *American Economic Review*, vol. 39, pp. 240–79, May.

Graham, E. M. (2001) *Fighting the Wrong Enemy: Anti-Globalisation Activists and Multinational Corporations*, Washington: Washington Institute of International Economics.

Rodrik, D. (1997) *Has Globalization Gone Too Far?*, Washington, DC: Institute for International Economics.

Stiglitz, J. (2002) *Globalization and its Discontents*, London: Allen Lane.

Srinivasan, T. N. (1999) 'Developing Countries in the World Trading System: From GATT, 1947, to the Third Ministerial Meeting of WTO, 1999', *The World Economy*, vol. 22, no. 8, pp. 1017–65.

Viner, J. (1950) *The Customs Union Issue*, New York: Carnegie Endowment for International Peace.

Wilcox, C. (1947) 'International trade organization: the London draft of a charter for an international trade organization', *American Economic Review*, vol. 37, pp. 529–59.

Winham, G. R. (1998) 'The World Trade Organisation: institution-building in the multilateral trade system, *World Economy*, vol. 21, no. 3, pp. 349–68.

Website

- World Trade Organization: **www.wto.org**

Chapter 6

Trade and growth, past and present

Introduction

Adam Smith in his *Wealth of Nations* broke with the mercantilist tradition when he argued that free trade is the best policy for all trading countries. He based his argument of the gains from trade on absolute cost differences. Each country should specialise in the commodities which it could produce more efficiently than other countries and import commodities which it would produce less efficiently. Ricardo was later to widen the scope of the analysis to take account of comparative cost differences. Even if a country had an absolute disadvantage in the production of both commodities with respect to another country, mutually advantageous trade could still take place. International specialisation of factors of production would result in an overall increase in output which could be shared by all trading countries.

Referring back to Chapter 2, specialisation which leads to real income gains can be represented by movements along a production frontier. This chapter also allows for the possibility that trade may enable a country to shift its production frontier outwards, so increasing the productive capacity of the economy. Trade can be the means by which countries gain increased access to enterprise, to physical and financial capital, and to new ideas and new technologies. All these things have the effect of increasing productive capacity. Trade in this instance is taking on a dynamic role. It is functioning as an engine of growth.

It is a significant point, however, that though mainstream economists tend to be unanimous in accepting real income gains from specialisation and exchange as in the pure theory of trade, they are much more divided on the supposed dynamic benefits of trade. The pendulum swings one way and then another. At one point of time the majority of economists may appear to believe in the likelihood of significant dynamic gains from trade. At other times they are much more sceptical.

'Let goods be homespun'

In the 1930s Keynes, well known previously for his staunch support of laissez-faire trade policies, switched his allegiance to protectionism, not only to promote domestic employment to counteract the slump in the UK, but also for what he saw as the advantages of self-sufficiency for economic growth. Some of his ideas would fit neatly today into the anti-globalisation movement. For example:

> I become doubtful whether the economic cost of self-sufficiency is great enough to outweigh the other advantages of gradually bringing the producer and consumer within the ambit of the same national economic and financial organisation . . . as wealth increases, both primary and manufactured products play a smaller relative part in the national economy compared with houses, personal services and local amenities which are not the subject of international exchange . . . I sympathise with those who would minimise economic entanglement between nations. Ideas, knowledge, art, hospitality, travel – these are things which should of their nature be international. But let goods be homespun wherever it is reasonably and conveniently possible.
>
> (J. M. Keynes, *Collected Writings*)

The liberal revival

After World War II Keynes changed his mind again and converted back to his early liberal views on trade. The liberal revival, in which international economics focused on the dynamic gains from trade, dates from the end of World War II. It was very much influenced by what was perceived at the time as the German economic miracle. This started with West German currency reform in 1948, and continued with the abolition of all the wage, price and exchange controls which had been inherited from the Nazi period. The excellent performance of the West German economy in the 1950s and 1960s was generally regarded by economists as a model of successful export-led growth.

In the early post-war period, however, developing countries tended to have a somewhat different perspective on the supposed benefits of free trade. In Latin America and in the newly independent ex-colonies of Africa and Asia, there was little faith in the ability of trade to promote growth and development. Instead the majority of policy-makers in developing countries supported trade protection in order to stimulate domestic manufacturing, which was believed to provide a better 'engine of growth'. Many inefficient infant industries grew up behind tariff walls in developing countries, often at the expense of much needed investment in the agricultural sector.

By the 1980s the pendulum had swung again, in favour of free trade and against protection in developing countries. Economists were emphasising the dynamic benefits of trade, both for developed and developing countries. Of course some economists had never wavered from free trade principles. In 1987, the Austrian economist Haberler, then approaching his ninetieth year, reaffirmed his long-held belief that orthodox trade theory applies just as much to developing as to developed countries. Why, he asked, should a different theory apply to Argentina and Australia, or to Brazil, Portugal and Spain? Today, the World Bank economists also strongly emphasise the dynamic gains from trade, claiming that the global trading system benefits all countries. Development policies need to give greater support for liberalised trade, thereby broadening participation and fusing its participants closer together.

The World Development Report 2000 argues that trade liberalisation benefits economies in two important ways. First, there is the reallocation of resources which comes about when tariffs are lowered and relative prices change to reflect differences in comparative advantage. Second, the report goes on: 'much larger benefits accrue in the long run as economies adjust to technical innovations, new production structures, and new patterns of competition'. These are the supposed dynamic gains from trade.

Objectives

When you have completed this chapter, you should be able to:

● distinguish between the *static and dynamic gains* from trade;

● describe the *'vent for surplus'* and *'staples' theories* of trade and growth;

● outline and discuss the circumstances under which trade is likely to function as an *'engine of growth'*;

● discuss the role of *trade liberalisation* in today's global economy with specific reference to developing and transition economies;

● consider the phenomenon of *de-industrialisation* and explain its relationship to trade;

● consider whether *regional trading agreements* can substitute for the liberalisation of the global trading system.

Static and dynamic effects of trade

Referring back to Chapter 2 (p. 17), in Figure 6.1 the production possibility curve nn' is a locus of all possible efficient production points for two commodities, x and y. If all resources available to the economy were to be devoted to the production of commodity x, On' amount of x could be produced. Similarly, if all resources available to the economy were to be devoted to the production of commodity y, On amount of y could be produced. At the pre-trade equilibrium determined by preferences, the indifference curve ii' will be at some point such as e where x and y in combination are produced and consumed.

Specialisation is represented by movements along the production frontier. For example, considerations of comparative advantage may suggest moving to a point such as e^*, representing less y and more x being produced. The increased output of x can be traded internationally, giving a net gain to the economy. Trade at the international terms of trade TT' enables a higher level of satisfaction to be achieved. The post-trade equilibrium, on a higher indifference curve, is e'. In Figure 6.1 the *static* gains from trade are represented by the equilibrium which is located on the indifference curve II'. The static gains derive from *specialisation* (movement from e to e^*) and international exchange (movement from e^* to e').

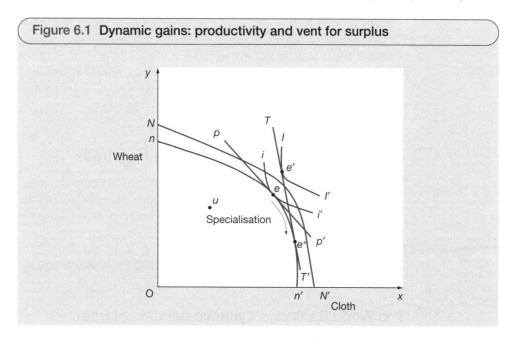

Figure 6.1 Dynamic gains: productivity and vent for surplus

The dynamic gains from trade are represented by a shift outwards in the production possibility curve from *nn'* to *NN'*. The reasons which have been advanced for productivity shifts as a consequence of trade are diverse. They originate in the classical arguments of Smith and Mill, but can be traced through to the present day, in the policy pronouncements on trade of the World Bank.

Classical economics and productivity gains from trade

A development economist, Hla Myint, first drew attention in 1958 to what he saw as the 'neglected elements in classical economics': those elements which stressed the *dynamic* as opposed to the *static* gains from trade. These elements can be found in the writings of Adam Smith and J. S. Mill.

● In Adam Smith's *Wealth of Nations* can be found the view that when foreign trade widens the extent of the market and permits greater division of labour, it also raises the skills of labour.

As human skills improve in consequence of increased trade, the productive capacity of the economy expands. This was widely recognised by the classical economists as a dynamic benefit of trade.

By opening a more extensive market for whatever part of the produce of their labour may exceed the home consumption, [trade] encourages them to improve its productive powers, and to augment its annual produce to the utmost, and thereby to increase the real revenue and wealth of society. (Smith, *Wealth of Nations*, book I, 1776)

● The classical economist J. S. Mill in his *Principles of Political Economy* regarded increases in productivity as the indirect effects of trade, which must be counted as 'benefits of a high order'. Mill stressed that trade is an important channel for the dissemination of knowledge. The rate of learning of the population is raised, thereby increasing the productive capacity of the economy. Trade is beneficial because it 'places human beings in contact with persons dissimilar to themselves and with modes of thought and action unlike those with which they are familiar' (*Principles of Political Economy*, bk. 3, ch. 17, 1848).

Externalities and productivity gains from trade

Moving to the present day, modern growth theory suggests that externalities can provide a link between trade and productivity gains. Knowledge, in Paul Romer's growth model (1986), is regarded as a 'natural externality'. It is a natural externality because it spreads from one person to another and from one firm to another. It cannot be kept secret. Knowledge is an important engine of growth, and since trade is a channel for the dissemination of knowledge, this constitutes a powerful dynamic benefit of trade.

The World Bank and dynamic benefits of trade

The *World Bank Report 2000* lists a number of dynamic benefits of trade which are particularly important for developing countries. The World Bank believes that these benefits are 'much larger' than the static gains from trade. They accrue in the long run as economies adjust to technical innovations, new production structures and new patterns of consumption.

● Trade has a powerful 'disciplinary' effect on domestic firms. It *forces them to become more efficient*, to bring prices closer to marginal costs, thus reducing the distortions which would otherwise be created by monopolistic structures.
● Trade provides firms with access to *up-to-date capital equipment* and high-quality intermediate inputs. This enables firms to raise their productivity.
● Productivity levels rise when firms are exposed to the *'best practices'* of overseas competitors. Demanding international clients force firms to re-engineer their products once they begin to sell their goods and services abroad.
● The dynamic benefits of trade set off a *cumulative chain of events* which tends to concentrate economic activity in a city or a region. For example, firms producing intermediate inputs are attracted to cities or regions producing exports. These intermediate inputs will be tailored specifically to the needs of the export industries. This leads in a cumulative fashion to higher productivity in the booming city or region.

If we now bring together early classical ideas and the latest World Bank pronouncements, it seems that the sources of dynamic gains from trade are as follows:

● Trade *widens the extent of the market* and encourages businesses to innovate, make greater use of capital equipment and enjoy economies of scale.
● Trade has an important *educative effect*. It is the means whereby skills and technology are transferred from one economy to another. It suggests new goods to consumers and inculcates new tastes.

● Trade *promotes international competition.* It inspires entrepreneurs to look for new ways of reducing costs. It is also a most effective way of putting inefficient monopolies out of business.

● A combination of externalities and increasing returns, operating in a cumulative fashion, means that trade can often operate as an engine of growth in a particular *location.* Producers tend to operate more efficiently in proximity to a dense network of customers, suppliers, employees and information.

Vent for surplus and staples theory

Refer again to Figure 6.1. Any point inside the production possibility curve, at u for example, represents some surplus productive capacity in the economy. The economy could move out to the production frontier, producing and consuming more of both goods x and y.

The development economist Myint pointed out that in the writings of Adam Smith can be found the suggestion that trade can provide a 'vent' or outlet for productive capacity which may be in surplus before a country is opened up to trade.

> By opening a more extensive market for whatever part of the produce of their labour may exceed the home consumption, [trade] encourages [countries] to improve productive powers, and augment annual produce to the utmost, and thereby increase the real revenue and wealth of society. (*Wealth of Nations*, book I, 1776)

According to Myint, vent for surplus is another neglected element in classical economics. He draws a contrast here between Ricardo and Smith. For Ricardo, the gains from trade were associated with a reallocation of fully employed resources. In terms of Figure 6.1, this means a movement along the production possibility curve nn'. For Smith, trade provided a vent for labour and natural resources that were in surplus before trade. This meant that exports could increase, and this need not be at the expense of output for domestic consumption. In effect the economy is moving out from a point such as u within the production frontier, to the production frontier where all resources are fully employed.

'Vent for surplus' is a uniquely interesting way of approaching the question of the dynamic gains from trade, because it requires us to think very carefully about the relationship between trade and growth, from both a theoretical and an empirical (real-world) standpoint.

Theoretical problems with 'vent for surplus'

What Smith and Myint had in mind was a situation where exports could increase in a relatively 'costless' fashion. There need be no revolutionary changes in techniques, or dramatic increases in productivity. Unused land is brought into cultivation by employing previously under-utilised labour. The expansion process keeps going by drawing on surplus productive capacity. It is an attractive 'something for nothing' process.

However, all the classical economists, including Smith, assumed that economies were subject to Say's Law. Say's Law follows the writings of the French political economist, Jean Baptiste Say, in arguing that supply creates its own demand. In a flexible market economy there can be no long-run underutilisation of resources. If demand is greater than supply, prices will fall until the excess demand is absorbed. What, then, is the meaning of u? How can underemployment persist inside the production frontier? What is the meaning of surplus productive capacity?

There are *four possible answers* to this theoretical conundrum. Take your pick!

- Smith's 'vent for surplus' argument is *wrong*. This is what Ricardo argued. He praised Smith for his theory of absolute advantage, but said that his vent for surplus theory was a *remnant of mercantilism:* a mistaken approach and one which was at variance with the rest of his work.
- Smith is right about the impact of trade on the employment of resources but he *confuses involuntary and voluntary underemployment.* Smith is writing about a situation of voluntary unemployment of labour in the pre-trade situation. People prefer to be idle, to consume large amounts of leisure in the pre-trade situation. Because there is only a limited range of goods available in the domestic economy, people prefer leisure to goods. It is only when a large variety of goods are made available through international contacts that people decide to increase their working hours.
- Smith was writing about a situation in which *some goods are produced jointly.* Sheep, for example, produce both meat and wool. But the domestic economy may not require both meat and wool in the proportions occurring naturally. Without foreign trade some of the joint products will be 'overproduced' domestically. For example, the domestic economy may be able to absorb all the meat which is produced but not the wool. Trade means that wool can be exchanged abroad for other goods which are in demand locally.
- Say's Law does not operate in poor underdeveloped economies. It is only when economies start to develop that a *price mechanism and appropriate economic organisation emerges.* At this point surplus capacity can be removed by price adjustments. But there is no self-equilibrating price mechanism before this juncture.

Myint himself favoured this last explanation of surplus productive capacity. He argued that the existence of underemployed resources in poor and isolated economies and regions was so commonly observed that Smith assumed it implicitly and never felt the need to comment on it, or explain. Underdeveloped economies lack suitable investment opportunities and a good internal transport system. Their internal economic organisation is not sophisticated enough to absorb surplus productive capacity. It is international trade itself which has usually introduced and extended the market economy in isolated societies.

Empirical evidence for vent for surplus

Myint wrote that the classical 'vent for surplus' theory provides a good explanation of the experience of certain developing countries in the nineteenth and early twentieth centuries. The countries which he had in mind were those where peasants' own export production was important. Examples of this are rice from South-East Asia, cocoa from the Gold Coast and Nigeria, and rubber from Malaya.

In Malaya (now Malaysia) in the late nineteenth century, 'plantation' rubber was produced on a large scale, using migrant workers from India. It found itself increasingly under competition from the Malayan peasant 'smallholder' sector. Between 1910 and the outbreak of World War I in 1914, the smallholder acreage and output grew at a phenomenal rate. The context was very much that of Smith's 'vent for surplus'. There was plenty of unused land which the Malayan peasant could cultivate with the aid of family labour. The peasant farmer used very little physical capital. Exports fitted into the existing traditional agricultural system. There was no reduction in, or reallocation away from, domestic food production.

In the Gold Coast (now Ghana) in West Africa, peasants were the driving force behind cocoa production. Between 1890 and 1910 output of cocoa rose from virtually nothing to a situation in which the Gold Coast was the leading world producer. Again, there was no reallocation of resources from the production of domestic foodstuffs. Capital requirements were modest. Exports grew as farmers pushed the margin of cultivation outwards from the coast, cutting down the tropical forest and planting the cleared land with cocoa trees. Family labour provided the necessary inputs, supplemented by some migrant labour from north of the forest belt at peak harvesting times.

Staples theory

A 'staple' is a raw material or resource-intensive commodity. Common staples are minerals, wheat, cotton, hides and meat. Staples theory is very similar to the vent for surplus. It tries to explain the wheat, minerals and livestock that were exported from North America, Argentina, South Africa and Australia during the nineteenth and early twentieth centuries. In this case the trade expansion was accompanied by massive inflows of physical and financial capital from Europe, and large-scale immigration from Europe, especially in the period 1890–1920.

In Canada, for example, economic historians tell the story of Canadian development as successive exploitations of natural resources: furs from the Hudson Bay Company, later the cod fisheries of Newfoundland, and finally the prairie wheat boom before World War I. Rising prices for these commodities stimulated export production. There were linkages from the export sector to domestic manufacturing. New industries and an improved transport infrastructure emerged from behind a tariff wall. Very substantial flows of capital and labour into Canada also accompanied the growth of Canada's exports.

In Argentina, development centred on the staples of wool, hides, wheat, corn, linseed and foreign meat. It has been estimated that between 1880 and 1929 Argentina's export-led growth, based on staples, trebled per capita GNP. There was massive immigration from Europe and a substantial inflow of financial capital from Britain, other European countries, and the US. Important linkages were established with the domestic economy: refrigeration plants, meat-packing industries and trade in domestically produced consumer goods and services all sprang up in the wake of staple export industries.

What have 'vent for surplus' and 'staples' theories in common?

Both are *dynamic* trade models, which focus on the *demand-generating* character of foreign trade. Linkages are very important in determining the pattern of development which stems from the export expansion. It has also been suggested that both models make use of the concept of a land frontier. This concept was first employed by the American historian Frederick Turner and has been used extensively by geographers. Rising prices and expanding markets in the world economy result in an extension of the land frontier. In the case of North America, the frontier was on the prairie. In Australia it was the 'outback', and in Argentina the pampas. In tropical lands, forests and jungles were cleared. In all cases substantial human resources were required to clear the land and provide the necessary infrastructure. It has been pointed out that an integral part of the story of vent for surplus and staple theory is international and regional mobility of factors.

'Vent for surplus' and 'staple' trade theories have much in common. However, their outcomes in terms of growth and development have been very diverse. Ghana, despite its prosperous beginnings, has suffered the decline common to all primary producers in Sub-Saharan Africa. Malaysia is now a dynamic middle-income developing country, but nevertheless it has many problems of an ethnic and social character. Argentina is a country in the temperate zone, but despite a promising start it has tended to stagnate under a variety of political and economic constraints. Canada, Australia and the United States have diversified away from resource-based export-led growth and development and have been rewarded throughout the past half century with high per capita incomes.

Why this diversity?

The precise relationship between trade, growth and development continues to exercise the minds of economists. There is no single approach and no simple answer to the issue of the dynamic gains from trade. All we can say is that economists on the whole are fairly optimistic. They believe that the dynamic gains from trade are positive and significant, though there is some dissent from this point of view, as we will see in the next section.

Is trade an engine of growth?

So far in this chapter we have learned that the gains from trade can be 'static', i.e. arising through the reallocation of resources as economies engage in specialisation and exchange, or 'dynamic'. Dynamic gains can arise on the side of supply ('productivity approach') or on the side of demand ('vent for surplus'). In all cases we would expect to see, in a real-world situation, a close association between trade (i.e. the value of imports and exports as a percentage of national income) and changes in the level of per capita national income.

If there is a close association between trade and changes in per capita income, we might feel justified in claiming that trade is an engine of growth. Indeed many economic historians, as well as economists, have taken just this approach. It is, however, an oversimplification of a highly complex economic relationship.

The direction of causation is by no means clear. Does increased trade lead to higher economic growth or do increasing levels of real income encourage more open, trade-orientated economies? The engine of growth hypothesis is often assumed to have applied particularly to the historical experience of today's industrialised economies. Britain, for example, as the leading industrialised nation of the nineteenth century, is usually assumed to have based her industrial primacy on exports of manufactured goods, particularly textiles. But when statisticians and econometricians get to work on the evidence, it is often their conclusion that it is internal supply conditions, rather than externally generated demand, which accounts for much of the observed increase in per capita income.

Even in situations where at first sight there appears to be a close relationship between exports and economic growth, research on trade volumes and values tends to rule out a strong and significant 'engine of growth' relationship. For example, most economic historians have taken Canada as an example of strong export-led growth. The prairie wheat boom which took place between 1890 and 1911 appears at first sight to have triggered off enormous development in Canada, resulting in rising real incomes, and the growth of manufacturing, urbanisation and service sector activities. On closer examination, however, statisticians have been unable to attribute a significant amount of economic growth to trade. No more than one-fifth of the observed increases in national income in Canada between 1890 and 1911 can be attributed directly to the activities of the export sector. So trade as an engine of growth may not be as strong as the staples theory would suggest.

The engine of growth in developing countries

Many development economists over the years have been sceptical about the extent to which trade has acted as an engine of growth in today's developing countries. Development economists observed that although trade had grown remarkably in many developing countries, often dating back to the nineteenth century, its spread effects to the domestic economy at large appeared to be very limited. Often trade had developed in an enclave, with minimal spillovers to the domestic economy. Why? These are three of the reasons which have been put forward by sceptical development economists. They have been subject to lengthy, but on the whole inconclusive, empirical investigation.

● Foreign-owned plantations and mining concerns tended to send back their profits to shareholders abroad. This constituted *a leakage of national income* to foreign countries. These leakages tended over time to reduce the spread effects from export growth. Profits were not reinvested beneficially in their countries of origin.

● The *technologies of production* employed by many foreign enterprises were ill-suited to the resource endowments of poor countries. Developing countries tend to be capital-scarce and labour-abundant. Foreign enterprises use relatively *capital-intensive* techniques of production. They *import* capital and managerial skills. This constrains the local employment-generating capabilities of the export sector. It also has unwelcome effects on the *balance of payments*, because of the need to import scarce factors of production.

● Developing countries have principally exported foodstuffs and raw materials, i.e. primary products, and have imported manufactures. Over time the *terms of trade* for primary products have declined relative to manufactures. One reason for this is the strong monopoly bargaining power of companies in rich countries, which has kept the prices of manufactures artificially high. Another reason is the lower income elasticity of demand for primary products relative to manufactures. As world incomes have grown, the demand for primary products has grown more slowly than the demand for manufactures. The prices of manufactures have, in consequence, outstripped the prices of primary products.

The engine of growth in developing countries: recent evidence

In the 1960s and 1970s doubts about trade as an engine of growth had far-reaching effects on trade policy in developing countries. Many developing countries that were unhappy with the growth-generating capacity of primary products embarked on policies of industrialisation through import-substitution industries (ISI). They closed their markets to imports of manufactured consumer goods and capital goods, and began to substitute domestically produced manufactured goods for imports, usually supported by a combination of tariffs on imports and subsidies to domestic producers.

Partly as a result of ISI policies, changes occurred in the composition of the exports of developing countries in the last three decades of the twentieth century. The share of primary products in developing countries' exports is now less than 50 per cent and declining. Developing countries in which exports of primary products account for 80 per cent or more of total exports are those countries which are relatively small in size. They are heavily concentrated in Africa.

David Dollar's cross-section studies

It is against the background of changing trade patterns for developing countries that economists embarked in the 1990s on a re-examination of the relationship between trade and growth in developing countries.

In 1992 David Dollar of the World Bank published a study in which he ranked developing countries according to the extent to which they were outward-orientated. The study took cross-section data for a large number of developing countries. The countries were divided into four groups depending on how open their economies were. If a country had low tariffs, minimal subsidies and a market-determined exchange rate, it fell into the 'most open' quartile. A country with a high level of protection and an overvalued exchange rate fell into the 'most inward' quartile. In between, the second

Table 6.1 Outward-orientation ranking for a sample of developing countries (1976–88)

Most open quartile	Second quartile	Third quartile	Most inward quartile
Thailand	India	Senegal	Algeria
Colombia	Brazil	Iran	Liberia
Pakistan	Turkey	Malawi	Zambia
Malaysia	Panama	Cameroon	Rwanda
Korea	Indonesia	Argentina	Tanzania
Peru	Botswana	Congo	Zaire
Taiwan	Uruguay	Jamaica	Iraq
Mauritius	Ethiopia	Guatemala	Uganda

Source: Adapted from Dollar (1992).

and third quartiles represented greater or lesser degrees of openness. The countries were classified according to data relating to the period 1976–88 (Table 6.1).

David Dollar found a statistically significant relationship between output growth and outward orientation. But he readily admitted that the results should be interpreted with caution. As he concedes in his article, there is the possibility that the causation runs in the other direction: from poor growth performance to inward orientation. Countries may be inward-looking precisely because they have poor economic performance. And there may be important variables which have been omitted. Countries which successfully adopt trade policy reform may owe their success to factors other than, or in addition to, their support for free trade.

David Dollar used a cross-sectional approach to testing the engine of growth hypothesis, looking at a range of countries over a given period of time. His methodology has been called into question by other economists. Their main criticism has been that David Dollar's trade variable picked up other effects, particularly macro-economic stability, which we know has a strong positive effect on economic growth.

Another way of testing the engine of growth hypothesis is to focus on the effect of trade on the growth of total factor productivity (TFP) rather than on the growth of output. Recalling the earlier section of this chapter, which focused on the productivity gains from trade, we can speculate that trade will have a positive effect on productivity in the economy. Empirical work of this type aims to capture the effects of trade working through increases in productivity. Jonsson and Subramanian (2001) have carried out such an exercise for South Africa, where substantial trade liberalisation took place in the 1990s. These researchers reported a significant negative relationship between changes in tariffs and TFP growth across the manufacturing sectors in South Africa. As tariffs were reduced, productivity rose. Time-series studies for South Africa confirmed the cross-section results. The researchers concluded that trade liberalisation has contributed significantly to TFP growth in South Africa – an encouraging result for the engine of growth hypothesis.

◯ Trade, technology and growth

Economists working on the engine of growth hypothesis in the 1990s have tended to concentrate more and more on the possibility that trade promotes growth through its effects on investment and technology. It is difficult to disentangle the two effects, since investment usually incorporates new technologies, and new technologies tend to require more investment. Empirical work in this area tends to be very encouraging to the engine of growth hypothesis. Large international markets bring technological spillovers. Firms can enjoy economies of scale in international markets, especially in research and development. Trade tends to have a positive effect on investment, and thereby affects the rate of technological progress and economic growth (Coe and Helpman, 1995).

Trade liberalisation

Towards the middle of the 1980s policy-makers in developing countries began to reassess and remove restrictions on foreign trade. In the 1990s, they were joined by policy-makers in transition economies who similarly began to liberalise their trade policies in the move from 'plan' to 'market'. Trade liberalisation generally involves:

● relaxing trade protection;
● opening up the economy to foreign investment; and
● the adoption of flexible exchange rates.

To be successful, it is generally agreed that trade liberalisation needs to be accompanied by other market-driven reforms:

● the elimination of price controls;
● abolition of state-owned trading monopolies;
● free entry for firms into production services and trade activities;
● financial liberalisation via interest rate reform and the relaxation of credit controls;
● institutional reforms to promote the market mechanism.

◯ Why trade liberalisation?

Why was trade liberalisation so widespread in the 1980s and 1990s? Dornbusch argued that there were four 'overlapping' reasons for trade liberalisation:

● *Anti-statism.* Trade policy reform was part of an intellectual swing away from the state. Trade protection was seen as one of the manifestations of a bureaucratic and over-intrusive state which hindered enterprise and innovation. Trade liberalisation was part of the wider shift towards market forces.
● *Poor economic performance.* Trade was seen as a way of improving economic performance. Economists such as Anne Kreuger and Bela Balassa argued that outward-orientated countries were the fastest-growing ones. Hong Kong, Singapore, Korea and Taiwan were cited as outstanding examples of trade-led growth.

● *Information.* Consumers had become much more knowledgeable about the goods available on world markets and the prices at which they could be obtained. It was no longer possible for governments to 'ration' these goods through high-tariff distorted prices. The poor wanted food and cheap durable goods. The rich wanted luxury goods – but at prevailing world prices.

● *IMF and World Bank pressure.* The IMF and the World Bank have made their support for developing and transition economies dependent on these countries adopting trade liberalisation policies. The IMF and the World Bank have backed up their policies with a large body of empirical evidence pointing to the success of trade-led economies. In particular, the IMF and the World Bank have argued that trade liberalisation

  ● encourages technological progress and organisational change;
  ● ensures that relative prices reflect scarcities and bring efficient allocation of resources;
  ● exposes the economy to customer demand, the profit motive and competition.

What have been the consequences of trade liberalisation?

This is a very contentious issue, as evidenced by the anti-globalisation protests in Washington, Seattle, Prague, Cape Town, etc., but mainstream opinion among economists still largely supports the view that trade liberalisation has been beneficial in developing and transition economies.

Joseph Stiglitz on liberalisation

Joseph Stiglitz is an exception to this rule. The supposed benefits of trade liberalisation have been called into question by Stiglitz, the winner of the Nobel Prize for Economics in 2001 who is a former chief economist of the World Bank. His views, though not representative of mainstream liberal economics, indicate a remarkable and challenging shift of opinion on the part of one prominent economist.

Stiglitz argues (2002) that it is the elites in developed countries who support trade liberalisation. They do not see the impact of such policies on the ground in poor economies.

● When comparative advantage requires resources to move from low-productivity uses, jobs are destroyed. *New jobs in high-productivity sectors cannot be created instantaneously.* It takes capital and entrepreneurship to create new firms and jobs and most developing countries lack just these resources.

● The most successful developing countries, such as those in East Asia, opened themselves to the outside world *in a slow and sequenced way.* They dropped protective barriers carefully and systematically, phasing them out only when new jobs were created.

● Workers in richer countries worry about jobs when trade is liberalised. Yet the plight of unemployed workers in many poor countries is significantly worse. They have *few safety nets* in the form of savings, and no unemployment benefits. They live in countries which already have unemployment at 20 per cent or more, and their chances of finding alternative employment are slim.

● Western countries have pushed trade liberalisation for the products which they export, but at the same time continue *to protect those sectors in which competition from poorer countries is seen a threat.* Poor countries find it difficult to penetrate the markets of rich countries.

Stiglitz concludes: 'Liberalization has thus, too often, not been followed by the promised growth, but by increased misery. And even those who have not lost their jobs have been hit by a heightened sense of insecurity' (Stiglitz, 2002).

Trade policy reform in transition economies

Transition economies are the former centrally planned economies of Central and Eastern Europe and the states of the former Soviet Union, China and Vietnam. They are moving at varying paces towards a liberalised market structure.

The World Bank has compared the experience of two transition economies, Estonia and Ukraine. *Estonia* has benefited from rapid trade liberalisation. Very early on in the transition to a market economy, Estonia removed all export barriers, eliminated quantitative import barriers, and made its new currency fully convertible. The result was a rapid reorientation of trade, adjustment to new quality standards, and a boost to export revenues. Export growth contributed 11 per cent per year to growth in GDP during the 1990s.

By way of contrast, *Ukraine* has suffered stagnation because of slow trade liberalisation. Ukraine maintained price and trade controls. It kept its structure of state trading and state procurement intact. Instead of embracing multilateralism, it entered into an extensive network of bilateral trade agreements. The exchange rate was maintained at an equilibrium position below the market rate in order to benefit exporters.

In consequence, goes the World Bank argument, Ukraine suffered falling trade which made a negative contribution to growth in the 1990s. Reforms were undertaken in the mid-1990s but they remained incomplete. The economy is still riddled with imperfections. Competition for import licences and quotas also encourages corruption in business and government.

Not all observers would agree that the key distinction between Ukraine and Estonia is their different attitudes to trade liberalisation. Estonia has special advantages in its close proximity and ties to western Europe. Being a Baltic sea port is an important boost to trade. So too is the Estonian Currency Board which underpins the exchange rate (see Chapter 10). Nevertheless, there is a measure of agreement among economists that in transition economies exports can be a major source of growth. The move to market-based economies has involved opening up to world markets, and a reorientation of exports. Establishing free trade could be expected to yield particularly large returns in transition economies for two reasons:

● Because the legacy of central planning was a bias towards large and inefficient firms. Opening up a planned economy to foreign competition brings large gains in output and efficiency.
● Because import protection in centrally planned economies had cushioned entire sectors and industries, not just individual firms. Trade liberalisation encourages significant restructuring at the industry level, bringing large productivity gains.

Economists working with trade models and projections have arrived at the following broad predictions for likely future changes in trade and output in transition economies.

1 Central and eastern Europe has a large untapped potential for trade with established market economies. It has relatively skilled labour and can compete in medium- and high-skill-intensive products. Those countries which have made rapid progress in liberalising their trade can expect to come close to fulfilling their estimated trade potential.
2 The states of the former Soviet Union are in a region of the world which previously traded very little with outside countries. In 1989 trade between the former Soviet republics amounted to more than four-fifths of their total trade. Liberalisation has been very slow, especially in the Central Asian republics, and they are far from exploiting their trade potential. Projections indicate that the states of the former Soviet Union will send increased supplies of energy to Europe, principally oil and natural gas, in return for capital-intensive intermediate goods and high-quality consumer durables.
3 China offers a dramatic example of export-led growth. In 1978 China was the world's thirty-second-largest exporter. Today it is the tenth-largest exporter and predictions are that its exports will continue to accelerate. China's exports are labour-intensive, with clothing, toys, sports goods and footwear dominating the export mix. They are providing a strongly effective engine of growth.

Regional trading arrangements versus liberalisation

A regional trading arrangement (RTA) is a preferential trade agreement between countries in a particular region. Countries not belonging to the RTA are, by definition, discriminated against in foreign trade.

The European Common Market, set up under the Treaty of Rome in 1957, began an important debate in the economics literature on the benefits and costs of RTAs. Bhagwati termed the RTAs of the late 1950s and early 1960s, which included the European Common Market, as the first regionalism. The first regionalism sparked a controversy led by Viner's work of 1950 in which he questioned whether RTAs are necessarily welfare-improving. To the extent that RTAs are trade-creating, i.e. promote trade between member countries, they can be expected to bring the static and dynamic gains which are associated with trade. But RTAs can also be trade-diverting, i.e. they discriminate against trade with non-members, and this reduces the static and dynamic gains from trade, if non-members are potential low-cost sources of supply to the RTA for certain goods and services.

Until one looks carefully at a particular RTA, it is impossible to say whether the benefits of trade creation are outweighing the costs of trade diversion. It is very much down to empirical investigation. For many years, economists tended to discount the likelihood of trade diversion, believing that it was of relatively low real-world significance. However, the more careful and detailed empirical studies carried out in recent years have demonstrated strong evidence of trade diversion in the MERCOSUR (Uruguay, Brazil, Paraguay and Argentina) and NAFTA RTAs.

In the 1980s began what Bhagwati termed the 'new' or 'second' regionalism. The US had previously looked unfavourably on RTAs, regarding them as breaching multilateral free trade principles. In the 1980s the US administration changed its mind and began to promote RTAs, which then grew in number at an unprecedented rate. There are now almost 100 regional trading arrangements, some of which are detailed in Table 6.2.

Economists studying the second regionalism have been mostly concerned with dynamic questions of trade diversion and trade creation. Some of the newer questions being asked by economists are:

● Do RTAs act as building blocks or stumbling blocks to the emergence of free trade?
● Do RTAs encourage what Bhagwati has referred to as the 'spaghetti bowl' effect, where numerous criss-crossing preferential trading agreements and tariff rates increase transaction costs between countries and lead to 'hidden' protectionism?
● Are RTAs essentially political rather than economic in intent? Do they simply provide opportunities for bureaucrats and politicians to gain credence as national and regional players, without requiring from them a wholehearted commitment to the principles of free trade?

Answers to questions such as these are waiting for more detailed empirical investigation. An example of the type of empirical work required is provided by Vamvakidis, an IMF economist. Vamvakidis (1999) asks a straightforward question: 'If an economy decides to liberalise, is it better to join an RTA or adopt non-discriminatory liberal trade policies?' To answer this question, he compares the growth performance of countries that liberalised broadly, with that of countries that joined an RTA. The data comprised time-series evidence for the period 1950–92. The results suggested that economies have grown faster, in both the short and long run, after liberalisation, as compared with joining an RTA. The results also suggested that liberalisation leads to higher investment ratios. In fact the impact of RTAs on growth was negative in most cases. Vamvakidis' empirical work has led him to the conclusion that an economy is likely to be better off in a liberalised world trade situation, than in a regional trading arrangement.

On the question of the impact of RTAs on non-member countries, a recent empirical study has concluded that regional arrangements have small, but negative spillovers on the rest of the world. The World Bank has concluded that if further research supports the view that RTAs have a negative impact on non-members, certain policy measures are indicated.

Table 6.2 Regional trading arrangements (examples)

RTA	Member countries	Year established
ASEAN: Association of South East Asian Nations	Brunei, Darussalam, Cambodia, Indonesia, Laos, Malaysia, Myanmar, Philippines, Singapore, Thailand, Vietnam	1977
CARICOM: Caribbean Community and Common Market	Antigua and Barbuda, Bahamas, Barbados, Belize, Dominica, Grenada, Guyana, Haiti, Jamaica, Monserrat, Trinidad and Tobago, St Kitts and Nevis, St Vincent and the Grenadines, Surinam	1973
CEFTA: Central European Free Trade Area	Bulgaria, Czech Republic, Hungary, Poland, Romania, Slovak Republic, Slovenia	1993
CIS: Commonwealth of Independent States	Azerbaijan, Armenia, Belarus, Georgia, Moldova, Kazakhstan, Russian Federation, Ukraine, Uzbekistan, Tajikistan, Kyrgyz Republic	1994
COMESA: Common Market for Eastern and Southern Africa	Angola, Burundi, Comoros, Democratic Republic of Conga, Djibouti, Egypt, Eritrea, Ethiopia, Madagascar, Malawi, Mauritius, Namibia, Rwanda, Seychelles, Sudan, Swaziland, Uganda, Zambia, Zimbabwe	1994
EC: European Community (now EU)	Austria, Belgium, Denmark, Finland, France, Germany, Greece, Italy, Luxembourg, Netherlands, Portugal, Spain, Sweden, United Kingdom	1957
GCC: Gulf Co-operation Council	Bahrain, Kuwait, Oman, Qatar, Saudi Arabia, United Arab Emirates	Not available
MERCOSUR: Southern Common Market	Argentina, Brazil, Paraguay, Uruguay	1991
NAFTA: North American Free Trade Agreement	Canada, Mexico, United States	1994
SPARTECA: South Pacific Regional Trade and Economic Co-operation Agreement	Australia, New Zealand, Cook Islands, Fiji, Kiribati, Marshall Islands, Micronesia, Nauru, Niue, Papua New Guinea, Solomon Islands, Tonga, Tuvalu, Vanuatu, Western Samoa	1981

- A *'model accession clause'* should be established for RTAs. In the model accession clause the conditions non-members must meet in order to join the RTA should be made explicit. Any country which can comply with these conditions should be allowed to negotiate access to its chosen RTA.
- The WTO should commit members of RTAs to *phase out preferential market access* within a specific time frame. It should be made clear that preferential access can only be a temporary feature of RTAs.
- Policy-makers who believe that the rise of RTAs elsewhere is having a negative effect on their economies should be encouraged to *pursue multilateral trade liberalisation* through the WTO.

CASE STUDY 6.1

Waiting patiently for the single regional market **FT**

When neighbouring Dominica became overwhelmed by mounting economic problems in July, it was not surprising that Barbados was among the first to offer help.

Notwithstanding changes of government over the past three decades, Barbados has maintained a formidable policy of co-operation with, and support for, its neighbours.

In the case of Dominica, financial assistance will be supported by technical help in overcoming that island's problems.

As a founding member of the Caribbean Community (Caricom), Barbados has taken the lead in moving the community towards a single market and economy in the belief that the region's small economies, if they remain divided, will be unable to make the best use of increasing liberalisation of international trade.

The effort to create the regional common market will gather pace later this year from facilities to be located in Bridgetown, the island's capital.

'The region has no choice but to transform itself into a single market and economy,' says Owen Arthur, prime minister of Barbados.

'The Caribbean will be part of a wider hemispheric economic arena with the Free Trade Area of the Americas scheduled for 2005. The regional single market and economy is needed before the region can deal with the hemispheric free trade area and the rest of the world,' says the premier.

The island's foreign policy has been aggressive in pursuit of its economic objectives. Foreign missions have moved on from traditionally diplomatic duties to be agencies for economic development, dealing as much with the problems of nationals in foreign lands as with encouraging prospective investors in the island.

Barbados has also made its mark in representing the interests of not only the Caribbean but the wider developing world, in forums such as the UN and its agencies, the British Commonwealth, the World Trade Organisation, and in negotiating trade agreements with the EU.

It has spoken with more than self-interest about the economic and environmental hazards that confront developing small island states.

It is in its concentration on relations with its immediate neighbours, however, that has in the past made Barbados the vanguard in attempts to seek increased functional co-operation with the islands of the Windward and Leeward group of the eastern Caribbean.

'We are interested in links with the eastern Caribbean islands because it is natural for Barbados,' says a government official.

'We have always been interested in developments in these islands, and it is recognised in the region that the Barbadian model has staying power for long-term economic and social development.'

The eastern Caribbean islands profit from the economic expansion in Barbados, the minister says. There is a framework for co-operation in sectors such as tourism and international business.

The value of such co-operation is recognised in the other islands. 'Close ties have always existed between Barbados and the islands of the Organisation of Eastern Caribbean States,' says Ralph Gonsalves, prime minister of St Vincent and the Grenadines.

The OECS is comprised of the Windward and Leeward Islands.

'It is evident that, although Barbados is more developed than we are, our economic fortunes are linked. Continued development in Barbados will benefit us, while Barbados will gain from political stability and economic expansion in our islands.'

Mr Arthur contends that the region has to find new ways of dealing with its problems, and that increasing regional co-operation is the answer.

'Caribbean economies are facing a crisis, with some countries being better able to manage than others. We have traditionally looked to multilateral institutions for help, but now we are helping ourselves. One way is through the creation of a stabilisation fund that will help Dominica and other countries that are not doing well.

'The Caribbean has reached a new platform of co-operation. It took the Europeans 50 years to get where they are. We started in 1989 and we have achieved much.'

Making economic priorities the basis of foreign policy has led Barbados to conclude tax treaties with several countries, including the US.

Barbados has gained significantly from these agreements as industrialised countries move against jurisdictions that offer preferential tax regimes.

Plans to take advantage of expected changes in regional politics guide foreign policy. Barbados has signed a double taxation agreement and a bilateral investment treaty with Cuba. It aims to benefit from any thaw in relations between Havana and Washington.

'We are an excellent location for international investments to be channelled,' says the government spokesman.

'In the case of the US, when the Cuban embargo is lifted, an obvious investment conduit will be Barbados. But it will take the US some time to negotiate these agreements with Cuba.'

Source: Canute James, *Financial Times*, 6 September 2002. Reprinted with permission.

Comment on case study 6.1

Regional trading agreements can be just as important for small developing countries as for large industrialised economies. CARICOM, which embraces Caribbean countries, was formed in 1973. One of the founding members was Barbados, which has taken on the role of leading nation in CARICOM.

Small economies suffer from disadvantages associated with small domestic markets. They are unable to enjoy scale economies in production, and also lack bargaining power when negotiating on economic matters with larger and more powerful countries. This is particularly important as small countries need to harness the benefits of liberalisation and export-led growth. As the Barbados Prime Minister Owen Arthur points out, the Caribbean really has no choice. It needs to pursue its RTA vigorously in order to deal with the rest of the world. By 2005 the Free Trade Area of the Americas is scheduled to be in operation, and the Caribbean will be part of this broader economic area.

RTAs have important political as well as economic objectives. Barbados as a leading nation in CARICOM represents the interests of its neighbours at the WTO, in negotiations with the EU, and at the UN. It speaks out on wider economic and environmental issues. Closer to home, Barbados is leading a movement for co-operation with small islands in the eastern Caribbean, the Windward and Leeward Islands, which at present are excluded from CARICOM. Recently it has been involved in international efforts to help CARICOM member Dominica overcome its financial problems.

Like many developing countries, members of CARICOM hope that the RTA will increase the flow of inward investment. They offer to industrialised countries a transparent and co-ordinated tax regime. This is important because many industrialised countries are now taking action against so-called offshore 'tax havens'. CARICOM also hopes to benefit from improved political relations between the US and Cuba. When the embargo on trade and investment in Cuba is eventually lifted by the US, a country like Barbados hopes to act as a trusted third party in deals between the US and Cuba.

Growth, trade and de-industrialisation

De-industrialisation usually refers to a decline in employment in the manufacturing sector. In most developed countries employment in manufacturing industry has diminished over a long period, but the trend has accelerated in recent times. The IMF has estimated that in developed countries the share of manufacturing employment in total employment halved between 1975 and 1995, falling from 28 per cent to 16 per cent of total employment.

The reason why this trend attracts attention is the possibility that it is the result of growing competition from low-cost labour-intensive imports from the developing world. Some economists have argued along these lines. Statistics referring to the disappearance of the manufacturing base frequently surface in calls for protection in developed countries. Is there any justification in this argument?

First, it is necessary to consider the range of possible causes of de-industrialisation in developed countries. They can be grouped under three headings: rising incomes, differential productivity growth and foreign trade.

Rising incomes

Colin Clark was a pioneering economic statistician, working in the 1940s, who combined his search for statistical 'facts' with great imaginative insights. He attempted to find, in his own words, 'the conditions under which we can hope for the greatest degree of economic progress in the future' (C. G. Clark, *The Conditions of Economic Progress*, 1940).

To Clark we owe the important observation that as economies grow over time, the structure of output, comprising primary, secondary and tertiary economic activities, changes. The greater part of primary activity is agriculture. As national income grows, the share of primary production in output and employment falls. Manufacturing (secondary) activity rises relative to primary production, and, at a later stage, service (tertiary) activity rises relative to manufacturing.

The explanation for this phenomenon lies, if Clark is to be believed, in the income elasticity of demand for different goods and services. As incomes rise, initially the demand for primary products falls relative to the demand for manufactures. Manufacturing output and employment will take up a smaller and smaller share of a growing national income relative to primary output and employment, irrespective of what is happening to foreign trade.

Productivity growth

There are greater opportunities for productivity growth in manufacturing, as compared with primary production. For a given increase in output, the employment implications will be lower in manufacturing than in primary production. Other things being equal, output growth in manufacturing will be associated with rising productivity and shrinking employment. This is to be expected in any economy, especially one which is investing and enjoying technological progress. These are the *supply-side* implications of economic growth for structural change and, again, they will happen irrespective of changes in international trade.

Foreign trade

There are two ways in which external factors may affect the manufacturing base, only one of which has protectionist implications.

First, a country may be financing imports of manufactures through booming primary or tertiary sector exports. For example, a country which discovers oil can happily allow this commodity, and allied activities, to dominate output and employment at the expense of the manufacturing base. Likewise, growing service sector activities, tourism, insurance, transport and commercial services will reduce, relatively speaking, the manufacturing base, and be reflected in foreign trade. Changes of this type are part of the dynamics of economic activity and have implications for a country's foreign trade. They will be reflected in the structure of domestic employment.

Second, as the protectionists claim, the disappearance of a strong manufacturing employment base in a developed country may be due to competition from labour-intensive manufactured imports. These imports are likely to originate in the relatively labour-abundant poor countries of the world. Hence this argument perceives a strong link between growing north–south trade, and the decline of the manufacturing base in the north.

What is the evidence for this proposition? Although some economists have argued along these lines, there is no firm evidence to suggest it is labour-intensive imports from developing countries which are bringing about a decline in the manufacturing base of developed countries. A recent study suggests that 80 per cent of the observed decline in manufacturing employment in industrial countries between 1963 and 1994 was attributable to changing preference patterns (demand) and productivity changes (supply) *within* industrial countries. North–south trade has had a negligible impact on de-industrialisation (Rowthorn and Ramaswamy, 1999). (See Chapter 9 for a discussion and analysis of exchange rates and their influence on trade.)

Summary

● The dynamic gains from trade, arising on the side of supply, can be represented by a shift outwards in the production possibility curve. 'Vent for surplus', arising on the side of demand, can be represented by an economy moving out from an unemployment equilibrium inside the production frontier.

● The World Bank believes that there are many dynamic benefits of trade which are particularly important for developing countries. Dynamic benefits are much larger than the static gains from trade.

● Vent for surplus implies long-run underutilisation of capacity which appears to run counter to Say's Law. The best explanation is that poor economies' economic organisation is not developed enough for price adjustment to remove surplus productive capacity.

● Staples theory refers to exports of raw materials or resource-intensive commodities accompanied by large-scale migration and capital from Europe. It is often used to tell the story of Canadian development, and like vent for surplus makes use of the concept of a land frontier.

● It is difficult to test the engine of growth hypothesis. David Dollar's cross-section studies have been heavily criticised. Other studies have looked at the effect of trade on the growth of total factor productivity, rather than on the growth of output.

● Trade liberalisation in developing and transition economies is usually accompanied by other market-driven reforms. Often it has come about under IMF and World Bank pressure, something which has been criticised by the prominent economist Joseph Stiglitz.

● Regional trading arrangements are growing in number and importance, but they may have fewer benefits for economic growth than trade liberalisation measures.

● In most developed countries employment in manufacturing industry has diminished over a long period. Very little of this decline is attributable to the growth of labour-intensive imports from developing countries.

Key concepts

● Static versus dynamic gains
● Productivity gains from trade
● Vent for surplus
● Staples theory
● The engine of growth
● Trade liberalisation
● Regional trade arrangement (RTA)
● De-industrialisation

Questions for discussion

1 What are the dynamic gains from trade? Can they be quantified?

2 What has happened to the long-run terms of trade of primary commodities relative to manufactures? Are there any policy implications for developing countries which can be derived from this trend?

3 Outline the 'productivity' and 'vent for surplus' trade theories. Have they any relevance to present-day issues in the world economy?

4 The World Bank argues that trade liberalisation in developing countries is 'good for growth'. Explain. Does empirical evidence support this view?

5 A developing country's trade minister asks your advice on proposals to join a regional trading arrangement. What advice would you give?

6 Would trade policy reform prevent falling living standards in transition economies?

7 Should workers in poor countries worry about their jobs when trade is liberalised?

8 Discuss instances where trade might promote growth through its effect on investment and technological progress.

Suggested reading

Coe, D. T. and Helpman, E. (1995) 'International R&D Spillovers', *European Economic Review*, vol. 39 (May), pp. 859–87.

Dollar, D. (1992) 'Outward-orientated developing economies really do grow more rapidly', *Economic Development and Cultural Change*, vol. 40, no. 3, pp. 523–44.

Dornbusch, R. (1992) 'The case for trade liberalization in developing countries', *Journal of Economic Perspectives*, vol. 6, no. 1, pp. 69–85.

Findlay, R. and Lundahl, M. (1994) 'Natural resources, "vent for surplus", and the staples theory', in *From Classical Economics to Development Economics*, pp. 68–93, Aldershot: Edward Elgar.

Jonsson, G. and Subramanian, A. (2001) 'Dynamic Gains from Trade: Evidence from South Africa', *IMF Staff Papers*, vol. 48, no. 1, pp. 197–224.

Myint, H. (1958) 'The Classical Theory of Trade and the Underdeveloped Countries', *Economic Journal*, vol. LXVIII, pp. 317–37.

Romer, P. M. (1986) 'Increasing returns and long-run growth', *Journal of Political Economy*, vol. 5, pp. 1002–37.

Rowthorn, R. and Ramaswamy, R. (1999) 'Growth, Trade, and deindustrialization', *IMF Staff Papers*, vol. 46, no. 1, pp. 18–41.

Stiglitz, J. (2002) *Globalization and its Discontents*, London: Allen Lane.

Vamvakidis, A. (1999) 'Regional trade agreements or broad liberalization: which path leads to faster growth?', *IMF Staff Papers*, vol. 46, no. 1, pp. 42–68.

Viner, J. (1950) *The Customs Union Issue*, New York: Carnegie Endowment for International Peace.

Williams, J. H. (1929) 'The theory of international trade reconsidered', *Economic Journal*, June, pp. 195–209.

Young, A. (1928) 'Increasing returns and economic progress', *Economic Journal*, December, pp. 527–42.

Chapter 7

International factor mobility

Introduction

The pure theory of trade assumes that factors of production are immobile between countries. According to the Heckscher–Ohlin model, it is factor endowments within a nation that provide the basis for trade. Perfect factor mobility would have the effect of substituting for international trade. Assuming perfect competition, factors would move between countries until the marginal productivities and prices of factors were the same in all countries. Then there would be no basis for trade.

In the real world there is neither perfect factor mobility, nor perfect factor immobility. There are different degrees of factor mobility across countries and through time. Labour, capital, natural resources, managerial skills and technology move with varying degrees of freedom from country to country.

This chapter is concerned with the causes and consequences of international factor movements. Although it is organised into capital flows and labour flows, much of what is said applies broadly to all factors of production, especially to those movements of skills and technologies which come about at the present time through the medium of multinational companies.

Capital movements do not necessarily imply the transfer of capital goods between countries. Rather we are concerned with financial transactions between countries, one country being the lender, and the other being the borrower. The assumption is that this transaction provides extra purchasing power in the borrowing country, allowing it to undertake investment. It is possible that capital goods may indeed be imported by the borrowing country using borrowed funds, but equally well the capital goods could be of domestic origin. Or the borrowed funds may be spent in other ways: for example, on domestic or imported consumer goods, or on inventories. It is assumed, however, that it is *finance for investment* which comes from abroad, and qualifies as a (financial) capital movement.

An important complication relating to financial flows between countries is the distinction between foreign direct investment and portfolio investment.

Portfolio investment refers to the purchase by individuals or institutions of foreign paper assets, either equities or bonds. Portfolio investment does not imply taking managerial control over a foreign company, or control over its physical assets.

Foreign direct investment (FDI) refers to the flow of funds to purchase a stake in a foreign company, thereby giving the purchaser control over the management of the company, or over its physical assets. If a company engages to a significant degree in FDI, acquiring substantial controlling interests in foreign companies, then it is usually referred to as a multinational enterprise (MNE) or as what is the same thing, a transnational corporation (TNC).

In economic theory, portfolio investment flows between countries can be explained by interest rate differences between the two countries. Theory suggests that capital moves from country A to country B because the interest rate (return on capital) is higher in B than in A. The process will continue until interest rates are equalised between A and B, and the marginal return on capital is the same in both countries. Then the process will come to an end. Few economists believe, however, that interest rate differentials satisfactorily explain capital flows, especially FDI. Multinational enterprises invest abroad because of specific business opportunities abroad, rather than because of calculations of interest rates and return to capital abroad. In fact, although this is a very popular area in present-day economics for theorising and research, as yet no single theory has emerged to explain FDI in the international economy.

Labour migration, by way of contrast, is a relatively straightforward phenomenon. People have moved from one world region to another, and from one country to another, since the beginnings of recorded history. Sometimes the push has clearly come from climatic changes and natural disasters. This has been the case particularly where large-scale population movements have been observed. Wars have also brought major population disturbances. In 1971, in a massive migration, 10 million refugees left Bangladesh for safety in India, though the majority subsequently returned. A desire for political and religious freedom has always been an important driving force for labour flows. However, it is also widely recognised that economic motivations play a key role in the movement of labour across national boundaries. A desire for higher wages, secure employment and better opportunities in terms of training and education all serve to attract individuals and families, encouraging them to move from one country to another.

Objectives

When you have completed this chapter, you should be able to:

● appreciate labour and capital flows in a *historical context*;

● discuss *reasons for capital flows*: rates of return, risk diversification, tariffs, location of raw materials and capital market imperfections;

● explain why a firm may wish to establish *subsidiaries and affiliates* abroad;

● outline the possible costs and benefits of *multinationals* from the perspective of the 'host' country;

● provide details of *Europe's FDI* abroad during the 1990s;

● define *labour migration* and discuss its likely benefits and costs;

● discuss present patterns of labour *migration into Europe*.

Capital and labour flows in history

Between 1870 and 1914, unprecedented quantities of financial capital flowed from Europe to Canada, Australasia, the United States, Latin America and Russia. Britain and France were the main capital exporters. Alongside capital flows, many millions left Europe to settle temporarily or permanently in Canada, the US and Latin America. Europeans went to Australasia and South Africa, with smaller numbers to East Africa and Asia. Chinese and Indians migrated to all parts of Asia and Africa to work on plantations and in trade.

The peak years for capital and labour flows were between 1907 and 1913. Britain, as a major source of capital, invested £1070m abroad during this period. Sixty per cent of the investment went to Canada, Australasia, Argentina and the United States (Table 7.1).

The reasons for the surge in labour migration and foreign investment in the period 1870 to 1914 have been discussed over time by many economists and economic historians. Key figures in international economics, such as Ragnar Nurkse and W. A. Lewis, as well as historians such as Jeffrey Williamson and Walter Rostow, have been encouraged to write about this period. Their broad conclusions are summarised below and provide a useful context in which to place the later debates.

● The period 1870 to 1914 approximated to a classical economic system in the world economy. There was heavy reliance on the price mechanism, there were only limited immigration controls for labour, and capital could move more or less unhindered

Table 7.1 British overseas investment 1907–1913

Destination	Amount (£m)	Share
New World	300	28%
Canada	250	23%
Australasia	50	5%
United States	160	15%
Latin America	240	22%
Argentina	110	10%
Brazil	80	7%
Mexico	30	3%
Chile	20	2%
Other Empire	160	15%
China and Japan	40	4%
Europe	50	5%
Russia	50	5%
Miscellaneous	70	6%

from country to country. Rising tariffs in Europe and the US, however, were already distorting the pattern of international trade, and there were political restrictions on overseas investment in some countries. For example, the French would not invest in Germany after the Franco-Prussian War.

● Britain was the most important exporter of capital. This was not because Britain had high savings, but because Britain had an unusually low rate of domestic investment at that time by international standards. British foreign investment went mainly to the regions of recent European settlement, plus Argentina.

● The other major capital exporter was France. Before 1880, most French investment went to Europe, Turkey and Egypt. Thereafter Russia, the Balkans and Scandinavia became important destinations for French investment.

● By the end of the nineteenth century, the distinction between portfolio investment and foreign direct investment had emerged. A number of US companies were operating abroad, in Canada, Britain and Germany. There were subsidiaries of British firms in Canada, Australia, New Zealand and South Africa.

● A high proportion of portfolio investment involved control by the investing country. Japan, for example, received large amounts of portfolio investment but this was controlled by the overseas investor. The present-day definition of portfolio investment would classify this as direct investment, because it involved control.

● Companies were floated in London in the 1880s to finance gold, silver and diamond mines in the colonies. Land and plantations were also popular for portfolio investment. Many of these companies failed. For example, seventy gold and silver mining companies were floated in London between 1880 and 1883. Twenty-four failed within three years, and thirty-six failed within five years.

● Until the 1880s, Britain was also the main source of outward migration. Later, in the 1890s, Italy and Spain emerged as the main sources of migrants, to be followed at the turn of the century by Austria-Hungary. France was not a country which sent out many migrants. Germany and France were countries which received migrants, from Italy, Belgium and eastern Europe, especially Poland.

● The number of Chinese living abroad increased by 5 million between 1880 and 1992. Chinese migrants went principally to southern Asia, Malaya and the Dutch East Indies. In Australia, labour unions opposed the employment of Chinese labour. There was also anti-Chinese legislation in California and Canada.

Why did international capital and labour flows increase so rapidly towards the end of the nineteenth century? Taylor and Williamson (1994) have provided an integrated model which stands up well to empirical investigation. They argue that high transport costs in the previous centuries had ruled out trade in natural resources and resource-intensive commodities. The economies of the New World had cheap resources, but lacked labour and capital to exploit them. As transport costs fell in the nineteenth century, labour flowed in to exploit natural resources.

Empirical evidence (Figure 7.1) shows a strong positive correlation between real wages and the growth of labour supplies between 1870 and 1913 in a cross-section of countries. Countries with low real wages such as Italy, Spain and Sweden showed low growth in labour supplies. These countries provided *migrants* to the New World.

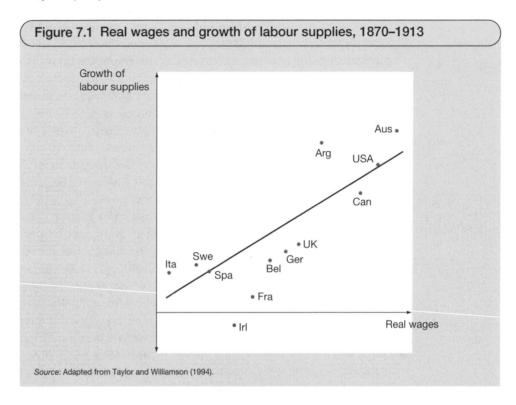

Figure 7.1 Real wages and growth of labour supplies, 1870–1913

Source: Adapted from Taylor and Williamson (1994).

Countries like the US, Canada, Australia and Argentina had significantly higher growth in labour supplies, principally migrant labour attracted by high real wages. Other Old World countries – France, the UK, Germany and Belgium – were clustered around the middle. Ireland showed a negative growth of labour supply, indicating rates of emigration higher than the rate of growth of population.

Migrant labour increased labour supplies in the New World and enabled the exploitation of natural resources. In the US, immigrants accounted for 40 per cent of the population increase between 1870 and 1913. Labour force growth made capital relatively scarce and encouraged massive capital inflows from the Old World. In particular, high dependency rates, brought about by high fertility and low infant mortality rates among migrant families in the US, depressed domestic savings rates and pulled in foreign investment.

Theory of capital movements

We noted in the Introduction that capital and labour move from one location to another in expectation of higher rates of return. A simple economic model, based on assumptions of perfect competition leads to the conclusion that residents of country A will purchase assets in country B because the productivity of capital in B is greater than in A. However, maximisation of rates of return as a motive for capital flows does not always stand up well to empirical evidence. As a simple example, capital flows are often 'two-way', from A to B, and from B to A. Why should this happen, if the productivity of capital in B is greater than in A?

Because empirical evidence is often inconsistent with the rates of return approach, economists give additional reasons for capital flows over and above rates of return. These are explanations which reflect the complexities of business behaviour. The most important additional reasons for capital flows are:

- risk diversification
- tariffs and other forms of trade intervention
- location of raw materials
- capital market imperfections.

Risk diversification

Empirical evidence suggests that risk diversification is an important reason for foreign investment. This applies to both FDI and portfolio investment. Foreign assets provide opportunities to reduce risk. Individuals and firms can reduce risk by distributing their investments across industries and countries. If a recession occurs in one country, this does not necessarily imply problems in all countries. Business cycles occur at different times in different countries. Governments also vary in their capabilities for macro-economic management, thus influencing the likely rates of return on investment in different countries at different points of time. International diversification can help explain the phenomenon of 'two-way' capital flows which appear to contradict the underlying theory of capital movements based solely on differences in the productivity of capital.

Tariffs and other forms of trade intervention

Multinational firms may invest abroad in order to get round a tariff wall. The EU's common external tariff has encouraged Japanese and US companies to invest in EU countries to overcome EU trade protection. In some circumstances, tariff protection may make production in a foreign country highly profitable and risk-free, in which case trade protection will encourage the inflow of foreign investment. Similarly, governments may offer incentives in the form of subsidies, investment allowances, tax holidays and free factories to encourage foreign firms. The aim is to boost local employment, and probably also to save foreign exchange by cutting imports.

Location of raw materials

The mining and processing of raw materials usually requires a high degree of vertical integration of operations. Vertical integration of firms can result in the flow of capital from one country to another. For example, the processing of raw materials like copper, aluminium and petroleum usually takes place close to the source of the raw materials. Firms involved in exploiting raw materials will find it necessary to set up processing facilities in these locations. Capital will flow from the parent company to finance processing activities abroad. Companies involved in operations such as these are usually large multinationals with significant integrated investment worldwide.

Capital market imperfections

Other things being equal, local entrepreneurs are likely to be able to produce goods and services at a lower cost than foreign entrepreneurs operating in the same market. Local businesses are familiar with local factor markets, government regulations and so on. But local businesses frequently have problems in raising capital. Their lenders may lack information about the credit ratings of local businesses. Or lenders may simply prefer, as borrowers, the large multinational company as opposed to the small local enterprise. In either case, the capital market fails to reflect the true profitability of domestic enterprise. It favours the larger and better-known multinational firm.

Multinational enterprises and factor mobility

Vast multinationals operate worldwide. Such companies are decisive forces in determining both trade and factor flows in the modern world economy. Understanding the organisation and strategy of such companies can shed light on the way factors of production (labour, capital, management and technology) move from one country to another.

In a narrow sense, multinational companies are simply the media through which factors flow internationally. In a broader sense factor mobility encompasses everything which multinational enterprises do when they establish and operate affiliates or subsidiaries in foreign countries. Usually the process begins with a transfer of financial capital from the parent company to the affiliate or subsidiary. However, this is not necessary to the process. In the modern world economy, finance can be raised anywhere in the world, including in the country in which the subsidiary is located. The necessary element in multinational enterprise is not the transfer of finance, but the transfer of managerial control. MNEs are not simply a means of transferring financial capital from countries where the returns are relatively low to countries where the returns are relatively high. Rather, it is the managerial and technological advantages of multinational firms which are transferred abroad.

J. H. Dunning (1974) provided a useful framework in which to discuss the reasons why a firm will become an MNE. His analysis was based on a consideration of three aspects of business behaviour:

● ownership
● location
● internationalisation.

Ownership is the special expertise a MNE has developed and now wishes to exploit in a wider market. The firm may have developed a cost-reducing process, or research and development may have resulted in a new product. The firm will have advertised widely to create a brand image. Even its distribution systems may be so effective as to offer 'ownership' advantages. Spreading all this knowledge over more and more customers by selling in foreign markets is a very effective business strategy. However, it does not give us reasons why the firm decides to locate abroad rather than simply export its products. To explain this, we need to refer to the other two aspects of business behaviour.

Location refers to factors which make production abroad an attractive option. Transport costs may have ruled out the export of domestically produced low-value bulky commodities such as cement. Tariff walls may provide an incentive to locate in a country, so that the firm can gain access to protected markets. Many services, such as 'meals out', cannot be exported at all. Hence the need for McDonald's to move worldwide to provide the Big Mac. When McDonald's 'goes global' it offers local franchises. Local firms know all about local customs, local markets and so on. This raises a further question as to why other MNEs do not simply license or franchise suppliers abroad to produce their products. Why tie up capital and managerial skills when local enterprise can do the job better? Of course, there are many MNEs like McDonald's, which make full use of franchising opportunities. But licences and franchises are not always the answer. To understand why, we refer to Dunning's third aspect of business behaviour.

Internationalisation explains why a firm chooses to operate its own plant rather than licensing others to do so. There are two basic reasons for internationalisation. First, the firm may not be able to agree with prospective licensees the terms under which they will be allowed to operate. How will the contracts be enforced? What royalties will be payable? Second, even if acceptable terms can be agreed, what safeguards are in place to prevent the product or process in question being copied? Will the licensee defect and set up a competitive firm? How high are barriers to the entry of new firms?

The Dunning approach is helpful in explaining why a domestic firm might decide to become a multinational. However, empirical evidence indicates that when it is translated into a theory of factor mobility, the Dunning approach does not perform at all well. In particular, it seems that it cannot explain real-world flows of FDI between countries with similar factor endowments.

A more promising empirical approach to multinationals suggests that business activity is determined by a trade-off between proximity advantages and concentration advantages. Proximity advantages are those which encourage a firm to be physically close to foreign markets. Concentration advantages are those which make it profitable for a firm to concentrate its activities at home in a single location. Foreign direct investment takes place when proximity advantages outweigh concentration advantages.

Benefits and costs of multinationals to the host country

The 'host' country is the country which receives capital and other factors of production from the multinational enterprise. Factor mobility, through the medium of a multinational enterprise, has many effects on the host country. The balancing out of benefits and costs is a complicated issue, but some of the more important considerations are highlighted below.

Economic benefits and costs

- *Balance of payments:* the initial transfer of financial capital to the host country will benefit the host country's balance of payments. Once the affiliate or subsidiary begins operating in the host country, remittance of profits and dividends may contribute a drain on the host's balance of payments.
- *Employment and national income:* the affiliate will contribute net value added to the host country's national income and employment. If the workers and other resources taken up by the company would otherwise be unemployed, there will be very significant net value added.
- *Externalities:* these may raise the productivity of other firms in the host country. For example, the MNE may train workers who subsequently leave to take up employment with other local firms. The MNE may also provide valuable technical assistance to local suppliers to meet the need for locally sourced inputs.
- *Economic management:* The MNE may have different economic goals from the host country, which complicates the host government's economic management function. The host government, for example, may be interested in building up the economy's research base to foster exports and economic growth. But there are examples of MNEs which do not undertake R&D in the host country because they wish to protect intellectual property rights. Or the host government may wish to boost tax revenues, but the MNE may be able to avoid local taxes and circumvent exchange controls. At one extreme, the MNE may simply pull out, shifting production from the host country to country C, if it dislikes the host's economic policies.

In addition to economic benefits and costs, there may be political and social implications for the host country from the activities of an MNE.

- Key people in the MNE may be of a *different political persuasion* from that of the host country. Many countries, especially in the developing world, have been keen to exclude MNE executives from the media (television, radio and the press), because they may have unacceptable political views.
- There may be complicated *legal issues* relating to the jurisdiction of the MNE and the host country. In disputes with the host country, MNEs may seek support from their home government, leading to a jurisdictional dispute between the two countries. This can be particularly important in relation to trade policy and trade disputes.
- MNEs may run counter to *nationalist sentiments*. Nationalists may oppose the concept of an independent world economy. MNEs are often suspected of undermining the host nation's sovereignty, bringing in alien cultural and social values. Alternatively, MNEs may be regarded as important agents of social and political change, encouraging diversity, co-operation and achievement within a strong multiethnic environment.

Europe's foreign direct investment

Changes in Europe's foreign direct investment in the 1990s reflected the important changes in the economic environment. Forces of particular relevance to Europe included liberalisation in central and eastern Europe, European integration, the introduction of the euro, and the restructuring of Europe's public sectors.

Research has indicated a number of interesting real-world trends in the 1990s.

- In the countries which now form the euro area, mergers and acquisitions have been a major determinant of outflows of FDI and portfolio investment since 1998. Euro area companies have invested in foreign firms to acquire technical expertise and to strengthen their global market positions.
- The largest share of euro area merger and acquisition investment has gone to the US, followed by the UK and Latin America (Figure 7.2). The largest proportion of euro area investment went into service sector activities (39 per cent), followed by manufacturing (31 per cent) and finance (18 per cent). High-tech industries (biotechnology, computer equipment, electronics and communications technology) accounted for about half of the FDI in manufacturing.
- Spain provides a good example of trends in European FDI. During the 1990s Spain changed from being a net recipient of FDI to an important investor in Latin America. Spanish FDI was drawn to Latin America by market opportunities and cultural ties. The major destinations were Argentina, Chile, Cuba and Mexico (Batiz-Lazo *et al.*, 2002). Spanish mergers and acquisitions have been important in Mexico, Brazil and Argentina. Cuba does not permit foreign private enterprises to operate in the economy, so investment has come about through co-operation agreements with Spain.
- Spain's investment in Latin America has been heavily weighted towards the banking sector. The major Spanish banks have acquired Latin American financial institutions. Utilities (electricity, gas, water) and telecommunications have also been important recipients of Spanish FDI.
- During the 1990s the countries of central and eastern Europe had significant increases in FDI inflows (Figure 7.3). Countries in negotiation with the EU for membership, particularly the Czech Republic, Hungary and Poland, succeeded in attracting FDI. Investors from abroad hoped to take advantage of new markets that will be *within* the EU, after accession.
- Hungary is an outstanding example of a transition economy which has received large inflows of foreign funds since the early 1990s. Among the countries of central and eastern Europe it ranks first in terms both of the volume and of the length of time over which it has attracted foreign capital. Research on the costs and benefits of FDI in Hungary indicate, on the benefit side, that foreign-owned firms have higher productivity than domestic firms, and that they produce positive spillover effects on other firms in the same sector. On the negative side, FDI in Hungary has increased regional disparities in the country. Most of the FDI is

concentrated around the capital, Budapest, moving outwards towards the EU border with Austria. The poorer areas of Hungary, moving south and east towards Romania, Ukraine and the former Yugoslavia, have received scarcely any FDI.

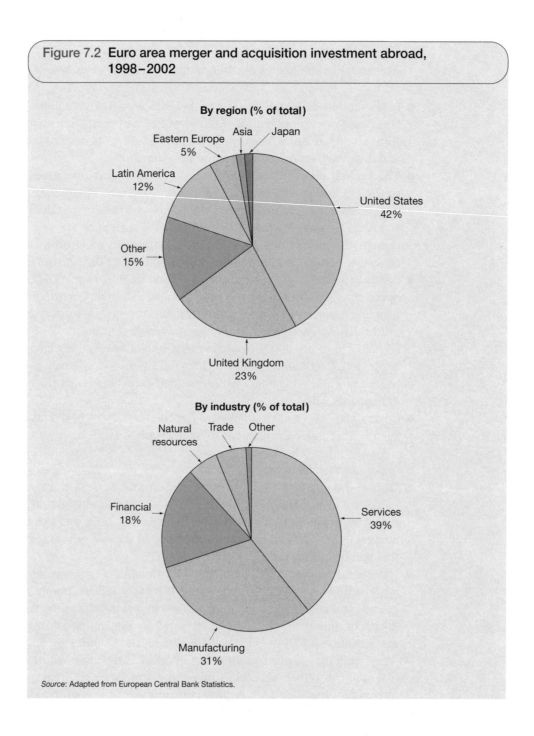

Figure 7.2 Euro area merger and acquisition investment abroad, 1998–2002

By region (% of total)

Eastern Europe 5%
Asia
Japan
Latin America 12%
United States 42%
Other 15%
United Kingdom 23%

By industry (% of total)

Natural resources
Trade
Other
Financial 18%
Services 39%
Manufacturing 31%

Source: Adapted from European Central Bank Statistics.

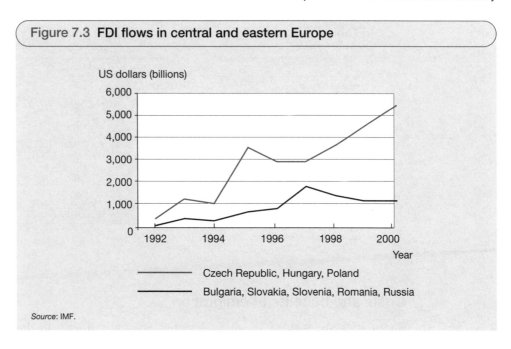

Figure 7.3 **FDI flows in central and eastern Europe**

US dollars (billions)

Czech Republic, Hungary, Poland

Bulgaria, Slovakia, Slovenia, Romania, Russia

Source: IMF.

Labour migration

In many countries in recent years, anti-immigration sentiments have increased. There have been tensions between different ethnic groups, sometimes erupting in violence and disturbances. Immigrants are often subjected to discrimination and abuse.

Often there is confusion between migrants, refugees and displaced persons (Table 7.2). Indeed, when countries have low quotas for immigration, economic migrants often seek asylum status (Table 7.3).

The 1990s was a period of strong international migration, comparable with the periods 1875–1914 and the 1960s. High growth rates in the destination countries have attracted migrants, transport costs have fallen, and there is much better information about opportunities in other countries. The fall of the Berlin Wall also made it much easier for migrants to leave the Soviet bloc.

Table 7.2 **International labour movements, year 2000**

Category	Number (millions)
Migrants	150
Refugees	18
Internationally displaced persons	23

Source: Financial Times, 25 July 2002.

Table 7.3 Asylum seekers in selected OECD countries, year 2000	
Country	*Number (000)*
Australia	16
Belgium	40
Canada	36
Italy	18
Germany	80
Netherlands	40
US	50
UK	96

Source: *Financial Times*, 25 July 2002.

Costs and benefits of emigration

Economics suggests that, on balance, everyone will gain in the long run from a freeing up of the international market for labour. Dani Rodrik, Professor of Economics at Harvard University, has suggested that even a marginal liberalisation of international labour flows would bring gains to the international economy far greater than the prospective gains from free trade. How does the economist see the costs and benefits of migration, both for the country of emigration and the country of immigration?

● *Surplus labour*. Many countries of emigration have surplus labour in the agricultural sector. High rates of population growth bring overcrowding on the land. An impoverished rural labour force tries to wrest a living from the land. In these circumstances emigration has often been a safety valve. As labour leaves the economy, the marginal product of those remaining on the land rises. There was surplus labour in Ireland in the nineteenth century. Irish emigrants went to Britain and to the US, where they found employment in farming, construction and new industries. Surplus labour in agriculture was also true of central, southern and eastern Europe in the nineteenth and early twentieth centuries. Hungary, Poland, Russia, southern Italy, Greece and Turkey all had large migrant populations. It used to be said that Italians from the south of Italy felt more at home when they visited New York than when they went to northern Italian cities such as Milan or Turin. In the 1950s, 1960s and 1970s there was a large exodus of surplus labour from the Indian subcontinent, from the Caribbean and from Sub-Saharan and North Africa, destined for Europe's towns and cities. Emigration of surplus labour should have raised the productivity and real income of those left behind, as well as raising the incomes of the migrants.
● *Remittances*. Many poor countries with shortages of foreign exchange rely heavily on the money sent back home by migrants to boost the credit side of the balance of payments. Turkey depends heavily on the remittances of migrants

working in Europe. The same is true of Greece. Parents of migrants from the Indian subcontinent can expect to receive money from their children. This applies even when the children marry, or are joined by other members of the extended family. Temporary migrants, for example seasonal agricultural workers with short-term work permits, usually remit very large proportions of their earnings. Often they are best described as target workers, saving for a particular purpose – say to finance education at home or to set themselves up in business. These remittances are a much-valued financial inflow for the country of emigration.

● *Brain drain.* The downside of emigration for the country is the loss of skilled, educated and talented people. Even where there is surplus labour on the land, it is the young and the more enterprising who emigrate. Contrary to what economic theory tells us, productivity may not rise on the land as the 'surplus' labour exits. Rather, many farms become moribund, the refuge of the very old, the very young, and those who are unable to adjust to life abroad.

The brain drain from South Africa

South Africa is a country suffering from a large exodus of skilled labour. The occupations involved are medicine, engineering, accounting and business. An estimated 20 per cent of workers with these skills have already left South Africa. For some of the skills the figures are higher. It is estimated that 35 per cent of doctors who graduated from the University of Witwatersrand in the 1990s have since emigrated.

For a country like South Africa, which has a shortage of skilled workers, emigration can be a disaster. As skilled labour exits, it becomes more and more difficult to maintain aggregate growth rates and employment levels. Every skilled worker who leaves brings about a loss of unskilled jobs. The ratio is possibly as high as ten unskilled jobs for every skilled migrant.

The causes of South Africa's skills exodus are many. On the 'push' side violent crime, AIDS and political uncertainty play a large part. On the 'pull' side, nearly a million South Africans hold British passports and can freely enter the UK to work. Other favoured destinations are Canada, the US, Australia and New Zealand. Finally, falls in the value of the South African rand have increased economic uncertainty and have caused many skilled workers to look abroad.

On the positive side, South African companies are beginning to train black South Africans to fill the gaps left by white emigrants. The polarisation in South Africa between black and white in terms of employment, which is one of the legacies of apartheid, may now at last be starting to break down.

Costs and benefits of immigration

What are the implications of immigration for the host country?

● *Transfer of technology.* New technologies of production which will benefit the receiving country are frequently diffused via immigration. There is a long history of such international transmissions of technology, going back in the UK to the Flemish weavers of the fourteenth century, who brought new technologies to the English woollen trade. In the present day, the multinational firm frequently acts as the medium through which new technologies cross national borders, via the movements of skilled personnel between head office, affiliates and subsidiaries.

● *Labour costs.* The impact of immigration on real wages in the host country has always been a controversial issue. Employers may be anxious to keep wages down in certain occupations and will welcome low-cost labour from abroad. Jobs which migrants are prepared to take may be the ones which are difficult to fill at existing wage rates: in hotels and hospitals, and other service sector occupations. Agriculture, too, frequently relies on cheap labour from abroad at peak harvest times. Opposition to immigration may come from local workers who fear the impact of competition from low-wage labour on their own levels of remuneration.

● *Demography.* High migration can boost consumer spending and lead to a more buoyant and innovative economy. Immigrants tend to have a younger age profile than the economy as a whole. They have young families and a high youth dependency ratio, i.e. the proportion of children to those of working age. Real consumption growth is positively correlated with the youth dependency ratio. Countries with a high youth dependency ratio tend to be more flexible and dynamic than those with a low youth dependency ratio.

● *Social-sector capital expenditure* refers to the extra investment required in the social infrastructure to cope with immigration. The social costs of immigration are reflected in the need for increased social capital (schools, housing, hospitals, transport) which must be met in the short run, before the migrant workers begin to contribute to national output.

Australia's need for people

Australia has always been heavily dependent on immigration. The present population numbers are less than 20 million, of whom a quarter were born abroad and a further 19 per cent are the children of immigrants. Low fertility rates mean that the population could decline by 2050 without further immigration.

There are powerful political lobbies in Australia which oppose further immigration. It is unlikely that Australia will accept the large numbers of unskilled workers and refugees in the future that it welcomed in the past. However, to maintain the present growth of national income, the workforce needs to increase by 1.25 per cent per year, which requires an annual migrant intake of at least 140 000. For that reason, the Australian government has raised the annual quota for migrants to 100 000. Of these 58 per cent are to be skilled workers, and the remainder must have close relatives in Australia. Despite the rise in the quota, on present projections Australia will be an ageing economy by mid-century. In some states, such as Tasmania, the population will have halved by 2050.

Migration in Europe

As well as sending migrants to the New World, Europe has always attracted immigrants. Almost half of the EU's 15 million immigrants today come from other European countries, particularly from southern, central and eastern Europe (see Figure 7.4).

Germany, Italy, the UK, France and the Netherlands have the greatest *flows* of immigrants at the present time, but it is Switzerland which has the largest *stock* of migrant people (Figure 7.5). In the past, Switzerland attracted many migrants into farm and hotel work. Eventually, the Swiss introduced strict immigration laws, arguing that the infrastructure was over-extended. This significantly reduced the flow of migrant labour.

EU countries

Under EU rules there is complete freedom of movement of labour between member countries. There is, however, some controversy surrounding migrant labour from EU accession countries.

Before the fall of the Berlin Wall, relatively few migrants from eastern and central Europe found their way into EU countries. For those who managed to leave the Soviet bloc and Yugoslavia, it was a one-way journey. Nearly a million workers left Poland for EU countries in the early 1980s, but few expected to be allowed to return. The picture in the twenty-first century is very different. There are now estimated to be about four million workers in the EU who come from central and eastern Europe, plus two million who come from the former Yugoslavia.

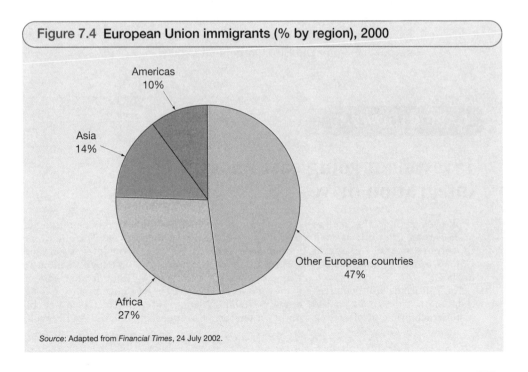

Figure 7.4 European Union immigrants (% by region), 2000

Americas 10%

Asia 14%

Other European countries 47%

Africa 27%

Source: Adapted from Financial Times, 24 July 2002.

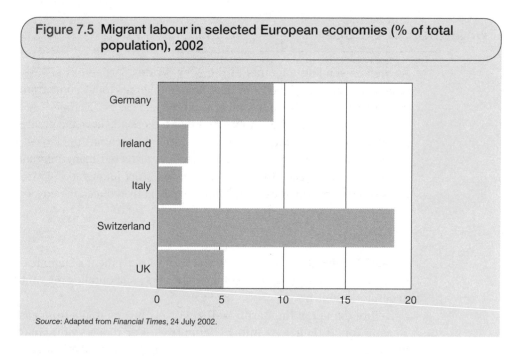

Figure 7.5 Migrant labour in selected European economies (% of total population), 2002

Source: Adapted from *Financial Times*, 24 July 2002.

Controversies attach to migrant labour from the EU accession countries. The European Commission has estimated that one-third of a million migrant workers will move each year from the accession countries, i.e. from the Czech Republic, Cyprus, Estonia, Hungary, Poland, Slovakia, Slovenia, Estonia, Malta, Lithuania and Latvia. Most migrants are expected to wish to work in Germany and Austria, where there will be strong competition for certain jobs. Under pressure, accession states have been forced to agree that they will accept restrictions on migration for up to seven years after the EU enlargement in 2004.

CASE STUDY 7.1

Investment going east boosts EU integration drive

FT

If all goes to plan, the leaders of 25 European countries plan to celebrate the European Union's eastward enlargement in 2004.

The politicians will doubtless claim most of the credit for the historic achievement of ending the cold war division of Europe. But they should spare a toast for business people.

PSA Peugeot Citroën, the French carmaker's announcement this week of plans to build a new € 700m ($688m, £443m) plant in eastern Europe, is a timely reminder of the role of west European companies in the integration process.

Peugeot said it was looking at four former communist states now preparing for EU accession – the Czech Republic, Hungary, Poland and Slovakia. Together

▶

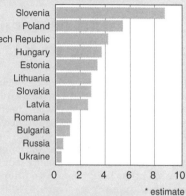

FDI inflows
$bn

- Czech Republic
- Poland
- Hungary

1996 97 98 99 2000 01 02*

Eastern Europe share of global FDI inflows (%)

1996 97 98 99 2000 01 02*

Annual wage in selected eastern European countries 2000 ($'000)

Slovenia
Poland
Czech Republic
Hungary
Estonia
Lithuania
Slovakia
Latvia
Romania
Bulgaria
Russia
Ukraine

0 2 4 6 8 10

* estimate

Sources: UNCTAD; EBRD

with Cyprus, Estonia, Latvia, Lithuania, Malta, and Slovenia, these states are in the last stages of negotiating EU accession.

Investment has long been laying the economic groundwork for the politicians. The first tentative foreign investments in the region were made even before the fall of the Berlin Wall in 1989. By the mid-1990s, a trickle became a flood. While EU politicians repeatedly postponed accession talks, business people pressed ahead with the construction of new plants and the modernisation of old ones.

In the process, they helped draw the ex-communist states out of Russia's orbit and into the EU's. The EU is now the accession states' biggest source of foreign investment and largest trade partner, accounting for up to 70 per cent of imports.

The process survived the Asian and Russian economic crises of the late 1990s and is now weathering the global economic slowdown. According to Unctad, the United Nations Conference on Trade and Development, global flows of foreign direct investment plunged 40 per cent last year. Only central and eastern Europe (a region which includes Russia) saw an increase, albeit of only 2 per cent to $27.2bn.

Willem Buiter, chief economist at the European Bank for Reconstruction and Development, the region's multilateral bank, said: 'The Peugeot announcement is a harbinger of things to come.'

Source: Stefan Wagstyl, *Financial Times*, 31 October 2002. Reprinted with permission.

Comment on case study 7.1

The EU is the largest source of investment funds for the EU accession countries. EU enlargement will begin in 2004, but since 1989, when the Berlin Wall came down, EU businesses have been involved in the construction of new plants and the modernisation of old manufacturing complexes in central and eastern Europe. In 2001, despite a world economic slowdown, FDI in central and eastern Europe rose to $27.2 billion.

PSA Peugeot Citroën, the French car manufacturer, has announced plans to build a new plant in eastern Europe. Possible locations are any one of four of the accession states, the Czech Republic, Hungary, Poland and Slovakia.

The third graph above also indicates one of the reasons for strong popularity of the accession countries with EU investors, namely cheap labour. In central and eastern European countries, there is diversity in wage levels, but they are, on average, 20 per cent of the wage level in the current EU countries.

CASE STUDY 7.2

Central and eastern Europeans already sampling life in EU

Flush with funds from cleaning houses in London, Marysia already knows how she will spend her illegally earned wages.

A 21-year-old Polish media student, she will work for about three months, long enough to buy the upmarket digital recorder she needs for her radio journalism studies, and then return to Poland.

She is one of tens of thousands of central and east Europeans already working in the European Union, well before their native countries join the EU. Many, like her, are temporary migrants, planning to return home after a few months.

Some enter the EU with legal short-term work permits, including seasonal agricultural workers in Germany, Italy and Spain. Others, like Marysia, work illegally but are widely tolerated for doing jobs that many others do not want.

Such arrivals from central and eastern Europe have become common only in the last decade.

Before the fall of communism, migrants from the region generally left home for good, with little hope of return, such as the 800,000 who left Poland in the grim 1980s. The collapse of the Berlin Wall was followed by a surge of migrants, led by ethnic Germans from Russia and elsewhere who had special settlement rights in Germany. They were accompanied by refugees from the Yugoslav wars who also went mainly to Germany.

However, since the early 1990s migration between east and west Europe has become much more fluid, with movements into the EU often being offset by movements back to the ex-communist states.

The Organisation for Economic Co-operation and Development says there are about 3m east Europeans in the EU, 2m of them refugees from the former Yugoslavia. Most of the rest are Poles, Romanians and Albanians, who have established ex-patriate communities where newcomers can often find accommodation and work.

For the most part the current controversies in the EU about immigration have not affected immigrants from central and eastern Europe. Very few are asylum seekers. And, as white Europeans, they adapt more easily to life in western Europe.

Nevertheless, there are fears that the accession of new states to the EU planned for 2004 could prompt a bigger wave of immigration from the candidate countries – the Czech Republic, Cyprus, Estonia, Hungary, Latvia, Lithuania, Malta, Poland, Slovakia and Slovenia.

Source: Financial Times, 24 July 2002. Reprinted with permission.

Comment on case study 7.2

Not all migrants work legally. Marysia is an illegal short-term migrant from Poland, working as a cleaner in London. She intends to stay for about three months before taking up studies in Poland. The money which she earns in London will purchase a digital recorder which she needs for her studies as a student of journalism.

Since the fall of the Berlin Wall, there have been many short-term migrants like Marysia from central and eastern Europe. Often they take up seasonal work in agriculture in Germany, Spain and Italy. They do not attract the publicity which asylum-seekers get. Because they are white and speak European languages, they adapt easily to life in Europe.

EU enlargement in 2004 is likely to increase the numbers of migrants from central and eastern Europe in EU countries. Not all EU countries are happy with this prospect.

Summary

● Capital movements are financial transactions between a borrower country and a lender country. They are divided into portfolio investment and foreign direct investment (FDI).

● Labour migration refers to the movement of people across national boundaries. The influences on labour migration include social and political upheavals and natural disasters, as well as economic motivations such as higher wages and secure employment.

● There was an important historical surge in labour migration and foreign investment in the period 1870–1914, which has been widely studied by economic historians. In the US, immigrants accounted for 40 per cent of the population increase between these dates.

● Factors influencing capital movements include rates of return, risk diversification, tariffs, the location of raw materials and capital market imperfections.

● The multinational enterprise can be studied in terms of three aspects of business behaviour: ownership, location and internationalisation. Alternatively we may explore the trade-off between proximity advantages and concentration advantages.

● There were important changes in FDI in Europe in the 1990s. The euro area has invested heavily in the US, the UK and Latin America. Spain has changed from being a net recipient of FDI to an important investor in Latin America.

● Hungary is a European transition economy which has received large inflows of foreign funds since the early 1990s. Most of the FDI has been concentrated in areas which border the EU.

● Labour migration can also have costs and benefits for the country of emigration and the country of immigration. South Africa is a country suffering from an exodus of skilled labour. Australia is a country which is still heavily dependent on immigrant labour to maintain the present growth rate of national income.

Key concepts

- Foreign direct investment
- Portfolio investment
- Rates of return
- Risk diversification
- Ownership, location and internationalisation
- Multinational companies
- Host country
- Migrants, refugees, and displaced persons
- Surplus labour
- Remittances

Questions for discussion

1 Explain the difference between portfolio investment and foreign direct investment.

2 Is there a conflict between the interests of host countries and the interests of MNEs?

3 Why do host countries offer incentives to MNEs?

4 Historically, Italy and Ireland sent millions of people abroad, but are now destination countries for migrants. Why?

5 What are the basic motives for portfolio investment? What additional reasons are necessary to explain FDI?

6 What are the motives for the international migration of workers? How important are economic criteria in migration?

7 How can South Africa solve its 'brain drain' problem?

8 Why is Australia unlikely to accept large numbers of unskilled workers and refugees? What effects will reducing the inflow of migrants have on the economy?

Suggested reading

Batiz-Lazo, B., Mendialdua, A. B. and Zabalandikoetxea, S. (2002) *Growth of the Spanish Multinational in Latin America during the 1990s*, Milton Keynes: Open University Business School.

Dunning, J. H. (1974) *Economic Analysis and the Multinational Enterprise*, London: George Allen and Unwin.

Dunning, J. H. (1981) *International Production and the Multinational Enterprise*, London: George Allen and Unwin.

Lewis, W. (1978) *Growth and Fluctuations, 1870–1913*, London: George Allen and Unwin.

Markusen, J. R. (1995) 'The boundaries of multinational enterprise and the theory of international trade', *Journal of Economic Perspectives*, vol. 9, no. 2, pp. 169–89.

Nurkse, R. (1954) 'International investment today in the light of nineteenth century experience', *Economic journal*, no. 64, pp. 744–58.

Rostow, W. W. (1952) *The Process of Economic Growth*, New York: Norton.

Taylor, A. M. and Williamson, J. G. (1994) 'Capital flows to the new world as an intergenerational transfer', *Journal of Political Economy*, vol. 102, no. 2, pp. 95–371.

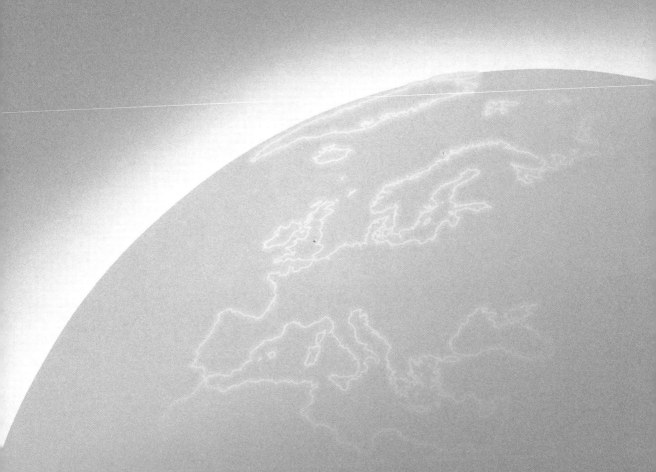

Part 2

International monetary economics

Chapter 8

Balance of payments accounts

Introduction

This chapter is concerned principally with the UK's balance of payments, and that of the euro area, whose accounts are drawn up by the European Central Bank. But most of the principles underlying the accounts will be found to have a more general application.

The standard definition of the balance of payments is that it is a statistical record of all the economic transactions which have taken place during a given time period between the residents of a country and the rest of the world.

The balance of payments provides an overall view of the international position of a country. There are a number of reasons for studying it closely. First, as we will see in Chapter 10, there are significant links between trade balances, capital flows and key macro-economic variables such as the levels of output, employment and prices. Therefore, when governments are formulating and debating economic policy, they need an accurate picture of the external position. Many central banks are now legally independent of their governments. Where this is the case, as in many industrialised countries, the government will 'anchor' its economic policy in an inflation target. The exchange rate, which is linked to trade and capital flows, then becomes an important intermediate target on the road to price stability.

In the second place, there are individuals and groups of individuals (firms, foreign exchange dealers, brokers and banks) who find it necessary to monitor carefully the country's external balance. If the external accounts appear sustainable, then there will be little chance of the currency depreciating. But if there are persistently large trade deficits and outflows of financial capital, there is the possibility of falling values for the domestic currency, and at worst a currency crisis and capital flight. If a country maintains a fixed exchange rate, then the level of reserves in the balance of payments accounts will also be carefully watched. If reserves fall below a critical level, there will be growing expectations of a currency devaluation and behaviour will adjust accordingly.

When you have completed this chapter, you should be able to:

● understand the reasons why a country or group of countries, such as the euro area, need *balance of payments statistics*;

● describe how a balance of payments account is drawn up and explain the main items in the account;

● show how the *current account*, *capital account* and *financial account* are constructed;

● discuss the role of the *international investment position* as indicating a country's status as a net debtor or net creditor in the world economy;

● explain and comment on the *euro area balance of payments* and international investment position.

The UK balance of payments

We begin with some general comments on the structure of the UK balance of payments.

Table 8.1 gives the summary balance of payments figures for the UK, year 2001. It has two main sections, the current account and the financial account.

Although Table 8.1 is based on official data, it is not the full balance of payments table for the UK. The UK official balance of payments statistics are drawn up on accounting principles, in which each item is entered twice, once as a debit and once as a credit. This is normal double-entry book keeping practice and means that, as in any system of accounts, total debits and total credits are always equal. Debit entries are those which involve payments to foreign residents. Credit entries are those which involve payments from foreign residents. If debits exceed credits, the item will have a minus sign. If credits exceed debits, the item will have a plus sign.

Table 8.1 has been adapted from official data. It is a simplified balance of payments table which shows net balances. For example, under 'Trade in goods' the figure is £33 534m. This means that the UK had a net negative balance in terms of traded goods in 2001. Imported goods exceeded exported goods by a value of £33 534m. On trade in services, there was a positive balance. Earnings from services sold abroad exceeded UK spending on services purchased from abroad by £11 073m in 2001.

Also note that the figures in Table 8.1 are reported as being 'not seasonally adjusted'. This means that no allowances have been made for seasonal changes in the various items. For an economy like the UK, this probably does not matter a great deal. Seasonal variations in international transactions in the UK tend to be small relative to the overall magnitude of the balance of payments, and short-lived in their effects. A deficit in one part of the year is likely to be offset by a surplus in another part of the year. For some economies, seasonal variations will be of

Table 8.1 UK balance of payments summary sheet (2001)

Not seasonally adjusted	£ million (net balances)
Current account	
Trade in goods	−33 534
Trade in services	11 073
Total trade	−22 461
Total income	9 162
Total current transfers	−7 154
Current balance	−20 453
Capital balance	1 499
Financial account	
Direct investment	20 065
Portfolio investment	−49 102
Financial derivatives (net)	8 432
Other investment	36 813
Reserve assets	3 083
Net financial transactions	19 291
Net errors and omissions	−337

Source: Adapted from UK government statistics.

much greater significance. An economy heavily dependent on crops like citrus fruits, for example, will have export earnings heavily influenced by the timing of the harvest.

Given time, all statisticians will ensure that seasonal adjustments are carried out on their data. Revisions are generally made on a monthly, quarterly and annual basis.

The balance of payments records credit and debit transactions associated with 'residents' and the concept of residency perhaps needs some explanation. Individuals who are resident in the UK do not necessarily have to be nationals of the UK or citizens of the UK. Residency only refers to a person's place of habitation. More complex is the question of firms. Are they 'resident' in the UK or 'resident' overseas? A company is resident in the country in which it is registered. Its foreign branches and subsidiaries are viewed as foreign residents. Hence transactions between a multinational company registered in the UK and its overseas branches and affiliates are regarded as international trade and are entered in the balance of payments accounts.

We can now turn to the presentation of the various items in the balance of payments. It will be observed that they are grouped under two main headings: the current account and the financial account. There is also a smaller capital account. We will examine each in turn.

The UK current account

Under the current account are trade in goods, trade in services, total income and total current transfers. Trade in goods, services, income and current transfers give rise to the current account balance which is the sum of all credits and debits under those four headings.

Trade in goods

Exports and imports of physical products are often referred to as merchandise trade. Data on exports and imports of goods are collected initially from a variety of UK, EU and world sources. The raw data are revised at a later date, using figures from HM Customs and Excise. In 2001, the value of imports of goods exceeded the value of exports of goods. The recorded deficit was £33 534m.

Table 8.2 provides a breakdown of UK trade in goods in 2000 and 2001. In this case the figures have been seasonally adjusted. As would be expected, the data show the heavy dependence of the UK on both imports and exports of manufactured and semi-manufactured goods.

Table 8.2 UK trade in goods (£ million)

Seasonally adjusted	2000	2001	Seasonally adjusted	2000	2001
Exports			**Imports**		
Food, beverages and tobacco	9 908	9 754	Food, beverages and tobacco	17 805	18 785
Basic materials	2 603	2 622	Basic materials	6 307	6 461
Oil	15 584	14 926	Oil	9 048	9 534
Other fuels	1 473	1 551	Other fuels	968	1 272
Semi-manufactured goods	47 665	51 002	Semi-manufactured goods	49 864	53 558
Finished manu-factured goods	109 018	110 750	Finished manu-factured goods	132 424	134 283
Unspecified goods	1 685	1 039	Unspecified goods	1 846	1 285
Total	187 936	191 644	**Total**	218 262	225 187

Source: Adapted from UK government statistics.

Trade in services

Under this heading come items such as travel, insurance and business services. Data sources include Lloyds of London and the Civil Aviation Authority. In 2001, earnings from services sold abroad exceeded payments for services purchased from abroad. The recorded surplus was £11 073m. Table 8.3 provides a breakdown of trade in services in 2000 and 2001. The figures have been seasonally adjusted. The largest individual items are transportation, travel and financial services.

Table 8.3 Trade in services (£ million)

Seasonally adjusted	2000	2001	Seasonally adjusted	2000	2001
Exports			**Imports**		
Transportation	12 615	12 220	Transportation	15 972	15 808
Travel	14 446	12 632	Travel	25 385	26 382
Communications	1 567	1 276	Communications	1 727	1 741
Construction	116	114	Construction	53	47
Insurance	3 927	3 832	Insurance	695	763
Finance	12 802	12 988	Finance	2 783	3 032
Computing and information	2 539	2 408	Computing and information	806	784
Royalties and licence fees	5 274	5 666	Royalties and licence fees	4 048	4 101
Other business	21 605	23 082	Other business	11 299	10 269
Personal, cultural and recreational	1 134	1 070	Personal, cultural and recreational	703	703
Government	1 174	1 519	Government	1 890	2 104
Total	**77 199**	**76 807**	**Total**	**65 361**	**65 734**

Source: Adapted from UK government statistics.

Total trade

Referring back again to Table 8.1, the trade balance is arrived at by combining the trade in goods and the trade in services. In the UK in 2001, total trade showed a deficit of £22 461m.

Total income

Again referring back to Table 8.1, this is principally interest and dividends on foreign direct investment and portfolio investment. In the UK in 2002, it showed a surplus of £9162m. Table 8.4 provides a breakdown of UK total income in 2000 and 2001. The figures are seasonally adjusted.

Table 8.4 UK total income (£ million)

Seasonally adjusted	2000	2001	Seasonally adjusted	2000	2001
Credits			**Debits**		
Compensation of employees	1 014	1 049	Compensation of employees	871	869
Investment income:			Investment income:		
Earnings on direct investment abroad	44 588	43 844	Earnings on direct investment abroad	27 110	28 075
Earnings on portfolio investment abroad:			Earnings on portfolio investment abroad:		
Earnings on equity securities	9 820	10 401	Earnings on equity securities	9 916	13 640
Earnings on debt securities	23 080	24 496	Earnings on debt securities	20 883	21 046
Total portfolio investment	32 900	34 897	Total portfolio investment	30 799	34 686
Earnings on other investment abroad	55 750	59 129	Earnings on other investment in the UK	67 145	67 088
Earnings on reserve assets	985	961			
Total investment income	134 223	138 831	Total investment income	125 054	129 849
Total	135 237	139 880	**Total**	125 925	130 718

Source: Adapted from UK government statistics.

Total current transfers

The final item on the current account (Table 8.1) is total current transfers. Net contributions to EU are the most important items under this heading. Also included are items such as government transfers to foreign countries (for example, as part of an aid project), personal gifts, payments on insurance claims, taxes and subsidies. In 2001 the UK had a deficit on current transfers amounting to £7154m. These are listed for 2000 and 2001 in Table 8.5.

Table 8.5 UK current transfers (£ million)

Seasonally adjusted	2000	2001	Seasonally adjusted	2000	2001
Credits			**Debits**		
Central government: receipts from EU institutions:			Central government: payments to EU institutions:		
Abatement	2 084	4 560	GNP: 4th resource	4 243	3 859
Other EU receipts	–	1	GNP adjustments	136	−1
Other receipts	379	351	Other	6	24
			Other payments	3 630	3 521
Total central government	2 463	4 912	Total central government	8 015	7 403
Other sectors: receipts from EU institutions:			Other sectors: payments to EU institutions	6 334	5 675
Social fund	659	370			
Agricultural guarantee fund	2 554	2 268			
ECSC grant	–	1			
Other receipts	6 597	8 632	Other payments	7 956	10 259
Total other sectors	9 810	11 271	Total other sectors	14 290	15 934
Total	12 273	16 183	**Total**	22 305	23 337

Source: Adapted from UK government statistics.

The UK capital account

Readers should note that the role of the capital account in the balance of payments changed in the late 1990s. Most of the items which had previously featured in the capital account now go under the separate financial account. This change in accounting practice has also been adopted by other countries.

Referring back to Table 8.1, this shows the 'capital balance' of the UK in 2001, at £1499m. Table 8.6 provides a breakdown of the capital account in 2000 and 2001. The figures are seasonally adjusted.

Since 1999, the capital account refers to a very limited number of transactions which are transfers of wealth between countries, and which can broadly be described as 'non-market' in character. A good example is 'debt forgiveness', when the government of a developed country writes off some or all of the loans it has

Table 8.6 The UK capital account (£ million)

Seasonally adjusted	2000	2001	Seasonally adjusted	2000	2001
Credits			**Debits**		
Migrants' transfers	1 371	1 602	Central government:		
EU institutions:			Debt forgiveness	22	18
Regional Development Fund	989	543	Other capital transfers (project grants)	225	237
Agricultural Guidance Fund	82	26	Total central government	247	255
Other capital transfers	280	535	Other sectors:		
Total EU institutions	1 351	1 104	Migrants' transfers	461	430
			Debt forgiveness		
			Public corporations	231	300
			Total debt forgiveness	231	300
Total other sectors	2 722	2 706	Total other sectors	692	730
Total capital transfers	2 722	2 706	Total capital transfers	939	985
Sales of non-produced, non-financial assets	161	119	Purchases of non-produced, non-financial assets	121	341
Total	2 883	2 825	**Total**	1 060	1 326
			Balance	1 823	1 499

Source: Adapted from UK government statistics.

made in the past to a developing country. Debt forgiveness is counted as a debit on the capital account. Another example relates to the assets owned by migrants. When a UK resident migrates to another country, the assets he or she owns are transformed into the assets of that country. Similarly, when migrants enter the UK, their assets become a credit on the UK capital account.

In the UK case, credits on the capital account are principally the assets of foreign migrants entering the UK, and grants received by the UK from EU institutions such as the EU Regional Development Fund. Debits on the capital account include debt forgiveness and transfers of wealth abroad by UK migrants moving to another country.

The UK financial account

Referring back to Table 8.1, this shows all financial transactions between the UK and the rest of the world, under four headings: direct investment, portfolio investment, financial derivatives and reserve assets.

Direct investment

Direct investment (see Figure 8.1) is a financial flow, in which one firm takes control of another firm (by purchasing a majority of the shares). Alternatively, the firm transfers financial resources to start up a subsidiary or an affiliate abroad. In 2001 the surplus (inflow minus outflow) on direct investment in the UK was £20 065m.

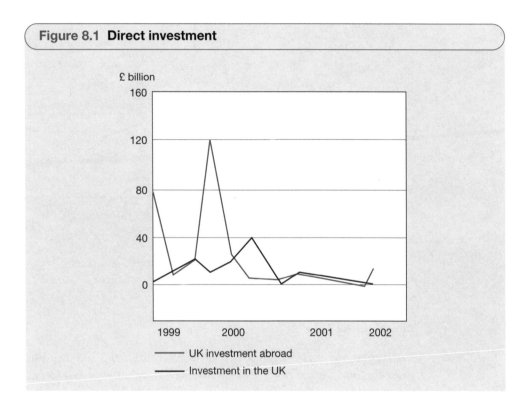

Figure 8.1 Direct investment

Portfolio investment

Portfolio investment (see Figure 8.2) takes place largely through banks and other financial institutions. It involves the purchase of bonds and equities. In 2001 UK portfolio investment showed a deficit (inflow minus outflow) of £49 102m.

Financial derivatives (net) and other investment

Financial derivatives are principally receipts from interest rate swaps. Other investment comprises bank lending and bank deposits in the UK and abroad. In 2001 UK financial derivatives (net) showed a surplus of £36 813m.

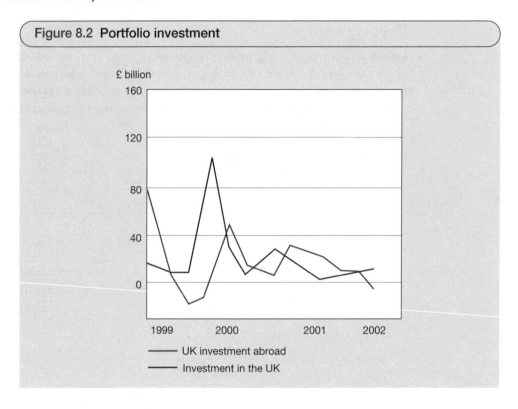

Figure 8.2 Portfolio investment

Reserve assets

Reserve assets include monetary gold, International Monetary Fund (IMF) special drawing rights, other reserves held in the IMF and holdings of foreign exchange (currency, bank deposits, and short-term paper such as equity, bonds and notes which can be easily translated into currency or bank deposits). Reserve assets represent the role played by the monetary authorities in foreign exchange markets. In the UK, these transactions are carried out principally by the Bank of England. In 2001 transactions in reserve assets in the UK gave a positive balance at £3083m.

Errors and omissions

Referring back to Table 8.1, the final item is an entry of −£337m for net errors and omissions. The balance of payments for any country follows the principles of double-entry book keeping. Every item is recorded as a debit and credit. Following accounting principles the sum of all the debits must equal the sum of all the credits. However, in practice, it is unlikely that the sum of all the debits will equal the sum of all the credits. When accountants and statisticians set to work to compile debits and credits for the balance of payments, there are bound to be some discrepancies. Some transactions, even legal ones, will slip through the net. The records kept by banks and customs and excise, on which the balance of payments is based, will have their own errors and discrepancies. The timing of the receipts in different categories will not coincide with the calendar year. To deal with these problems, the accounts have a particular category, errors and omissions, which is the figure necessary to make the sum of debits equal to the sum of credits. The statisticians will be anxious to keep the figure for errors and omissions as low as possible. They hope, through constantly revising the values of the various items recorded in the balance of payments, to improve information and provide a better and truer picture of external transactions.

The UK international investment position

Table 8.1, the UK balance of payments, is based on flows of goods, capital and finance during a particular period, in this case during the year 2001. However, flows give rise to stocks. Table 8.7, the UK international investment position, shows international investment as a stock, at the end of 2001.

The international investment position shows the extent of UK foreign assets and liabilities. It reflects not only the flows which took place in 2001, but also the accumulated credits and debits from previous years. If assets exceed liabilities, the country is a net creditor. If liabilities exceed assets, the country is a net debtor.

Referring to Table 8.7, the international investment position of the UK in 2001 showed net external liabilities of £39.9m. In other words, the UK is a net debtor country (see Figure 8.3). Does this matter? In one sense it does. The UK has to pay interest and dividends on this debt, and this will involve transfers of income abroad. If the inflow of foreign funds has been used productively in the past, then on the positive side enough income will have been generated to allow the UK

Table 8.7 UK net international investment position (2001)

	£ billion
International investment position	
Direct investment	297.7
Portfolio investment	−80.0
Other investment	−283.3
Reserve assets	25.6
Total	−39.9

Source: Adapted from UK government statistics.

comfortably to make these payments. However, this is not always the case. Some countries in the world have become so dependent over time on assets held by foreign firms, governments and individuals that they are effectively 'owned' by them and have very little room to manoeuvre, either in the economic or in the political sense.

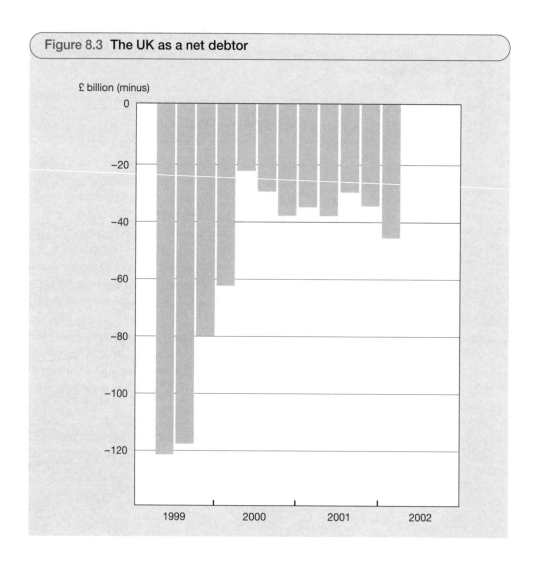

Figure 8.3 The UK as a net debtor

The euro area balance of payments

Table 8.8 shows the balance of payments for the euro area in 2001. It is based on statistics compiled by the European Central Bank. The ECB needs a variety of statistical materials for use in its role in managing the euro area. The balance of payments and international investment position (Table 8.9) are arrived at by aggregating individual country data. The countries are the 12 EU members which had adopted the euro by 2001 (i.e. the 15 EU members minus the UK, Sweden and Denmark).

Table 8.8 Euro area balance of payments summary sheet (2001)

Not seasonally adjusted	€ billions (net balances)
Current account	
Trade in goods	81.8
Trade in services	4.1
Total trade	85.9
Total income	−35.8
Total current transfers	−48.2
Current balance	2.0
Capital balance	8.5
Financial account	
Direct investment	−104.6
Portfolio investment	36.5
Financial derivatives (net)	−20.7
Other investment	1.1
Reserve assets	17.8
Net financial transactions	−69.9
Net errors and omissions	59.5

Table 8.9 Euro area net international investment position (2001)

	€ billion
International investment position	
Direct investment	459.3
Portfolio investment	−721.5
Other investment	−288.2
Reserve assets	391.2
Total	−152.1

The euro area current account

In 2001 the current account of the euro area showed a slight surplus of €2bn. Breaking down the current account shows that income and transfers were in deficit but were offset by a substantial surplus of €85.9bn on trade in goods and services.

A geographical breakdown of the external trade in goods of the euro area (Table 8.10) shows a surplus on trade in goods with all countries except Japan, Asia (excluding Japan) and Africa.

Table 8.10 Geographical breakdown of euro area trade in goods (2001) (€ billion)

	Exports FOB	Imports CIF	Balance
UK	198.2	150.0	48.2
Sweden	36.0	33.1	3.0
Denmark	25.1	20.5	4.6
Candidate countries	133.3	114.2	19.1
Switzerland	65.7	52.0	13.8
United States	177.6	135.2	42.4
Japan	34.2	56.8	−22.5
Asia exc. Japan	161.9	200.1	−38.2
Africa	59.3	72.4	−13.1
Latin America	49.2	39.9	9.2
Other countries	120.6	114.1	6.5
Total	1 016.3	988.3	73.0

Source: Adapted from ECB statistics.

The euro area financial account

The euro area balance of payments (Table 8.8) also shows flows of direct investment, portfolio investment, financial derivatives and other investment and reserves in and out of the euro area during 2001. A breakdown of the financial account for the six months January to July 2001 can be found in Table 8.11.

Table 8.11 shows an outflow of direct investment overall (January–July 2001). There is a net inflow of direct investment within the euro area, and a net outflow of direct investment ouside the euro area. Portfolio investment also shows an overall net outflow.

The European Central Bank, which holds reserves in the euro area, has a unique position in the world economy as a supra-national central bank and financial institution. Reserves on the financial account of the ECB are divided into monetary gold, special drawing rights, reserves held in the IMF, and holdings of foreign exchange. In 2001, transactions in reserve assets gave the ECB a positive balance of €17.8m.

Table 8.11 Financial account balance of the euro area, January–July 2001 (€ billions)

Direct investment	−93.9
Abroad	−161.7
Equity capital and reinvested earnings	−102.0
Other capital, mostly inter-company loans	−59.8
In the euro area	67.9
Equity capital and reinvested earnings	55.9
Other capital, mostly inter-company loans	12.0
Portfolio investment	−9.5
Equities	61.0
Assets	−81.8
Liabilities	142.8
Debt instruments	−70.5
Assets	−91.5
Liabilities	21.0
Combined net direct and portfolio investment	−103.4
Financial derivatives	−8.8
Other investment	98.4
Reserve assets	12.1
Financial account balance	**−1.7**

Source: Adapted from ECB statistics.

The euro area net international investment position

Table 8.12 shows the euro area international investment position in 2001. Like the UK, the euro area is a net debtor. Since the late 1990s, the euro area has had net external liabilities principally associated with accumulated stocks of foreign direct investment in the euro area. The implications of the euro area's international investment position are further discussed in Chapter 12.

Table 8.12 Net international investment position of the euro area (€ billions (ECU billions in 1997))

Year	Total	Direct investment	Portfolio investment	Financial derivatives	Other investment	Reserve assets
1997	32.7	177.6	−724.7	−5.9	222.4	363.3
1998	−147.9	152.2	−713.5	2.3	81.7	329.4
1999	−75.0	402.4	−752.8	10.1	−107.3	372.6
2000	−101.4	466.6	−666.8	7.0	−286.2	378.0
2001	−151.2	459.3	−721.5	7.0	−288.2	391.2

Source: Adapted from ECB statistics.

Summary

● The balance of payments shows the international position of a country. It *records transactions* between *residents of a country and the rest of the world over a given time period.*

● Governments need *information* from the balance of payments for economic management. Firms and individuals need this information when making certain decisions.

● The balance of payments is drawn up on *accounting principles*, with double-entry book keeping. Debits and credits, when both are summed, are equal.

● The balance of payments has *three* main sections: the *current* account, the *financial* account and a smaller *capital* account.

● The main items on the UK current account are trade in goods, trade in services, total income and total current transfers. These give rise to the *current account balance* which is the sum of all credits and debits under those four headings.

● The capital account lists a relatively small number of *transfers of wealth* between countries which could be described as *non-market* in character.

● The financial account shows all *financial transactions* between the UK and the rest of the world. It has four main items: direct investment, portfolio investment, financial derivatives and reserve assets.

● The international investment position (Table 8.7) shows the *stock of UK foreign assets and liabilities* at the end of 2001. It reveals the UK to be a net debtor country.

● The European Central Bank has a unique position in the world economy as a supra-national central bank and financial institution. It produces a balance of payments table for the euro area by aggregating individual country data. Other than that, the euro area balance of payments follows the same principles as the UK balance of payments.

Key concepts

● Double-entry book keeping
● Debit entries
● Credit entries
● Seasonally adjusted
● Concept of residency
● The current account

● The capital account
● The financial account
● Reserve assets
● Errors and omissions
● International investment position

Questions for discussion

1 Define the balance of payments. What policy insights does the trade balance offer?

2 What is the difference between the capital account and the financial account of the balance of payments?

3 Explain the significance of (i) the current account balance, (ii) the capital account balance, and (iii) the financial account balance.

4 A policy-maker asks you to point out in the UK balance of payments where transactions between the UK and the EU are recorded. What answer would you give? Comment on the EU/UK transactions you observe in the tables from the point of view of economic policy.

5 What can you deduce from the international investment position of the UK? Of the euro area? Are there any policy implications for the UK? For the euro area?

6 Explain how direct foreign investment features in both the financial account and the current account (over time) of the balance of payments.

7 Describe the reserve assets of the ECB as they feature in the euro area balance of payments. Why are such data collected? Would the ECB be concerned if the reserves suddenly declined?

8 Computer and information items feature strongly in UK exports of services. Explain what items are likely to be included under this heading. Why are such items of less significance in UK imports than in exports?

Suggested reading

Websites

● Office for National Statistics: **www.statistics.gov.uk**
● European Central Bank: **www.ecb.int**

Chapter 9

Foreign exchange markets

Introduction

Unless international trade is carried out via barter (not a common situation in the modern world), international transactions will involve a monetary transaction and the conversion of one currency into another. The exception, of course, is trade within a monetary union, which takes place via a common currency, but that discussion is deferred until Chapter 12. Foreign exchange markets are markets in which national currencies are bought and sold. Such markets can have a profound effect on international trade and investment.

In principle, the operation of a foreign exchange market is straightforward: a matter of supply and demand. The exchange rate is simply the equilibrium price of one currency in terms of another. In practice, however, foreign exchange markets are far from simple. Charles Kindleberger wrote in the 1970s that:

> the study of international finance is like a trip to another planet. It is a strange land far removed from the economics of an ordinary household. It is populated by strange creatures, hedgers, arbitrageurs, the gnomes of Zurich, the Snake in the Tunnel, the gliding band, and the crawling peg. It is an area in which it is unsafe to rely on ordinary household intuition. (Kindleberger and Lindert, *International Economics*, 1978)

Since Kindleberger, foreign exchange markets have become even more unfathomable. They may also have become more volatile. The international system of payments, and the foreign exchange markets on which the system depends, have been extensively liberalised. International capital flows freely to an extent which would have seemed inconceivable in the 1970s. In addition to FDI, there are today massive portfolio flows. Exchange rates are free to respond to market forces. Although world trade is larger than ever and is now valued at around $4000bn per year, on currency markets, $1000bn is traded *daily*. Currency values move rapidly in response to changing expectations and at times can be extremely volatile.

This chapter describes the system of international payments, and the foreign exchange markets which underpin the system. In order to simplify the analysis, this

155

chapter begins with simple models of the mechanism for international payments, and of exchange rate determination. The simple models are then modified in important respects to reflect the real world of foreign exchange markets. At the outset, however, it is worth noting that there are various layers of complexity in foreign exchange markets, and still many unresolved issues. It is not surprising that many people claim that international finance is difficult to understand, if not downright malign!

Objectives

When you have completed this chapter, you should be able to:

● understand the role of *firms, banks and brokers* in the mechanism of international payments;

● explain *spot* and *forward* rates, *swaps*, *futures* and *options*;

● understand the *appreciation* and *depreciation* of a currency in the context of the demand for, and supply of, one currency relative to another;

● discuss why the *values* of currencies rise and fall;

● define *nominal* and *real* effective exchange rates;

● outline movements in the euro effective exchange rate;

● define *absolute* and *relative* purchasing-power parities;

● demonstrate how *arbitrage* ensures consistency in *cross rates* in different locations;

● describe *international financial flows* and show how they are affected by, and in turn influence, the *foreign exchange market*.

The mechanism of international payments

The first stage in understanding the market for foreign exchange is to appreciate how international payments are made. Put at its simplest, when country A buys goods and services from country B, how are payments made?

Let us suppose that firm X in country A wishes to purchase raw materials from a supplier in country B. Suppose too that firm X has a bank account in country A, denominated in the domestic currency of country A. Firm X does not have to search around for someone to supply the appropriate foreign currency to make payment in the currency of country B because the commercial bank with which firm X does normal business will have a foreign exchange department and will be able to supply the foreign currency when firm X wishes to purchase raw materials.

Having quoted an exchange rate to firm X, the bank owes payment in a currency which it does not possess. This is when the bank has what is known as an *open position*. It can be a risky position, because prices move quickly in foreign exchange markets and, if the price of country B's currency rises relative to

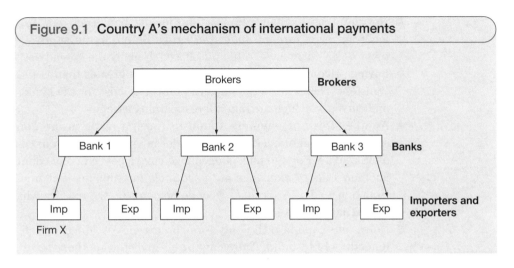

Figure 9.1 Country A's mechanism of international payments

that of country A, then the bank will make a loss. The bank will close its open position as soon as possible by acquiring country B's currency, either from one of its own customers who is an *exporter* selling goods and services to country B, or from another bank, or from a broker specialising in country B's currency (Figure 9.1).

Figure 9.1 shows the three levels of transactions involved in the payment mechanism. At the base of the pyramid are the import and export firms in country A. In the middle are the various commercial banks which deal with those firms. At the top of the pyramid are the specialised foreign currency brokers.

In practice, transactions between banks and their customers, who can be either firms or individuals, comprise the foreign exchange *retail* market. Transactions between banks themselves, and between banks and brokers, comprise the foreign exchange *wholesale* market. There is also the futures/options market, which is discussed later in this chapter. In this system, the principal form of foreign exchange will be the bank deposit, but foreign exchange may also comprise bank notes and coins, and commercial bills of exchange.

The simple model of international payments in Figure 9.1 can be modified in a number of important respects to reflect the more complex real-world situation.

● A *multinational company* might have bank deposits in many countries. When it transfers goods and services across national boundaries, it will use company cheques. There will be no shift in the ownership of bank deposits.
● An exporter who sells goods and services abroad might prefer to *keep their earnings of foreign currency overseas*. For example, most oil transactions are conducted in dollars. Many OPEC countries have traditionally kept the payments they receive in the form of large dollar deposits ('petrodollars') in London and other financial centres. US exporters have also kept their export earnings in the form of 'eurodollars', which are transformed into 'eurobank' loans to individuals and firms in the UK and other countries.

- Not all foreign exchange transactions involve bank transfers. There can be a physical transfer of *foreign notes and coins*. Before a tourist goes abroad, for example, foreign currency is often purchased. Usually the spread between the tourists' buying price and the tourists' selling price is greater than is the spread for bank transfers. This reflects the higher opportunity cost for the banks of holding notes and currency, which are non-interest-earning assets.
- Another form of payment found in foreign trade is the commercial *bill of exchange*. A bill of exchange is an order in writing to pay a fixed sum of money at a future date. Foreign bills of exchange have a payee in one country and a payer in another. Bills of exchange are *negotiable* instruments which can be transferred from one holder to another, via endorsements on the bill. They have a long history in international trade.
- Notes and coins are the only foreign currency holdings which need to be kept immediately to hand. They cannot be invested in *short-term money markets* where other assets can earn a rate of interest at least equal to that earned by domestic funds.

The massive sums which are now traded on a daily basis on foreign exchange markets reflect some important changes which have come about in the world economy. In the early 1970s, the Bretton Woods system of fixed exchange rates collapsed. The system of flexible exchange rates which replaced the Bretton Woods system has been associated with much greater volatility in exchange rates, leading to widespread speculation and hedging in foreign exchange markets. Liberalisation of capital markets has also been significant. Once countries stepped back from placing restrictions on flows of capital abroad, foreign direct investment and portfolio capital flows both accelerated. Finally, in the 1990s came the revolution in information technologies, with foreign exchange dealers able to connect worldwide, making millions of dollars' worth of electronic transfers instantaneously.

Exchange rates, swaps, futures and options

Spot and forward rates

The exchange rate is the price of one currency in terms of another. The market is based on the fact that foreign exchange is bought and sold. Quotations of price are available on a daily basis. For virtually every national currency, there is a *spot rate* for immediate delivery of the currency via a bank transfer. The price of the transfer approximates to the base rate. More risky and more complicated transactions, such as those involving bills of exchange, generally cost more than the base rate, i.e. the foreign currency price has been discounted. Table 9.1 shows the daily spot rate for the pound against major international currencies in Europe, the Americas, the Pacific/Middle East/Africa on 7 November 2002.

For currencies which are widely traded internationally, it is usually possible to get a price quote for forward delivery, either one month, three months or one year

Table 9.1 Pound spot and forward (selected countries), 7 November 2002

	7 Nov Closing	1 Month rate	3 Months rate	1 Year rate
Europe				
Czech Republic (koruna)	48.4	48.4	48.3	47.8
Hungary (forint)	375.3	377	380.8	396.6
Norway (NKr)	11.5	11.5	11.6	11.8
Romania (leu)	53 014.7	–	–	–
Russia (rouble)	50.3	–	–	–
Slovenia (tolar)	359.4	–	–	–
Switzerland (SFr)	2.3	2.3	2.3	2.2
Turkey (lira)	2569777	–	–	–
Euro	1.6	1.6	1.6	1.6
Americas				
Argentina (peso)	5.6	–	–	–
Brazil (R$)	5.7	–	–	–
Canada (C$)	2.5	2.5	2.4	2.4
USA ($)	1.6	1.6	1.6	1.5
Pacific/Middle East/Africa				
Australia (A$)	2.8	2.8	2.8	2.8
Hong Kong (HK$)	12.3	12.3	12.3	12.1
India (Rs)	76.3	76.4	76.6	77.5
Israel (Shk)	7.5	–	–	–
Japan (Y)	191.6	191	189.7	184.3
Saudi Arabia (SR)	5.9	5.9	5.9	5.8
UAE (dirham)	5.8	5.8	5.8	5.7

ahead. Forward rates can also be seen in Table 9.1. A forward rate is a promise to buy or sell foreign exchange at a specified date in the future, at a price already agreed. The aim is to allow the buyer (seller) of currencies to reduce the risk of future fluctuations in price because currency fluctuations can easily change an otherwise profitable foreign trade deal into a loss-making undertaking.

Swaps, futures and options

A foreign exchange swap is a spot sale of a currency combined with a forward purchase of a currency. Brokers and banks dealing in foreign exchange will try to balance out sales and purchases of a currency in order to reduce the risk associated with currency fluctuations. Sometimes this balancing out is best achieved over time. Hence an open position in spot selling is balanced by an open position in forward purchasing. Swaps are a significant part of present-day dealing in foreign exchange.

Forward contracts enable buyers and sellers of currency to reduce their exposure to risk, but they are inflexible. They cannot be bought and sold. Futures contracts (Table 9.2) are saleable up until the time of maturity. They perform the same function as a forward contract in reducing risk but, because they can be bought and sold, they introduce a valuable element of competition into the forward market.

It is also argued that, because a futures contract is a saleable product, it tends to be standardised and suitable for the small customer, whereas forward contracts are usually specially negotiated to meet the needs of specific buyers and sellers.

Options are contracts which give the holder the right to buy or sell a foreign currency at a specified exchange rate at some date in the future. The holder of the option is not obliged to exercise this right and that is the main difference between forward and futures contracts, and options. A 'European' option can only be exercised on the expiry date shown on the contract, whereas an 'American' option can be exercised up to the expiry date. 'Call' options give the right to acquire foreign exchange for the domestic currency. 'Put' options give the right to obtain the domestic currency for foreign exchange (Table 9.3).

Like futures contracts, options are tradable. They are arranged through the Chicago Mercantile Exchange (CME) which guarantees the contract. Futures contracts are particularly useful for dealing with risk on foreign exchange transactions which the individual or the firm may in the end decide not to enter into. If planned transactions are uncertain, and if in the end they do not materialise, then the foreign exchange option need not be exercised.

Table 9.2 Currency futures, 7 November 2002

Currencies	Date of maturity	Volume
Euro–sterling	December	140
Euro–$	December	238
Euro–yen	December	680
$–Can$	December	7 259
$–euro	December	20 633
$–euro	March	92
$–Sw franc	December	13 909
$–Sw franc	March	36
$–yen	December	15 023
$–yen	March	217
$–sterling	December	7 622
$–sterling	March	12

Table 9.3 Currency options 7 November 2002

Part 1 – US $/euro options (CME)

Strike price	Calls			Puts		
7 Nov	Nov	Dec	Jan	Nov	Dec	Jan
9 900	1.15	1.58	1.83	0.03	0.67	0.00
10 000	0.38	1.10	1.33	0.35	1.02	1.63
10 100	0.07	0.72	0.94	1.02	1.61	–
10 200	0.02	0.44	0.65	1.95	2.34	–

Calls: 3189; puts: 735; volume: 3924; previous day's open interest: 71 715.

Part 2 – US $/yen options (CME)

Strike price	Calls			Puts		
7 Nov	Nov	Dec	Jan	Nov	Dec	Jan
8 100	1.28	1.64	2.08	0.03	0.35	0.58
8 200	0.42	1.00	1.45	0.11	0.66	0.94
8 300	0.04	0.58	0.99	0.83	1.32	–
8 400	0.02	0.33	0.65	1.77	2.08	–

Calls: 585; puts: 669; volume: 1254; previous day's open interest: 103 514.

Part 3 – US $/UK £ options (CME)

Strike price	Calls			Puts		
7 Nov	Nov	Dec	Jan	Nov	Dec	Jan
9 900	1.00	1.10	–	0.16	0.80	–
10 000	0.26	1.20	1.00	1.10	1.66	–
10 100	0.04	0.80	0.90	–	–	–
10 200	0.02	0.26	–	–	–	–

Calls: 144; puts: 39; volume: 183; previous day's open interest: 9979.

Notes: Strike price = contracting price for contracts expiring in the quoted month.
Open interest = number of contracts open as of previous day.
Volume = calls + puts.
Strike prices quoted in % intervals.

Forward contracts, swaps, futures and options are all ways of reducing the individual's or the firm's exposure to foreign exchange risk. But there are other risks involved in international transactions, especially on the capital account, which relate to the value of assets. Here, it is not just foreign exchange fluctuations which pose a risk, but also interest rate changes which will affect the value of an asset.

Derivatives are financial contracts with values linked to an underlying asset: bonds, stocks, commodities, loans, certificates of deposits and foreign exchange.

Repos (sale and repurchase agreements) are securities which are sold with a simultaneous agreement to repurchase them at a specified price at some future date. The US repo market is now very large. The repo market is also growing fast in the euro area at the expense of foreign exchange swaps and other money market instruments (see Figure 9.2).

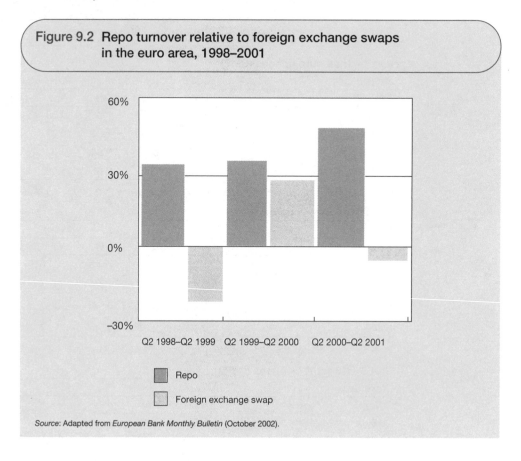

Figure 9.2 Repo turnover relative to foreign exchange swaps in the euro area, 1998–2001

Source: Adapted from *European Bank Monthly Bulletin* (October 2002).

The determination of the equilibrium exchange rate

The easiest way to approach the exchange rate is to think of it as a price determined by supply and demand for foreign currency. As with the mechanism of international payments, the simple model can then be modified in a number of important respects to reflect the more complex real-world situation.

Suppose that we are considering the demand in the UK for the US$. In Figure 9.3 *DD'* represents the UK demand for the US$. *SS'* represents the supply of the US$.

The equilibrium exchange rate between the pound sterling (£) and the US dollar ($) is given by the intersection of the demand and supply curves. The equilibrium exchange rate is *e*, and the equilibrium quantity of dollars supplied and demanded is *q*.

Why should firms or individuals in the UK wish to buy dollars?

● They may wish to *purchase goods and services* from the US.
● They may wish to *open a US bank account*.

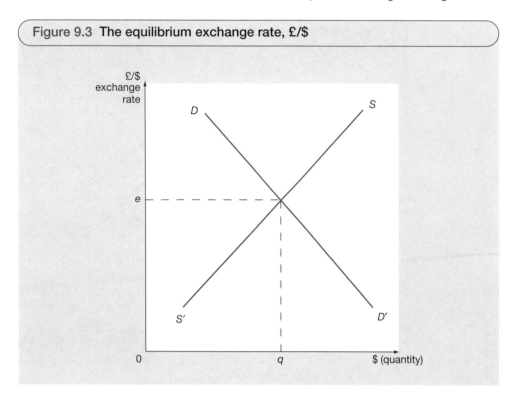

Figure 9.3 The equilibrium exchange rate, £/$

- They may be engaging in *speculation*, buying dollars in the expectation of making a windfall profit when the value of the dollar rises.
- They may be *hedging*: that is, acquiring the dollar today to avoid the risk of having to pay more for it at a future date when dollar payments need to made.

Appreciation and depreciation

If the dollar becomes more valuable, it is said to appreciate. More pounds will be required to purchase each dollar. If the dollar becomes less valuable, it is said to depreciate. Fewer pounds are required to purchase each dollar. In our simple model, appreciation of the dollar means depreciation of the pound and depreciation of the dollar means appreciation of the pound.

Consider Figure 9.4. Suppose there is an increase in demand for the dollar. The DD' curve shifts out to $D''D'''$ and the quantity of dollars demanded and supplied increases to q'. The exchange rate rises to e'. It requires more UK pounds to buy each dollar. The dollar has appreciated against the pound – or, what is the same thing, the pound has depreciated against the dollar. This could be because the UK is purchasing more goods and services from the US, or buying more US assets. Or there may be speculation or hedging in the expectation of a rise in value of the dollar.

A reduction in the demand for the dollar could be analysed in the same way. The demand curve shifts to D^*D^{**} and the quantity of dollars demanded and supplied falls to q^*. Now, the demand for the dollar has fallen, possibly because US goods, services and

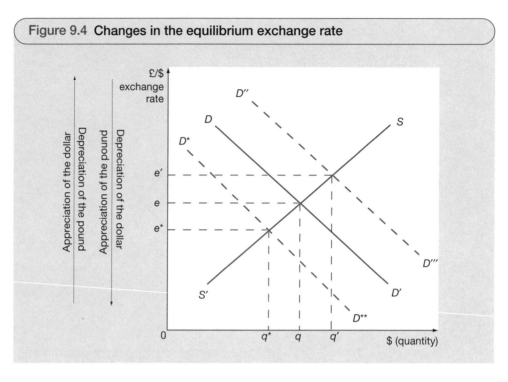

Figure 9.4 Changes in the equilibrium exchange rate

assets have become less desirable and/or because there is speculation and hedging in the expectation of a fall in the value of the dollar. On Figure 9.3 the fall in the £/$ exchange rate to e^* is equivalent to a depreciation of the dollar/appreciation of the pound.

The many and diverse factors which can prompt a slide in the value of one currency relative to another are illustrated in Case Study 9.1.

CASE STUDY 9.1

Dollar falls   **FT**

The dollar continued to slide yesterday as traders sought out higher yielding currencies

The greenback has been on the defensive since Wednesday when the US Federal Reserve cut the fed funds rate by 50 basis points to 1.25 per cent.

The biggest gainer was the pound, which now offers a 275 basis point premium over US rates. Sterling rose to a two-and-a-half year high of $1.593.

The euro also pushed higher to $1.015, despite a disappointing 1.2 per cent fall in German industrial production in September.

Ray Attrill, director of research at the economic consultancy 4Cast, said the unanimous approval by the UN Security Council of a resolution on Iraq had also been negative for the dollar.

'There is a concern that this takes us one step closer to a war that will most likely be negative for the dollar,' said Mr Attrill.

When the dollar stabilised after a steep fall in the second quarter, there was a sense of anticlimax in the foreign exchange market.

The long awaited collapse of the dollar had fizzled out after a mere 15 per cent fall against the euro.

Now traders are bracing for a second leg in the dollar's fall.

Recent economic data has suggested that the US has come to a virtual standstill. This is making it ever harder for the US to attract the inflows necessary to fund its current account deficit. With the deficit set to reach $480bn this year, the US needs to attract around $1.9bn every working day just to prevent the dollar from falling.

Analysts said that there were now signs that capital inflows into the US are slowing.

'The dollar has not been falling because people are selling it,' said Paul Meggesyi, currency strategist at JP Morgan. 'It is simply that commercial flows are asserting themselves as capital inflows slow.'

It is unlikely that hot money flows are going to save the dollar either. With rates at 1.25 per cent, there is unlikely to be much interest in the short end of the US yield curve.

'It is almost unthinkable to sustain a current account of 5 per cent of GDP, with

short term interest rates of 1.25 per cent and real interest rates of −1 per cent,' said Mr Meggesyi. 'Real interest rates in the eurozone and Japan are closer to a positive 0.7 per cent.'

Yesterday high yielding currencies continued to forge higher, with the Australian and New Zealand dollars amount the gainers.

The fact that there had been no aggressive euro buying by fund managers makes a more sustainable rally in the European currency more likely.

Source: Christopher Swann, *Financial Times*, 10 November 2002. Reprinted with permission.

Comment on case study 9.1

Why do the values of currencies rise and fall? Case Study 9.1 illustrates the diversity of factors behind the fall in the value of a currency, in this case of the dollar. First, a cut of 1.25 per cent in the US Fed funds rate could be expected to halt the decline in the fall of the value of the dollar if it were taken to be indicative of the government's commitment to supporting US economic recovery. However, if a cut in the rate is taken to indicate the likelihood of even greater problems ahead, as apparently happened in this case, then action on the part of the Fed may cause the dollar to tumble further. The gainers in this case study were sterling and the euro, both of which appreciated. The euro appreciated in spite of the fact that German industrial production had recently fallen. Other gainers were Australian and New Zealand dollars.

One observer, a director of an economic forecasting consultancy, said that the likelihood of war with Iraq lay behind the fall in the value of the US dollar. Also significant was the recession in the US which was making it difficult for the US to attract capital inflows. The US current account deficit in 2002 is around $480bn. The US needs to attract $1.9bn of financial capital each day just to prevent the value of the dollar from falling. But interest rates are so low that even speculative flows are discouraged. The real interest rate in the US in November 2002 is negative. In the eurozone and Japan, it is positive. If fund managers actively start to buy the euro, and the value of the euro rises, then the dollar could slide even further.

Nominal and real effective exchange rates

The exchange rates we have been discussing so far in this chapter are bilateral rates. Table 9.1, for example, lists bilateral rates for the pound sterling, spot and forward, against currencies in Europe, the Americas, and the Pacific/Middle East/Africa. Bilateral rates indicate the value of currencies between two countries. But countries have many trading partners, and it is often helpful to construct an index which shows different currency values, weighted by their importance in a given country's international trade.

Table 9.4 Effective exchange rate of the euro

Year	Nominal effective exchange rate of the euro	Real effective exchange rate of the euro	Bilateral euro exchange rate: US dollar	Bilateral euro exchange rate: Japanese yen
1997	99.1	99.4	1.134	137.1
1998	101.5	101.3	1.121	146.4
1999	95.7	95.7	1.066	121.3
2000	85.7	86.5	0.924	99.5
2001	87.3	88.9	0.896	108.7

Source: Adapted from European Central Bank statistics.

The *nominal effective exchange rate* is an index number of the weighted average of bilateral exchange rates using trade shares as the weights.

The *real effective exchange rate* adjusts the nominal effective rate for price inflation and is designed to measure a country's price or cost competitiveness. The formula for the real effective exchange rate is:

$$RER = NR \times P_{\text{dom}} / P_{\text{row}}$$

Figure 9.5 Effective exchange rates of the euro, the dollar and the yen

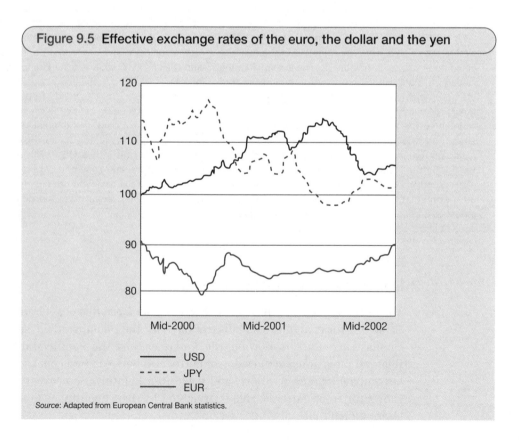

Source: Adapted from European Central Bank statistics.

where *RER* is the real effective exchange rate, *NR* is the nominal effective exchange rate, P_{dom} is the domestic price level *or* domestic unit labour costs, and P_{row} is the price level of the 'rest of the world': actually the price level of major trading partners.

The euro effective exchange rate

The eurozone has twelve major trading partners with their currencies listed below.

US (dollar)	Japan (yen)
Switzerland (franc)	UK (sterling)
Sweden (krona)	Denmark (krone)
Norway (krone)	Canada (dollar)
Australia (dollar)	Hong Kong (dollar)
Korea (won)	Singapore (dollar)

The effective exchange rate (nominal and real) is the weighted average of the bilateral rates, weighted by trade shares. Of particular significance are two of the major euro trading partners, the US and Japan. They dominate movements in the euro's nominal and real effective exchange rates (Table 9.4 and Figure 9.5).

Purchasing-power parities

The equilibrium exchange rate is the one which satisfies the demand for, and the supply of, a particular currency. If markets for goods, services, factors and currencies are all working perfectly, both nationally and internationally, the equilibrium exchange rate will also bring 'balance' to the current account and the capital account of the balance of payments. A discussion of the relationship between balance of payments and exchange rates is deferred to the next chapter. However, it is helpful to note at this point that the equilibrium exchange rate which 'clears' the balance of payments can be discovered by looking at purchasing-power parities (PPP).

Absolute version of PPP

Suppose that a Big Mac costs 2 euros in France and 2 dollars in the US. This implies that the exchange rate should be parity between the dollar and euro – a 1:1 exchange rate. If the actual exchange rate is 1 euro = 1.5 dollars, this suggests that the dollar is undervalued and its price should increase to only 1 dollar = 1 euro.

The implication of purchasing-power parity is that, by looking at domestic prices for the same commodity in different countries, it is possible to estimate by how much a currency is overvalued or undervalued in quoted exchange rates, and, therefore, whether the value of the currency is likely to go up or down.

The Swedish economist Gustav Cassel drew attention to the properties of PPP when he was writing in the inter-war period. Cassel was keen to find out the appropriate exchange rates for various European countries following the dislocation of international trade and payments after World War I. He believed that a study of domestic price levels would indicate the appropriate par values for European currencies: 'the exchange rate or external value of a currency is determined by the domestic value, or the purchasing power parity, of the foreign currencies concerned' (Gustav Cassel).

Relative purchasing-power parity

A weaker version of absolute purchasing-power parity refers to *changes* in price levels and exchange rates. It says that exchange rates adjust from a general level to reflect inflation differentials between two economies:

$$\%\Delta R = \%\Delta Pd - \%\Delta Pf$$

where

ΔR is the change in the exchange rate;
ΔPd is the change in the domestic price level, or the domestic inflation rate;
ΔPf is the change in the foreign price level, or the foreign inflation rate.

For example, if the price level in the eurozone rises by 5 per cent and the price level in the US rises by 10 per cent, the relative PPP predicts a 5 per cent depreciation of the dollar against the euro.

Empirical evidence

PPP, in both the 'strong' absolute version and the 'weak' relative version, has been extensively tested over time. At best, the results can be described as mixed. Some of the more significant empirical findings are listed below.

● As an historical example, Britain went back to the gold standard in 1925, returning to the old, pre-war value of the pound. PPP would suggest that this was a mistake since inflation had been much greater in the UK than the US since 1914. The pound, therefore, should have been devalued. In reality, it *was* a mistake to return to pre-war parities and it pitched the UK into a decade of unemployment and depression between the two world wars.
● Calculations of PPP by Balassa in 1964 suggested that developing countries' currencies were undervalued relative to those of developed countries. However, Balassa realised that all other evidence pointed to the contrary, i.e. that developing countries' currencies were overvalued, and should have been devalued. Balassa resolved the paradox by pointing out that purchasing-power parity calculations tend to suggest, misleadingly, that the currency of low-income countries is undervalued. This is because the international exchange rate is based only on traded goods. Traded goods tend to cost the same in both rich and poor countries, but non-traded goods (haircuts, for example) will cost less in the low-income country than the high-income country. This is not reflected in PPP and the exchange rate. Balassa's argument was supported by his own empirical work which showed that as a country's per capita income fell more and more below that of per capita

Table 9.5 Price of a litre of olive oil, 2002	
Place	*Price* (€)
Brussels	4.67
Frankfurt	8.23
Madrid	3.74
Milan	5.54
Paris	5.14

income in the US, its currency based on PPP estimations appeared to be increasingly overvalued.

● PPP performs well in predicting changes in exchange rates in the long run, in periods of high inflation. For example, during the first half of the 1970s, Brazil experienced 150 per cent domestic inflation. The changes in the rate of exchange between the cruzeiro and the US dollar during this period exactly reflected differences in the domestic inflation rates between Brazil and the US.

The PPP approach is generally agreed to be more useful in predicting long-term trends in exchange rates, especially in periods of inflation. It is less useful in predicting short-term and medium-term changes in exchange rates. In the short and medium term, exchange rates deviate from PPP because of speculation and changes in expectations, and interest rate changes. PPP concentrates on goods and services but the prices of assets are also important. This means that interest rates are also influences on exchange rates.

Finally, it should be noted that even *within a currency zone* (monetary union) there will be important real factors bringing differences in relative prices for the same commodity. Tamin Bayoumi and Ronald MacDonald (1999) have shown significant differences in the long-run trends in relative prices within the United States and within Canada. Both the US and Canada are, in effect, monetary unions.

Table 9.5 also shows differences in relative prices at one point in time within another monetary union: the eurozone. The price of olive oil in Frankfurt in 2002 is more than double the price in Madrid, indicating that important structural factors are at work in determining relative prices – the sort of factors which are ignored in PPP approaches.

Arbitrage

Economists usually make the assumption that the prices for the same currency in different places in the world will be the same: that dealers and brokers in New York, London, Tokyo, Frankfurt and Paris will quote the same price.

The reason why prices are equalised in this way is the process known as *arbitrage*. Arbitrage is the simultaneous purchase and sale of a currency to take advantage of differences in price in two locations. For example, if the euro/dollar

Table 9.6 Exchange cross rates, 6 November 2002

		C$	DKr	€	Y	NKr	SKr	SFr	£	$
Canada	C$	1.00	4.79	0.64	78.46	4.75	5.87	0.94	0.41	0.64
Denmark	DKr	2.09	10	1.35	164.0	9.92	12.27	1.97	0.86	1.34
EU	€	1.55	7.43	1.0	121.8	7.37	9.12	1.46	0.64	1.00
Japan	Y	1.28	6.10	0.82	100	6.05	7.48	1.20	0.53	0.82
Norway	NKr	2.12	10.08	1.36	165.3	10.00	12.37	1.99	0.87	1.35
Sweden	SKr	1.70	8.15	1.10	133.6	8.08	10.00	1.61	0.70	1.09
Switzerland	SFr	1.06	5.08	0.68	83.28	5.04	6.23	1.00	0.44	0.68
UK	£	2.43	11.62	1.56	190.5	11.52	14.25	2.29	1.00	1.56
USA	$	1.58	7.45	1.00	122.1	7.39	9.14	1.47	0.64	1.00

Note: Danish kroner, Norwegian kroner, Swedish kronor per 10, Yen per 100.

exchange rate is more favourable in Paris than in London, a dealer can purchase in Paris and sell in London, making an immediate profit. All it needs is an electronic transmission of data. By buying low and selling high, the price of a currency in different locations will be equalised. Any profits will be transitory.

If we introduce a third currency in addition to the euro and the dollar, there is a possibility of triangular arbitrage. If the exchange rate between the euro and the dollar is known, and the exchange rate between the euro and the pound sterling is also known, then the exchange rate between the dollar and the pound can be calculated. It is implicit in the other two rates.

The 'third' implicit exchange rate is often referred to as the cross rate. Table 9.6 shows the cross rates for nine major currencies and nine locations. Arbitrage will ensure consistency of cross rates in different locations. Table 9.6 demonstrates that cross rates are consistent.

For example, the price of £ sterling quoted in New York (USA) which is 0.641, is the same as 1 divided by the price of the dollar quoted in London (UK) which is 1/1.599 = 0.641. Arbitrage has brought consistent cross rates.

Arbitrage can be applied to many commodities in the world economy: those which are homogenous such as sugar, wheat or cocoa. Prices will be equalised in markets in different parts of the world, though costs of transport will need to be taken into account. Transport costs do not apply to currencies.

International financial flows

There is an important link between what is happening in financial markets and what is happening in foreign exchange markets. This link needs to be clarified. Economists do not always agree on *how* the transfer of financial assets between countries feeds into foreign exchange markets, so the analysis presented in this section may well oversimplify what will turn out to be important theoretical disagreements.

Essentially, this section draws attention to the fact that, since the mid-1990s, international financial flows have increased hugely in importance in the world economy. We are not too concerned with foreign direct investment (FDI) which can be thought of as a traditional long-run capital movement which responds to real factors such as technology and innovation. Rather the problems relate to the bewildering array of short-term and medium-term internationally traded assets which are increasingly dominating financial flows.

The issues can be illustrated by looking at the net financial flows which have taken place between two of the world's key financial markets in the period 1995–2002. Figure 9.6 shows the financial flows between the euro area and the US between 1995 and 2002. Net financial flows to the US from Europe reached a peak in 2000 when purchases of US equities by euro area residents reached 108bn euros.

Figure 9.6 shows the breakdown of net financial flows between FDI, bonds, notes and equities. FDI refers to the flow of funds to purchase a stake in a foreign company, thereby giving the purchaser control over the management of a company or its physical assets. Although the volume of FDI has increased in recent years, arguably its characteristics have not changed in any dramatic way. It responds to real rates of growth, innovation and so on. It is best analysed within the context of the profit-maximising firm. Equities, bonds and notes are paper assets which do not give managerial control

Figure 9.6 Financial flows between the US and the euro area, 1995–2002

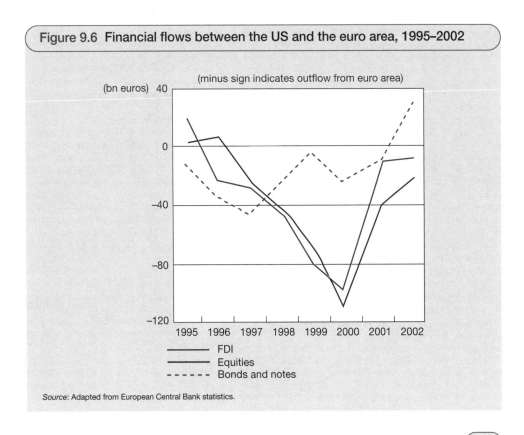

Source: Adapted from European Central Bank statistics.

Table 9.7 New international bond issues

Part 1 – US dollars

Borrower	Amount m	Coupon %	Price	Maturity	Fees %	Spread	Book-runner
Korea Development Bank	300	4.25#	99.835	Nov 2007	Undisc.	+135 (7 Nov)	Barclays Capital
Korea Development Bank	425	5.50#	99.552	Nov 2012	Undisc.	+148 (12 Aug)	CSFB JP Morgan
Dow Chemical (a)	500	5.75#	99.425	Nov 2009	Undisc.	+225 (9 Aug)	Saloman Smith Barney
Lloyds TSB Bank plc (b,S)	150	6.90	100.60	Undated	Undisc.	–	Goldman Sachs
Inter-American Development Bank	137	0.50#	70.07	Nov 2012	Undisc.	–	UFJ International

Part 2 – Euros

Borrower	Amount m	Coupon %	Price	Maturity	Fees %	Spread	Book-runner
North Rhine Westphalia	1bn	–	(c)R	Feb 2008	0.10R	+1 3(swaps)	DKW/SSSB/ WestLB
Bancaja4 FTH, Class A(d)‡	970.5	–	100.00 R	Jun 2034	0.05R	–	Bancaja/ Dresdner KW
Provide-VR 2002–1 plc(g)‡	102.9	–	–	Feb 2045	none	–	DZ Bank
Banque PSA Finance	500	4.625	99.405 R	Feb 2008	0.25R	+53 (swaps)	ABN Amro/BNPP/ HSBC
Irish Nationwide B/S‡	250		99.938 R	Feb2006	0.25R	–	BNPP/SG Inv Banking

Part 3 – Swiss francs

Borrower	Amount m	Coupon %	Price	Maturity	Fees %	Spread	Book-runner
Oest Kontrollbank (j)	250	2.00	99.49	Nov 2007	0.20	−11 (swaps)	UBS Warburg
Generalitat Valenciana	250	2.00	99.21	Dec 2007	0.20	+24 (4.5Jan07)	BNP Paribas

Part 4 – Norwegian kroner

Borrower	Amount m	Coupon %	Price	Maturity	Fees %	Spread	Book-runner
New Zealand	500	6.25	100.44 R	Jan 2008	0.25R	+4(6.75 Jan07)	Deutsche Bank

Source: Financial Times, 7 November 2002.

over a firm. *Equities* have become very widely traded in the world economy, though it is often difficult to obtain information on specific cross-border sales. The emergence of stock markets in many developing and transition economies is indicative of the scale of equity movements. *Bonds and notes* have also become very widely traded across national boundaries in recent years, and they may require a little more explanation.

Bonds and notes

Length of maturity distinguishes bonds from notes. Bonds have a maturity of less than ten years. For our purposes, bonds and notes can be considered simply as bonds. Bonds are issued both by governments and corporations. They have a face value which indicates the amount which will be paid back at maturity, and interest payments (coupon payments) which are paid each year. The borrower who issues the bond denominates them in the currency of the host country, i.e. the market of another country. The sale is conducted by an underwriter (book-runner) which is either a bank or a financial institution, which is conducting the sale for a fee.

Table 9.7 is taken from the *Financial Times*, showing new international bond issues in November 2002. The borrowers are banks, such as the Korea Development Bank, and firms such as Dow Chemicals. The underwriters are banks and financial intermediaries such as Goldman Sachs. The bonds are denominated in international currencies such as US dollars, euros and Swiss francs.

In addition to FDI, equity, and bonds and notes, there are significant cross-border flows of short-term money market assets in the modern world economy. These are assets with maturity of less than one year and include various forms of commercial paper, certificates of deposit, government securities and short-term corporate debt. The distinguishing feature of this category of financial flows is that they are highly liquid, i.e. they can easily be turned into cash.

Financial markets and the foreign exchange market

When an investor decides to take up an asset which is denominated in a foreign currency, there is a risk associated with the possibility that the foreign currency may depreciate. The decision to invest abroad depends on a comparison of the respective rates of return on domestic and foreign assets. These rates of return depend not only on the rates of interest on the respective assets, but also on any gains and losses associated with the appreciation or depreciation of the foreign currency relative to the domestic currency.

Suppose that a resident of the UK decides to purchase a US asset, denominated in dollars, which returns 10 per cent. If the dollar appreciates in the period between purchasing the asset and its maturity, the rate of return will be greater than 10 per cent. There will be gains from an appreciation of a dollar-denominated asset when the time comes to switch back the funds into sterling. Equally well there could be a loss, if the dollar depreciates in value. This could reduce or even wipe out any rate of interest on the asset. The implication is that when deciding whether to invest in the domestic economy, or whether to purchase foreign assets, the investor must take into account:

● the domestic interest rate, or expected rate of return on domestic assets;
● the foreign interest rate or expected rate of return on foreign assets;
● any anticipated changes in the exchange rate.

The link between the foreign exchange market and financial flows is through the rates of return on domestic versus foreign assets which depend not only on the rates of interest in domestic and foreign financial markets, but also on gains and losses associated with any appreciation or depreciation of the currency in foreign exchange markets.

Earlier we considered the position of importers (and exporters) facing a foreign exchange risk. The importer in an 'open position' is taking a foreign exchange risk, because spot exchange rates vary day by day. A depreciation of the domestic currency could leave the importer out of pocket on a deal. If an importer wishes to 'cover' the open position, it is necessary to engage in hedging. Hedging usually involves buying forward. The importer buys forward to meet the foreign exchange cost at the expected date of delivery of the imported goods. Hedging is a way of avoiding gambling on the future value of a currency.

Whatever applies to the importer or exporter of goods and services also applies to the investor. Here, the distinction between short- and medium-term financial flows and FDI is probably critical. With FDI, the decision to invest abroad is heavily influenced by the commercial instincts of multinationals. 'Real' factors such as scale economies, cost-reducing innovations, productivity gains and so on are likely to be key determinants of the scale and direction of FDI. Short- and medium-term investors will be more concerned about the foreign exchange risk associated with their investments. To avoid the foreign exchange risk they will engage in covered interest arbitrage.

⬭ Covered interest arbitrage

The investor purchases foreign currency at the spot rate to make the foreign investment. Simultaneously, the investor sells (swaps) the foreign currency forward to cover the foreign exchange risk. When the investment matures, the investor will have the equivalent amount of the domestic currency to offset the foreign exchange risk.

Short-term investment, such as the purchase of a ninety-day Treasury bill denominated in a foreign currency, is particularly susceptible to depreciation of the currency expressed as an annual percentage. For example, if we return to the US asset which returns 10 per cent per annum, if the dollar depreciates 10 per cent during the ninety-day investment period, this represents a loss of 40 per cent on the capital invested, calculated on an annual basis, which needs to be set against the 10 per cent return.

⬭ Speculation

So far in this chapter, the emphasis has been on the activities of those who wish to avoid a foreign exchange risk, or cover an open position. But while the hedger will try to cover a foreign exchange risk, the speculator seeks out risk, and maintains an open position in the hope of making a profit.

Speculators operate in both the spot and forward markets. The speculator who operates in the spot market purchases the currency today and holds on to it for resale at a future date. If the currency appreciates, the speculator makes a profit. If it depreciates, the speculator makes a loss.

Speculation in the forward market is an activity which gives even higher returns than speculation in the spot market, but at the risk of even greater losses. This is because speculating in the forward market is usually done on a 10 per cent basis, i.e. the speculator only puts down 10 per cent of the money when the forward contract is made. If the speculator is right and the price of the currency goes up, when the forward delivery is made it can be immediately resold at the higher spot rate and the profit taken. There has been no need to use large amounts of one's own funds, or to borrow, in order to meet the initial 10 per cent deposit. But if the speculator is wrong and losses are incurred, then the low margin has encouraged the speculator to gamble and the extent of losses will probably be much greater than in the spot market.

CASE STUDY 9.2

A difficult week for the US

Foreign investors have bought $650bn in US equities over the past 25 years, according to estimates from State Street, the US bank. Since most of the equity purchases took place in the late 1990s, foreign investors are currently sitting on a 20 per cent loss. State Street therefore expects that foreigners will have a reduced appetite for buying more US assets, especially with the dollar still 15–20 per cent above its long-term valuation.

On top of this, foreigners are about to lose out on the dollar. State Street's Foreign Exchange Flow Indicator shows aggressive selling of the dollar – in other words, hedging of their currency risk. There is certainly the risk of a vicious circle developing, as negative returns lead to further dollar selling.

Source: Financial Times, 16 October 2002. Reprinted with permission.

Comment on case study 9.2

Since 1977, $650bn of US equities have been purchased by foreign investors. The graph shows the take-off in the late 1990s. Since equity markets have performed badly since mid-2001, this means that the majority of investors have already suffered a 20 per cent loss on their investments.

The case study also points out that in addition to the 20 per cent loss, investors will lose out from a depreciation of the dollar. The anticipated return on an asset denominated in a foreign currency has two parts – the rate of return (interest rate) in the host country, and the appreciation or depreciation of the host country's currency. Estimates put the dollar at 15–20 per cent overvalued. If the dollar depreciates, the value of equities will fall. There is some indication that investors are already selling dollars to hedge against future currency losses. Selling dollars will cause a further deterioration in the value of the dollar. A vicious circle may develop. As the value of the dollar falls further, hedging against losses on equities will reinforce the downward trend.

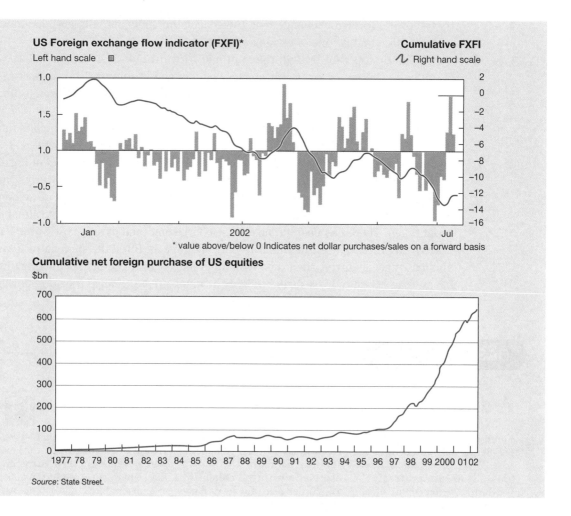

US Foreign exchange flow indicator (FXFI)*

Left hand scale ☐

Cumulative FXFI

∿ Right hand scale

* value above/below 0 Indicates net dollar purchases/sales on a forward basis

Cumulative net foreign purchase of US equities
$bn

Source: State Street.

Summary

- Foreign exchange markets are not easy to understand. Since the 1970s they have become more *complex* and probably more *volatile*. Yet they are important, *affecting* both international *trade* and *investment*, and in turn *being affected by* the flows of goods, services and capital across national boundaries.

- *International payments* can be understood via a *pyramid* of institutions, with firms and individuals at the base, banks in the middle, and specialised brokers at the apex.

- Exchange of one currency for another can involve many different types of transaction. These include spot and forward rates of exchange, swaps, forward contracts and futures contracts, options, derivatives and repos.

- The exchange rate can be thought of as a *price determined by the supply of, and demand for, a foreign currency*. If a currency becomes more valuable in terms of another, it is said to appreciate. If it becomes less valuable in terms of another, it is said to depreciate. There are many diverse reasons for the rise or fall in the price of a currency.

● Exchange rates can be *bilateral* or a weighted average of bilateral rates, which is the *effective* exchange rate. Effective exchange rates can be *nominal* or *real*. Real effective exchange rates are nominal rates corrected for differences in inflation in trading countries.

● *Purchasing-power parity* determines the equilibrium exchange rate which brings 'balance' to the current and capital account of the balance of payments. PPPs can be expressed in *absolute* or *relative* terms. The *empirical evidence* for PPPs is very mixed.

● *Arbitrage* equalises the price for the same currency in different parts of the world. Arbitrage ensures consistency of cross rates in different locations.

● There are important links between *financial markets* and *foreign exchange markets*. Financial markets deal in equities, bonds, notes and other paper assets, such as government securities and short-term corporate debt. When deciding whether to purchase an asset denominated in a foreign currency, the investor must take into account any *anticipated changes in the exchange rate*, as well as domestic and foreign interest rates.

Key concepts

- Spot exchange rates
- Forward exchange rates
- Swaps, futures and options
- Derivatives and repos
- Equilibrium exchange rate
- Appreciation and depreciation

- Nominal and real effective exchange rates
- Purchasing-power parities
- Arbitrage
- Open position

Questions for discussion

1   Discuss the respective roles which the following play in the foreign exchange market:
    individuals
    commercial banks
    foreign exchange brokers
    financial intermediaries.

2   What factors have influenced the value of the euro in international markets since its launch in January 1999?

3 Outline purchasing-power parity theory in the context of the determination of long-run exchange rates. How well does the theory stand up to empirical evidence?

4 Explain the difference between spot exchange and forward exchange. What is the function of the forward market? What is the function of a futures contract?

5 What is a foreign exchange risk? How can it be covered?

6 Explain the role of arbitrage in foreign exchange markets. In your answer pay particular attention to triangular arbitrage and cross rates.

7 Does it ever make sense to invest abroad at a lower interest rate than at home? Give reasons for your answer.

8 What are the principal currencies traded on foreign exchange markets? Back up your answer with current statistics. Why are these currencies preferred over others?

Suggested reading

Bayoumi, T. and Macdonald, R. (1999) 'Deviations of exchange rates from purchasing power parity: a story featuring two monetary unions', *IMF Staff Papers*, vol. 46, no. 1, pp. 89–102.

Cassel, G. (1928) *Post-War Monetary Stabilisation*, New York: Colombia University Press.

Hartman, P. (1999) *Currency Competition and Foreign Exchange Markets: The Dollar, the Yen, and the Euro*, Cambridge: Cambridge University Press.

Joshi, V. (1990) 'Exchange Rate Regimes in Developing Countries', *Public Policy and Economic Development: Essays in Honour of Ian Little*, Oxford: Clarendon Press.

Walmsley, J. (1992) *Foreign Exchange and Money Market Guide*, New York: John Wiley.

Chapter 10

The exchange rate and economic policy

Introduction

When exchange rates were discussed in Chapter 9, no role was assigned to official intervention by the government or the central bank to influence or maintain currency values. This omission will now be remedied.

Central banks can play a vital role in the determination of exchange rates. As international trade expanded in the nineteenth century, monetary systems evolved to cope with the needs of both domestic and international commerce. Initially the mainstay of international trade was the commercial bill of exchange drawn and accepted by banking houses such as Barings or Rothschilds. The French and English central banks played a key role in this system of payments. The central banks would agree to buy and sell precious metal – gold in the case of Britain, and gold and silver in the case of France. Precious metals were exchanged at a fixed rate against the national currency. This yielded a franc–sterling exchange rate for commercial bills. Later in the nineteenth century, Germany and Japan adopted a gold standard and in 1879 the major European economies and Japan were joined on the gold standard by the US, which pegged the value of the dollar, the 'greenback', to gold. The 'greenback' dollar had first been issued during the American Civil War when it was pegged to the price of silver, as well as to gold.

Under the gold standard, central banks intervened in markets, buying and selling currencies in order to maintain par values. When the gold standard effectively ended in 1914, there was in principle a spectrum of alternatives ranging from the free float, in which exchange rates respond to market forces without any official intervention, through to a monetary union which has a common central bank fixing exchange rates between participating countries. At the present time the United States occupies a position close to the freely floating end of the spectrum, intervening in the foreign exchange market very infrequently. At the other end of the spectrum, the euroarea has replaced its system of fixed exchange rates (the ERM) with the euro single currency. In between these two come various types of 'managed floats' and 'pegged rates' with a greater or lesser degree of flexibility. Variants of all these exchange rate regimes can be found in the world economy of today, and will be discussed in this chapter.

Chapter 10 is concerned with the choices policy-makers exercise in relation to exchange rate regimes, and the factors which influence those choices. The analysis is organised historically, moving from the gold standard which operated until the beginning of World War I, through to the Bretton Woods gold exchange system which held from 1945 to the early 1970s, and then to the present-day 'managed flexibility' and euro system. The strengths and weaknesses of the different exchange rate regimes will become apparent. This is an area which has attracted significant debate and controversy among economists.

Objectives

When you have completed this chapter, you should be able to:

- describe the functioning of the *gold standard* as it operated between 1880 and 1914;
- explain and comment on the *gold exchange standard*, set up at Bretton Woods;
- give reasons for the *breakdown of the Bretton Woods system* in the early 1970s;
- explain how the exchange rate system of *managed flexibility* is designed to function;
- discuss the relationship between *output, inflation and exchange rates* under managed flexibility;
- describe the role of the exchange rate with an *inflation 'anchor'*;
- comment on the *volatility* of flexible exchange rates;
- explain the *different exchange rate regimes* which are, in principle, available to policy-makers;
- describe and comment on the *currency board* system.

The gold standard (1880–1914)

It is customary to date the gold standard from the last two decades of the nineteenth century, the period when most major trading countries decided to link their currencies to gold, though the system, in fact, had been evolving since the late seventeenth century. The gold standard was a system of fixed exchange rates, in which countries converted their currencies to gold at fixed unvarying rates. Britain was the first country to tie the currency, the pound sterling, to gold. The official gold–silver ratio in Britain was always more favourable to gold rather than to silver. During the nineteenth century, as the prestige of gold increased relative to silver, Britain benefited, enhancing her role as leader in world trade and payments. Other countries had maintained a silver standard, pegging their currencies to silver, but this had fared less well than gold. The final blow to the silver standard came with the expansion of silver mining in the 1870s. With increased supplies, the value of silver plummeted. Gold, which was relatively scarce, became the preferred standard, underpinning an international system of trade and payments which lasted until World War I.

The impact of falling silver prices in the 1870s on countries which had previously adhered to a silver standard was quite dramatic. Countries on the silver standard found their currencies rapidly depreciating against those of gold standard countries. In response, Austria-Hungary adopted the gold standard in 1892. Japan adopted the gold standard in 1886, and Russia likewise in 1897. By the end of the nineteenth century, the silver standard was effectively at an end. The demand for silver was falling year by year, and the price of silver declining.

The United States had maintained what was effectively a bimetallic (gold and silver) standard until the mid-nineteenth century. As silver prices fell, US farmers suffered heavily from falls in the export prices of their crops. The collapse of the silver standard attracted considerable rural unrest. In 1896, there was a presidential campaign, in which the Democrat candidate, William Jennings Bryan, campaigned for a return to silver but was defeated. The US Congress finally passed the Gold Standard Act of 1900 which once and for all committed the US to the gold standard system of fixed exchange rates, which was by then the standard of her major trading partners.

In the nineteenth century, many developing countries had been on a silver standard. India was one such country. With the switch to gold, India was obliged to close her silver mints. There were higher interest rates to pay on India's foreign debt to Britain which was denominated in gold. The silver-based Indian rupee depreciated and the debt burden increased. However, India's exports did become more competitive. As the rupee depreciated, export prices fell. India's exports increased in volume and there is even some evidence of rising real incomes for exporters in India at that time.

Economists and economic historians over the years have praised the gold standard, arguing that it 'automatically' ensured that countries achieved equilibrium in the balance of payments. To understand how this might come about, consider the following simple model.

Assume:

● there are no constraints on the buying and selling of gold within countries;
● gold is allowed to move freely between countries;
● prices and wages are flexible, both upwards and downwards;
● national currencies are either of gold, or are backed 100 per cent by gold.

Now assume that the quantity theory of money holds in all economies:

$$MV = PT$$

where M is equivalent to the stock of money, V is the velocity of circulation of money, P is the general price level, and T is the volume of transactions (or level of output) in the economy. Holding V and T constant, with the level of output at full employment, yields a proportionate relationship between the general price level and the stock of money. If the money supply doubles, prices double. If the money supply falls by half, prices are halved.

Suppose now a country with balance of payments problems: say that it has a surplus of imports on its current account. A simple mechanism of adjustment can be illustrated as follows:

Import surplus
↓
Gold outflow
↓
Fall in money supply
↓
Fall in domestic prices
↓
Rise in exports
↓
EQUILIBRIUM

The import surplus results in a gold outflow which is equivalent to a fall in the domestic money supply. Assuming a quantity theory of money, this results in a fall in the domestic price level and a rise in exports as foreigners increase their purchases. The rise in exports balances out the import surplus and equilibrium is restored.

The simple model of the gold standard outlined above can be modified to incorporate a Keynesian theory of the demand for money and to allow for short-term capital movements (see Figure 10.1).

Suppose a demand for money function DD'. This is based on the Keynesian 'speculative' demand for money to hold as an asset. At low market rates of interest, the demand for money will be high, because no-one wants to hold fixed-interest securities such as bonds. Because rates of interest are low, investors believe that, on balance, interest rates will rise. If rates of interest do rise, the price of bonds will fall. Anyone holding bonds will make a capital loss. Conversely, at high rates of interest, no-one wants to hold money. They prefer to hold bonds because the likelihood is that interest rates will fall. If this happens the price of bonds will rise, and holders of bonds will make a capital gain. There is an inverse relationship between the demand for money to hold as an asset, and the rate of interest.

Now return to the country with an import surplus and a gold outflow. SS' represents the stock of money. As gold flows out of the economy, the schedule shifts to $S''S'''$. The rate of interest rises from r to r'. This interest rate rise attracts short-term financial capital into the deficit country and compensates for loss of gold due to the import surplus. Equilibrium is restored.

◯ 'The rules of the game'

A major attraction of the gold standard model is that it functions to maintain equilibrium in the balance of payments without the necessity for central bank or other government intervention. At least that is the theory. In practice, we know that

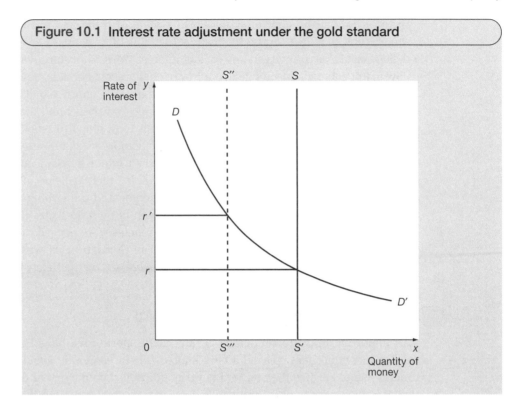

Figure 10.1 Interest rate adjustment under the gold standard

countries did not always follow what Keynes was later to call 'the rules of the game'. This happened before 1914 and increasingly after World War I, leading eventually to the total collapse of the gold standard.

● Even before 1914 countries were often very reluctant to let gold flow out of their economies to pay for imports. Before World War I, there was insufficient gold flowing between countries to bring about automatic adjustment. In France in the 1880s and 1890s, for example, the withdrawal of gold to pay for imports required special permission from the Bank of France. In Germany, the Reichsbank was similarly obstructive to importers who wished to pay their foreign suppliers in gold. Countries tended to regard their gold reserves as a sign of their power and prestige, and governments were reluctant to see them decline.

● Countries in deficit should have allowed the money supply to fall and prices to fall in order to restore equilibrium. But central banks were often reluctant to see the money supply fall because it would have a deflationary effect on the economy, causing unemployment to rise. Instead, the central banks engaged in expansionary open market operations to offset the fall in the money supply – a policy referred to as 'sterilising the reserves' or 'sterilisation'.

Although in theory the fixed exchange rates of the gold standard brought automatic adjustment to the balance of payments, in practice there was a certain degree of official intervention even during the heyday of the system in the decades before World War I.

Britain's role at the centre of the world system of trade and payments meant that she was able to attract short-term finance. The Bank of England, when faced with a trade deficit, would often intervene by raising interest rates. Short-term capital would then flow in from abroad, offsetting the outflow of gold brought about by an import surplus.

After World War I, the gold standard disintegrated. Countries had an even stronger tendency to flout the 'rules of the game'. France and the United States in particular allowed gold to flow into their economies but took steps to ensure that domestic prices and incomes did not rise so that their exports become uncompetitive. This meant that other countries could not reduce their imports from France and the USA and were forced into deflationary policies to solve their balance of payments problems. Between 1929 and 1933 employment, income and trade fell in the world economy. As countries emerged from the Depression in the mid-1930s, the gold standard had been destroyed for ever. Sterling area currencies were pegged to sterling. The US dollar and the French franc were floating. The German mark was at the old gold parity with very extensive exchange controls exercised by the Reichsbank.

Central banks under the gold standard

An important point to recognise is that, at the period we have been considering, governments normally played a very limited role in economic management. Governments had to balance the budget, but economic policy, to the extent that it operated at all, was the preserve of central banks. Research has indicated that the practice of central banks did not follow the precepts of the gold standard. The gold standard required that countries follow agreed rules, with priority given to exchange rate stability above all other policy objectives. In fact, central banks had their own views about the ways in which the financial system should operate. Usually the central bank governors gave priority to domestic objectives over external goals.

The Bretton Woods system (1946–71)

The years between 1931 and 1936 were characterised by instability and competitive devaluations in the world economy. The value of international trade fell by 30 per cent. Countries employed tariffs and other import restrictions, attempting to 'export' their domestic unemployment through a balance of payments surplus.

When the Allies met in 1944 at Bretton Woods, New Hampshire, to reconstruct the world system of trade and payments, the experience of the inter-war period was uppermost in the minds of delegates, including those of the British delegation led by Keynes. The Bretton Woods system attempted to address those world economic problems which had manifested themselves in the 1920s and 1930s.

● The Depression of the early 1930s had brought declines in output and employment. There had been particularly severe falls in the prices of primary products. Rearmament in Europe had prevented a worsening of the international economic situation, but the Allies feared that depressed world trading conditions could re-emerge at any time, and undermine the reconstruction of post-war Europe. The Bretton Woods system was an attempt to combat world recession by co-ordinated international adjustment.

- There was insufficient gold in the world economy to finance the expanded trade flows envisaged by the Allies. The gold standard could operate now only if there was a widely accepted reserve currency. The key reserve currency before 1914 had been sterling, but in the inter-war period confidence in sterling had rapidly declined, and Britain had emerged from World War II in a very weak position. For the same reasons, French francs and German marks were also likely to present problems as reserve currencies in the immediate post-war period. The US had emerged strongly from World War II and the US dollar was the best candidate for a reserve currency. A new system of international payments would need to be devised, giving due weight to the dollar as a reserve currency in international transactions.

- At all costs, there must be no return to the protectionism of the inter-war period. In the United States, an average tariff level of 50 per cent (the Smoot–Hawley tariff) had been introduced in 1930, which worsened the Depression for the major trading partners of the US, and encouraged them to adopt 'beggar-my-neighbour' protectionist policies. The end result had been a downward spiral of exports, output and employment.

The system of international payments which was adopted at Bretton Woods set out to preserve the benefits of free trade which were already enshrined in proposals for an International Trade Organisation (ITO). At the same time, following Keynesian principles, countries were to be allowed to manage their economies in ways which would enable them to maintain full employment. Gold standard adjustment, which required reductions in the money stock, price level and output to correct balance of payments deficits, was rejected. Instead, the Bretton Woods system was to be that of fixed exchange rates under a gold exchange standard.

The gold exchange standard

Under the gold exchange standard:

- The United States agreed to maintain the *price of gold fixed at $35 per ounce*. At this price the US would exchange dollars for gold, and vice versa, without restriction. Other countries also fixed their currencies to gold and therefore to the dollar and to other currencies. Exchange rates were fixed, and could not be moved more than 1 per cent above or below par values.

- In order to discourage countries from engaging in competitive devaluations and adopting protectionist measures, the newly established International Monetary Fund (IMF) would provide *loans in gold or reserve currencies, to meet temporary balance of payments deficits*. Countries which were members of the IMF were to subscribe a quota, 25 per cent in gold and 75 per cent in their own currency. These quotas were the reserves of the IMF out of which it would provide loans. The quotas reflected the income level of the member country. Hence the US was assigned the largest quota. Quotas were to be revised every five years to reflect any changes in economic prosperity.

● If balance of payments difficulties were judged to be *fundamental* rather than temporary, then a country would be *allowed to devalue*, i.e. change the par value of its currency, but only with the prior approval of the IMF. Devaluation would make exports cheaper and imports more expensive. Providing imports and exports were appropriately price-elastic on the side of both supply and demand, there should be an improvement in the balance of trade.

● To reinforce the balance of trade effects of devaluation the IMF could impose conditions on its lending. Strict fiscal and monetary policies in the debtor country would curtail import spending and release resources to increase exports. Rising rates of interest associated with a reduction in the money supply would also encourage capital inflows, thus improving any deficit position on the capital account of the balance of payments.

Breakdown of the Bretton Woods system

Sterling had underpinned the gold standard, but it was the dollar which came to be the central reserve currency of the Bretton Woods gold exchange system. The United States, which had emerged from World War II as the dominant economy in the western world, held huge reserves of monetary gold which underpinned the value of the dollar. The US agreed to maintain the convertibility of the dollar at a gold price of $35. Other countries were very happy to hold dollars as a reserve currency. Dollars were readily convertible into gold, and could be held in dollar bank deposits which yielded an interest rate to their holders. Thus the gold exchange standard became effectively a dollar exchange standard. Britain, much weakened by World War II, managed to hold together the sterling area with a battery of exchange controls and other restrictions until the sterling area was wound up in the 1960s.

The US ran a balance of payments deficit from the 1950s onwards. Other countries were content to let this happen, especially countries in Europe which regarded US markets as a means of building up those gold and dollar reserves which had become vastly depleted during World War II. During the 1960s, the US balance of payments position rapidly weakened because of the need to finance the Vietnam War. The increasing strength of the German mark and the Japanese yen brought speculation against the dollar. In 1971, under the Smithsonian Agreement, the US effectively devalued the dollar by 10 per cent when it set a new gold price of $38 per ounce. Significantly, the US also abandoned its pledged gold convertibility for the dollar. Speculation against the dollar persisted, and by 1973 the world's major currencies were floating. The Canadian dollar, pound sterling, Swiss franc, yen and lira were all floating. Seven western European currencies were jointly floating. Floating currencies, which had seemed at first to be a temporary phenomenon, were confirmed by the IMF as a permanent system in 1978.

From the beginning of the float, all currencies had been subject to some form of intervention, either by central banks, or by government finance ministers. It was a 'managed' float, as opposed to a freely flexible system. When it was confirmed as a permanent system by the IMF, two conditions were imposed by the IMF on policy-makers:

● that countries should not engage in intervention which would destabilise exchange rates;
● that countries should not attempt to 'influence artificially' any exchange rate, in order to gain a trading advantage.

Bretton Woods, for and against

The Bretton Woods gold exchange system of fixed exchange rates performed very well in solving problems which had first occurred in the 1930s. It was able to sustain co-operation in exchange rate realignment, and to prevent the recurrence of the competitive devaluations which had destabilised the world economy in the 1920s and 1930s. As a system of fixed exchange rates, it was also able to create a more stable trading environment, and a more predictable macro-economic framework in which governments were able to pursue their objectives of full employment, price stability and economic growth.

Yet thirty years on from its demise, few economists would argue today for a reinstatement of the global system of fixed exchange rates of the kind that was overseen by the IMF. The Bretton Woods system was too inflexible. It could not adapt rapidly enough to changing economic and political circumstances.

A fundamental weakness was that the IMF had little or no influence on countries with a balance of payments surplus. They could not be forced to revalue. Yet their surpluses were a source of instability. Pressure could be put on deficit countries to devalue and IMF lending was made conditional on strict fiscal and monetary policies in debtor countries. But there was no corresponding requirement to oblige surplus countries like Germany and Japan to revalue their currencies, expand their economies, or lower their interest rates.

Also the Bretton Woods system was costly to administer. The IMF itself and its member countries were required to hold large reserves of gold, dollars and SDRs (IMF special drawing rights) which tied up resources.

Managed flexibility

The exchange rate system which had emerged in the world economy by 1973 is usually described as 'managed flexibility'. It is a system in which the forces of supply and demand interact on the foreign exchange market to produce an equilibrium price (exchange rate) and quantity of a traded currency.

A simple model of the demand and supply for imported goods and services under managed flexibility is illustrated in Figure 10.2. Suppose the euro area has an import surplus with respect to the US. This reduces the demand for euros from DD' to $D''D'''$. The exchange rate for the euro depreciates. European goods become relatively cheap in the US and exports from the euro area to the US will increase. Likewise, as the

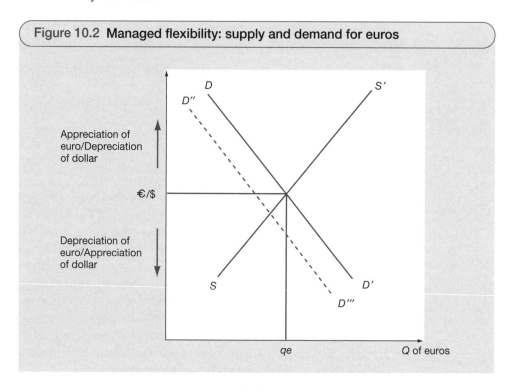

Figure 10.2 Managed flexibility: supply and demand for euros

dollar appreciates, the prices of imported US goods in the euro area increases. Imports into the euro area from the USA become less competitive and demand falls.

Elasticities

The ultimate impact of the euro currency depreciation on the trade balance will depend on elasticities. If the demand for Europe's exports is elastic, then the euro area's trade balance will improve with the depreciation of the euro, since the reduced price of exports leads to an increase in expenditure on them in the US. Likewise, if the demand in Europe for US imports is elastic, the rise in the price of US imports will significantly reduce expenditure on imports. A depreciating currency will remove a trade deficit, providing that the sum of the values of foreign and domestic elasticities of demand for imports is greater than 1 (unity). This is referred to as the Marshall–Lerner condition for a successful devaluation, named after the two economists Alfred Marshall and Abba Lerner who drew attention to it.

In practice, it is unlikely that currency depreciation will operate in such a straightforward fashion to eliminate deficits on the balance of trade. One reason is that the model just described assumes perfect competition, an unlikely real-world scenario. Also, the response of exports and imports to relative price changes will take time. Empirical evidence suggests in some cases lags of up to two years before the full effects of a depreciating currency become apparent in import and export volumes.

CASE STUDY 10.1

Weak dollar hits Hyundai figures

Hyundai Motor suffered a 2.4 per cent year-on-year drop in third-quarter profits because of the US dollar's weakness against the South Korean won.

However, unit sales grew 11 per cent from the previous year to nearly 450,000 cars as South Korea's largest vehicle maker increased its dominance of the domestic market and strengthened its position in the US.

The won has appreciated by 6.8 per cent against the dollar in the first nine months of this year, making Hyundai cars more expensive overseas and eroding the value of the company's foreign currency income.

Net profits reported yesterday were Won296.3bn ($245m), compared with Won303.5bn last year, in line with analysts' expectations.

Provisions for possible losses arising from the carmaker's generous 10-year warranty deal in the US also hit profits, according to Kim Hak-joo, analyst at Samsung Securities.

Hyundai is building a $1bn plant in Alabama to feed surging demand for its cars in the US. The company has shaken off its bargain-basement image in recent years and moved upmarket, while maintaining its traditional price competitiveness.

Hyundai has become the most popular non-Japanese car brand in the US, with 2.3 per cent of the market in October.

However, Mr Kim warned that fourth-quarter sales would be hit by last month's strike by port workers on the US west coast, which prevented Hyundai cars reaching the market.

Domestic sales increased in the third quarter but analysts warned that Hyundai was under pressure in its home market because of increased competition and the withdrawal of a tax break on luxury goods that had inflated car sales.

Hyundai and its affiliate Kia have about 70 per cent of the South Korean market.

DaimlerChrysler, the German carmaker, owns 10 per cent of Hyundai. The pair began work yesterday on a $233m plant in South Korea where they will jointly produce diesel engines.

Source: Andrew Ward, Financial Times, 15 November 2002. Reprinted with permission.

Comment on case study 10.1

The South Korean car manufacturer Hyundai sells its cars in the US. In fact they are the most popular non-Japanese cars in the US, with over 2 per cent of the US market. However, Hyundai have suffered from an appreciation of the South Korean won against the dollar. This has made Korean exports into the US more expensive, and has cut Hyundai's foreign currency income and net profits. As a car-maker, Hyundai also has to offer buyers a warranty. Its ten-year warranty deal is very generous and the company needs to make provisions for possible future losses in the US, arising out of the scheme.

Hyundai has also been hit by a strike of port workers in the US. This prevented its car exports reaching the US market. This will be less of a problem in the future because Hyundai is building a $1bn factory in Alabama to meet the rapidly growing demand for cars.

The company has made great efforts to improve the image of its cars and it has moved upmarket in the US. It has managed to do this while maintaining its price competitiveness. The case study indicates the extent to which price competitiveness in foreign markets can be undermined by exchange rate movements. Exchange rate movements will also affect the foreign exchange costs of Hyundai's projected FDI in the US, and the scale of the provisions which it needs to make for possible future losses in dollar earnings arising out of its generous warranty scheme.

The case study indicates that the supply conditions for Hyundai vehicles are probably quite elastic. Hyundai is South Korea's largest vehicle manufacturer and is about to build a $233m plant in South Korea with the German car manufacturer Daimler-Chrysler.

Money supply, output, inflation and the exchange rate under managed flexibility

When managing an economy, the government will need to have a policy towards exchange rates which is consistent with its broader macro-economic objectives. The elasticities approach to exchange rate adjustment cannot provide the answers, because it is only a partial equilibrium approach. It concentrates on exports, imports and the trade balance, and does not take into account the relationship between the exchange rate and the important macro-economic variables such as the price level, and the national income or output.

The system of managed flexibility allows central banks acting on behalf of the government to intervene in the foreign exchange market, buying and selling currencies to influence the exchange rate. The central bank does not have complete freedom to intervene in the market for foreign exchange because the IMF has a continuing role in providing surveillance over exchange rate policies, backed by the financial assistance which it offers to member countries who are experiencing balance of payments problems. IMF members are obliged to promote 'orderly' exchange arrangements. The Fund would immediately enter into discussions with a member country which appeared to be engaging in large-scale intervention in an exchange market. More specifically, central banks are supposed to conform to certain 'norms of behaviour'. They are allowed to 'iron out' short-term fluctuations in exchange rates, a technique known as 'leaning against the wind'. But they are not allowed to have undue influence over the long-run trend; that is why they are discouraged from engaging in 'excessive leaning'. This is because exchange rates are supposed to be determined by market forces.

○ 'Anchoring' macro-economic policy

Exchange rate policy is not decided by the central bank independently of the government, that is independently of the Treasury or Ministry of Finance. Even where the central bank is legally independent of the government, as is the case with the Bank of England, the government decides the broader macro-economic objectives. The central bank's actions are 'anchored' in the objectives which are set by the government.

It is possible to 'anchor' macro-economic policy in national income objectives, or in inflation, or in the money supply, or even in the exchange rate itself. The most popular anchor for industrialised countries is inflation. Inflation targeting is a monetary policy regime which has become increasingly popular among industrial countries which adhere to flexible exchange rates.

Figure 10.3 illustrates how inflation, anchored in monetary policy, might operate in practice, and the role of the exchange rate. The central bank has at its disposal *instruments* such as open market operations, the discount rate, and reserve requirements. These instruments can be used to influence money market interest rates, which are sometimes described as the *operational* targets. Money supply and

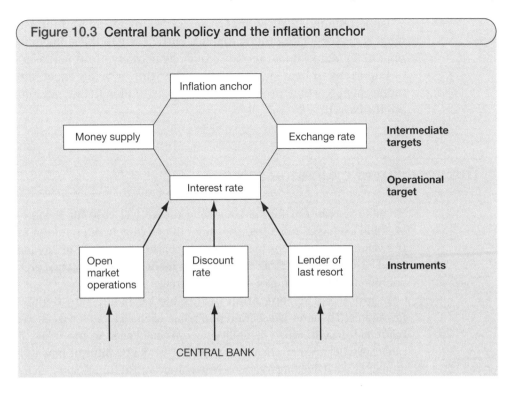

Figure 10.3 Central bank policy and the inflation anchor

the exchange rate are the *intermediate* targets on the road to the predetermined inflation 'anchor'.

As Figure 10.3 indicates, there is a key relationship between the interest rate (an operational target), the exchange rate (an intermediate target), and the all-important inflation anchor. How does the relationship work though? The critical point to appreciate is that a bilateral exchange rate is the relative price of money in two national economies. Factors which affect the demand and supply of money in one economy are critical in determining that country's exchange rate.

The equilibrium interest rate is the one which brings the demand for money, and the supply of money into equilibrium (refer back to Figure 10.1). If the central bank increases the money supply, the rate of interest will fall. This diminishes the attractiveness of home country assets relative to foreign assets (p. 173). Holders of assets denominated in the domestic currency switch to assets denominated in the foreign currency. In consequence, other things being equal, the home currency depreciates. This change originates in the financial account. It is reinforced by changes on the current account.

If the central bank increases the money supply, other things being equal, the price level will increase. If we assume a quantity theory of money, $MV = PT$, an increase in the money supply causes an increase in the price level (pp. 181–2 above). The prices of foreign goods and services remain unchanged; therefore the increase in the money supply has brought about a depreciation in the value of the currency.

Underpinning all these macro relationships are important assumptions about what is happening to other variables, particularly to the expectations of those who operate in financial and foreign exchange markets. However, as a rule of thumb, it is important to bear in mind that, other things being equal, an increase in the money supply will depreciate the currency. A fall in the money supply will appreciate the currency.

The volatility of exchange rates

Economists can put forward a strong theoretical case for flexible exchange rates. Flexible exchange rates permit a smooth and largely intervention-free adjustment in the values of currencies in response to market forces. As in any market, an unregulated currency market can be shown, in theory at least, to yield an efficient low-cost solution to the rationing of scarce resources.

In practice, the reputation of flexible exchange rate regimes has been less favourable. The inter-war period of flexible exchange rates was characterised by instability and default. Since flexibility was re-established in the 1970s, flexible exchange rates have behaved erratically. Although it would be difficult now to return to a global system of fixed exchange rates on the pattern of Bretton Woods, an important question is why today's flexible exchange rates are so volatile, and whether anything could or should be done about this.

In 1976, Dornbusch argued that the new system of flexible exchange rates was volatile because the domestic monetary policies of the various countries which underpinned the system were themselves chaotic. Indeed it was the chaotic nature of monetary policy in the late 1960s and early 1970s that had contributed to the breakdown of the Bretton Woods system in the first place. Dornbusch argued that if countries follow expansionary monetary policies regardless of underlying economic fundamentals, they can expect capital flight, speculation and all the other manifestations of instability which work through to the exchange rate. Dornbusch introduced the concept of 'overshooting'. When monetary policy is volatile, its effects on the exchange rate are amplified. This is because domestic prices and wages tend to be sluggish in their response to monetary policy changes. All the impact of instability is felt, in an amplified way, on exchange rates. Exchange rates are, in effect, shock absorbers for a volatile monetary policy.

One problem with Dornbusch's theory is that it really does not stand up to empirical evidence. Kenneth Rogoff (2002) has pointed out that although monetary policy is much more stable now than it was in the 1970s, with many conservative governments and central banks anchoring economic management in inflation targets, the volatility of the G-3 (Group of 3) currencies, the Japanese yen, US dollar and the euro, is little changed since the 1970s.

Economists have some alternative theories to explain exchange rate volatility, but none has gained universal acceptance. A large number of studies of G-3 exchange rates have been carried out, but volatility is still difficult to explain or predict.

Does volatility matter?

Again there is no agreement on this point among economists. Economists used to believe that flexible exchange rates, if they turned out to be unstable, would be harmful to economic activity in general and to international trade and investment in particular. In recent years, economists seem to be changing their minds. Kenneth Rogoff and Maurice Obstfeld have argued that the level of economic activity is largely determined within nations rather than between nations. Hence exchange rate volatility does not significantly affect economic activity within nations. However, conclusions of this nature may be more appropriate to the US than to other, more trade-dependent economies. Data from some European countries suggests that bilateral exchange rate volatility does affect trade and economic activity between countries, though admittedly not to a highly significant extent.

In a way, it is consoling that exchange rate volatility does not appear to be as damaging to economic activity as we once thought. It is consoling because we do not know whether it is in the power of the government and the central bank to do anything about it. If governments cannot solve the 'problem' of volatility, then there is a fundamental weakness in the system of managed flexibility, because it is very difficult to devise financial instruments which will hedge against exchange rate risks in the medium to long term.

Choice of exchange rate regime

The introduction to this chapter stressed that there has seldom been a simple choice for governments between 'fixed' and 'floating' exchange rates. Instead there is a spectrum of alternatives. The previous section was largely based on a situation in which industrialised countries operate managed flexibility in exchange rates, with economic policy 'anchored' to an inflation target.

In the remainder of the chapter, we consider some of the alternatives being pursued at present in the world economy. Discussions of the euro, monetary policy in the euro area, and the problems of the European exchange rate mechanism (ERM), which preceded the euro, are deferred to Chapter 12.

Exchange rate arrangements

Table 10.1 indicates the wider choice of exchange rate regimes which are, in theory at least, available to policy-makers in the world today.

The spectrum ranges from flexible to fixed exchange rate arrangements. *Pure flexibility* means market-determined exchange rates with no official intervention. *Managed flexibility* allows the central bank to influence the exchange rate, making small adjustments to the market-determined rate. A stronger level of intervention permits the central bank to intervene to keep the exchange rate within a *predetermined band* relative to other currencies, the band being *wide* (less intervention), or *narrow*

Table 10.1 Choice of exchange rate regimes

Exchange rate regimes

FLEXIBLE

    Pure flexibility

    Managed flexibility

    Wide target band

    Narrow target band

    Crawling peg

    Fixed peg

    Currency board

    Currency union

FIXED

(more intervention). A pegged rate system allows the central bank to fix the price of a currency relative to others. Again there are degrees of intervention. The *crawling peg* permits *small variations* around the parity (less intervention), whereas the *fixed peg* adheres to the *predetermined parity*. At the fixed end of the spectrum, a *currency board* links domestic money to a foreign currency and requires a firmly pegged exchange rate. The *currency union*, which is discussed in Chapter 12 in the context of the euro, fixes exchange rates between participating countries and transfers fiscal and monetary policy to a common central bank.

There are examples of all these exchange rate regimes in the world economy today. It is true to say, however, that the trend overall is towards greater exchange rate flexibility. The reason for this is financial liberalisation. All economies have become more open to international financial capital. But it can be very difficult to maintain a fixed exchange rate when financial capital is very mobile. When it becomes apparent that a currency needs to be devalued, capital quickly flows out and makes the fixed exchange rate even more precarious.

Nevertheless, pegged exchange rates do still feature in developing and transition economies. In small open economies, such as in the Caribbean, there has been a tendency to peg the national currency to the currency of the industrial country which is the main trading partner. Single-currency pegs, often to the euro or the dollar, are also used by a number of large developing and transition economies as a guard against inflation and instability.

Empirical evidence indicates, however, that a particular value for a pegged exchange rate in transition and developing countries can often be short-lived. Countries frequently find their currency under pressure and are forced to devalue, and accept a new and lower peg. Interestingly, it is rare for countries in crisis to exit a pegged rate in favour of flexible rates. The decision to opt for more flexible rates is likely to be taken by such countries in a period of relative tranquillity in exchange rates.

CASE STUDY 10.2

Zimbabwe tightens exchange controls amid economic gloom

Zimbabwe yesterday tightened exchange controls as Herbert Murerwa, finance minister, admitted that the country continued to face 'high inflation, foreign currency shortages and declining savings investment and output'.

Tabling a largely no-change budget with some minor tax adjustments, Mr Murerwa focused on exchange controls, increasing the proportion of earnings that exporters must sell to the central bank, at the hugely undervalued official exchange rate, to 50 per cent from 40 per cent.

He also tightened regulations on the use of the retained 50 per cent of earnings, saying this would have to be surrendered to

the central bank and held in the exporter's account. He did not say whether exporters would still get the parallel market rate of Z$1,500 to the US dollar rather than the official rate of Z$55.

Although this had been expected, the minister shocked parliament when, in a move to curb foreign currency leakages, he announced the closure of foreign exchange bureaux, but gave no details of how this would be done. This was a surprise given the fact that some bureaux are owned by influential members of the ruling Zanu-PF party.

He painted a gloomy picture of the state of the economy, forecasting that GDP would contract

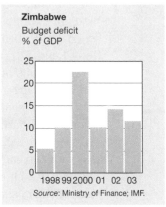

Zimbabwe
Budget deficit
% of GDP

Source: Ministry of Finance; IMF.

by 11.9 per cent this year and another 7.2 per cent in 2003, taking the decline over five years to more than 35 per cent.

Source: Tony Hawkins, *Financial Times*, 15 November 2002. Reprinted with permission.

Comment on case study 10.2

Not all economies have taken on board the message of economic liberalisation and exchange rate flexibility. Zimbabwe has substantial economic problems. National income has declined by over one-third in the past five years. There was a significant budget deficit of around 14 per cent of GDP in 2002. Savings and investment are in decline, and there are serious shortages of foreign exchange.

To cope with foreign exchange shortages, Zimbabwe has gone down the road of exchange controls. Foreign exchange bureaux will be closed down – a draconian measure which is likely to lead to political problems, as some of them are owned by the Finance Minister's party colleagues. The Zimbabwean dollar is pegged to the US dollar, but at the official rate it is massively overvalued. The official rate is 55 Zimbabwe dollars to the US dollar. The unofficial

'parallel' market rate is 1500 Zimbabwe dollars to the US dollar.

Zimbabwean exporters are required to hand over 50 per cent of their dollar earnings to the Zimbabwe Central Bank, to be converted into Zimbabwe dollars at the overvalued official rate. The remainder of export earnings also has to be surrendered to the central bank to be held in the exporter's account.

Economists of all persuasions are of the opinion that an economy like this is being mismanaged. The problem is not the pegged exchange rate as such but that the rate is massively overvalued. It is difficult to see how Zimbabwe can turn the situation around without a change in the direction of economic policy. The case study hints at large-scale capital flight, which increasing uncertainty about the economy will do little to stem.

The currency board system

Currency boards were once very common. They underpinned a wide range of colonial monetary systems. The model was the British West African Currency Board, set up in 1912, with the Bank of British West Africa as its agent. It issued special silver coins to circulate in the four territories of the Gold Coast, Nigeria, Sierra Leone and Gambia. In effect, it was a sterling exchange standard in which specially minted West African money was held at par with sterling. By 1950, on the eve of independence, the British colonial currency board system covered West Africa, East Africa, Hong Kong, Cyprus, Mauritius, the West Indies and Malaya. Currency boards operated in various other regions, territories and independent countries until the 1950s. Iraq had a currency board between 1931 and 1949. Ireland had a currency board between 1920 and 1939. Argentina has a more recent but unsuccessful experience of a currency board (1991). There were also earlier spells with currency boards in Argentina, in 1902–14 and 1927–9. Estonia, Lithuania, and latterly Bosnia, have operated with currency boards.

Table 10.2 shows the currency boards operating at the present time with their dates of establishment and currency peg.

A currency board issues domestic money in exchange for the reserve currency to which the domestic currency has been pegged. A currency board has a single function, that of supplying the domestic currency which is fully backed by reserves. It has no discretion to change the monetary base. In fact, it cannot acquire any domestic assets at all. Currency boards are therefore unlike central banks. They cannot engage in lending, or facilitate expansionary or restrictive macro-economic management.

What are the advantages of the currency board? Certainly it ensures that the domestic currency remains fully convertible into the reserve currency. There is macro-economic discipline too, because the central bank cannot increase the money stock

Table 10.2 Currency boards (1998)

Country	Date of establishment	Currency peg
Bermuda	1915	US$
Bosnia	1998	mark/euro
Brunei	1967	Singapore $
Cayman Islands	1972	US$
Estonia	1992	mark/euro
Falkland Islands	1899	£ sterling
Faroe Islands	1940	Danish krone
Gibraltar	1927	£ sterling
Hong Kong	1983	US$
Lithuania	1994	US$

and fuel inflation. Balance of payments adjustment is automatic on gold standard principles. If the country runs a balance of payments deficit, reserves will flow out. Since the currency board issues domestic money in exchange for the reserve currency, there will be a fall in the domestic money supply. Prices will fall, exports will become cheaper, imports more expensive, and the trade balance will improve. All these factors will create confidence and confer credibility on the currency board country.

But there are problems with currency boards. In the first place, they still tend to be tainted by their colonial ancestry. The European colonial powers which set up currency boards saw no reason why their colonies should have central banks. There was no way in which their colonies would be permitted to operate an independent monetary policy. Unsurprisingly, after independence virtually all developing countries immediately set up their own central banks for which there were strong nationalist political pressures. There are many in the developing world today who still regard the currency boards of the past as having been agents of exploitation.

One reason why currency boards were regarded as exploitative is that they were connected with 'seigniorage'. Historically, this was the charge made by the mint for turning metal into money. In the context of currency boards, it is the large difference between the costs of producing coins and notes, and their value as money. Currency boards earn seigniorage. In fairness, this should be given back to the currency board country but in practice this did not always happen.

Currency boards also tend to have a deflationary bias. Domestic currency is backed 100 per cent by external reserves. There is no fiduciary issue. The money supply can increase only if there is a trade surplus or capital inflow. This means that an economy which is growing in real terms will have problems in expanding the money supply. Admittedly capital inflows may be attracted to some countries, but certainly not to all. Countries which cannot attract capital will need to maintain a surplus on trade if they wish to generate liquidity. It is interesting to note that Keynes was a strong critic of the colonial currency boards for being deflationary. They were, he said, 'designed, probably on purpose, to promote a higher degree of conservatism in development' (Keynes, letter to the UK Colonial Office in 1943).

Balancing out the advantages and disadvantages leads to the suggestion that there are three sets of circumstances in which currency boards may be appropriate in the present-day world economy.

1 Currency boards may be appropriate for very small economies. The cost of acquiring enough reserves to start up the board will be small, as will be the seigniorage costs associated with operating it.
2 Currency boards may be appropriate where there is a need to restore confidence and credibility in an economy. If there has been a history of monetary mismanagement, even of hyper-inflation, a currency board will have much to recommend it.
3 If a country plans to use its exchange rate as an 'anchor' for economic policy, a currency board will be very appropriate. There will be no need for discretionary central bank monetary policy. The exchange rate 'anchor' will also be highly visible. This will be the case particularly for an open economy with liberalised trade and capital flows.

Summary

- Central banks and governments have a history of intervention in foreign exchange markets to maintain par values. The free float, in which exchange rates respond to market forces without official intervention, is very rare.

- The gold standard operated from about 1880 to 1914, though the system had been evolving since the late seventeenth century. Under certain assumptions, the gold standard can be shown to maintain equilibrium in the balance of payments without the necessity for central bank or other official intervention.

- The gold standard disintegrated after World War I. Countries flouted the 'rules of the game'. Central bank governors also had their own views about how the system should operate, and this brought problems.

- The gold exchange standard of Bretton Woods set out to avoid the protectionism of the inter-war period. The US agreed to maintain a fixed price for monetary gold at $35 per ounce. Other countries also fixed their currencies to gold and, therefore, to the dollar and to other currencies.

- The Bretton Woods system broke down in 1971 when the US abandoned convertibility and set a new price for monetary gold which effectively devalued the dollar. By 1973, the world's major currencies were floating. This was confirmed as a permanent system by the IMF in 1978.

- Managed flexibility is a system in which the forces of supply and demand interact on the foreign exchange market to produce an equilibrium exchange rate. The impact of currency changes on the trade balance depends on elasticities.

- When managing an economy, the government needs a policy towards exchange rates which is consistent with its macro-economic objectives. The central bank's actions may be 'anchored' in the objectives set by government. The most popular anchor for industrialised countries is inflation.

- Exchange rates under a system of managed flexibility are volatile. The volatility of the G-3 currencies has changed little since the 1970s. It does not seem that governments and central banks can do a great deal to reduce volatility.

- There is a spectrum of exchange rate regimes which ranges from flexible to fixed exchange rates. Pegged exchange rates can still be found in a large number of developing and transition economies. It is very difficult to exit pegged rates and adopt flexibility when a currency is under pressure.

- Currency boards were once very common. They can still be found in a few economies. A currency board has a single function: that of supplying domestic currency which is fully backed by reserves.

Key concepts

- The gold standard
- Bimetallic standard
- Rules of the game
- The Bretton Woods system
- Gold exchange standard
- Fundamental balance of payments problems

- IMF special drawing rights
- Managed flexibility
- 'Anchoring' economic policy
- Overshooting
- Crawling peg and fixed peg
- Currency board

Questions for discussion

1 How did the gold standard work? In your answer pay specific attention to the role of the rate of interest under gold standard conditions.

2 What were the main objectives of the international monetary system adopted in 1944 at Bretton Woods? When a disequilibrium emerged in a nation's balance of payments, through what mechanism was it supposed to be removed?

3 What are the principal problems associated with the system of managed flexibility for exchange rates?

4 Why should a rise in the value of sterling depress UK exporters and cheer up UK importers?

5 What are the various circumstances under which changes in the relative values of currencies can be expected to correct trade deficits?

6 A developing country's Finance Minister asks your advice on proposals to exit a pegged exchange rate system. What advice would you give?

7 Explain how a currency board differs from a central bank. Are there any circumstances where you would recommend that a transition economy replace its central bank by a currency board?

8 Do fixed or flexible exchange rates provide for greater 'discipline' on the part of policy-makers?

Suggested reading

Bennett, Adam G. G. (1993) 'The operation of the Estonian currency board', *IMF Staff Papers*, vol. 40, no. 2, pp. 451–70.

Dell'Ariccia, G. (1999) 'Exchange rate fluctuations and trade flows: evidence from the European Union', *IMF Staff Papers*, vol. 46, no. 3, pp. 315–34.

Dornbusch, R. (1976) 'Expectations and exchange rate dynamics', *Journal of Political Economy*, vol. 84, pp. 1161–76.

Eichengreen, B., Masson, P. *et al.* (1999) 'Transition strategies and nominal anchors on the road to greater exchange-rate flexibility', *Essays in International Finance*, no. 213, Princeton: Princeton University Printing Services.

Hamman, J. (2001) 'Exchange-rate-based stabilization: a critical look at the stylized facts', *IMF Staff Papers*, vol. 48, no. 1, pp. 111–38.

Obstfeld, M. and Rogoff, K. (2000) 'The Six Major Puzzles in International Macroeconomics: Is There a Common Cause?', in B. Bernanke and K. Rogoff (eds), *NBER Macroeconomics Annual 2000*, Cambridge, MA: MIT Press.

Rogoff, K. S. (2002) 'Why are G-3 exchange rates so fickle?', *Finance and Development*, vol. 39, no. 2.

Schuler, K. (1996) *Should Developing Countries Have Central Banks?*, London: Institute of Economic Affairs.

Schwartz, A. J. (1993) 'Currency boards: their past, present, and possible future role', *Carnegie-Rochester Conference Series on Public Policy* 39, pp. 147–87, North-Holland: Elsevier Science.

Chapter 11

Capital flows and financial crises

Introduction

In the last thirty years all regions in the world have suffered major or minor financial crises. In particular, there were problems in:

Mexico (1973–82)
Argentina (1978–81)
European Monetary System (1992–3)
Mexico (1994–5)
East Asia (1997–8)
Russia (1998)
Brazil (1999)
Turkey (2000–1)
Argentina (2001–2)

The crises of the 1970s and 1980s were explained by what have come to be called first-generation models. Economists argued that crises resulted from an overvalued exchange rate. Governments were pursuing expansionary domestic policies which depleted foreign reserves. The external value of the currency could not be maintained, leading investors to pull out of the country as the value of their assets began to fall.

In response to the crises in the European Monetary System (1992–3) and in Mexico (1994–5), economists modified the first-generation models. The second-generation models took account of the fact that in a system of flexible exchange rates, which had been the case in the world economy since the 1970s, foreign reserve depletion was no longer the critical factor. Neither, in the case of the EMS, were European governments set on a path of fiscal imprudence. Rather it was that many of their exchange rates were overvalued in the EMS. The cost of maintaining an overvalued exchange rate rises when people begin to expect a collapse. Governments have to weigh up the costs of maintaining an exchange rate (and this is heavily dependent on investors' beliefs about the future) against the benefits of maintaining the rate. Self-fulfilling expectations create a very unstable situation. If the government's credibility falls, a currency crisis results. Investors pull out, fearing further falls in the value of their assets.

When the East Asian crisis broke in 1997–8, economists such as Krugman doubted whether the first- and second-generation models could explain what was happening. The countries of East Asia were not plagued by inflation and government overspending, as had been the case in Latin America in the 1970s and 1980s. Nor were there the far-reaching exchange rate problems which had dogged the European Monetary System in the early 1990s. Between March 1997 and June 1997, the level of international reserves in Thailand had dropped by 6 billion US dollars. Nevertheless, at the end of this record fall, there were still 31 billion US dollars of foreign exchange reserves. Reserves were nowhere near a crisis level. When the Bank of Thailand floated the Thai baht – it had previously been in a 'basket' of pegged currencies – there was an ample stock of reserves. So where did the problem lie?

This explanation has given rise to many third-generation models which focus on the role of the financial sector in the currency crises which occurred during the second half of the 1990s. Loss of confidence on the part of the investors reverses cross-border financial flows and leads to a major crisis.

Chapter 11 explains the link between capital inflows and financial crises.

Objectives

When you have completed this chapter, you should be able to:

● distinguish between different *types of capital flows*;

● understand capital flows and financial crises in the context of *portfolio theory*;

● outline the *sequence of events* leading to a capital reversal and financial crisis;

● understand the reasons behind the *reversal of capital flows*: bank run, herd behaviour, irrational exuberance and bubble;

● discuss the variables which can predict a future crisis and identify '*early warning signals*';

● understand what is meant by the *contagion effect*;

● consider whether *new technologies* could help construct a global early warning system of financial crises.

CASE STUDY 11.1

Spanish investors worry about exposure to Brazil

Financial instability in Brazil is giving Spanish investors the jitters. Spanish companies have invested more than €50bn in Brazilian telecommunications companies, banks and power stations in the past 10 years, twice the amount invested in Argentina.

The prospect of a left-wing government coming to power after October's general elections could significantly alter the business environment for multinationals in Brazil.

Telefónica, Santander Central Hispano and Iberdrola have all invested heavily in Brazil, and when the economic crisis failed to spill over from neighbouring Argentina last year, investors heaved a sigh of relief. Now they are less sanguine.

Spanish companies have already suffered from the 22 per cent depreciation of the Brazilian real against the dollar this year, and the strengthening of the euro against the US currency.

The weakening Brazilian currency has hurt profits, but the worries go deeper.

Luis Ignacio Lula da Silva, the Workers Party's presidential candidate, is leading in the polls. His party is ambivalent about central bank independence, and is promising tax cuts and big increases in public spending. The election pledges have raised the spectre of a possible default on Brazil's $100bn government debt.

Telefónica, with $17bn invested in Brazil, last week blamed weaker currencies for a 23 per cent fall in Latin American revenues to €4bn in the first half of 2002.

SCH, Spain's largest bank, reports its first half results today. They are also expected to reflect Brazil's financial turbulence. Standard & Poor's downgraded the bank's credit rating last week citing heightened risk in Latin America. 'Increasing volatility in Latin America, especially in Brazil, is augmenting the latent risk SCH faces through its large accumulated investments in the region,' the ratings agency said.

Particularly worrying for investors is the €7bn in Brazilian government debt held by SCH's Brazilian units. According to José Luis de Mora, an analyst with Merrill Lynch, government debt accounts for 40 to 50 per cent of SCH's bank assets in Brazil, a high ratio in the context of falling prices for Brazilian debt.

Mr Mora rules out a Brazilian debt default: 'Brazil is not Argentina,' he says. Nevertheless, he expects Santander to lower its exposure to Brazilian government debt over the coming months. 'There will be trading losses,' he says.

Mr Mora estimates Santander's net profit will fall 2–3 per cent in the first half to €1.3bn. Banespa contributes about one-quarter of SCH group profit.

Iberdrola, Spain's second-largest utility, has plans to treble its investment in Latin America by 2006, when the region will account for one-third of its assets.

Nevertheless, the company says it will go ahead with a €1.1bn investment programme in Brazil, which currently accounts for about 7 per cent of the utility's assets.

Iberdrola took a €47m charge in the first half to reflect the impact of the real's depreciation on the group's Brazilian assets. The company says its investments in Mexico will be far more important in the future.

Source: Leslie Crawford, *Financial Times*, 29 July 2002. Reprinted with permission.

Comment on case study 11.1

This article illustrates the vulnerability of private capital flows to political instability in emerging markets. Spanish investors have moved strongly into Brazil over the past decade. Spanish banks and utilities have invested heavily in their Brazilian counterparts: banks, power stations and telecommunications.

Already Spanish investors have suffered from a depreciation of the Brazilian real against the dollar and the euro which has reduced the value of their Brazilian assets. Spain's largest bank, SCH, has had its Standard and Poor's credit rating downgraded because of increased problems in Brazil. With the left-wing government elected, Brazil's central bank may lose its independence. Also, a left-wing government in Brazil may engage in large-scale public spending and tax cuts. Expansionary policies may mean a default on Brazil's government debt. Of Brazil's debt, £7bn is held by SCH, and accounts for 40–50 per cent of SCH's bank assets in Brazil. This is a very high ratio.

Iberdrola, Spain's second-largest utility, has also run into problems in Brazil. Depreciation of the real has reduced the value of Iberdrola's Brazilian assets. The company will go ahead with its present programme in Brazil, but expects to look increasingly to Mexico in the future.

Portfolio theory and diversification

Financial capital flows fall into four categories (Figure 11.1):

- *Foreign direct investment* refers to the flow of funds to purchase a stake in a company, thereby giving the purchaser control over the management of the company and its physical assets.
- *Foreign portfolio investment* refers to the purchase of foreign paper assets, either equities or bonds. Portfolio investment includes a large variety of other short-term

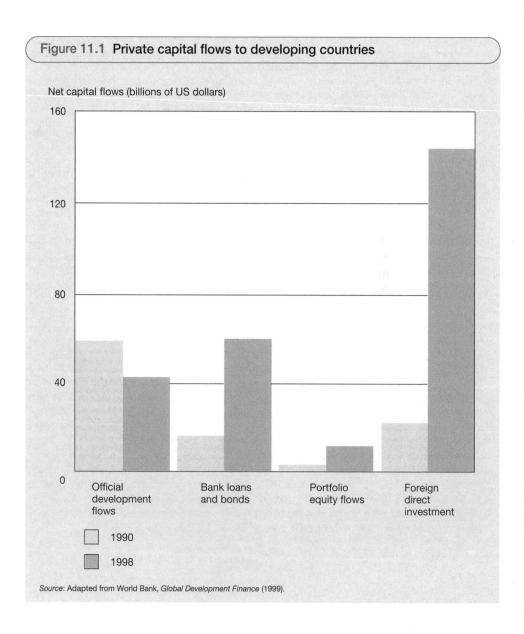

Figure 11.1 Private capital flows to developing countries

Source: Adapted from World Bank, *Global Development Finance* (1999).

instruments which can be grouped together as 'commercial paper'. Portfolio investment does not imply taking managerial control over a company, or over its physical assets.

- *Bank loans* refer to the loans which commercial banks make to overseas companies and governments. Multinational banks are heavily involved in this type of activity.

- *Official development flows* refer to the finance made available to developing and transition economies, on a concessionary basis. This finance can be *multilateral*, for example being provided by institutions like the IMF and World Bank, or *bilateral*, coming from major national aid donors such as France, Germany, Japan, UK and US. Bilateral official flows are often based on long-run historic ties of a political, strategic or economic nature between the donor country and the recipient economy. France, for example, is a major aid donor to her ex-colonies in Sub-Saharan Africa.

Equity and debt

The distinction between equity finance and debt is also an important one. Bonds, bank loans and official development flows are debt. The loan (plus interest) must be paid at its face value, irrespective of the country's economic circumstances. If a country's national income falls, it is still obliged to pay the debt – or default on its debt. Portfolio investment and direct investment are equity finance. The return is related to earnings. If there is a downturn in the economy, returns fall. Dividends, including those to foreigners, are no longer paid. The value of the asset falls. The foreign investor is, in fact, sharing the burden of the downturn in the domestic economy.

Trade in foreign assets can be explained in terms of portfolio choice and portfolio diversification. Agents in the international capital market can be individuals or, more likely, commercial banks, companies or non-bank financial institutions such as pension funds and insurance companies. Agents select assets on the basis of risk and expected return. Globalisation and liberalisation offer agents the opportunity to diversify their portfolios and reduce risk.

In an economy in which there are many barriers to investment abroad investors will find it difficult to acquire a diversified portfolio because they can only hold local assets. They will be obliged to 'put all their eggs in one basket'. Investors need diversified portfolios to reduce risk, and will pay a premium for diversification. It may even be that new and inefficient domestic firms will emerge simply to fulfil the demand from investors for diversified portfolios.

When barriers to investments abroad are removed, investors are no longer interested in investing in inefficient domestic companies. They can seek out efficient foreign companies. Inefficient local firms may in time be driven out of business. Ultimately, reducing barriers to investment across national boundaries is likely to result in markets which are financially integrated. A market which is financially integrated permits investors to diversify globally and reduce risk. Integrated markets lead directly to a more efficient allocation of resources.

Financial crises

In the 1990s private financial flows which crossed national borders grew rapidly and started to outstrip the growth in trade. Private flows increased as official flows declined (Figure 11.1). Why did cross-border flows increase so dramatically?

● Developed, developing and transition countries *liberalised their capital account transactions*, as part of the wider move to market orientation.
● There was a significant amount of *financial innovation* which created new investment opportunities (e.g. derivatives, hedge funds). This brought new risks of course.
● In Europe and the US, many post-war 'baby boomers' neared retirement. They sought high returns for their significant pension assets. Hence *pension and mutual funds* began to look abroad for profitable investment outlets.
● *Developing countries* continued to require huge amounts of financial capital to cope with their rapidly growing populations. They also began to constitute the fastest-growing market for the products of multinational companies. This attracted *private capital flows*. To some extent, these flows have come about at the expense of official development assistance (Figure 11.1).
● Innovations in *telecommunications and computer technologies* reduced transaction costs and enabled financial markets to 'go global'. This was particularly applicable to emerging markets in developing countries. Banking and financial markets, and the regulatory framework in developing countries, had previously been considered too weak to sustain significant capital inflows.

Economists have long held that foreign capital has a unique role to play in raising living standards. Foreign investment increases the number of resources available to an economy. Usually it stimulates jobs, skills and managerial and technical know-how. Often it provides market access, as multinationals search the world to source their goods and sell their products. Yet there is a downside. International capital flows expose recipient countries to waves of speculation and changes in investor sentiments. Volatile capital flows can lead to volatilities in exchange rates and holdings of official reserves. They can threaten banks and wreak havoc with stabilisation policies. Most seriously of all, in some of the most vulnerable economies in the world, the financial turbulence associated with financial crises can have massive implications for national income. Figure 11.2, adapted from the World Bank's *World Development Report* of 2000, illustrates this latter point. It shows the huge costs involved in resolving bank crises in five vulnerable economies in the 1990s.

This chapter is concerned with the reasons for capital inflows and their reversals. There are theoretical, empirical and policy issues. But it is important to recognise that *third-generation models*, which link currency crises to the behaviour of the financial sector, represent a new and developing area of economics. Through the 1960s, 1970s, and 1980s the parameters which determined the flow of funds across national boundaries were believed to be fairly well understood. Then in the 1990s the situation changed dramatically. Market-orientated reforms were implemented. The Berlin Wall came down and parts of the world which, for close on half a century, had been

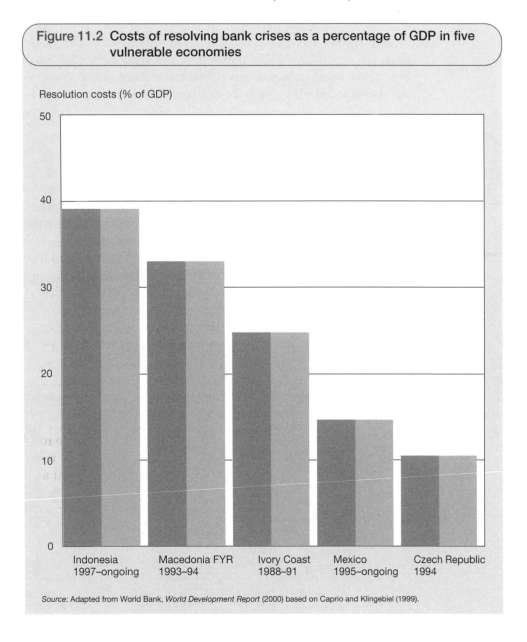

Figure 11.2 Costs of resolving bank crises as a percentage of GDP in five vulnerable economies

Resolution costs (% of GDP)

Source: Adapted from World Bank, *World Development Report* (2000) based on Caprio and Klingebiel (1999).

isolated from global financial markets, suddenly received massive financial flows to restructure their economies. Innovations in the financial sector put the spotlight on investor behaviour. In view of the scale and speed of the changes, it is not surprising that much of the research into capital flows is on the frontiers of economic knowledge. Adam Smith and the classical economists tended to believe that everyone reacts to markets in a similar way. Classical models of human behaviour assume uniform market reactions. But in the context of investor behaviour this assumption is invalid. Market-makers, speculators and portfolio managers all have very different goals and very different time horizons. It makes for interesting but difficult dynamics. In spite of tremendous progress during the last few years, the economics profession still does not understand fully the anatomy of a currency crisis.

The crisis in Asia

Capital flows into Asia rose sharply between 1990 and 1996, and at the time were seen essentially in a virtuous light. As interest rates began to fall in the US and Europe, institutional investors began to search for high returns in emerging markets. Fund managers were also looking to diversify internationally. Asia, and emerging markets elsewhere, had liberalised their economies to permit inward investment and had introduced a variety of reforms to their financial markets which proved attractive to investors. This virtuous circle scenario is illustrated in Figure 11.3.

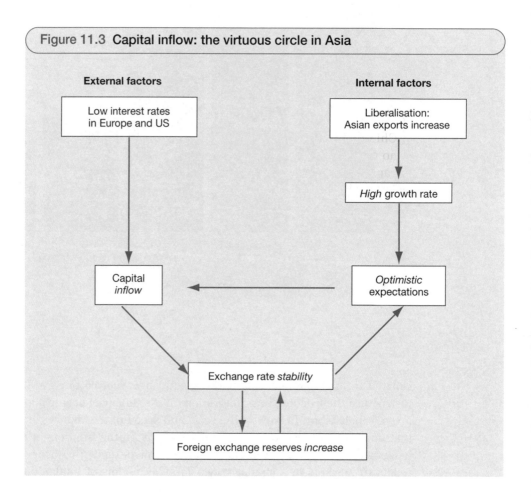

Figure 11.3 Capital inflow: the virtuous circle in Asia

Capital inflow was kick-started by falling interest rates in Europe and the US in the early 1990s. In Asia, liberalisation had increased exports and had led to a high growth rate, generating optimistic expectations about future returns on Asian investment. Portfolio inflows then underpinned the external values of Asian currencies. The value of the Thai baht, for example, increased significantly. In the early 1990s Thailand received most of the capital inflows to the so-called 'Asian Tigers'. Korea, Taiwan, Indonesia, Hong-Kong and Malaysia also received large volumes of foreign funds seeking profitable investment outlets.

The virtuous circle was interrupted in 1996–7. Rates of interest were still low in Europe and the US but liberalisation was virtually completed in Asia and the growth rate was falling. In Thailand, Malaysia, Singapore and Korea export-led growth was beginning to lose momentum. Japanese growth was also stalling and the depreciation of the yen began to undermine confidence in Asian prospects. The Thai baht was effectively devalued in 1997, and in July of that year the Thai government asked the IMF for assistance.

The benefits of high returns and diversification for investors from the US and Europe had evaporated. Private capital fled the markets of Thailand, Indonesia, Korea, Malaysia and the Philippines. The virtuous circle of capital inflow had become a vicious circle of capital outflow (see Figure 11.4).

The virtuous and vicious circles were common to all the Asian countries affected by the crisis of 1997. However, Takatoshi Ito, Professor of Economics at Hitotsobashi University in Tokyo, has shown in his empirical work that different Asian countries had differed markedly in the type of capital inflow which they had attracted:

- China and Malaysia still continued to attract *direct investment*. They had no significant portfolio flows. In fact, Malaysia was a net exporter of portfolio capital.
- Thailand's *portfolio inflows* (bonds, equities and commercial paper) were higher than direct investment. This may be a significant point, since portfolio capital can be easily withdrawn. It is much more difficult to withdraw direct investment which may already have been translated into factories and machinery.

The currency crisis in Asia

Probably because Thailand had relatively high portfolio flows, it is here where the crisis first began. By 1996 Thailand was in current account deficit on the balance of payments. Export growth was zero and the stock market was overvalued. When the crash came, Thai banks and finance companies had serious problems with loans which they had made, which now could not be enforced and became worthless assets. In May 1997 there was serious speculation on the value of the baht, and when it was floated its value immediately fell. Eventually agreement with the IMF was reached on a loan package. The conditions imposed on Thailand were strict monetary and fiscal policies, though Thailand had in any case always been fairly conservative in its budgetary policy. The Thai crisis was not the same as the

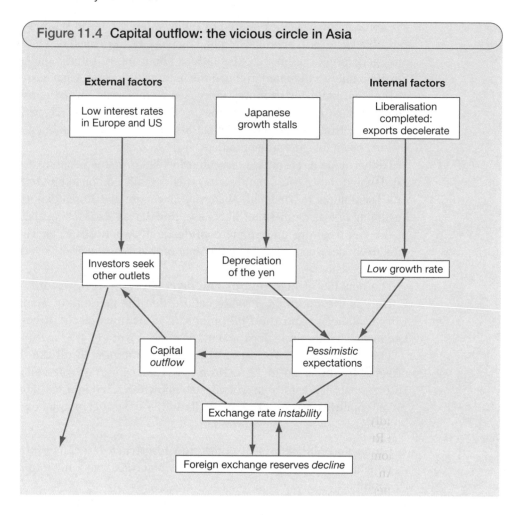

Figure 11.4 Capital outflow: the vicious circle in Asia

Latin American crises where fiscal imprudence had been an important contributory factor. Significantly, in Thailand strict controls were imposed on finance companies. Over fifty such companies were suspended before the IMF agreement was signed.

The role of financial intermediaries in the East Asian financial crises became very apparent when the Thai bubble burst. Essentially:

● Financial intermediaries in emerging markets had been perceived by investors to be *guaranteed* in some way by their governments, but this was not the case.
● In practice financial intermediaries were *unregulated*. They often engaged in very risky lending operations.
● Excessive lending to risky ventures by financial institutions had brought about *inflation of asset prices*.
● High asset prices made financial intermediaries appear more *profitable* than they were in reality.

The combination of high asset prices, deceptively 'profitable' intermediaries and perceived guarantees proved just too tempting for many investors. The circulatory nature of the process explains the severity of the crisis when the bubble eventually burst. Then:

- Falling asset prices made the insolvency of the financial intermediaries very apparent.
- The intermediaries promptly ceased trading.
- Asset prices collapsed.
- A financial crisis developed.

We can see, therefore, how portfolio behaviour – the desire of an agent to diversify a portfolio overseas in order to gain high returns at minimum risk – could end in a currency crisis and an outflow of capital. These are the underlying processes and sequences of events which are common to all recent financial crises.

The 1998 Russian crisis

It is also true that every crisis has its own special features. This was strikingly so in the Russian crisis of 1998, as this section demonstrates.

The 1998 Asian crisis had proved to be the final blow to the wavering Russian economy. The Asian crisis had resulted in a dramatic fall in Russia's crude oil prices. They halved in the first six months of 1998. Confidence in the value of the rouble rapidly evaporated. By June of 1998 Russia's domestic interest rates had soared. The Russian government was obliged to pay over 100 per cent interest on its rouble-denominated loans. Meanwhile, capital was fleeing the country.

An IMF rescue package was agreed in July 1998, but within weeks Russia had suspended IMF loan payments and devalued the rouble. This was a unilateral move which quickly sparked off a world crisis, deepening problems in Brazil which was already suffering a serious currency depreciation, and then spreading out to Argentina, Ecuador and Colombia (2001–2).

The Russian crisis is an interesting case study showing how vulnerable the former planned economies were to capital reversals. Stiglitz, the Nobel prizewinning econo-mist, was chief economist at the World Bank when the Russian crisis hit. In his book *Globalization and its Discontents* he describes the Russian economy as a 'rickety tower' which collapsed when oil prices fell. Capital flows into Russia were domi-nated by large official flows (on average $3.5 billion during 1993–6) and a surge in private portfolio inflows in the form of purchases of Treasury bills in 1996. But the fundamentals of the economy were weak: an overvalued exchange rate, corruption (the World Bank had identified Russia as the most corrupt region in the world), legal uncertainties and economic mismanagement. In Stiglitz's view, IMF policies had led Russia into deeper debt. Macro-economic failures compounded the problem, contributing to the enormity of the decline.

Examining the events leading up to the Russian crisis of 1998, it is by no means clear that the private capital flows which went into the economy during the 1990s could ever be rationalised by economists in terms of portfolio theory and diversification. As Stiglitz argues (2002):

> Russia was a nationally resource rich country. If it got its act together, it didn't need money from the outside; and if it didn't get its act together, it wasn't clear that any money from the outside world would make much difference.

In the end, of course, the IMF rescue package failed. When payments were suspended and the rouble was devalued, significant amounts of IMF money allegedly fled the country and turned up in foreign banks. Russia's erstwhile investors also repatriated as much capital as they could salvage from the wreckage.

Could any of this have been predicted? Although Russia received large capital inflows during the period 1990–7, a study of the Russian balance of payments indicates even to the non-specialist that there were large errors and omissions. Attempting to reconcile current account balances, official flows and reserves leads to the conclusion that even in the early 1990s there were large unrecorded private capital outflows. Capital was already fleeing the economy in the early 1990s. The overvalued exchange rate was just one of the factors encouraging capital flight. More important, perhaps, was the underlying social and political culture. As funds came in, they were more than matched by the funds flowing out.

Contagion

Economists (and investors) have sought to answer the question as to why turbulence in one capital market tends to spread to others. The phenomenon is referred to as 'contagion selling' of assets, or simply 'contagion'.

The contagion effect has been observed in all financial crises:

● In *Mexico* during the 1994 crash it was referred to as the 'tequila effect'. Investors reduced not only their exposure to collapsing Mexican assets, but also their exposure in other vulnerable markets such as Argentina and Brazil, as well as in countries such as Chile which were widely believed to be relatively safe.

● In the Asian crisis of 1997, capital outflow spread to Korea, a country which was initially believed to be far removed from any potential crisis. Korea held out until November 1997, at which point its currency came under heavy pressure. Foreign banks which had made loans to Korean banks started to withdraw their lending. By December 1997 Korea was obliged to agree an IMF assistance package. Interestingly this did not bring to an end the liquidity crisis. Eventually the monetary authorities in G-7 countries were obliged to put pressure on their commercial banks to maintain lending to the Korean banks. This marked the beginning of the end of the crisis in Korea.

● In Russia in 1998 the collapse of the rouble had widespread implications for equity markets throughout the world. Even on the US stock market there was a 'run for quality', though the real-world exposure of the US economy to Russia's collapsing currency was very minimal.

It is always possible that contagion occurs simply because countries have important 'fundamentals' in common. Local events in one country are symptomatic of wider problems. Problems emerge in one financial market and it is only a matter of time before they become apparent in other markets. A number of studies have concluded that the common 'fundamentals' in emerging markets are fiscal indiscipline and exchange rate mismanagement. The World Bank has suggested that closer policy co-ordination among the principal economies in a region might keep exchange rates in check and permit earlier action to contain a crisis. Co-ordination we now know must also extend to financial markets and particularly to regulation. Banking practices in emerging markets need to comply with the global rules for prudent banking behaviour established by the Basle Accord.

Herd behaviour

When investors and fund managers react similarly to financial crises, at more or less the same time, the suspicion is that they are behaving like a '*herd*'. They rush into new markets without appropriate information and pull out as soon as crisis threatens. By acting like a herd, markets are destabilised and volatility increases.

What are the causes of herd behaviour?

Economists have carried out a significant amount of theoretical and empirical research on herd behaviour in recent times. Herd behaviour is when some decide to make an investment, then observe that others are not making the investment, and in consequence change their minds. Or they decide against an investment and then change their minds and carry out the investment when they see others investing.

The reasons why investors are influenced by others' decisions fall into two broad categories.

- Investors, as individuals, often have *incomplete information* about financial markets and the countries in which they operate. Individuals may copy the behaviour of other investors or groups of investors in the belief that this group knows something they do not.
- Institutions and their managers have a *fear of being different*. This fear may be underpinned by incentives and bonuses. Fund managers may be penalised for below-market returns rather than be rewarded for above-market returns. They will aim to meet the average return for all funds. In these circumstances, 'word of mouth' will play an important role in herding. Investors will aim for conformity with other investment professionals by engaging in consultation and informal networking.

Empirical evidence suggests that there is a greater tendency to herd, and hence greater volatility, in emerging financial markets than in the markets of developed countries. Investors often have incomplete information about newly liberalised emerging markets. In such circumstances investors assume (wrongly perhaps) that others have inside knowledge. They tend to follow those with a *reputation* for picking winners. Weak reporting requirements and lax accounting standards add to the problem because they make it difficult to take decisions on the basis of 'fundamentals'.

'Herding' as discussed above may be unfortunate (and even reprehensible from the standpoint of its likely negative impact on pension funds), but it is *rational*. Eventually, however, herd behaviour may lead to *irrational exuberance*, producing a bubble which eventually bursts. Asset prices begin to rise to heights which cannot be rationalised by reference to fundamentals. Investors start to buy stocks which are already rising in price at an unprecedented rate. The positive feedback effect reinforces price rises and increases volatility. In the end, the bubble bursts and financial crisis ensues.

Early warning systems

Is it possible to predict a crisis? Can countries be identified in terms of their vulnerability to capital reversals? Using past data, economists have proposed models which could, in principle, act as early warning systems. There are a large number of models, but they can be broken down into two categories:

● Models which use a signals approach. Indicators have been isolated from past data. They include such things as the differential between foreign and domestic interest rates on deposits and indices of equity prices. If these indicators exhibit unusual behaviour over a two-year period, it is a signal of a risk of crisis.
● Models which use regression analysis to predict likely currency crises on the basis of past data. Variables indicating the probabilities of crises include:

– high foreign investment rates;
– high domestic credit growth;
– overvalued exchange rates;
– large current account deficits.

Regression models in current use were mainly formulated prior to the 1997 crisis in Asia. When used (retrospectively) to 'predict' (statistically) the 1997 crisis (Berg and Patillo, 1999) the results have been mixed. Some models give very poor results: no better than would have been achieved by guesswork, and significantly worse than would have been achieved by an informed observer such as an economist or even a financial journalist! It is highly likely that the models perform so badly because they do not incorporate important variables relating to portfolio behaviour, which is acknowledged to have been critical in determining the currency crises in Asia.

The problem seems to be that many of the important variables relating to financial markets and portfolio behaviour, which can trigger a currency crisis and capital outflow, are difficult to model statistically. Weak banking systems, political instability, social unrest and loss of investor confidence appear to have been significant causal factors but cannot easily be modelled. Of the variables which *can* be modelled statistically, three emerge as significant in regressions for 'predicting' the capital outflows and crises of the second half of the 1990s:

● high domestic credit growth;
● overvalued exchange rate;
● large current account deficit.

Of course these three are simply evidence of the economic 'mismanagement' from which many countries suffer from time to time. Translating them into early warning systems is another matter.

If, as is suspected, recent crises – especially the one in Asia – were triggered by investors withdrawing from shaky companies, it may be that the debt/equity ratios of companies are significant explanatory variables. In the Asian countries, prior to the crisis, the debt/equity ratios in the corporate sector were very high. Debt had to be honoured, irrespective of company profits. A high debt/equity ratio can be a problem. Equity finance, related to profitability, is a better bet for a company in a downturn. The corporate balance-sheet positions left companies in Asia very exposed. Asian economies were vulnerable because their corporate sectors were highly leveraged. Debt/equity ratios were high. There is emerging research in this area which suggests that adding corporate balance-sheet positions to second-generation models substantially improves the explanatory power of these models in the case of the Asian crisis. This is what we would expect when investor behaviour is a significant influence on capital flows.

Safety zones for emerging markets

The literature on early warning systems tends to concentrate on predicting the likelihood of capital outflows and currency crises. There is an alternative approach to dealing with the downside of portfolio flows which is to try and establish the fundamentals of an economy in which crises never occur. This is assumed to constitute a safe or near-safe environment for capital inflows.

Not only does this approach offer a positive guide for policy-makers in countries which wish to attract significant inflows of funds, but it also helps investors by providing a check-list of information needed in order to manage risk. It might even, in this role, help to deter the herding instinct which contributes to volatility.

The fundamentals which go to make up a safe or near-safe environment for capital inflows have been estimated from the positive experience of emerging markets from 1985 to 1998 (Osband and Rijckeghem, 2000). These are those markets which managed over a 12-month time horizon to avoid a currency crisis. The fundamentals can be listed as follows:

● *prudent government borrowing and spending*;
● *high international reserves*, measured either as a ratio to short-term debt or as a ratio to imports (the traditional measure);
● *low rate of growth of private domestic credit*, used as a proxy for the strength of the banking system;
● *competitive exports* and a *healthy current account* on the balance of payments;
● a *competitive, non-overvalued exchange rate*;
● *high growth rate of real GDP*, and of *industrial production* in particular;
● a *diversified export base* which helps the country withstand problems with the terms of trade and other external shocks.

Based on the above, it is possible to identify environments with such strong fundamentals that they face little or no risk of a currency crash in a 12-month time horizon. Levels that exceed the thresholds are deemed safe or near-safe. The researchers applied the filtering technique to a sample of emerging markets between 1995 and 1998, and were able to classify 47 per cent of the observed environments as safe or near-safe, which seems like good news.

But it means of course that over half of the environments were 'unsafe' in terms of selected fundamentals. This may be a fair reflection of the real world or it may be that the thresholds are set too high. Or they could even be too low. For example, if the global financial environment becomes more volatile in the future, the need for foreign exchange reserves will rise. On this basis, an environment which was safe or near-safe in the 1990s may no longer be so. Likewise, if trade begins to falter globally, then an even stronger and more diversified export base may be necessary to create a safe or near-safe environment for foreign investment.

A global early warning system

Can new technologies be used to construct an effective early warning system? The IMF is actively exploring the possibility of using modern computing power and data storage technology to gather information on up to one million financial instruments which are traded globally. The system will gather data on currency exchange rates, interest rates, commodity prices and stock market indices in order to provide a global early warning system. The aim will be to build up a model of financial markets to indicate where volatility will occur and how long it will persist.

The interesting question for economists is how the system intends to model human behaviour! This is not a sphere of activity in which market reactions are uniform or predictable. Added to this, outcomes are very much of the 'self-fulfilling prophecy' variety. When others invest, the message is to invest because prices and returns will rise. When others withdraw, the message is to withdraw because prices and returns will fall.

In these circumstances, the role of the IMF must be to convince investors not to withdraw capital if the fundamentals are in place. It requires the IMF itself to have confidence in the fundamentals, and particularly in the institutions which underpin them. Hence it is necessary for the IMF to strengthen its inspection and supervision procedures so that it does not fall into the trap of propping up incompetent or insolvent institutions.

Summary

● All regions of the world have suffered major or minor currency crises over the last thirty years.

● The crises of the 1970s and 1980s, principally in Latin America, were explained by a *first generation* of models which focused on government overspending and reserve depletion. A *second generation* of models took into account the costs and benefits of maintaining an exchange rate with self-fulfilling expectations creating an unstable situation.

● The *third generation* of models, derived from the experience of the Asian crisis in 1997–8, focuses on the role of the *financial sector* and the different types of capital flows to emerging markets.

● Trade in foreign assets is explained in terms of portfolio choice and portfolio diversification. *Cross-border flows* of private capital increased dramatically in the 1990s as a consequence of *liberalisation, financial innovation* and the growth of *pension and mutual funds*.

● The crisis in Asia turned a *virtuous circle* of capital inflow into a *vicious circle* of capital outflow. The role of *financial intermediaries* in the currency crisis was apparent when the Thai bubble burst.

● The Russian crisis of 1998 had a number of special features including the *capital outflow* which had been taking place since the early 1990s.

● '*Contagion*' is the process by which turbulence in one capital market spreads to another. It requires for solution much greater policy co-ordination and transparency, and IMF/World Bank surveillance.

● When investors and fund managers react similarly to a financial crisis they are behaving like a '*herd*'. Herd behaviour originates in incomplete information and a fear of being different.

● *Early warning systems* which are modelled on past data are rather poor at predicting crises. They may do better if they incorporate variables relating to corporate balance sheets and portfolio behaviour.

● *Safety zones*, which focus on the fundamentals which go to make up a safe environment for capital inflows, can be modelled statistically. The IMF is using modern computing power and data storage technology to build up a *global early warning system*.

Key concepts

- First- and second-generation models
- Foreign direct investment
- Portfolio investment
- Equity finance and debt
- Third-generation models
- Financial intermediaries
- Contagion
- Herd behaviour
- Early warning systems
- Safety zones

Questions for discussion

1 Why did the crisis in Thailand spread to South Korea? Why did the fall in the value of the Russian rouble cause a 'flight to quality' in the US?

2 What are the different types of financial capital which flow in and out of countries? What is the distinction between debt and equity finance? Why is the distinction important?

3 Why did official development flows decline in the 1990s? Why did private capital flows increase?

4 On balance, do you think developing and transition economies benefit from private capital inflows?

5 Should people nearing retirement in Europe opt for fund managers who have a very positive attitude to investment in emerging markets? Should they choose a fund manager with a 'fear of being different?'

6 Financial intermediaries have received great criticism for their role in the Asian crisis. Is this fair?

7 Why did financial capital flow both in *and* out of Russia in the 1990s?

8 Is it possible to predict financial crises?

Suggested reading

Berg, A. and Pattillo, C. (1999) 'Are currency crises predictable? a test', *IMF Staff Papers*, vol. 46, no. 2, pp. 107–38.

Bikhandani, S. and Sharma, S. (2001) 'Herd behaviour in financial markets', *IMF Staff Papers*, vol. 47, no. 3, pp. 279–310.

Gardner, R. N. (1956) *Sterling-dollar diplomacy in current perspective*, Oxford: Oxford University Press, expanded edition with revised introduction (1980) New York: Columbia University Press.

Osband, K. and Van Rijckeghem, C. (2000) 'Safety from currency crashes', *IMF Staff Papers*, vol. 47, no. 2, pp. 238–58.

Schinasi, G. J. and Todd Smith, R. (2000) 'Portfolio diversification, leverage, and financial contagion', *IMF Staff Papers*, vol. 47, no. 2, pp. 159–76.

Stiglitz, G. (2002) *Globalisation and its Discontents*, London: Allen Lane.

Part 3

The global economy

Chapter 12

The European Union in the global economy

Introduction

We must learn to trust each other again.

(Robert Schuman, France's Foreign Minister, 1950)

It is important for economists to recognise the political origins of the European Union (EU) of today. The EU (which has variously been known as the Common Market, the Six, the European Economic Community, and the Community) is undoubtedly the most challenging economic institution to have emerged from the deep and tragic problems of twentieth-century Europe. The architects of the EU, Robert Schuman and his associate Jean Monnet, were wholly committed to European unity after World War II. In 1950 they made a historic breakthrough on the road to Franco–German reconciliation by proposing the establishment of the European Coal and Steel Community (ECSC) to put French and German coal and steel production under a single jointly agreed authority. The Treaty of Paris which set up the ECSC in 1951 marked the first step towards European unity. Its driving force was as much political as economic.

The second point to bear in mind is the evolutionary principle which has been central to the success of the European ideal of the past half-century. Karl Otto Pöhl, the then president of the German Central Bank (Deutsche Bundesbank) put it this way when he said in 1990 that:

> the ambitious goal of an economic and monetary union cannot be achieved by a single revolutionary act, in a great leap forward, but only in an evolutionary process.

As the chronology of the EU (p. 223) makes clear, integration has been a long process. To make European unity a permanent reality, the member states needed to arrive at an understanding of the nature of the relationship between political stability and economic prosperity, and be prepared to work long and hard at developing institutions capable of carrying forward the dual economic and political agenda.

In the UK, however, there are many gaps in people's education and understanding as Europeans. The image of the EU for many in Britain is close to ex-premier Margaret Thatcher's view, who memorably claimed that:

most of the problems the world has faced have come from mainland Europe, and the solutions from outside it.

The British, as Europeans, are different. Fewer than one-third of British voters said in 2002 that they trusted the EU. Less than one-third believed that the EU was a 'good thing'. Compared with other European countries, there has been deep-seated disenchantment in Britain with the role of the EU in the global economy.

Where does the US, as the world's leading economic power, fit into this picture? For forty years after the end of World War II, the US believed that European integration was the key to political stability and material prosperity in the world economy. The cold war between east and west encouraged US support for western European unity. Then, from the late 1980s onwards, things started to change. In political terms, with the fall of the Berlin Wall, the political and ideological differences between the EU and the US became more apparent. Then, too, a number of US economists and policy-makers began to comment unfavourably on the economies of the EU which were seen as suffering from deep-seated structural weaknesses. In particular, critics cited inflexible labour markets, highly protected and subsidised agricultural sectors, and inefficient overextended public sectors. The US economist Paul Krugman, for example, has strongly criticised the EU:

> Its markets, though freer than they used to be, are still ludicrously over-regulated by US standards.

After the launch of the euro in 1999, there was more criticism of the EU from US economists and policy-makers, with strong scepticism expressed about the assumed benefits of monetary union in Europe.

Objectives

When you have completed this chapter, you should be able to:

- outline the *chronology of the EU*, from its beginnings in the European Coal and Steel Community in 1951 to the launch of euro coins and notes in the year 2002;
- discuss the objectives of the Treaty of Rome, and progress towards a *single market* for the EU;
- explain how the *European Monetary System* (EMS) works, and the key features of the *Exchange Rate Mechanism* (ERM);
- discuss the reasons why *sterling failed* within the ERM;
- comment on *European Monetary Union*, with specific reference to the euro, the role of the European Central Bank and the costs and benefits of the *single currency*;
- explain what is meant by an *optimum currency area*;
- outline and discuss the principles of *economic management* in the euro area in the context of the Stability and Growth Pact;
- explain the issues facing EU *accession countries*, especially in relation to monetary affairs and the single currency.

Chronology of the European Union

1950   Robert Schuman proposes that coal and steel production in France and Germany are put under a common authority.

1951   Start of the European Coal and Steel Community. Belgium, France, Germany, Luxembourg, Italy and the Netherlands sign the Treaty of Paris establishing the ECSC.

1957   Treaty of Rome. France, Germany, Italy, Belgium, Luxembourg and the Netherlands establish the European Economic Community (EEC).

1963   Charles de Gaulle, President of France, vetoes the UK's attempt to join the EEC.

1971   Breakdown of the Bretton Woods system.

1972   Introduction of the snake (exchange rate system) for Belgium, France, Germany, Italy and the Netherlands.

1973   The UK joins the EEC, together with Denmark and Ireland.

1979   Launch of the European Monetary System (EMS). Belgium, Denmark, France, Germany, Ireland and the Netherlands are given a 2.25 per cent margin up or down; Italy has a 6 per cent margin up or down.

1980   British tabloid newspaper, *The Sun*, launches an anti-EEC campaign focusing on Jacques Delors, EEC President.

1981   Greece joins the EEC.

1986   Portugal and Spain join the EEC.

1986   Single European Act signed.

1989   Spain joins EMS with a 6 per cent margin.

1990   UK joins ERM with a 6 per cent margin.

1992   Maastricht Treaty signed to establish a path to full European union. Britain granted opt-out on the Social Chapter and monetary union.

1992   Britain and Italy forced out of the ERM, on 'Black Wednesday'.

1993   ERM margins widened to 15 per cent, either up or down.

1993   Single European Market. The EEC becomes the European Union.

1995   Austria, Sweden and Finland join the EU.

1997   The UK signs the Social Chapter.

1999   Launch of the euro in eleven countries. UK, Denmark and Sweden keep their own currencies.

2002   Euro notes and coins become legal tender.

2004   Expected accession date for 13 candidate countries from eastern and southern Europe.

The Treaty of Rome and the internal market

The Treaty of Rome, which established the EEC in 1957, had as its objective the 'four freedoms', that is, the free movement of goods, services, financial capital and labour between member countries. It put in place a number of structures and institutions to achieve this objective, which have evolved into the following:

● the *European Commission*, which makes legislative proposals to the European Parliament;
● the *Council of Ministers*, which comprises the heads of government of all the member countries;
● the *European Parliament*, which has legislative, supervisory and budgetary powers. It is elected by voters in member countries, with a specific number of seats allocated to each country;
● the *Court of Justice* which interprets legal documents and settles disputes;
● the *Court of Auditors*, which is responsible for the management of the EU budget.

By the end of the 1960s, the EEC had eliminated tariffs on trade between its member countries, but a variety of non-tariff barriers remained on the movement of goods, services, financial capital and people. In 1986 the Single European Act was signed to remove these barriers. The Single European Act did not replace the Treaty of Rome, but aimed to complement it with a programme to establish a free internal market by the end of December 1992.

The internal market

The internal market is 'an area without internal frontiers in which free movement of goods, persons, services, and capital is ensured in accordance with the provisions of the Treaty of Rome'. The Single European Act is free-market and de-regulatory in intent. It supports the free market by:

● eliminating customs duties between member countries (Articles 12–17);
● eliminating quantitative restrictions between member countries (Articles 30–37);
● supporting the free movement of persons, services, and capital between member countries (Articles 48–73);
● promoting transport between member countries (Articles 74–84);
● establishing rules against the distortion of competition (Articles 85–94).

The single market, 1993 and after

The internal market of the EU was formally launched on 1 January 1993. The 15 members of the EU (2003) were committed to implement all the single market laws by 2003.

There are two major areas for concern in relation to the single market. One area concerns compliance with existing legislation. The other relates to new laws for a single financial market.

Compliance

Some national governments have been reluctant to implement single market legislation. Three countries – France, Greece and Portugal – have been singled out as falling behind in bringing legislation from the European Commission on the single market before their national legislatures. The European Commission reported in 2002 that there were 200 legal cases being taken against France to force it to comply with EU legislation. Only five of the EU's 15 members had fully harmonised national laws in accordance with EU laws. They were the UK, Sweden, Denmark, Finland and the Netherlands.

Financial markets

Goods and services now move freely between EU countries, but there is still no fully integrated financial market. The aim of a single financial market is to allow firms and stock exchanges, authorised to trade in one country of the EU, to operate in all member states. The European Commission has argued for the following changes, to promote a single financial market:

● investment banks should be allowed to operate across the EU if they are authorised to operate in their home country;
● stock exchanges should be allowed to operate trading screens across the EU;
● individuals should be able to buy shares anywhere in Europe, probably with less red tape and lower prices than at present.

A reservation expressed in some member countries (see Case Study 12.1) is that the European Commission may take a bureaucratic and regulatory approach to the single financial market, which could hinder, rather than encourage the free flow of funds across national boundaries.

CASE STUDY 12.1

City warns EU over single financial market

The City of London has warned the European Union that its planned single financial market 'needs a high-profile political push' if it is to succeed.

A discussion paper sent to Frits Bolkestein, the single market commissioner, urges the EU to cut through a 'thicket of obstacles' and put market-based policies at the heart of its financial services programme.

The paper has been drafted by international financial institutions under the leadership of Sir Nigel Wicks, a former senior Treasury official, and Dame Judith Mayhew, the senior Corporation of London official who represents City interests to the EU.

It proposes eight 'fundamental principles and practices' to be 'formally enshrined in the

most authoritative manner' in EU laws to secure the market's completion. It is a rare example of the City looking beyond its boundaries and burying internal differences to produce a common strategy. The document was completed just before the unveiling tomorrow in Brussels of plans from the Paris-based Eurofi financial services pressure group for cementing the single financial market with a European system of securities regulation.

The initiatives reflect concern that the planned single financial market lacks both a strategy and a champion and that it risks fragmenting, often through political compromises when legislation is being agreed in Brussels. However, rather than focus on the regulatory framework, the Wicks paper – to be circulated to EU governments – stresses markets are created and developed by market participants and not by rules and regulations.

It says non-legislative solutions, such as self-regulation or the use of ombudsmen, should be the first answer to single-market problems. If legislation is used 'as a last resort', it should be proportionate, cost effective and deal with clear market failure. EU treaties should be changed to force the European Commission to consult market participants at all stages of the legislative process. Regulation should take account of different types of risk, such as those faced by professional operators and retail clients.

The Wicks paper underlines the importance of financial markets operating ethically and calls on the Commission to be proactive in policing EU financial market laws.

The paper proposes a 'European Financial Markets Forum', comprising national regulators, market participants and experts, to develop further standards and principles needed in the single market. In addition, a committee from financial markets should regularly brief EU leaders, finance ministers, the Commission and European parliament on progress and obstacles to the creation of a single market.

Source: Peter Norman, *Financial Times*, 25 November 2002. Reprinted with permission.

Comment on case study 12.1

If the EU is to realise its objective of a single market for goods, services, people and capital, it needs to make rapid progress in establishing a single financial market. This case study illustrates concern in the City of London about a single financial market.

The City of London rarely has a common strategy on issues which arise within the EU because there are too many internal differences between different interest groups within the City. The EU single financial market is, however, an exception. The City has buried its differences to come up with a single view.

The view is that the European Commission should try as far as possible for a market-based solution, rather than one based on EU regulations and EU legislation. For example, the City prefers, wherever possible, self-regulation or the use of the ombudsman to resolve disputes, rather than a legislative solution. If legislation is used it must be very much as a last resort. The case study also calls for the European Commission to consult widely among participants in the financial market in order to take the single market further. Participants include national regulators, financial services operators and retail clients, all of whom have a stake in the single financial market. The case study indicates that the City recognises the importance of financial markets being required to operate ethically.

The European Monetary System and the Exchange Rate Mechanism

From the mid-1970s onwards, the European Economic Community members grappled with the establishment of a new European Monetary System which aimed for greater exchange rate stability in Europe, together with harmonised macro-economic policies. The Bretton Woods system had collapsed in 1971. By 1979, problems were also emerging in the system of 'managed flexibility' exchange rates, which had replaced the Bretton Woods system. The dollar had become overvalued and many currencies linked to the dollar, as well as the dollar itself, were subject to destabilising speculation.

The EEC members responded in 1979 by establishing the European Monetary System to bring greater stability to European exchange rates. The EMS was based on a European currency unit, the ECU, which was an average of the 'basket' of national currencies in the EMS. From the beginning, UK sterling was in the 'basket' because the ECU was also used as a unit of account for EEC transactions. However, though the UK was a founder member of the EMS, it did not initially join the *exchange rate mechanism* (ERM) of the EMS because the UK had no confidence that it could maintain the value of sterling within the ERM.

The Exchange Rate Mechanism (ERM)

The Exchange Rate Mechanism pegged the currencies of individual member countries of the EEC to the 'central unit' of currency, the ECU. Countries were permitted to diverge from the ECU by 2.25 per cent in either direction if they were in the narrow band, and 6 per cent in either direction if they were in the broad band. A country whose currency departed from its designated band was expected to take steps to remedy the situation. It had to adjust domestic policies, particularly the interest rate, in order to restore the agreed parities. If it was successful, then there was no need to realign the value of its currency. On the other hand, if parities could not be sustained, then realignment of the currency would be required. All central banks of the member countries could intervene at this stage, buying and selling currencies to establish new ERM parities.

The system could revalue currencies as well as devalue currencies. This was a major difference between the ERM and the Bretton Woods system of exchange rate determination (see Chapter 10 above). Under Bretton Woods, it was very difficult for the IMF to persuade creditor countries to revalue their currencies, as this would harm exports. All the pressure for adjustment fell on debtor countries. In the ERM, by way of contrast, revaluation was more common than devaluation.

The UK and the ERM

Although the UK was a founder member of the European Monetary System, it did not join the ERM in 1979. In 1990, this decision was revised and Britain joined the ERM. Two years later the ERM was in great difficulty with heavy speculation against the currencies of Sweden, Portugal, the UK, Ireland and Italy. On 16 September 1992 ('Black Wednesday') Prime Minister John Major took the UK out of the ERM. Italy was also obliged to withdraw from the ERM at this point, because of heavy speculation against the lira. Following the withdrawal of the UK and Italy, speculation continued in the ERM against the currencies of France, Belgium and Denmark. By August 1993, with the establishment of 15 per cent margins upwards or downwards for the ERM currencies, the ERM was effectively at an end as a fixed exchange rate system, though it still operated at the wider band within the EMS.

Controversy still surrounds the UK entry into and exit from the ERM. Debate is fuelled by the fact that the UK needs to fix its exchange rate against other European currencies if it were to enter the European Monetary Union. Why did the UK 'fail' in the ERM and would this experience be repeated within the European Monetary Union? The UK entered the ERM in 1990 at an agreed value for sterling of DM 2.95 against the German mark. UK entry was followed by a sharp recession in the UK between 1990 and 1992. Was this a coincidence or was the entry value for sterling at DM 2.95 set too high? Did it bring about a UK recession and a collapse in overvalued UK exports? Economists are divided on this issue. Some believe that the recession was triggered by an overvalued pound. Manufacturers, heavily dependent on exports, saw their sales and profits slump. Other economists believe that there were already weaknesses in the UK economy in 1990–2, principally a collapsing residential property market and soaring domestic interest rates.

Verdict on the ERM

What lessons did the EU draw from the experience of the ERM up to 1993?

- There was no formal mechanism to bring about currency realignments. After 1987 it had became very difficult to *realign currencies*. Once the system came under speculative pressure, central banks could not cope. This meant that countries like Italy with high rates of inflation persisted with overvalued exchange rates.
- The emergence of new *global financial markets* had made it very difficult to maintain a system of fixed exchange rates. Huge volumes of currency transactions had begun to dominate the world economy, undermining the attempts of the European central banks to support agreed parities.
- *Low US interest rates* and *high German interest rates* had encouraged massive currency outflows from the US to Germany. Germany had embarked on reconstruction after the collapse of the GDR and the reunification of the two halves of the country. Portfolio and direct investment from the US was needed to finance reconstruction in Germany but had the effect of destabilising the exchange rate system.

Exchange rate instability and trade flows

One of the main reasons for the EEC adopting the European Monetary System and its Exchange Rate Mechanism was the belief that *fixed exchange rates would promote trade* within member countries by reducing uncertainty and removing the need to develop costly financial instruments to hedge against exchange rate risk. An IMF researcher, Giovanni dell'Ariccia, has analysed the effects of exchange rate volatility on trade flows within the EEC between 1975 and 1994. He found that exchange rate volatility did affect trade flows. High volatility meant lower trade flows and vice versa. In the EEC, between 1974 and 1995, the volume of international trade decreased when the exchange rate became more volatile. This finding justifies the attempts which were made by the EEC member countries to find a monetary system and Exchange Rate Mechanism which would bring stability to the trade in goods and services among member countries.

CASE STUDY 12.2

Economists rake over coals of ejection from ERM

At a conference today to mark the 10th anniversary of Britain's ejection from the European exchange rate mechanism, Andrew Crockett, general manager of the Basle-based Bank for International Settlements, and a leading contender to be the next governor of the Bank of England, will dip his toe into murky waters.

He is to speak on the question of whether DM2.95 was the right rate for the centre of the pound's permitted band within the ERM.

Like most British policymakers, he has a personal interest in the debate: he was head of the international side of the Bank of England during the crisis. But the issue is not just of historical significance.

As the Treasury deliberates whether to attempt once more to fix the exchange rate against other European currencies, and having promised its answer by June, the level of the pound is again a pressing question.

Memories of the vicious recession of 1990–92, which coincided almost exactly with Britain's membership of the ERM, suggest at first glance that DM2.95 was too high. In the subsequent decade, inflation in Germany has averaged 2 per cent a year, while in Britain it has averaged 2.5 per cent. So if the pound's rate against the D-Mark was overvalued then, it ought to seem even more overvalued today.

Surprisingly, however, many economists would dispute that conclusion. It has become an increasingly widely held view that even at its current rate, equivalent to about DM3.17, the pound is not too far off a sustainable long-term level.

Brintons, the Kidderminster-based carpet manufacturer, is typical of the businesses that suffered during the recession of the early 1990s. John Pilling, its managing director, says the experience of watching a profit of almost £8m turn into a loss of more than £2m shaped his conviction that Britain should stay out of the euro.

But the pound's level in the ERM was only part of the company's problems. The killer was a UK residential market battered by high interest rates and the housing slump.

Source: Ed Crooks, *Financial Times*, 16 September 2002. Reprinted with permission.

Comment on case study 12.2

The year 2002 marked the tenth anniversary of the UK leaving the Exchange Rate Mechanism of the European Monetary System. Although the UK had been a founder member of the EMS in 1979, it was unable to join the Exchange Rate Mechanism through the 1980s because of problems with sterling. Eventually, when the UK joined in 1990, the stay was destined to be short-lived. Within two years, Britain was outside the ERM again and the system itself effectively ended a short time after that.

The case study makes clear that economists are still undecided about why sterling failed within the ERM. Essentially there are two schools of thought on this. The first says that the UK joined with too high a rate for sterling, at DM2.95. This devastated UK manufacturers who found that they were unable to compete in European markets. The carpet manufacturer, Brintons, based in the UK Midlands, believes that its profits plummeted because of the overvalua-

tion of the pound in the ERM. According to this point of view, the crisis in manufacturing, brought about by an overvalued pound, was a critical element in the recession in the UK in 1990–2.

The alternative view is that the UK was already entering into a recession in 1990, brought on by the sharp decline in residential property prices. The house price boom of the late 1980s had ended with soaring interest rates and a collapse of confidence in the housing market. Manufacturers like Brintons were particularly affected by the UK's domestic recession and would have been massively hit even if the UK had remained outside the ERM.

This case study demonstrates that the issue of fixed versus floating exchange rates still divides economists. If the UK decides to enter the European Monetary Union and adopt the euro, at what rate should the pound be fixed? Is the current rate too high? Too low? The Treasury and the Bank of England face some difficult decisions.

European Monetary Union

The EU Summit of 1991, which culminated in the Maastricht Treaty, laid the foundations for monetary union among EU countries:

- the creation of a *common currency*, the euro, launched in 1999;
- the establishment of a *European Central Bank*, the ECB, to oversee monetary policy in the euro area.

The euro

The euro was introduced on 1 January 1999. Between January 1999 and January 2002, national currencies still existed in the euro area but were fixed in value to the euro, and therefore to each other. On 1 January 2002, the euro was introduced in note and coin form. Six months were allowed for national currencies to be withdrawn from circulation. Then, on 1 July 2002, the euro became the only legal tender in the twelve EU countries which had signed up to monetary union.

The euro and the IMF

How does the euro fit in to the post-Bretton Woods system of managed flexibility for exchange rates, which is overseen by the IMF? The IMF has designated the euro a 'freely usable' currency, replacing the mark and the franc. The other 'freely usable' currencies are the dollar, sterling and the yen. This means that the euro is equally acceptable as these currencies as a medium of exchange in international transactions, and is widely traded in international foreign exchange markets.

The European Central Bank

The euro single currency is administered by the ECB which has its headquarters in Frankfurt, Germany. It is an autonomous institution, independent of political influence. Its monetary policy is anchored in price stability. The ECB has observer status at the IMF where it is consulted on the role of the euro in the international monetary system, and on the place of the EU in the global economy.

What are the costs and benefits of the single currency

Economists and politicians have debated this question extensively since 1991. On the positive side:

- A single currency removes exchange rate uncertainty between countries of the EU which signed up to the euro. This should have a beneficial effect in increasing the *volume of trade* between member countries since exchange rate volatility can discourage trade (see Case Study 12.3).
- Reduced exchange rate uncertainty between EU member countries should also encourage direct and portfolio *investment* by firms trading across national

boundaries. In empirical studies, exchange rate uncertainty has been shown to have strong deterrent effect on capital flows.

● Price differences between euro area countries for the same goods and services should diminish as price differences become more transparent. Effectively, increased *competition* and greater *transparency* should *drive down prices* in the euro area with the introduction of a single currency.

On the negative side:

● It is possible that the single currency changeover could be used by some businesses and individuals as a smokescreen for *raising prices*. For example, following the introduction of the euro, Greek consumers boycotted businesses which raised the prices of their goods and services.

● A single currency rules out *exchange rate realignment* between member countries of the euro area. Under both fixed and flexible exchange rates, real exchange rate realignment can take place. This may be necessary as the economic structures of countries change over time, and as countries grow and develop at different rates. If exchange rate realignment cannot take place, then the burden of adjustment will fall on national income and employment. In some countries, income and employment may well decline.

● A single currency rules out the option of using the exchange rate to accommodate *country-specific economic shocks*. For example, suppose that the UK were a member of the euro area and the price of oil collapsed. This would affect only the UK as an oil producer, and not the other member countries. The UK would not be able to respond to the shock with an exchange rate policy. The ECB would intervene only if all countries were affected by an economic shock.

CASE STUDY 12.3

Single currency 'boosts eurozone trade'

The creation of the euro has boosted trade between eurozone countries significantly, according to new research, reinforcing the argument that the single currency has created a more genuine single market in Europe.

The Treasury last week identified the effect on trade as one of the most important issues in its assessment of the five economic tests for joining the euro, due to be published by next June.

The research, by economists at the Inter-American Development Bank in Washington, suggests that, in the three years since the euro was launched, trade between countries in the eurozone has been increased by 12–19 per cent as a result.

However, in an anti-euro paper published today by the Institute of Economic Affairs, Patrick Minford, professor of economics at the University of Wales, said increased trade between closely integrated countries was not necessarily linked to currency union.

Arguing that the costs of a changeover would far outweigh the benefits of foreign exchange savings, Prof Minford said Britain's foreign exchange rate risk was likely to increase because half its trade was with the dollar area, against which the euro has been more volatile than the pound.

Source: Ed Crooks and Scheherazade Daneshkhu, *Financial Times*, 9 September 2002.

Comment on case study 12.3

One of the advantages claimed for the single currency is that it should boost the volume of trade within Europe. In fact, a positive effect on trade flows is one of the economic tests for entry to the euro which was identified by the UK Treasury.

This case study refers to research carried out by economists at the Inter-American Bank in Washington. The research shows that in the three years following the launch of the euro, trade between countries in the euro area increased by just over 12 per cent. This is claimed to offer strong support for the positive effects of a single currency on trade flows.

Not all economists would, however, accept this interpretation of the evidence. Patrick Minford has long been an opponent of UK entry into the euro area. He claims that increased trade in the euro area is the result of factors other than the introduction of a single currency. What is more, Professor Minford believes that with a single currency the UK could suffer more, rather than less, exchange rate volatility. This is because the UK trades heavily with the US and the euro has been more volatile against the dollar than is the pound sterling against the dollar.

All this suggests that there are deep-seated differences among economists about the costs and benefits of a single currency. These differences are unlikely to be resolved by a single piece of empirical evidence.

The UK and the euro

The question of whether the UK should enter the monetary union is debated extensively in the UK press and elsewhere. Both sides of the argument rely on assessments which take into account the following questions:

● How appropriate is the ECB's euro area fiscal and monetary approach to the UK?
● How will UK trade with countries within and outside the euro area be affected by the UK joining the euro area?
● What is the 'correct euro rate' for sterling? Is the present rate appropriate (€0.63 to the euro, December 2002)? If not, why not?
● How are prices in the UK likely to be affected by entry into the euro area?
● How would the UK cope with country-specific economic shocks if it were part of the euro area?
● Are businesses in the UK likely to benefit from being located in the euro area? How will the financial services sector be affected?

There are no easy and straightforward answers to these questions. Failing to join the euro, however, is likely to have serious political costs. EU countries outside the euro are not regarded as 'fully paid up' members of the 'European club'.

The optimum currency area

In order to analyse systematically the likely effects of a single currency, economists can use the framework of the *optimum currency area* to assess possible costs and benefits.

The concept of the optimum currency area goes back to the 1960s, and an article in the *American Economic Review* by Robert Mundell. Mundell argued that an optimum currency area, i.e. one which benefits from a single currency, is a matter of *factor mobility*.

A currency area is a geographical entity, a cluster of regions or countries which maintain fixed exchange rates within the area, but flexible exchange rates with trading partners outside the area. The euro area is an extreme case of fixed exchange rates in the form of a common currency. Similarly the individual states of the US have a common currency in the dollar.

Following Mundell's argument, the optimum size of a currency area depends on factor mobility. The optimum currency area could comprise a country or a number of countries but it must be characterised by factor mobility. Then, within the country or group of countries, the single currency has the advantage of reducing transaction costs. Flexible exchange rates are not necessary to bring about balance of payments adjustments between regions or countries because this role is taken on by factor mobility. Changes in factor prices and factor movements can be relied upon to balance the internal accounts. But where there is very limited factor mobility between countries, or even within a country, flexible exchange rates can provide the means of adjusting balance of payments disequilibria. Regions in surplus can revalue; those in deficit can devalue.

From the perspective of the optimum currency area, the key question for the euro is how mobile are factors of production within and between the countries of the euro area. If factors are mobile within the euro area, then following Mundell's argument the euro area will gain from a single currency because there will be benefits from reduced transactions costs. In other words, the euro area would be an optimum currency area. However, immobilities and rigidities in factors of production in the euro area may offset the benefits of a single currency because a single currency means that there is no way of adjusting to balance of payments disequilibria.

Of course, in the real world, factor mobilities are not the essence of an optimum currency area. Of more relevance for success is political credibility. Currency areas need to implement economic policies which co-ordinate the macro-economic policies of their various regions. When the currency area is a sovereign state this is less of a problem. A European country like Switzerland has three regions and four languages but has no difficulty in operating a single currency, the Swiss franc, because the country is politically integrated. But when a currency area embraces a number of sovereign states, it is much more difficult to ensure the co-operation necessary for macro-economic policies to converge in support of a single currency.

Economic management in the euro area

Macro-economic decision-making in the euro area is based on the Eurosystem. The Eurosystem comprises the European Central Bank (ECB) and the national central banks of the 12 member states which have adopted the euro (2003). Policy-making is vested in the ECB Governing Council which comprises the governors of the euro area national central banks. The Governing Council of the ECB appoints the Executive Board of the ECB, which comprises the president, vice-president and four members. Central banks in EU member states which have not adopted the euro belong to the European System of Central Banks but not to the euro system (see Figure 12.1).

Price stability

What are the objectives of the ECB? The ECB has the statutory task of providing price stability in the euro area and 'support for general economic policies'. Table 12.1, which compares the mandates of the ECB with those of the Bank of England, the US Federal Reserve and the Bank of Japan, shows the strong commitment of the ECB to price stability.

Although all central banks anchor macro-economic management in price stability, it is possible to argue that the ECB puts an even greater emphasis on the avoidance of inflation than do most other central banks. The two policy instruments available to the ECB to ensure price stability are interest rates and money supply, particularly the broad monetary aggregate, M3. The ECB is one of the few remaining central banks to use monetary aggregates as an inflation indicator.

To monitor price developments, the ECB uses a harmonised index of consumer prices in the euro area (HCIP), together with other price and cost indicators (Table 12.2).

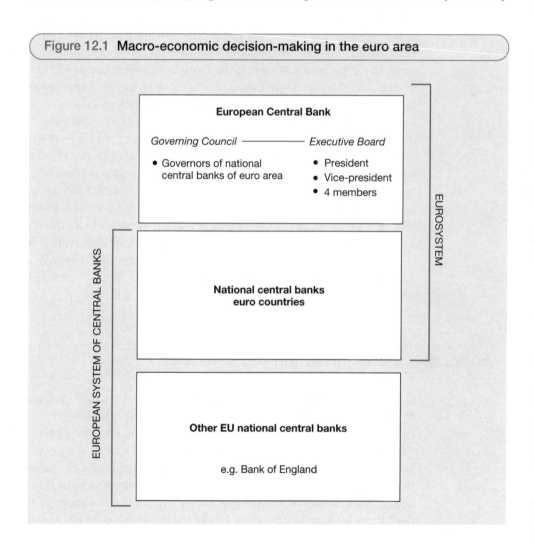

Figure 12.1 **Macro-economic decision-making in the euro area**

Table 12.1 Objectives of central banks in the euro area, the United Kingdom, the United States and Japan

ECB	Bank of England	Federal Reserve System	Bank of Japan
• Price stability • Without prejudice to price stability, support of the general economic policies in the Community	• Price stability • Subject to price stability, support of the economic policy of the government including its objectives for growth and employment	• Stable prices • Maximum employment • Moderate long-term interest rates	• Price stability, contributing to the sound develop ment of the national economy

Source: Adapted from the *ECB Monthly Bulletin*, November 2002.

Table 12.2 Monitoring prices and costs in the euro area (seasonally adjusted, annual percentage changes)

	1999	2000	2001
Harmonised index of consumer prices (HICP), and its components			
Overall index	1.1	2.3	2.5
of which:			
Goods	0.9	2.7	2.5
Food	0.6	1.4	4.6
Processed food	0.9	1.1	2.9
Unprocessed food	0.0	1.7	7.2
Industrial goods	1.0	3.4	1.5
Non-energy	0.7	0.7	1.1
Energy	2.4	13.3	2.8
Services	1.5	1.7	2.5
Other price and cost indicators			
Industrial producer prices	−0.4	5.5	2.2
Unit labour costs	1.3	1.1	–
Labour productivity	0.9	1.4	–
Compensation per employee	2.3	2.5	–
Total hourly labour costs	2.2	3.4	–
Oil prices (€ per barrel)	17.1	31.0	27.8
Commodity prices	−5.9	16.7	−7.6

Source: Adapted from the *Annual Report*, European Central Bank, 2001.

The Stability and Growth Pact

Monetary Union requires a single monetary policy. The member countries of the euro area are expected to exercise *fiscal discipline* in order to complement the ECB monetary policy which is geared to price stability. Under the Stability and Growth Pact, fiscal policy has to lead, in the medium term, to a budget which is 'close to balance or in surplus'. Countries which are in a situation of imbalance (see Table 12.3) are required to make appropriate adjustments, reducing the deficit by at least 0.5 per cent per year.

The ECB also monitors developments in output, demand and labour markets in the euro area. Because euro area countries are required to exercise fiscal discipline, they are restricted in the extent to which their governments can use public spending to boost employment. The euro area, under the direction of the ECB, relies on increased flexibility in labour markets to promote growth and employment in its member countries.

Unemployment and structural reform

Unemployment is high in the euro area – over 8 per cent. The unemployment rate for the young, those under the age of 25, is a particular problem at 16 per cent in 2001 (Table 12.4).

The ECB has concluded – a view not without its critics – that the existence of high and persistent levels of unemployment and low labour market participation in a number of euro area countries indicate that further and more comprehensive labour

Table 12.3 Fiscal positions in the euro area 2000/2001

Government surplus (+) or deficit (−) as a % of GDP

	2000	2001
Euro area	−0.8	−1.3
Belgium	0.1	0.0
Germany	−1.3	−2.7
Greece	−0.8	−0.3
Spain	−0.4	0.0
France	−1.3	−1.5
Ireland	4.5	1.7
Italy	−1.7	−1.4
Luxembourg	5.8	5.0
The Netherlands	1.5	0.2
Austria	−1.9	0.1
Portugal	−1.9	−2.2
Finland	7.0	4.9

Source: Adapted from ECB Statistics.

Table 12.4 Unemployment in the euro area (% of labour force)			
	1999	*2000*	*2001*
Total	9.8	8.8	8.3
Under 25 years	19.2	17.4	16.5
25 years and over	8.5	7.7	7.2

Source: Adapted from ECB Statistics.

market reforms are needed. In particular, the EU has called for more strongly based national initiatives such as:

● flexible wages and increased wage differentiation;
● reform of tax and benefit systems to encourage job search;
● improved education, training and life-long learning;
● an expansion in the use of part-time contracts.

CASE STUDY 12.4

Spain sets eurozone example with second balanced budget

Spain yesterday shamed its larger European partners by presenting a balanced budget bill for the second year in a row.

The 2003 budget is the first to be drafted under a new 'zero deficit' law which forbids Spain's central and regional governments to spend more than they can collect in taxes.

Cristóbal Montoro, finance minister, told parliament that the government's fiscal balance next year would show a deficit of 0.5 per cent of gross domestic product, but that this would be compensated by an equivalent surplus in the social security fund, which is allowed under European Union accounting rules.

Fiscal prudence has been one of the hallmarks of José María Aznar's government. The prime minister, a former tax inspector, inherited a budget deficit of 6.6 per cent of GDP when he came to power in 1996. The spending overhang was progressively reduced until last year, when Mr Aznar succeeded in eliminating Spain's chronic deficits altogether.

'We did our homework, and this allowed us to reap the benefits of higher economic growth,' Mr Montoro told parliament. The finance minister was critical of the European Commission's decision to give EU members such as Germany, France and Portugal more leeway with their fiscal deficits. Mr Montoro said sluggish economic growth should not be used as an excuse for prolonging fiscal deficits. 'The EU's growth problem does not reside in public finances, but in the absence of structural reforms,' he said.

In addition to tightening public spending, a number of external factors have helped Spain balance its budget: rapid economic growth in the late 1990s increased employment and therefore contributions to the social security system. Membership of the eurozone brought about a dramatic fall in real interest rates, which lowered the government's debt servicing costs. Finally, Spain is the largest net recipient of EU aid. In 2003, Spain will receive €16bn ($15.7bn) in EU funds, equivalent to more than 2 per cent of GDP, against payments of €8.5bn to the EU.

Source: Leslie Crawford, *Financial Times*, 26 September 2002. Reprinted with permission.

Comment on case study 12.4

The Stability and Growth Pact of the Economic and Monetary Union (EMU) requires that fiscal policies in member states should result in budgets which are 'close to balance or in surplus'. Three of the larger EU countries, France, Germany and Italy, have been granted an extended period – an extra two years until 2006 – to balance their budgets.

Smaller EU countries, particularly the Netherlands, Austria and Spain, have criticised the Brussels plan to delay until 2006 the dates for balanced budgets in the three large economies. Spain had already achieved a balanced budget by 2001. Its budget for 2003 has been drafted under a new 'zero-deficit' law which prevents national and regional governments in Spain from spending more than they raise through taxation. Although there will still be a deficit in the budget, this will be balanced by a surplus on the social security fund.

Offsetting deficits in this way is allowed under EU accounting rules.

The Prime Minister of Spain, a former tax inspector, has progressively reduced, and finally eliminated, Spain's budget deficits. Spanish ministers are critical of EU rules allowing greater leeway in achieving balanced budgets. They reject the argument that slow growth requires a fiscal deficit, arguing that countries like France, Germany and Portugal should concentrate on structural reforms to raise the rate of growth.

It must be conceded that Spain has had help from other factors in balancing the budget. Rapid growth has increased employment and contributions to the social security system. Membership of the EU has lowered interest rates and the costs of servicing government debt. Spain is also fortunate in receiving substantial amounts of EU funding way in excess of her financial contribution to the EU.

CASE STUDY 12.5

Labour market: Structural problems run deep

If the task of reducing unemployment depended on glitzy public relations, then Germany's jobless queues would be considerably shorter than the current 4.12m.

The launch in mid-November of a government 'roadshow' to support his labour market reform plans was the latest gesture by Chancellor Gerhard Schröder aimed at increasing public awareness of the country's nagging unemployment problem.

Accompanied by music and video clips, the chancellor used a speech in Wolfsburg, home of carmaker Volkswagen, to launch the nationwide tour, urging greater awareness that 'joblessness is a problem that should pre-occupy everyone in society'.

While acknowledging that the chancellor's social message may be right, economists and business leaders remain deeply sceptical that such public relations events will help tackle the long-standing problems posed by Germany's creaking labour market.

They argue that measures to increase labour market flexibility – billed by the government as its flagship reform project for the next four years – have yet to prove their worth.

The measures, focused on streamlining job placement schemes for the unemployed and improving job opportunities for the low paid, were labelled this month as 'the biggest labour market reform in German history' by Wolfgang Clement, economics and labour minister.

The government's motivation for wanting to act decisively is clear enough. Unemployment has remained stuck above 4m for months, with little prospect of falling next year.

In addition to bringing misery to those affected, the figure weighs heavily on government finances, increasing welfare costs and cutting tax revenues.

Source: Hugh Williamson, *Financial Times*, 25 November 2002. Reprinted with permission.

Comment on case study 12.5

Membership of the euro area gives very little leeway for an individual member country to reduce unemployment through macro-economic management. Interest rates and money supply are determined by the European Central Bank. Fiscal policy must be directed at ensuring balanced budgets in the medium term. This is the context in which to place this case study on German unemployment.

Economists and business leaders are sceptical that simply increasing the level of public awareness will do much to solve the German unemployment problem. The German unemployment rate is historically high at over 4 million. This brings a great deal of unhappiness and discontent to those affected and also has budgetary implications in terms of higher welfare payments and falling tax revenues.

Following EU principles, the German government has introduced measures aimed at increasing labour market flexibility. They include new job placement schemes and better job opportunities for the unemployed. Unfortunately these measures have had little success to date.

One of the problems that Germany has is its long tradition of compromise with important social groups such as trade unions. The unions are committed to what they see as social justice, and are sceptical about labour market reforms. On the other hand, economic advisors are advocating restrictions on collective bargaining and greater flexibility for firms negotiating wages in local labour markets. The German government aims to reduce unemployment by 50 per cent within three years, but most observers are sceptical that this goal can be achieved, given the rigidities of the labour market in Germany.

Accession countries and the euro

The candidate countries are in the final stages of preparation for accession to the EU. Although countries such as the UK and Denmark, which were members of the EU before the introduction of the euro, were given the option of joining or staying out of the euro area, this does not apply to accession countries. They are obliged to join the euro area at some point of time, the only issue open to negotiation being the date of entry.

Should accession countries join the euro area at an *early date*? Some economists argue that early entry to the euro area would benefit accession countries. It would reduce transactions costs associated with the internal market and remove the uncertainty arising out of flexible exchange rates.

Only those accession countries that can meet the Maastricht criteria are eligible for entry to the euro area. This means:

● membership of the European Monetary System (EMS) and Exchange Rate Mechanism (ERM) for at least two years, with the domestic currency maintained within the 15 per cent band against the euro;
● a public sector deficit of less than 3 per cent of GDP and a national debt of less than 60 per cent of GDP;
● low rates of inflation.

Two of the largest of the accession countries, Hungary and the Czech Republic, have substantial fiscal deficits (2003) and would have problems in meeting the Maastricht criteria in the near future. But it could be argued that the prospect of membership of the euro area can provide the necessary political motivation for these countries to embrace fiscal discipline, as it did in the case of the earlier entry of Spain, Greece and Portugal. Poland, for example, plans to adopt the euro at an early date and regards prospective euro entry as providing the government with justification for tighter fiscal and monetary policies at home.

Alternatively, should euro entry by accession countries be *deferred as long as possible*? The argument here is that the present euro area functions in a way which is most suited to EU members who are mature high-income economies, whereas the strict fiscal and monetary policies imposed by the ECB may not suit many accession countries, particularly those recently emerging from strait-jacket communism. Structural reforms will be needed in those countries before euro entry is contemplated. The Maastricht criteria are wholly concerned with macro-economic management. They have little, if anything, to offer in relation to fundamental economic reforms and the long-run development of transition economies.

Small open economies in the euro area

Some of the accession countries – Malta is a case in point – are small, flexible and open economies for which a single currency should be especially suitable. Maintaining an independent currency is an expensive luxury for countries such as Malta. This also applies to Malta's Mediterranean neighbour Cyprus, another accession economy. Although membership of the euro area would have undoubted advantages for countries like Malta, there are other aspects of EU membership which are less attractive to them, and for which special terms may need to be negotiated. For example, by any standards Malta is an overcrowded island economy. Its population of 400 000 people occupies an area of around 300 sq. km. The EU has granted Malta exemption from certain aspects of the single market which relate to property and labour movements. If the Maltese government believes that an influx of non-Maltese workers from other EU countries would destabilise the local labour and property markets, then reserve powers are available to the government to introduce restrictions on the movement of labour and the purchase of property.

For small open economies, however, there remains the overriding disadvantage of being tied even more closely to EU countries as major trading partners when there are other trade blocs which could provide significant trading opportunities, particularly those based on the United States, China and Japan. Although membership of the euro area brings small economies reduced transactions costs and exchange rate stability to boost trade with other EU countries, these benefits may be offset to some extent by reduced trading opportunities with the rest of the world.

Summary

- The European Union (EU) has its origins in Franco-German reconciliation after World War II. It has followed an evolutionary process, with EU integration coming about over a long period, from 1950 to the present day.

- The Treaty of Rome of 1957 established the objectives of the 'four freedoms' – free movement of goods, services, financial capital and labour between member countries.

- The EU Single Market was launched in 1993. There are two main outstanding issues: lack of compliance with single market legislation, and the lack of a fully integrated financial market.

- The European Monetary System (EMS) was established in 1979. The Exchange Rate Mechanism (ERM) of the EMS was effectively ended as a fixed exchange rate system in 1993.

- The Maastricht Treaty, following the EU Summit of 1991, laid the foundations for monetary union in EU countries. The common currency, the euro, was launched in 1999. The European Central Bank (ECB) oversees monetary policy in the euro area.

- The single currency has costs and benefits which have been extensively debated by economists. The effects of a single currency can be analysed systematically within the framework of an optimum currency area.

- Economic management in the euro area is based on the Eurosystem, headed by the European Central Bank (ECB). It gives high priority to price stability, using interest rates and the money supply (M3) as indicators.

- There is a view that the existence of high and persistent levels of unemployment in a number of euro area countries indicates that comprehensive labour market reforms are needed.

- Accession countries have particular problems in relation to entry into the euro area. There is a debate over whether they should enter at an early date, or defer until significant structural reforms have taken place.

Key concepts

- The four freedoms
- The Single Market
- European Monetary System
- Exchange Rate Mechanism
- Single currency
- Optimum currency area
- European Central Bank (ECB)
- Stability and Growth Pact
- Labour market flexibility
- Maastricht criteria

Questions for discussion

1 Explain the 'four freedoms' as set out in the Treaty of Rome. To what extent have they brought about *efficiency gains* in EU countries? Have there been any other benefits? Other costs?

2 From the standpoint of UK businesses, what are the likely advantages and disadvantages of a single EU financial market?

3 What type of economy is likely to benefit from joining a monetary union?

4 What lessons can EU countries draw from the experience of the Exchange Rate Mechanism (ERM) of the European Monetary System?

5 'The success of US monetary union should not be taken as an indicator of the consequences of monetary union for Europe, since the US is institutionally very different' (George Akerlof). Explain and discuss.

6 'Britain will eventually find that it is in its own interest, politically and economically, to enter the euro area' (Robert Mundell). Do you agree?

7 Explain how economic management is conducted within the euro area. What is the relationship between the European Central Bank (ECB) and the various national central banks of the euro area member countries?

8 What is the euro area Stability and Growth Pact? What happens when a country refuses to honour its obligations under the pact?

9 What are the implications of a euro area country breaching the code of fiscal discipline?

10 Why is labour market reform considered to be a central plank of euro area economic policy? How can a national government increase labour market flexibility?

Suggested reading

Dell'Ariccia, G. (1999) 'Exchange rate fluctuations and trade flows: evidence from the European Union', *IMF Staff Papers*, vol. 46, no. 3, pp. 315–34.

European Central Bank Annual Reports, Frankfurt: European Central Bank.

European Central Bank Monthly Bulletins, Frankfurt: European Central Bank.

Mundell, R. A. (1961) 'The theory of optimum currency areas', *American Economic Review*, no. 51, pp. 717–25.

Website

● European Central Bank: **www.ecb.int**

Chapter 13

Europe's transition economies in the global economy

Introduction

This chapter is concerned with the transition economies of Europe: the countries of central and eastern Europe which are still engaged in the painful transition from a fully planned to a fully market-based system of economic organisation. China and Vietnam have also followed the path of transition but without the clear political agenda which has marked out transition in Europe.

The transition experience of Asia is referred to from time to time in this chapter because it provides some interesting and important points of comparison with the European case. In the European transition economies, a massive political agenda has been as important as the economic agenda in pushing transition forward. There is an old tradition in political economy which says that free markets and political liberty go hand in hand. Political and economic liberty are, in fact, interdependent. Like most of the fundamentals in economics, this idea can be traced back to Adam Smith. The transition economies of Europe, prior to the fall of the Berlin Wall in 1989, were highly authoritarian and undemocratic. The Soviet Union had been a communist dictatorship since 1917. In central Europe communism was imposed in the aftermath of World War II. Market liberalisation after 1989 was seen as a necessary accompaniment to the political reform which was demanded by millions of people in central and eastern Europe.

It is important to recognise the far-reaching implications of the dual political and economic agenda in Europe, because there have been misgivings in some official quarters over the outcome to date of European transition. Joseph Stiglitz, when he was the chief economist at the World Bank, described transition as a 'bitter and disappointing failure'. What he had in mind was the disastrous fall in national output in Russia and in some European transition economies after 1989 and the associated social failures. As we enter the second decade of transition, economists and policy-makers understandably have a more measured approach to reform.

The fall of the Berlin Wall in November 1989 was an occasion for hope. It also inspired a sense of euphoria and triumphalism, and for some, a belief that the transition to a market economy and democratic society would be simple and short. But ten years of experience has demonstrated that the transition is complex and long and that the upheavals and stresses can be harsh . . . But the disappointed hopes of some should not be allowed to overshadow the remarkable achievements.

(European Bank for Reconstruction and Development, 1999)

There is, in the final sentence of the ERBD's report on transition, a recognition of the difficulties in pursuing simultaneously economic liberalisation, and a 'root and branch' political agenda. Comparisons have been drawn between the Chinese and European political and institutional approaches to transition. China had learned from her catastrophic Great Leap Forward and Cultural Revolution of the mid-twentieth century and took the decision to base economic transition on existing political and social institutions. The path to a market economy was via a gradual political process of incrementalism ('crossing a river by grasping for stones one at a time') and non-ideological pragmatism ('the question is not whether the cat is black or white, but whether or not it catches mice').

Europe rejected incremental reform for very good reasons. Critics of gradual reform in Europe feared that unless the power of vested interests in the European transition economies was broken, sectional interests would soon reassert themselves. The political agenda in Europe, therefore, was based on 'root and branch' political and institutional change.

Although China adopted a gradualist approach to political and social change, its economic performance did not suffer. In fact it has been superior to even the best performing transition economies in Europe, causing some economists to question the democratisation-liberalisation link. Has China's very positive experience with transition come about *because of* its cautious approach to political change, or *despite* its refusal to expouse the liberal political creed? Economists and policy-makers have reached no firm conclusion on this point. In the IMF and World Bank there has been some movement towards the view that the gradualist political approach in Asia enabled adjustment to come about without massive job-shedding by state-owned enterprises, and without the fiscal and financial instability which beset economic transition in Europe. The 'shock therapy' approach adopted in the transition economies of Europe, with their 'root and branch' agenda of political and economic reform, brought enormous social and economic dislocation.

One of the important lessons of transition in Europe has been that the path to a market economy can have unwelcome social consequences (see Case Study 13.1). Political and economic liberty are worthwhile goals and may be, as the classical economists indicated, very much interdependent. But the path to freedom can have unintended social costs.

● Many of the intellectuals who supported the transition have seen their *values and culture collapse*. In the transition economies of Europe the 'high culture' of music, art and literature has given way under market pressures to a range of imported goods and services which appear to reflect some of the least attractive aspects of western materialism.

- *Income distribution* now fails to reflect any commonly accepted notion of social justice. Black-marketeers, criminals and sharp operators on the margins of the law have exploited newly emerging opportunities in Europe's transition economies. The boundary between legitimate and illegitimate economic activity in many of the former centrally planned economies is very blurred.
- The *safety nets* which people take for granted in most developed countries have fallen away in transition economies under the pressure of mounting government debt. There is no longer any job protection or universal health and education. Authoritarian regimes may have lacked the basics of personal freedom, but they still managed to deliver a minimum level of health, education, job security and pension provision for the working population.

This then is the background to the present chapter, which looks at Europe's transition economies with particular reference to the external consequences of reform: foreign trade, exchange rates, currency and capital markets and EU enlargement. Over the period 2000–2 a process of recovery began in transition economies. Central and eastern Europe did record positive growth rates (Table 13.1). Foreign direct investment is increasing. But there are still high rates of unemployment which leave many in the poorest countries unable to feed themselves and their families. Other surveys suggest that even the high unemployment figures in national statistics may be underestimates. Twelve years after the fall of the Berlin Wall, the output of central and eastern Europe is, on average, one-third below its 1989 level.

Table 13.1 Economic indicators for selected central and eastern European countries

Country	GDP growth rate %		Unemployment rate %	
	2000	2001	2000	2001
Bosnia and Herzegovina	9.1	8.0	39.4	40.0
Croatia	3.7	4.1	22.6	23.1
Hungary	5.2	3.8	8.9	8.0
Romania	1.8	5.3	10.5	8.6
Slovenia	4.6	3.0	12.0	11.8
Macedonia	4.5	−4.1	45.0	42.0
Estonia	7.1	5.0	7.7	7.7
Latvia	6.8	7.7	7.8	7.7
Lithuania	3.8	5.9	12.6	12.9
Azerbaijan	11.1	9.9	1.2	1.3
Moldova	2.1	6.1	1.8	1.7
Russian Federation	9.0	5.0	9.8	8.7
Ukraine	5.9	9.1	4.2	3.7

Source: Adapted from various national statistics.

> **Objectives**
>
> When you have completed this chapter you should be able to:
>
> ● outline the *timetable of the transition* process in Europe, which began in the late 1980s;
>
> ● discuss the process of transition from the standpoint of *economic theory*;
>
> ● explain what is meant by a gradual or *incrementalist* perspective on transition;
>
> ● discuss the types of *institutional reforms* appropriate to transition economies;
>
> ● outline the past and current *GDP levels* in Europe's transition economies and make appropriate comments and comparisons;
>
> ● discuss the important question of *poverty levels* and income distribution during the transition;
>
> ● explore issues relating to *trade liberalisation* and the exchange rate;
>
> ● comment on the significance of *capital flows* to Europe's transition economies;
>
> ● explain why Europe's transition economies have future *accession to the EU* as a major objective.

CASE STUDY 13.1

Viewpoint

Irina Kryachuk, a charming young doctor from Kiev, has a lot to say about the legacy of communism in her country. Her professional life is dominated by one of the ugliest reminders of Ukraine's Soviet past.

She is a haematologist, treating blood cancer among the 160 000 'liquidators' who cleaned up the site of the Chernobyl nuclear reactor disaster in 1986.

The end of communism has brought the end of the ordeal for most Ukrainians. But Ms Kryachuk is ambivalent about the transformations that have shaken her country since inde-

pendence from the Soviet Union in 1991.

For starters, she hasn't been paid her 200 hryvnia ($44) monthly salary since April. She is reluctant to complain, however, because of the enormity of the problem she faces on a daily basis. 'We work extremely hard,' she says. 'A high percentage of our patients die, simply because that is the field of medicine we are in. Emotionally it is devastating. And we are doing it for free.'

She recounts a visit by American doctors from the National Cancer Institute last year. 'The thing that surprised them the most is how we could be so

enthusiastic about our work when we were not getting paid,' she says.

But like most Ukrainians, Ms Kryachuk gets by. Her husband left medicine to publish a commercial journal on pharmacology and, because of his income, the couple has firm roots in Ukraine's growing middle class.

'We are relatively well off,' she says, but laments the fact that her husband cannot practise medicine because of the economic situation. 'Wherever two doctors are married, one of them has to leave the profession in order to earn a living for the family. We lose a lot of good professionals that way.'

She also believes that post-Soviet society, for all its faults, is a more mobile society. 'From the standpoint of discrimination against women, society has improved since the days of the Soviet Union. They would always take more men into the Communist party than women, and everything depended on the Communist party. Now more depends on one's abilities.'

And those with abilities have found their horizons are far wider than before. Ms Kryachuk recently attended medical conferences in Paris and Salzburg, paid for by the Soros Foundation.

'This would have been unheard of before, under communism. To travel, that was only for the top nomenklatura.'

Source: Financial Times, 10 November 1999. Reprinted with permission.

Comment on case study 13.1

The case study illustrates the unwelcome social consequences of transition in the Ukraine. A decade after independence from the former Soviet Union, life for the majority of the Ukraine's 50 million people is hard. Ukraine also has the sad legacy of Soviet rule, in the form of the Chernobyl nuclear site with its huge environmental and human health costs.

The Ukraine economy is plagued by default, pension debt and wage arrears. This young doctor has not been paid for six months. When paid, her monthly salary is equivalent to only $44. Her family, nevertheless, is relatively well off because her husband has left the medical profession to go into commercial publishing.

Despite the current difficulties of the Ukraine economy, the doctor still finds positive reasons for supporting the liberalisation programme. She has been able to travel abroad, a privilege previously only granted to the higher echelons of the Communist Party. Finance from abroad has enabled her to attend conferences to increase her medical knowledge. As a woman she also finds less discrimination. The Communist Party, on which everything hinged, was heavily dominated by men.

This case study illustrates the support for liberalisation which can still be found among many younger, middle-class people in central and eastern Europe who appreciate the greater freedom for travel and education within the global economy. There are millions of mainly younger people in central and eastern Europe who have language and computer skills which can command well-paid jobs in new companies created with foreign capital. Unlike their elders, the young do not dream of restoring the stability and security of the communist era.

Timetable of transition

Transition has had important social and political dimensions as well as the purely economic. In the following 'timetable' important events are highlighted. They are markers in a process that has been described as the greatest theme of the late twentieth century.

In the early 1980s nearly half of the world's population lived in centrally planned economies. Now, only Cuba and North Korea describe their economies as centrally planned. Even in those economies, significant reforms are underway, especially in the area of state ownership.

No-one could have predicted how quickly the system of central planning would unravel after 1989. Looking at the timetable of events, the interaction of economic forces with military and social processes is very apparent. Underlying the changes are significant differences in the performance of different transition economies. Progress has been very impressive in central Europe and the Balkans. Countries like the Czech Republic, Slovakia and Hungary have now completed their privatisation programmes and we might question whether they should still be described as 'transition' economies. CIS states have had a much more disappointing economic performance. The ten transition economies which have already been accepted as full candidates for accession to the EU have the brightest prospects.

Timetable of transition

1960s   Economic reforms begin in Hungary.

1980s   Economic reforms begin in China.

1985   Mikhail Gorbachev (General Secretary of the Communist Party of the Soviet Union) launches *perestroika*.

1986   Chernobyl nuclear reactor disaster.

1989   March – Russian reformers win victory in multi-party elections.
June – Solidarity wins parliamentary elections in Poland.
September – Hungarian Foreign Minister orders dismantling of the fence between Hungary and Austria.
November – fall of Berlin Wall.
December – 'Velvet Revolution' in Prague.

1990   German Economic and Monetary Union.

1991   Baltic states and Ukraine leave the Soviet Union. Soviet Union dissolved. Boris Yeltsin becomes Russian President.

1992   War breaks out in Bosnia.

1993   Czechoslovakia splits into Czech Republic and Slovakia. Opening of Prague stock market.

1995   Dayton Peace Accord ends fighting in Bosnia.

1997   Czech Republic, Hungary, Slovenia, Poland and Estonia begin EU accession talks. Russian financial crisis. Russian government defaults on debts.

1999   Kosovo crisis. NATO halts air war.

2000   Growth starts to rise in transition economies. Inflation halved to single digit figures.

2001   Czech Republic, Slovakia and Hungary complete their privatisation programmes. Romania privatises its largest industrial enterprise.

2002   Protests in Poland. Calls for higher pensions, curbs on foreign capital and state support for industry.

2002   EU recognises ten transition economies as full candidates for accession: Bulgaria, Czech Republic, Estonia, Hungary, Latvia, Lithuania, Poland, Romania, Slovak Republic and Slovenia.

From plan to market

From the standpoint of economics, 'transition' describes the process of moving from a planned to a market-based system of economic organisation. Adam Smith's 'invisible hand' teaches us that a competitive market economy will deliver an efficient allocation of resources. We can also expect that a competitive market economy will promote economic growth through its effects on investment and innovation.

In principle there is no reason why a planned economy should not perform as well as a market economy, given a perfect planning system. This was shown in the famous Lange–Lerner analysis, a highly theoretical approach based on the abstract concept of an ideal social planner.

Of course, in practice, neither markets nor plans work out as theory indicates. There are market failures as well as planning failures. In real-world situations, planning failures have been more catastrophic than market failures because of the complexity of decisions, and the difficulty of collecting the information required for an economically efficient solution. The planned economy has also contributed to political failures, with lack of transparency and the centralisation of power.

The practical problems of the European centrally planned economies before transition have been well documented in the literature.

● Centrally planned economies initially enjoyed rapid growth, but by the 1970s, stagnation had set in. Policy-makers were unable to restore the initial dynamism of these economies.
● Consumers were not sovereign in centrally planned economies. Decisions on what to produce were taken by planners and bureaucrats. Shortages of critical goods and services were endemic in the system.
● The objective of enterprises was to meet predetermined targets. These were usually based on output in the previous period and did not respond to changes in demand or costs in the short or medium term.
● Prices were part of the accounting mechanism and not a guide to resource allocation.
● Rationing was the accepted method of dealing with chronic shortages of imported goods and services and foreign exchange.

When the decision was taken to abandon central planning in favour of the market mechanism, there were very few policy-makers who were trained in economics and had confidence in market solutions. There were huge gaps in the state of knowledge of orthodox market economies:

● Many policy-makers in centrally planned economies *identified markets with instability*, disorder and chaos. Stability was perceived as being synonymous with lack of change, not with equilibrium in markets.
● The planned economy had the merit of delivering a job to every citizen. There was understandable opposition to market reforms which might result in increased

unemployment, even if unemployment was of a 'temporary' character, leading to the emergence of new and more productive employment opportunities.

● The planned economy did not encourage an intuitive understanding of the *macro-economic picture*. It was based on compartmentalisation of the economy into a large number of small tasks. The interrelationships at the macro level between price level, exchange rate, interest rate and balance of payments, which are taken for granted by market economists, were not appreciated because there had been no need for policy-makers to visualise the entire economic system.

● Failures in the economy were perceived as *failures by individuals* and not as failures of policy or of institutions. A common phrase was 'Who is to blame?' People and personalities were more important than theories and their applications.

The background of the transition from plan to market, therefore, was lack of knowledge of the functioning of market economies, together with a reluctance to believe that free markets could ever organise economic activity with greater efficiency and dynamism than a centrally planned economy.

◯ The policy prescriptions

Transition can be described as the replacement of state ownership of assets and the planning machinery with private property and the market mechanism. This description tends to conceal the complexity of real-world transition, which in practice embraced the following three strategies:

1 Drastic *macro-economic stabilisation* involving fiscal and monetary restraint. Strict control was exercised over government spending and revenue, the supply of base money and the level of interest rates. All European transition economies have undergone stabilisation at some point, though there have been large variations in the timing of these policies.

2 *Deregulation and liberalisation of markets*, to bring administered prices closer to market levels. Large inefficient firms in state ownership (coal, steel and heavy industry, in particular) were restructured or privatised. The banks and other parts of the financial system were also restructured and regulated on market principles.

3 Economies were *opened up to trade and capital flows*. Trade regimes have been liberalised, tariffs and non-tariff barriers reduced, and exchange rates made fully convertible. New trade patterns have emerged, with the emphasis on growing exports to EU markets. The aim has been to harness both static and dynamic gains from trade. Capital inflows also play an important part of the transition story, with both foreign direct investment and portfolio flows into Europe's transition economies.

All three of the strategies listed above have attracted controversy. Have stabilisation policies led to falls in output? What kind of privatisation is appropriate? Has the financial sector played a positive or negative role? Has the speed of reform been too fast or too slow?

Controversy has been fuelled by the fact that transition has brought many unexpected consequences. Gérard Roland, Professor of Economics at the University of

Berkeley, California, has listed these 'surprises' in a paper (2001) which attempts to portray what has been learned from the transition process over the past ten years. The surprises were:

● large output falls after liberalisation which were not predicted by economists;
● divergence in economic performance between central Europe and the countries of the former Soviet Union;
● the development of the Mafia phenomenon: instead of the emergence of markets, the Mafia emerged in many economies;
● the huge economic success of China's transition over the past two decades.

The surprises of transition have led economists to begin to think again about transition, and to see it in a more dynamic way. This has involved looking at reform strategies from an evolutionary-institutionalist perspective. Instead of calling for 'root and branch' economic and political changes, quickly, comprehensively and simultaneously, the evolutionary-institutionalist approach suggests that adequate institutions must be developed gradually to underpin the market economy. Institutions cannot develop overnight. They require a 'trial and error' approach which focuses particularly on:

● the establishment of a minimum legal environment for business;
● security of property rights and law enforcement;
● political stability;
● the development of business and market networks;
● the building of long-term business relationships.

There is an increasing consensus among professional economists that the 'Washington consensus' view with its so-called trinity of transition (liberalization, stabilization, and privatization) is a misguided recipe for successful transition. While professional economists do not deny the need to liberalize, stabilize, and privatize, they increasingly recognize that these policies cannot achieve their goals without the institutional underpinnings of capitalism appropriate to the specific conditions of each country. In practice there has been a growing convergence within the academic community, if not a consensus, toward the evolutionary-institutionalist perspective. (Gérard Roland, 2001)

Institutional reforms

Economists are now in agreement that too little thought was given to institution building in transition economies. There is the need for a good legal system, an equitable and transparent tax system, political stability, and more. Political reform remains top of the agenda. As Table 13.2 demonstrates, there is a clear positive relationship between political freedom and market reform. In countries which are, politically speaking, partially free or not free, the state continues to be dominated by powerful business groups. The state is still the source of highly concentrated business power.

Also of concern are the high levels of 'unofficial' and unregulated activity in many economies following liberalisation (Table 13.3).

Table 13.2 Democracy and market reform in transition economies

Political institutions	Advanced market liberalisation	Average market liberalisation	Limited market liberalisation
Free (democratic)	Poland		
	Czech Republic		
	Hungary		
	Slovenia		
	Slovakia		
	Romania		
Partially free		Albania	
		Moldova	
		Ukraine	
		Russia	
		Azerbaijan	
Not free			Belarus
			Tajikistan
			Turkmenistan
			Uzbekistan

Source: Adapted from Aslund, Boon and Johnson (2001).

Table 13.3 Share of the unofficial economy, % total GDP

Country	1990	1995
Bulgaria	25.1	36.2
Hungary	28.0	29.0
Poland	19.6	12.6
Romania	13.7	19.1
Belarus	15.4	19.3
Estonia	19.9	11.5
Georgia	24.9	62.5
Latvia	12.8	35.3
Moldova	18.1	35.7
Russia	14.7	41.6
Ukraine	16.3	48.9

Source: Adapted from Aslund, Boon and Johnson (2001).

To complete the transition in Europe from plan to market, therefore, requires further far-reaching changes in institutions, in three important respects:

- *Governance*: this involves strengthening the legal system and systems of corporate governance, strengthening tax administration, improving government accounting and introducing fiscal transparency.
- *Enterprise restructuring*: there is a need for the elimination of loss-making activities in large-scale enterprises. Many of the enterprises are newly privatised which have been permitted to run up massive debts.
- *Financial sector reform*: particularly in Russia and the other CIS economies the banking system is underdeveloped, with insufficient regulation and supervision. Steps need to be taken to reduce debt and insolvency.

To conclude this section, between 1989 and 1992, 26 European countries started out on the path from plan to market. Although fundamental changes to institutions can only come about gradually, nevertheless it is anticipated that most of these countries will have completed the transition within the next decade. At that point they will face the same problems and opportunities as their western European neighbours, albeit from a very different historical perspective.

GDP levels and GDP growth levels in Europe's transition economies

It was noted in the introduction that there were significant falls in the level of national income after 1989 in most of Europe's transition economies. Only four transition economies had reached or exceeded their 1989 national income level by the year 2000. All four were in central Europe. They were Poland, Slovenia, Slovakia and Hungary (Figure 13.1).

At the other end of the scale were five CIS countries where national income more than halved between 1989 and 2000. They were Georgia, Tajikistan, Turkmenistan, Ukraine and Moldova. Most CIS countries including Russia suffered significant declines in national income and did not begin to recover until after the end of the Russian currency crisis in 1998 (Chapter 11).

It is also apparent from Table 13.1 that by 2000 most of the transition economies had begun to enjoy some growth in national income. This growth was particularly significant among some of the countries which had performed badly in the 1990s. In the case of Russia, strong growth in 2000–1 was due, partly at least, to favourable export prices for oil. Azerbaijan has also enjoyed an oil boom. Capital inflows have played a part too in the more recent surge in other CIS country growth rates.

Taking the transition period as a whole, from 1989 to 2002, there have been significant differences in economic performance between countries. As a group, CIS countries saw a significant decline until after the Russian crisis in 1998. The Baltic states and central Europe performed less badly.

What has determined the different economic performances of Europe's transition economies since 1989? A number of economists have researched this question

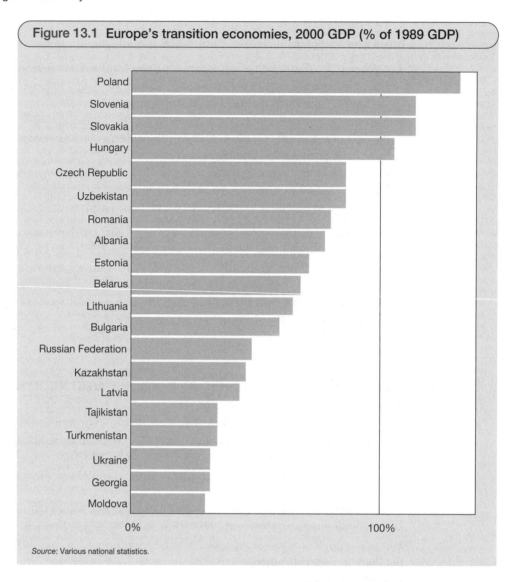

Figure 13.1 Europe's transition economies, 2000 GDP (% of 1989 GDP)

Source: Various national statistics.

using broadly similar research methodologies. The results of their research can be summarised as follows:

● *Stabilisation* of the economy was a necessary condition for recovery of output. Growth could not occur until the fiscal deficit was reduced and inflation brought under control. Countries with high inflation and budget deficits had relatively low growth rates.

● *Liberalisation of markets* (internal and external), and *structural reforms* such as the privatisation of large, inefficient state enterprises, were significant factors in promoting growth. In the early years, however, such changes may bring negative growth, and may explain the poor performance of some transition economies.

● *Different initial conditions* are important in determining differential growth rates. Important considerations under this heading are:

  – *distance* from western Europe, which tended to disadvantage CIS countries relative to the Baltic states and central Europe;
  – *political and social dislocation*: wars disadvantaged some countries, in the Balkans for example;
  – *length of time under communist rule* was a hurdle: the longer the period, the more disadvantageous for growth.

● *Legal and political institutions.* Over time, initial conditions have become less and less important in explaining differential economic performance, but the quality of institutions has become more important. Sustaining growth requires continuous, institutional improvement. A favourable climate for property rights is particularly significant.

The sequencing of changes

A question for empirical research is whether more emphasis on institutional reform at the beginning of the transition might have avoided the disastrous declines in output in transition economies during the 1990s. This is, of course, a counterfactual question. We can never be certain whether things would have been different if attention had been paid, for example, to judicial changes, the rule of law and the regulatory framework for competition. However, empirical evidence does tend to suggest that the importance of appropriate institutions increases over time. In the beginning the priority must be stabilisation but institutions become highly important in later stages. 'Good macro- and micro-economic policies can get growth started even with poor institutions but as time goes on, institutional development must proceed apace or growth will falter' (Oleh Havrylyshyn, 2001).

Privatisation

Finally, in explaining differential economic performance there is some evidence to indicate that if privatisation is badly carried out it can actually be harmful. Good privatisations are generally beneficial, but there have been damaging effects from poorly designed policies in some cases. Much of this comes down to deficiencies in corporate governance and lack of competition.

Poverty during the transition

The UN's human development index is based on three dimensions of human development:

● a long and healthy life, as measured by life expectancy at birth;
● knowledge, as measured by the adult literacy rate and school enrolment ratio;
● a decent standard of living, as measured by GDP per head.

Table 13.4 Countries suffering setbacks in the human development index

HDI now lower than 1975	HDI now lower than 1980	HDI now lower than 1985	HDI now lower than 1990
Zambia	Romania	Botswana	Belarus
	Russian Federation	Bulgaria	Cameroon
	Zimbabwe	Burundi	Kenya
		Latvia	Lithuania
		Lesotho	Moldova
			South Africa
			Ukraine

Source: Adapted from UNDP *Human Development Report* (2001).

Although all regions of the world have made progress in human development over the last two decades, there are differences in performances across countries. The transition economies of Europe are numbered among those which are calculated by the UN to have suffered significant setbacks in human development (Table 13.4).

Transition in Europe has entailed massive social costs, especially in the Balkans and CIS states. As national income declined in the 1990s, social expenditure could not be maintained. Falling per capita income and rising levels of unemployment exacted a heavy toll in terms of human welfare. Life expectancy, particularly for males, fell. Average life expectancy dropped from 69 to 65 in transition economies in the 1990s, recovering more recently to 67. Secondary school enrolment ratios, particularly for females, declined (Table 13.5).

Table 13.5 Countries where girls' net secondary enrolment ratio declined, 1985–97

Asia and the Pacific	Latin America and the Caribbean	Sub-Saharan Africa	Central and eastern Europe and CIS
Mongolia	Bolivia	Angola	Bulgaria
	Ecuador	Congo	Croatia
	Haiti	Ivory Coast	Estonia
		Guinea	Georgia
		Mozambique	Kyrgyzstan
			Latvia
			Romania
			Russia

Source: Adapted from UNDP *Human Development Report* (2001).

In all the transition economies the number of poor households rose. In Russia it has been estimated that, by the end of 1995, 40 per cent of the population was living in poverty.

What are the causes of the increase in poverty in Europe's transition economies?

● high rates of unemployment, particularly amongst the unskilled;
● wage arrears – in Russia in the 1990s only 40 per cent of the workforce was paid in full and on time;
● the real value of social benefit payments has declined: in the 1990s in Russia, pensions and allowances were only a quarter of their value before transition;
● structural change, particularly the decline of heavy industry (coal, metallurgy, chemicals) and of agriculture, has brought increasing regional disparities in per capita incomes;
● deterioration in the quantity and quality of publicly provided goods and services – health, education, subsidised housing and utilities – has reduced the social wage.

Leaving aside the humanitarian arguments, why are so many economists and policy-makers so concerned about poverty levels in Europe's transition economies? The severity and depth of poverty certainly took many observers by surprise. As Table 13.1 indicates, even though transition economies have had positive growth rates since 1999, unemployment remains high and could well be underestimated.

Opinion surveys also indicate that many more people regard themselves as poor than are counted as such in the official estimates. Some work carried out by the World Bank showed that in Russia very large numbers of the population regard themselves as poor and are very pessimistic about the future. They are dissatisfied with liberalisation and negative about future economic and social reforms. These results indicate to economists and policy-makers that it will be difficult in the future to sustain a faster reform agenda in some of Europe's transition economies unless there are significant inroads into widespread poverty and alienation.

Trade liberalisation and the exchange rate

Trade under COMECON

In the pre-transition decades, the economies of central and eastern Europe, under Soviet domination, belonged to CMEA, the Council for Mutual Economic Assistance, known as COMECON, which is the English acronym. The exception to the rule was Yugoslavia, which was not a COMECON member. In 1989 over 60 per cent of overall foreign trade was still within the COMECON bloc, though east–west trade had been growing steadily since 1965.

The COMECON system had fundamental flaws which go a long way towards explaining the poor economic performance of its members before 1989. It was a system in which the state dominated international relations, far removed from the free market principles which underpinned the trade of the west.

- Trade relations were handled by *foreign trade organisations* (FTOs). Enterprises could not trade on their own account. FTOs specialised in particular products and an industrial country would have as many as fifty FTOs. The Soviet Union's oil FTO was the world's single largest oil exporter.
- Foreign trade was a *planned economy activity*. There was no doctrine of comparative advantage to promote specialisation and exchange. If domestic resources were insufficient to permit planned output, imports were required. Exports were considered as a means of paying for necessary imports.
- COMECON, in theory, was supposed to *co-ordinate national plans*. Trade between COMECON members was 'residual' in character. In practice the technical problems involved in co-ordinating various national plans were insurmountable. Trade within COMECON was basically bilateral and inter-governmental.
- There were *multiple exchange rates* for various purposes:

  - the *'official' exchange rate*, which was generally overvalued;
  - the *'commercial' exchange rate*, calculated as the amount of domestic currency needed in exchange for a unit of foreign currency;
  - *'non-commercial' exchange rates* for foreign tourists;
  - *'subsidised' exchange rates* on a product-by-product basis to encourage certain exports or imports.

In January 1990 the COMECON countries decided to move to world prices and abandon multiple exchange rates. The system had been under pressure for twenty years or more, and accelerated with reforms in Hungary and Poland, when private businesses began to trade on their own account. It was a common complaint that COMECON goods were poor in quality by the standards of the west. The planning system had failed entirely to promote dynamic gains from trade.

Liberalisation

Liberalisation in international trade was supposed to bring to transition economies the benefits of specialisation and dynamic gains from competition. The transition economies were expected to reduce tariffs and introduce exchange rate convertibility. Most of the transition economies of Europe took up relatively low exchange rates in the post-COMECON world. Czechoslovakia, for example, devalued the currency by 90 per cent in the first year of transition. This gave a boost to exports. However, not all COMECON countries were able to reorient their trade patterns and trade fell (Table 13.6). The worst-affected countries were Armenia, Azerbaijan, Georgia and Latvia, whose external trade virtually ceased when COMECON collapsed. For some transition countries, the break-up of the COMECON arrangements was probably the single most important factor in explaining the fall in output. However, there was clearly no alternative to the break-up of COMECON, as countries like Poland, Hungary and Czechoslovakia had already insisted on leaving the Soviet-dominated trading bloc. Table 13.6 shows Hungary and Estonia to be the only countries with significant exports of high-technology goods as a percentage of manufactured exports.

Quality of exports and FDI

One of the key reasons for the collapse of COMECON was the fact that its trade was based on goods of low quality which could not compete in world markets. The argument was that exposure to competition would force innovation and improvements in product quality. Has this happened? To some extent, yes. The Czech Republic, Hungary, Poland and Slovenia have significantly increased the quality of their exports. Much of this quality improvement has been associated with foreign direct investment.

For example, Hungary had strong inflows of FDI during the 1990s. This has made a strong impact on productivity levels and quality in the export sector. This is because the Hungarian workforce is well educated, even though capital and technology are at low levels. FDI supports quality export activity. Interestingly, research indicates that this effect of FDI on quality in the export sector is strongest in areas close to the EU border: for example, the north-east of Hungary.

Other countries have failed to show significant improvements in the quality of exports. Russian, Slovakian and Bulgarian exports are comparable to imports from Turkey and India, i.e. towards the lower end of the world quality spectrum.

Table 13.6 The structure of trade in European transition economies

Part 1

Country	Imports of goods and services (as a % of GDP)		Exports of goods and services (as a % of GDP)	
	1990	1999	1990	1999
Armenia	46	50	35	21
Bulgaria	37	52	33	44
Croatia	–	48	–	61
Czech Republic	43	65	45	64
Estonia	–	83	–	77
Hungary	29	55	31	53
Kazakhstan	–	40	–	45
Latvia	49	58	48	47
Moldova	–	65	–	50
Poland	21	32	28	26
Romania	26	34	17	30
Russian Federation	18	28	18	46
Slovakia	36	67	27	62
Turkmenistan	–	62	–	42
Ukraine	29	52	28	53

Part 2

Country	Primary exports (as a % of merchandise exports)		Manufactured exports (as a % of merchandise exports)	
	1990	*1999*	*1990*	*1999*
Armenia	–	34	–	63
Bulgaria	–	–	–	–
Croatia	–	24	–	76
Czech Republic	–	12	–	88
Estonia	–	31	–	69
Hungary	35	13	63	85
Kazakhstan	–	74	–	25
Latvia	–	43	–	57
Moldova	–	73	–	27
Poland	36	21	59	77
Romania	26	21	73	78
Russian Federation	–	57	–	25
Slovakia	–	14	–	82
Turkmenistan	–	–	–	–
Ukraine	–	–	–	–

Part 3

Country	High-technology exports (as a % of manufactured exports)	
	1990	*1999*
Armenia	–	6
Bulgaria	–	–
Croatia	–	11
Czech Republic	–	13
Estonia	–	25
Hungary	–	28
Kazakhstan	–	11
Latvia	–	11
Moldova	–	8
Poland	11	10
Romania	5	6
Russian Federation	–	14
Slovakia	–	8
Turkmenistan	–	–
Ukraine	–	–

Source: UNDP *Human Development Report* (2001).

Exchange rates

Since the collapse of the COMECON multiple exchange rate system, there has been a diversity of exchange rate strategies in transition countries. The Baltic states and Bosnia have currency boards. Other transition countries have moved towards managed flexibility. For transition economies seeking EU membership, the importance of the euro in currency boards and in managed flexibility has been increasing. Countries seeking accession are advised by the European Central Bank to orientate their currencies towards the euro. For example, Lithuania has re-pegged its currency, moving from the dollar to the euro in February 2002.

Box 13.1 Exchange rate strategies for accession countries

Monetary and exchange rate strategies

In the pre-accession phase, no single exchange rate strategy is prescribed, although an increasing degree of orientation towards the euro would be in line with further economic and financial integration with the euro area. However, the unilateral adoption of the euro as legal tender ('euroisation') is incompatible with the rationale and multilateral framework of EMU. Following EU accession, ERM II should not be seen as a mere 'waiting room' for the adoption of the euro, but as a meaningful policy framework within which to prepare the accession economies for monetary union and to achieve further real and nominal convergence. Euro-based currency boards may be judged compatible with ERM II, subject to an assessment on a case-by-case basis.

Source: Europe Central Bank (2001).

Capital flows

Capital flows have been an important part of the transition story in Europe. But there have been significant differences between countries, and groups of countries, in terms both of the total capital inflow and of its composition, i.e. when disaggregated into:

- foreign direct investment (FDI)
- portfolio investment
- IMF credit and loans
- exceptional financing.

Total capital flows

The key facts are as follows:

- The highest total capital inflows have been into Baltic countries where flows averaged 10 per cent of GDP during the second half of the 1990s.
- The next highest total capital inflows, around 5 per cent of GDP, were into CIS countries (excluding Russia) and the countries of central–eastern Europe,

principally Slovenia, Poland, Hungary and the Czech Republic. Slightly lower levels of capital inflow were recorded in the countries of south-eastern Europe (Albania, Bulgaria, Croatia and Romania).

● Russia was unusual in having net *outflows* over the period 1995–2000, because of significant capital outflows. This is usually interpreted as 'capital flight' i.e. private capital seeking more secure and possibly less transparent homes.

The picture on total capital inflows is given by Figure 13.2.

Composition of capital flows

There were also significant differences in the composition of capital flows in the 1990s between countries and groups of countries.

● In central–eastern Europe (Slovenia, Poland, Hungary, Czech Republic) capital inflows were principally foreign direct investment (purchase of a stake in a

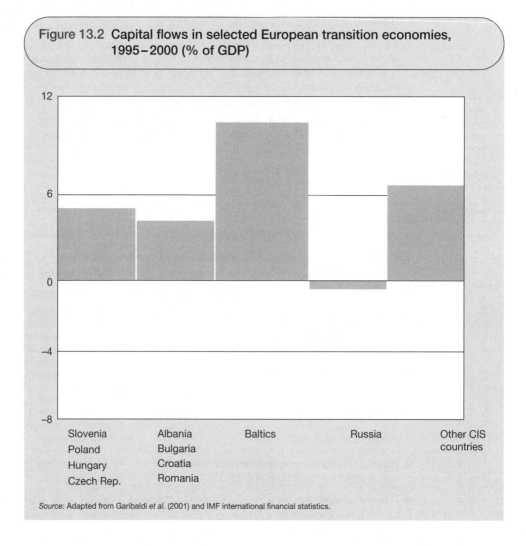

Figure 13.2 **Capital flows in selected European transition economies, 1995 – 2000 (% of GDP)**

Source: Adapted from Garibaldi *et al.* (2001) and IMF international financial statistics.

company). There was also significant portfolio investment (equities, bonds and other commercial paper) and private lending. IMF lending was negative, indicating *repayment of loans.*

● Baltic countries received large FDI. They also received significant inflows in the form of private lending to banks and companies, but virtually no IMF assistance.

● For south-eastern Europe (Albania, Bulgaria, Croatia and Romania), the bulk of the capital inflow was FDI and private loans to banks and companies. There was also some debt rescheduling (see below), as part of an IMF assistance package. Bulgaria was the main recipient of IMF credit.

● In the CIS countries there was very little private lending and virtually no portfolio investment. Inflows took the form of FDI and large amounts of lending by the IMF and World Bank, plus what is known as *exceptional financing,* i.e. permission granted by the IMF to increase a country's external debt. This mainly took the form of debt forgiveness and debt rescheduling.

● In Russia exceptional financing was a very important source of capital inflow throughout the transition. Whereas IMF credit and loans and exceptional assistance decreased in most transition economies after 1995, in Russia and in other CIS countries it actually accelerated after the Russian currency crisis in 1998. There was also a 'bubble' in portfolio investment in Russia before 1998, which collapsed in 1999. Recovery in foreign direct investment and portfolio investment is proving to be very slow (Case Study 13.2).

CASE STUDY 13.2

Foreigners remain on the sidelines despite market's strong performance

The Russian capital markets may be booming, and portfolio investors are eyeing shares and bonds with a growing appetite. But foreign direct investors, nowhere more than in the financial services sector, are still holding back.

Individually, finance professionals have been arriving in Moscow in large numbers as a shake-out takes place among employers elsewhere. But collectively, whether for banks or insurers, pension funds or advisers, most managers have been keeping a respectful distance from Russia when it comes to committing their own corporate resources.

After a peak in 1997 and a plummet in 1998 with the August financial default, the Russian markets have proved among the best relative performers in the world for investors at the turn of the millennium. Ratings have risen, and economically the Russian 'story' has looked increasingly positive under the administration of President Vladimir Putin.

But direct investment continues to be sluggish across all sectors, and many of the funds which are coming in to the country are Russian offshore money returning home from havens such as Cyprus and Luxembourg. Financial services has accounted for a fraction of the modest overall amount in the past few years.

Russian companies have begun to seek full foreign listings in New York, London and Frankfurt, and a sharp rise is likely in the coming months in their efforts to raise funds through the issue of bonds.

In part, the explanation is the still relatively modest size and limited profitability of many parts of the financial services sector. Despite its relatively strong performance, Russia still holds a very small absolute total share of emerging market funds, with mainstream foreign pension funds continuing to hesitate about investment within the country.

In the build-up to domestic pension fund reform, coming against a backdrop of continued public suspicion of institutions and the financial markets alike, domestic mutual funds are still starved of funds, while regulation means there are high fixed costs for those operators who are present.

Another issue is protectionism. In the insurance sector, for example, domestic compa-nies have been lobbying hard for more time to establish themselves before they are exposed to the liberalisation sought as a condition for Russia's membership of the World Trade Organisation.

In banking, the state's Sberbank and Vneshtorgbank hold the vast majority of deposits, and a considerable share of lending, as well as benefiting from other privileges linked to the guarantee of the state.

Just as Russian industrialists are keen to have first pick of state-owned oil and other assets coming up for privatisation, so some Russian fund managers are attempting to ensure forthcoming guidelines on pension reform give them the best chance of controlling future funds, to the exclusion of their foreign rivals.

Finally, there is bureaucracy, an unclear regulatory and legal environment, and the cultural issues surrounding operating in the Russian market that hold many foreign operators at bay, particularly during uncertain economic times elsewhere.

But policy initiatives such as the introduction of compulsory car insurance, the creation of private pension schemes, and bank sector restructuring all suggest the market is set to become larger and more attractive.

If the Russian economy continues to grow and reform, once the first generation of restructuring has taken place by Russian operators, the foreigners may start to come in, too.

Source: Andrew Jack, Financial Times, 16 September 2002. Reprinted with permission.

Comment on case study 13.2

Russia is apparently recovering in 2002 from the crisis of 1998. Overseas investors are arriving in Moscow. Many of these investors, working on their own behalf or for banks, insurance funds and pension funds, have lost their jobs in US and European finance centres because of the stock market downturn.

Russia's private capital inflows have been slow to recover after 1998. Capital flight has reversed to some extent, coming back to Russia from offshore tax havens. But foreign portfolio investment in Russia is lacking impetus for growth.

There are various reasons why portfolio investment and private lending to Russia is likely to be slow growing. There is mistrust and suspicion of Russia's financial institutions. Foreigners also have to overcome protectionist sentiments in Russia. Domestic insurance companies in Russia have lobbied the WTO for more time to adjust to foreign competition. Pension funds in Russia are trying to exclude foreign rivals.

There is an unwelcoming cultural and legal environment in Russia which tends to deter foreign capital when times are hard. When better days return, these barriers may not seem so much of a deterrent to capital inflows for investors balancing out risk and return.

International banks

The growth in private capital flows to transition economies has been accompanied by a surge in the growth in the operations of international banks in central and eastern Europe (Table 13.7). Only one of the top ten banks is non-European (Citibank from the US). None are UK-based.

Table 13.7 **The ten largest international banks operating in central and eastern European countries, 2001**

Rank	Bank	Originating country	Total assets (€ million)	Market share (%)
1	KBC	Belgium	24	11
2	BA/CA	Austria	22	10
3	Erste Bank	Austria	20	9
4	Unicredito	Italy	18	8
5	Citibank	US	15	7
6	Société Générale	France	15	7
7	ING	Netherlands	12	6
8	Raiffeisen	Austria	11	5
9	Banca Commerciale Italiano	Italy	10	5
10	Commerzbank	Germany	8	4

Source: Adapted from various bank sources.

In these banks at the present time, total deposits as a percentage of GDP exceed total loans as a percentage of GDP. This reflects the fact that they are mostly banks of EU origin which historically have had cautious lending policies. But it does indicate a potential for *higher lending* to the more stable, faster-growing transition economies of Europe.

Causes of capital flow to Europe's transition economies

Detailed research by economists into the reasons for capital flow into these economies has yielded few surprises.

● *Inward direct investment* is heavily influenced by traditional economic fundamentals. Countries which attract large amounts of direct investment tend to have:

  – macro-economic stability;
  – liberalised trade;
  – favourable national resource endowments;
  – no direct barriers to inward investment;
  – a high level of economic reforms.

● *Portfolio investment* is poorly explained by traditional economic fundamentals (Garibaldi *et al.*, 2001). Here it is the *quality of governance* in Europe's transition economies which seems to be critical. Secure markets seem to be important, and also the protection of property rights. But none of the economic fundamentals which explain FDI have any robust role in explaining portfolio flows.

EU accession and transition economies

◯ Conditions for accession

The Rome Treaty, modified by the European Single Act, and the Maastricht Treaty has set out the conditions for accession to the EU. Any European country, including European transition economies, must satisfy the following conditions:

● They must be *stable democracies*, committed to the rule of law, respect for human rights and protection of minorities.
● They must be *market economies*, committed to economic and monetary union. In particular, they must support:

- free movement of goods, services and capital workers;
- the Common Agricultural Policy;
- fiscal harmonisation.

In addition, accession countries are now required to be committed to the Maastricht convergence criteria for economic and monetary union:

● a stable exchange rate;
● public debt less than 60 per cent of GDP;
● public sector deficit no greater than 3 per cent of GDP;
● inflation rate not greater than 1.5 per cent above the EU economy with the lowest inflation, and interest rate no greater than 2 per cent above the EU nation with the lowest interest rate.

◯ Why join the EU?

The difficulties for transition economies in satisfying the EU conditions, especially the Maastricht convergence criteria, cannot be overestimated. Yet five economies (the Czech Republic, Hungary, Estonia, Poland and Slovenia) opened negotiations with the EU in March 1998. Five other economies (Bulgaria, Latvia, Lithuania, Romania and Slovakia) began negotiations for entry in February 2000. In many transition economies the objective of EU membership unites people of many different political and economic philosophies. Why?

● Trade flows are already bringing the two halves of the continent together. In 2000 western Europe accounted for 70 per cent of the exports of the European transition economies (excluding Russia). The comparative figure for 1989 was 40 per cent.
● The EU is the most important source of private capital for Europe's transition economies. The transition economies also look to the EU for managerial and technological inputs.
● The overriding political and social factors pushing accession forward should not be underestimated. Most of the younger people in transition economies, together with the better-off and well-educated, are eager to discard the legacy of the communist past. However, in Poland, which was at one time the most pro-EU of

the accession countries, opinion polls indicate that there has been a decline in support for the EU over the past two years.

EU attitude to accession

In principle the EU member countries welcome wider union. This would bring more secure and predictable economic and political benefits. Three other European countries are also becoming involved in accession talks, i.e. the small economies of Malta and Cyprus, plus Turkey. The EU president is on record as saying it is still too early to set a firm date for accession. Reasons for slow progress include EU dissatisfaction with the pace of reform, in particular the pace of market liberalisation. Particularly criticised are the Czech Republic, Bulgaria and Romania. Romania has been singled out by the EU for the scale of its inefficient, loss-making state industries. Russia has been told that it is nowhere near achieving EU membership conditions.

A way of measuring the policy framework of transition economies, in terms of the requirements of EU membership, can be the index of economic freedom (IEF). The IEF looks at the policy, regulatory and legal framework of individual countries. A country with the appropriate framework is assigned a value of 5. A value of 1 is reserved for countries with the worst economic freedom indicators.

Table 13.8, calculated for the transition countries closest to EU membership, shows that the IEF index for these countries is still well below that of the average EU country.

There are other reasons why some EU member countries have doubts about the accession of transition economies. In summary they are:

● The high costs of extending the CAP to transition economies, which have a higher share of agriculture in their GDP. The EU average share of agriculture is 3 per cent. Agriculture in Hungary and Poland is valued at 7 per cent of GDP.

Table 13.8 The IEF index for those transition economies closest to accession

	Degree of openness	Fiscal policy and size of gov.	Monetary policy and financial sector policies	Price system distortion	Rule of law	Average
EU average	4.52	2.45	4.11	4.11	3.93	3.82
Czech Rep.	4.5	3.0	4.5	3.5	4.5	4.0
Hungary	3.0	2.5	3.0	3.5	3.5	3.1
Poland	3.0	2.75	2.0	3.5	3.5	2.95
Slovakia	4.0	2.25	3.0	3.0	3.0	3.05
Slovenia	2.0	2.75	3.5	2.5	2.5	2.65
CEE average	3.3	2.65	3.2	3.2	3.4	3.15

Source: Adapted from Barbone and Zalduendo (1996).

● The costs of restructuring the transition economies, which would need to be met from EU funds. All their regions would qualify for EU funds, crowding out the present major beneficiaries such as Greece, Portugal, Spain and Ireland.

● Fears of large future flows of migrant workers into EU countries. There are strong incentives to migrate, with huge disparities in wages and working conditions. EU members like Austria are vociferous in their demands that the EU anticipate large waves of migrant labour from transition economies.

CASE STUDY 13.3

Poland seeks more EU compensation

Poland will seek higher production quotas and extended tariff protection – among other potentially controversial measures – to compensate for lower direct payments to its farmers after it joins the European Union.

Warsaw's amended negotiating stance on farming, details of which were made available to the FT, will seek to transfer funds earmarked for rural development to top up direct payments to farmers.

Poland fears it will be unable to tap all those funds – which carry exacting bureaucratic and co-financing requirements – especially in its first year of membership.

After joining the single market, Poland will also ask to keep import tariffs on products including grain, hops and tobacco, which it says are especially sensitive to competition from subsidised EU imports.

Polish officials want to level the playing field in view of the European Commission's proposal to offer candidates just 25 per cent of the direct payments extended to existing members, rising to full levels over 10 years.

Poland's new negotiating stance marks the opening salvo in talks on the financial aspects of membership, expected to be hard-fought on both sides. Leszek Miller's government is expected to formally approve the new stance next week. Poland is the largest country hoping to join the EU in 2004.

But Poland's request for tariff protection is likely to face stiff opposition among existing EU members.

Source: John Reed in Warsaw and Michael Mann, *Financial Times*, 27 September 2002. Reprinted with permission.

Comment on case study 13.3

In 2004 Poland expects to join the EU. Poland is the largest of the EU accession countries and its negotiating stance is, therefore, very important. Poland has a large agricultural sector. It is proposing that rural development payments from the EU should be diverted instead to making direct payments to farmers. This is unlikely to be popular with existing EU members.

Opposition from EU members is also likely to be strong when Poland asks to be permitted to maintain tariffs on imports of cereals, hops and tobacco.

There is no level playing field here because these products attract significant EU subsidies at the present time. Accession countries will only get 25 per cent of the existing subsidy, rising to 100 per cent over a ten-year period, once they are in the single market. Poland believes that this is unfair and that domestic producers will lose out to competition from EU imports in the short and medium term – hence its wish to maintain tariffs on accession. Negotiations between Poland and the EU are likely to be protracted.

Summary

- In Europe, transition countries have had a massive political agenda as well as an economic transformation. China has taken the path to the market, but without root and branch political reform.

- The downside of European transition has been the decline in GDP. In 2001 the output of transition economies was, on average, one-third below its 1989 level.

- In practice planning failures have been more catastrophic than market failures. The problems of the European centrally planned economies have been well documented.

- When the decision was taken to abandon central planning in favour of the market there were few policy-makers in these countries who were trained in economics or who had confidence in market solutions.

- There have been many unexpected consequences of transition, including the large output falls after liberalisation. Economists now believe that too little thought was given to institution-building in transition economies.

- By 2000 most transition economies had begun to enjoy some growth. As a group, CIS countries have performed significantly less well than central Europe and the Baltic states.

- The transition economies of Europe have suffered significant setbacks in human development: life expectancy, school enrolment rates and other aspects of human welfare have deteriorated.

- Some transition economies did not benefit from trade liberalisation when COMECON collapsed. Neither has the quality of their exports improved. There have also been differences between countries in terms of total capital inflow and its composition.

- Transition economies are anxious for EU membership. Ten economies have been recognised as full candidates for accession. Some EU members are doubtful about accession, especially the costs of extending the CAP to countries like Hungary and Poland.

Key concepts

- From plan to market
- Root and branch economic reform
- Evolutionary-institutionalist perspective
- Governance
- Sequencing of changes
- Capital inflows
- Capital flight
- EU accession

Questions for discussion

1 There have been very significant differences in the economic performance of transition economies. Why?

2 Has the 'Washington consensus' of liberalisation, stabilisation and privatisation worked in transition economies?

3 Some economists call for far-reaching changes in institutions in Europe's transition economies. What changes do they have in mind? Will they work?

4 Which transition economies have suffered setbacks in human development? Why?

5 Explain foreign trade and exchange rates under COMECON. What has 'trade liberalisation' meant? What has 'exchange rate liberalisation' implied?

6 There have been significant differences in capital flows to transition economies. What are these differences? Why do they occur?

7 Why do transition economies want to join the EU? Should EU members welcome their accession?

8 'Unlike their elders the young do not dream of restoring the stability and security of the communist era.' Why?

Suggested reading

Aslund, A., Boon, P. and Johnson, S. (2001) 'Escaping the under-reform trap', *IMF Staff Papers*, vol. 48 (special edition), pp. 88–108.

Barbone, L. and Zalduendo, J. (1996) *EU Accession and Economic Growth: The Challenge for Central and Eastern European Countries*, Washington, DC: World Bank.

Bornstein, M. (1973) *Plan and Market: Economic Reform in Eastern Europe*, London: Yale University Press.

From Plan to Market (1996) World Development Report, Oxford: Oxford University Press.

Fischer, S. (2001) 'Ten years of transition: looking back and looking forward', *IMF Staff Papers*, vol. 48 (special edition), pp. 1–8.

Garibaldi, P., Mora, N. *et al.* (2001) 'What moves capital to transition economies', *IMF Staff Papers*, vol. 48 (special edition), pp. 109–45.

Havrylyshyn, O. (2001) 'Recovery and growth in transition: a decade of evidence', *IMF Staff Papers*, vol. 48 (special edition), pp. 53–87.

Kaser, M. (1967) *Comecon: Integration Problems of the Planned Economies*, Oxford: Oxford University Press.

Lange, O. (1938) *On the Economic Theory of Socialism*, Minneapolis: University of Minnesota.

Roland, G. (2001) 'Ten years after . . . transition and economics', *IMF Staff Papers*, vol. 48 (special edition), pp. 29–52.

Stiglitz, J. E. (1999) *Whither Reform? Ten Years of the Transition*, World Bank Annual Conference on Development Economics, Washington, DC: World Bank.

United Nations (2001) *Human Development Report 2001*, published for the United Nations Development Programme (UNDP) New York, Oxford: UNDP.

Chapter 14

International institutions

Introduction

After World War II, the post-war planners in both the US and Britain were determined to break with the economic nationalism and isolationism which had characterised the inter-war period, and had led to the decline in international trade. There was a positive political side to the agenda. The belief was that freedom in international transactions would promote world peace. A new liberal economic order was designed to provide the foundations for world prosperity.

At Bretton Woods in New Hampshire in 1944, the British delegates were led by Keynes and Lord Halifax. The US experts were led by Harry Dexter White. The Bretton Woods agreement set up two of the important institutions of the post-war world: the International Monetary Fund (IMF) and the International Bank for Reconstruction and Development (IBRD or World Bank).

The story of Bretton Woods, and the Anglo-American discussions which led up to it, have been told in Richard Gardner's classic study of international relations. He described Bretton Woods as 'the greatest ever adventure in economic diplomacy'. Reading his account of the events of those days, it is not difficult to recapture the extraordinary efforts that were made to create a new liberal world order. There is a famous scribbled verse, salvaged from the official papers at the end of the Bretton Woods conference, which recalls the sense of excitement among the negotiators:

> *In Washington Lord Halifax*
> *Once whispered to Lord Keynes,*
> *'It's true they have the money bags,*
> *But we have all the brains.'*

Gardner's study reminds us that the objective of Bretton Woods was nothing less than the reconstruction of a multilateral system of world trade and payments. But the objective was something less than free trade. It was a system in which tariffs were to be reduced to moderate levels and were to be made non-discriminatory. In Britain the experience of the inter-war period had destroyed faith in unqualified free trade. Britain had supported free trade and the gold standard in the 1930s, but these policies had brought widespread unemployment. In the United States there was also a strong attachment to intervention in trade, in the form of 'reasonable, moderate, and decent levels of taxes'. On the monetary side there was little commitment to markets in the form of freely fluctuating exchange rates. The planners at Bretton Woods required currencies to be convertible, but they intended to fix the rates at which currencies could be exchanged, and to maintain controls on financial flows.

It is important to recognise that in the history of the Bretton Woods institutions the market mechanism did not go unchallenged. As Joseph Stiglitz has pointed out in his recent critique of the World Bank and the IMF, these institutions, in their original conceptions, were based on the recognition – which we owe to Keynes – that markets often do not work well. Stiglitz reminds us that:

> over the years since its inception, the IMF has changed markedly. Founded on the belief that markets often work badly, it now champions market supremacy with ideological fervour . . . Keynes would be rolling over in his grave were he to see what has happened to his child.   (Stiglitz, 2002, p. 13)

Turning now from the IMF and World Bank to GATT, in October 1946 a preparatory committee gathered in London to work on a charter for an International Trade Organisation within the framework of the United Nations. The final drafting of the ITO charter took place in 1947, but by this time the US business community was arrayed against multilateral trade. The ITO was replaced by GATT, and eventually by the WTO (Chapter 5). In GATT there was a commitment to reducing tariffs, preferences, quantitative restrictions and other impediments to trade. These were clear steps towards multilateralism but did not ensure unfettered free trade.

Parallel to the Bretton Woods system were developments in the United Nations. In June 1945 the United Nations Charter was signed in San Francisco. It is significant that much of the debate on post-war international institutions actually took place at first within the United Nations. The ITO was first perceived as a specialised agency of the UN. The Bretton Woods conference itself was initially a United Nations-sponsored monetary and financial conference. By 1947, however, it was clear that the United Nations was becoming divided into two hostile camps reflecting an increasingly divided world economy. On one side was ranged the US and her European allies. On the other side was the Soviet bloc. The Soviet Union did not ratify the Bretton Woods agreements. The IMF, the World Bank and GATT increasingly came to be regarded as instruments of US policy. The voting policies of the IMF and the World Bank, as compared with the United Nations, tended to reinforce this impression. The principle which applied in the UN was 'one country, one vote'. All countries had the same influence in the decision-making process. In the IMF and the World Bank votes were weighted according to the financial contribution of the member country. Rich countries such as the US had a much greater influence over decision-making.

This chapter discusses the role of those international institutions which have governed the world economy since World War II: the IMF, the World Bank and the specialised UN agencies. We will see that they have attracted a fair amount of blame over the last half-century, as well as their share of praise.

The IMF

The IMF was set up in 1944, with 44 member countries. Its full title is the International Monetary Fund. It comprises 180 member states at the present time. From the beginning it was located in Washington, USA.

The quota system

The basis of IMF power and influence is its financial resources, currently worth around $270 billion. These resources come from the subscriptions of member countries. Each member's subscription or quota is determined on the basis of its national income. Rich countries have a higher subscription than poor countries.

On joining the IMF a country pays 25 per cent of its subscription in the form of widely accepted foreign currencies: the euro, dollar, yen or pound sterling. The remainder of the quota is paid in the country's own currency. Quotas are reviewed every five years.

Since its inception, the IMF has been a large holder of gold reserves because many quotas were paid initially in gold. Today the IMF is one of the world's most important holders of gold reserves.

Objectives of the IMF

The IMF is governed by articles of agreement which provide the legal framework for the international monetary system. When it was set up the international monetary system, as overseen by the IMF, covered five areas:

● *Convertibility.* The IMF determined the circumstances in which countries made their national currencies convertible with other currencies.

- *The exchange rate regime.* The IMF decided on the ways in which currency values were to be corrected, and the choice to be made between fixed and flexible exchange rates.
- *Balance of payments adjustment.* The IMF resolved how balance of payments surpluses and deficits were to be accommodated between countries.
- *Reserve assets.* The IMF held reserves from which debtor countries could borrow in limited quantities. Initially the reserve assets of the IMF were gold, sterling and the dollar. In 1970 the first special drawing rights (SDRs) were allocated to members. Essentially the IMF created a special drawing account for each member. Members could draw SDRs proportional to their share in Fund quotas, when they were in difficulties. SDRs were, therefore, to be counted as reserve assets. The currencies of the major industrial countries went to make up the SDR.
- *International management.* The IMF provided machinery for consultation and collaboration on international monetary problems.

In Chapter 10 ('The exchange rate and economic policy') we learned how the Bretton Woods system broke down in the early 1970s. The Bretton Woods system was essentially one of fixed exchange rates. In the late 1960s, when the US ran into persistent balance of payments problems, the system collapsed. By 1973 all major currencies were floating, and by 1978 a system of managed flexibility had emerged. Essentially, the central banks of individual nations had taken over the responsibility for the first three of the above objectives: convertibility, the exchange rate regime and balance of payments adjustment.

In the system which emerged by 1978, the forces of supply and demand interacted on the foreign exchange market to produce an equilibrium price (exchange rate) and quantity of every traded currency. But it was a managed system, in which national central banks intervened, buying and selling currencies to influence the exchange rate within target bands.

The IMF still had a role to play in relation to convertibility, exchange rates and balance of payments adjustment, but it was a *much reduced role*. It was given the responsibility of ensuring that:

- individual countries or groups of countries did not engage in *destabilising speculation* over exchange rates;
- individual countries or groups of countries did not attempt to *influence artificially* the value of exchange rates in order to gain a trading advantage.

This still left the IMF with two of the roles which had been assigned to it in 1944, i.e. holding reserve assets which debtor countries could borrow, and a management role in providing the machinery for collaboration and consultation on international and monetary issues.

Lending reserve assets

The IMF is able to make loans to debtor countries that are experiencing balance of payments problems. Loans take the form of the currencies supplied by financially strong countries (euro, dollar, sterling) plus SDRs. If necessary the IMF can supplement its own resources by borrowing from financially strong member countries.

IMF loans are provided under an 'arrangement'. This sets out the conditions of the loan: that is, its 'conditionality'. Usually a country has to agree to carry out specific economic programmes and broader reforms in order to qualify for assistance.

The IMF has different types of loans, or 'facilities', to meet the specific needs of members. Some have very low, i.e. 'concessionary', rates of interest. There are also different repayment periods.

The main facilities available in 2001 were:

- *Poverty reduction and growth facility* (PRGF). This is concessionary finance (interest rate 0.5 per cent) for low-income countries, to be repaid over a period of between five and ten years.
- *Stand-by arrangement* (SBA). This is short-term finance to meet balance of payments problems, and has to be repaid within two to four years. It is the most widely used IMF facility and attracts a market-related rate of interest.
- *Compensatory finance facility* (CFF) is one of the oldest forms of IMF lending. It assists countries suffering an unexpected fall in export earnings because of a collapse in world commodity prices.
- *Supplemental reserve facility* (SRF). This was introduced in 1997 to meet the need for large-scale financing for countries suffering from massive capital outflow. The loans are short-term (one to one-and-a-half years) and attract high rates of interest.
- *Contingent credit lines* (CCL) introduced in 1999 are designed to help a country avoid 'financial contagion' (see Chapter 11). Its aim is to help avoid a crisis by boosting confidence in the economy. The loans are short-term.

The IMF will also provide emergency assistance to countries which are coming out of war or civil disturbance, or who have experienced a natural disaster.

International management

The IMF supports consultation and collaboration among its member countries. Countries meet together in *'groups'*. The two major groups, in terms of influence over policy, are the G-7 and the G-20.

Group of seven (G-7)

Canada
France
Germany
Italy
Japan
United Kingdom
United States

The G-7 major industrial countries have held annual economic summits (meetings at the level of head of state or government) since 1975. Since 1987, the G-7 Finance Ministers and central bank governors have met at least semi-annually to monitor developments in the world economy and assess economic policies. The managing director of the IMF participates in the discussions.

Group of Twenty (G-20)

Argentina,	Japan,
Australia,	Korea,
Brazil,	Mexico,
Canada,	Russia,
China,	Saudi Arabia,
France,	South Africa,
Germany,	Turkey,
India,	United Kingdom,
Indonesia,	United States,
Italy,	European Union euro area

The G-20 was formally established at the G-7 Finance Ministers' meeting on 26 September 1999. The inaugural meeting took place on 15–16 December 1999 in Berlin. The G-20 was formed as a new forum for co-operation on matters pertaining to the international finance system. It promotes discussion among key industrial and emerging market countries.

The membership of the G-20 comprises the Finance Ministers and central bank governors of the G-7 countries, plus the central bank governors of 12 other key countries, the president of the European Union (if not a G-7 member), the president of the European Central Bank, the managing director of the IMF, and the president of the World Bank.

Reform of the IMF

The IMF has always been dogged by controversy. In 1946 Keynes had assured a friend that the inaugural meeting of the IMF would be 'just a pleasant party'. In the end what had appeared to be quite straightforward agenda items for its first meeting proved to be highly controversial. An example was the choice of city for the IMF headquarters. Britain and the other member countries had to give way on the decision to locate IMF headquarters in the United States, but they had hoped at least for it to be located in New York. Washington, being the capital city of the wealthiest and most powerful member, would symbolise dominance of the US in the IMF. Keynes commented, 'the Fund, as an international institution, should not be associated too closely with the capital of any nation'. But in the end the US view prevailed and Washington became the headquarters of the IMF.

From the 1950s through to the present day there have been calls for reform of the IMF. Issues relating to exchange rates and convertibility peaked in the 1970s. These have been discussed in Chapter 10. Those aspects of the IMF which survive intact from the Bretton Woods days – that is, its role as *international lender* and its role in *international monetary management* – have also been the subject of criticism over a long period. *Lending policies* were criticised from an early date because of the conditions placed by the IMF on weak deficit countries which needed short-term finance to cope with a balance of payments shortfall. IMF loans usually required countries to stabilise their economies. This meant that countries seeking IMF assistance faced policies of raising interest rates, reducing credit, tightening up on the money supply, increasing taxes and reducing government spending. The effects on their national income and employment were often disastrous. The poorer the country, the nastier the medicine. Rich countries in temporary difficulty were given a much easier adjustment programme than developing countries. Latin America was typically subjected to very stringent conditions, starting with devaluation and a credit squeeze, and ending all too frequently in political instability and capital flight.

As far as the *management role* was concerned, certain countries in continental Europe and in the developing world felt that they were effectively excluded from the decision-making process. In the 1950s collaboration and consultation, where it existed, was largely bilateral, restricted to the US and Britain. In the developing world the UNCTAD pressure group (United Nations Conference for Trade and Development) was formed in 1964 to uphold the interests of developing countries in the international economy. Its aim was to counteract the exclusivity of the Bretton Woods institutions, which were dominated by the interests of richer countries.

Stiglitz on reform of the IMF

Stiglitz, in his capacity as chief economist at the World Bank between 1997 and 2000, came into conflict with the IMF on a number of occasions. His proposals for reform of the IMF are set out in his book *Globalization and its Discontents* (2002). They echo some complaints which have been present in debates on the IMF since its beginnings in the 1940s. But there are important *new problems*, associated with short-term capital flows and the currency crises of the 1990s in Argentina, East Asia and Russia, and the role which the IMF has played in these crises. Stiglitz's proposed reforms cover the following areas:

● The IMF needs to *disclose the poverty and unemployment impact* of its conditionality requirements. Countries should be told about the likely consequences of following IMF stabilisation policies. Greater transparency in this and other aspects of IMF policy is a key area for reform.
● The IMF should pay more attention to improving safety nets in vulnerable countries. Most developing countries have weak safety nets; they especially lack

unemployment insurance. Even in developed countries, the small business and agricultural sectors need better safety nets to cope with economic adjustment.

● The IMF is a major creditor in the world economy, and is also *dominated by creditor countries*. That is why it spends so much time and money on 'bailouts'. The appropriate way of dealing with financial crises is through bankruptcy, not through IMF-financed bailout of creditors. Such a reform would have the advantage of discouraging reckless lending to emerging markets.

● Responses to financial crises in developing and transition economies need to be placed within the *social and political context* of these economies. Excessive attention is often given to the needs of outside investors. The problems of small businesses and workers in the local economy are ignored. In the long run, this leads to political and social instability and chokes off the same capital inflows which the IMF is desperately trying to encourage.

The Washington consensus

Not all economists would agree with the need for deep-seated reforms to the IMF as called for by Joseph Stiglitz. However, there is a wider concern among economists about what is termed the 'Washington consensus', which features in the Bretton Woods institutions, the IMF and the World Bank.

The 'Washington consensus' (so named by Williamson, 1989) refers to the principles which guide the experts of the IMF and the World Bank who are based in Washington. For developing countries and transition economies, these principles are the ones which have to be accepted if they wish to gain access to the funds of the major official lenders.

The emphasis in the Washington consensus is on 'market-friendly' economic reform. For the IMF the most important aspects of reform are still geared to stabilisation, i.e.

● fiscal and monetary austerity;
● exchange rate liberalisation;
● relaxation of controls on trade;
● relaxation of controls on capital movements.

Economists have criticised the adverse effects of the Washington consensus on trade and production. Although the IMF is praised for making developing and transition economies aware of the dangers of overspending, a number of critics have pointed out the downside of IMF involvement (e.g. Eichengreen, 1999). The downside is that the IMF itself does not bear the cost of failure.

Spokespersons for the Bretton Woods institutions claim that they have learned from their mistakes. There is a fundamental contradiction however, in the way that the agencies respond to errors. They do not pay the costs . . . An IMF staff member flying home in a chastened frame of mind represents one sort of response to liberalisation attempts which have collapsed, a local health worker trying to help undernourished infants recover from the effects of a dramatically-reduced national income is quite another. (Lance Taylor of the MIT, 1997)

The concerns of economists about the Bretton Woods institutions have tended in the past few years to be overshadowed by the noisier challenges of activists in the global movement. It is useful to remember that the real debate has always surrounded the institutions, with many reservations about IMF/World Bank policies on the part of mainstream observers.

CASE STUDY 14.1

IMF's favourite sons could spell trouble for their parent

Four months ago, Pedro Malan, the Brazilian finance minister, gave an eye-catching demonstration of confidence in his country's underlying economic health when he repaid a $4.2bn (£2.7bn) loan to the International Monetary Fund before it came due.

Now, though Mr Malan's star pupil status has helped to secure a fresh $30bn of IMF lending, the markets are sending his country to the bottom of the class.

Mr Malan and Arminio Fraga, Brazil's central bank governor, may soon also see their fortunes decline if, as seems likely, they lose their jobs after October's elections.

While that would mark the end of a double-act that has achieved a remarkable turnaround in Brazil, economists point out that the country's underlying weaknesses might undermine even the most perfect policy-makers.

In any case, the effects of political uncertainty show the dangers of investors, or the IMF, placing too much faith in the ability of individuals to turn a country round. Wall Street and the IMF like dealing with Mr Fraga and Mr Malan.

Both are at home with international policymakers: Mr Fraga, with a doctorate from Princeton, is a former executive at George Soros's fund management firm. Mr Malan is a former executive director of the IMF's sister institution, the World Bank.

When Mr Malan spoke at New York meetings of the Institute of International Finance, the grouping of leading financial institutions, he received a tumultuous reception. Speakers paid tribute to his role in giving Brazil international respectability.

'These guys are respected both by the markets and the IMF,' says Frederick Jaspersen, Latin America director at the Institute of International Finance. 'They are good, and the Fund knows it.'

But this in itself could be a problem, as questions are raised about the Fund's treatment of its 'favoured sons'.

As the IMF became embroiled in the 1990s with a series of problem countries – Russia, Mexico, Indonesia – observers often noted that the Fund's management tended to latch on to one or a group of reformers in each country.

They spoke the same language of orthodox economics, moved in the same circles as IMF senior managers, were often US-educated and were generally deemed trustworthy by Washington.

In his farewell speech to the IMF last year, Stanley Fischer, the Fund's former second-in-command, paid tribute to a list of such luminaries, which included Mr Malan. He emphasised that the Fund supported policies, not people. But he said: 'Often we do our job by reinforcing people struggling under enormous pressures to do the right thing.'

Described by one Group of Seven official as the 'great man' theory of policy-making, this style occasionally left the IMF out on a limb when the favoured son turned out to be less influential or reliable than it imagined.

Source: Alan Beattie, *Financial Times*, 16 August 2002. Reprinted with permission.

Comment on case study 14.1

It is unusual for a country to be able to pay an IMF loan even before it becomes due, but this is what happened in Brazil in April 2002. It confirmed the IMF's faith in the Brazilian Finance Minister and in the governor of Brazil's central bank. Both these individuals speak the language of IMF policy-makers. The governor of the central bank has a degree from Princeton, the prestigious US university. The Finance Minister is himself a former executive director of the World Bank.

But some have criticised the IMF for focusing so much on favoured individuals rather than on policies. The IMF has a tendency to listen to those who share its views. They speak the language of market economics, are often US-educated, and move in the same circles as senior IMF people. The problems arise when the 'favoured son' runs into political problems at home. Often these politicians become too closely identified with the IMF. If their economy goes down, they lose their jobs. The IMF is unwise to rely on individuals who may turn out in the end to occupy very shaky positions.

The World Bank

The World Bank was established in 1944; its full name is the International Bank for Reconstruction and Development. It is made up of three organisations:

- the *International Finance Corporation* which is a private sector bank;
- the *International Development Agency* (IDA) which provides loans to developing and transition economies at concessionary rates;
- the *Investment Guarantee Agency*, which insures investors against risk.

Objectives of the World Bank

The objectives of the World Bank have changed substantially since its founding. The US proposed an International Bank in 1943, to finance post-war reconstruction in continental Europe. The idea was taken up by Keynes with great enthusiasm. One of the first applicants for emergency assistance to the new institution was Britain herself, much to the disgust of the US administration which argued that the Bank was 'not intended to deal with special needs of that sort!' In the end it was Marshall Aid from the US which financed European reconstruction, and the World Bank turned instead, though slowly at first, to granting loans to developing countries, many of which were moving from colonial status to independence.

The World Bank borrows on world markets and lends to needy countries for development purposes. Because the World Bank is heavily creditworthy, it can borrow at relatively low rates of interest. Very poor countries can then borrow from it at concessionary rates. The less poor pay a rate of interest which is marginally above the rate at which the World Bank can borrow.

In theory, the World Bank is the institution which provides long-term development finance for developing and transition economies at relatively low rates of interest, whereas the IMF is the institution which provides developing countries and transition countries with short-term finance to tide over balance of payments problems. In practice, the distinction between the two types of lending is now very blurred. This is because the World Bank has tended to move away from providing finance for specific projects, e.g. a school or a hospital, and towards programme aid which assists developing and transition economies with broad economic and structural change. This type of finance is referred to as structural adjustment lending, and it is conditional on certain policies being followed. The types of policy measures which have been requested in return for World Bank finance are shown in Table 14.1.

During the 1990s it became increasingly apparent that there were problems with the conditions imposed by the World Bank on its long-term lending.

● Many countries *failed to comply* with the conditions. Some countries which did not comply with the conditions even managed to get a second loan from the World Bank (Mosley, 1987).

● When countries did comply with the conditions, this often had the effect of depressing incomes and investment, resulting in a *negative effect on long-term growth*.

● Loans in foreign currency often enabled countries to *postpone making difficult decisions*. Such loans kept in power unpopular and corrupt governments. Foreign exchange also enabled money to be spent on luxury imported consumer goods.

● When *rates of return* are compared, policy-based programme lending has frequently *performed worse* than old-fashioned project lending which has tended to be favoured by bilateral aid donors.

Table 14.1 Types of policy measure required for structural adjustment lending

Trade policy	Remove import quotas
	Cut tariffs
	Improve export incentives
Resource mobilisation	Reform taxes
	Reform interest rate policy
	Strengthen management of external borrowing
	Improve financial performance of public enterprises
Efficient use of resources	Revise agricultural prices
	Reduce agricultural subsidies
	Revise energy prices
	Revise industry incentives
Institutional reform	Improve support for industry
	Improve support for agriculture

Source: Adapted from Mosley (1987).

The debt problem

The World Bank has another problem, which it shares with the IMF. Huge proportions of GDP and the export earnings of developing and transition economies go to service debt. Much of this debt comprises interest payments on past borrowings from official and private sources.

Most of the debt of African and other low-income countries is owed to the official multilateral and bilateral agencies which have provided them with concessionary finance. By contrast the typical middle-income debtor country owes more than half

Table 14.2 Aid, private, capital and debt

Part 1

	Official development assistance received (as % of GDP)		Net foreign direct investment flows (as % of GDP)	
	1990	1999	1990	1999
Developing countries	1	1	1	3
Least developed countries	12	7	–	3
Arab States	–	–	1	0
East Asia and the Pacific	1	1	2	3
Latin America and the Caribbean	0	0	1	5
South Asia	1	1	–	1
Sub-Saharan Africa	–	–	0	2
Eastern Europe and the CIS	–	–	–	3
OECD	–	–	–	–
High-income OECD	–	–	–	–

Part 2

	Other private flows (as a % of GDP)		Total debt service (as a % of GDP)	
	1990	1999	1990	1999
Developing countries	0	0	4	6
Least developed countries	1	0	3	3
Arab States	0	0	6	4
East Asia and the Pacific	0	0	4	5
Latin America and the Caribbean	0	1	4	8
South Asia	0	0	3	3
Sub-Saharan Africa	0	1	4	5
Eastern Europe and the CIS	–	1	2	5
OECD	–	–	–	–
High-income OECD	–	–	–	–

Source: Adapted from World Bank: *World Development Report* (2000).

its debt to the commercial banks and other private lenders. Because of higher interest rates, the debt service ratios of middle-income countries can be substantially greater than those of low income debtors – see, for example, the position of Latin America and the Caribbean in Table 14.2.

Debt relief initiatives can take the following forms:

- *Debt reduction* is any response which *reduces the debt* owed by a country. Debt reduction does not mean simply exchanging one form of debt for another. For example, when official debt is swapped for equity, dividends are paid to private creditors rather than interest being owed to official lenders. But this does not necessarily reduce the debt. In the long run it could actually increase it.
- *Debt relief* is any measure which *reduces the present value of payments due*. In the long run, however, this may actually increase the debt and benefit the creditor. For example, rescheduling a debt will reduce payments in the short run. But unless a country can increase its capacity to service the debt in the long run, the debt burden over time can increase.
- *Debt forgiveness*. Public pressure has obliged the World Bank and IMF to forgive, i.e. completely wipe out, the debts of some of the poorest countries in the world economy.

Debt relief, reduction or forgiveness can mean increased leverage for the World Bank and the IMF. IMF/World Bank approved policies have to be followed. Sometimes these policies have unintended consequences. The IMF often insists on the currency being devalued as part of a stabilisation package. This raises the debt burden because debt is repayable in foreign currency. So, for example, devaluation in Moldova in 2002 increased its debt burden to an equivalent of 75 per cent of government revenue. In a country with already desperately low spending on health and education, this can be little short of a disaster.

CASE STUDY 14.2

Debt relief missing targets says IMF study

A flagship international debt relief scheme for the world's poorest countries is failing to free many countries from debt as it becomes clear that its forecasts were too optimistic, the International Monetary Fund and World Bank have admitted.

In a study for the joint ministerial steering committee linking the two institutions, which meets at the end of this month, fund and bank staff say that half of the 20 countries going through the process are likely to exceed their sustainable debt targets. But the bank's governing board, which met earlier this week, showed no enthusiasm for making the scheme more gen-

erous despite pressure from non-governmental organisations, bank officials said.

The staff study – a copy of which has been seen by the *Financial Times* – asserts: 'Earlier projections often contained overly optimistic macroeconomic assumptions, reflecting . . . inadequate analysis of the likely sources of growth and the expected impact of planned policies.'

Falling commodity prices have pushed several of the highly indebted countries, which are heavily dependent on agricultural exports, off track in hitting debt-to-export targets.

The report considers various proposals from NGOs and a bill currently in the US Congress to deepen the relief available, but concludes that they would be too expensive and an inefficient way of delivering extra money to poor countries.

Jacob Kolster, a senior bank official, said the bank's governing board, representing its shareholder countries, had met earlier in the week and backed this conclusion.

'There was no general sentiment in the bank's board to modify the heavily indebted poor countries (HIPC) initiative,' he said. The IMF's board meets today to consider the report.

Some rich nations, including Nordic countries and the UK, have proposed minor modifications to the scheme which would increase slightly the amount of debt relief on offer. But bank officials say even these have been opposed by the US and Japan.

The report also warns that litigation against debt-ridden poor countries from some governments and commercial creditors is jeopardising their development. Iraq, for example, is suing Uganda for non-payment of sovereign debt, while the private military company Executive Outcomes, which was involved in the civil war in Sierra Leone, is suing the government there for $30m in unpaid fees.

A spokesman for Executive Outcomes defended the litigation, saying that the government 'owe us the money rightfully'.

NGOs reacted with anger to the report, saying it proved the scheme was insufficiently generous. 'The knowledge that life-saving debt cancellation is being held up while creditors tinker with a failed programme is enough to bring thousands of people to the streets of Washington,' said Mara Vanderslice, at Jubilee USA Network.

A group of international NGOs including Oxfam, Cafod and Christian Aid released a report this week suggesting a deepening of the relief available under the scheme.

Source: Alan Beattie, Financial Times, 6 September 2002. Reprinted with permission.

Comment on case study 14.2

As a consequence of the work of the Jubilee 2000 movement, the IMF and the World Bank jointly agreed a new debt relief plan for some of the world's poorest countries. Previously very few countries had qualified for debt forgiveness. After the new IMF/World Bank initiative (HIPC), 20 countries qualified for significant debt relief.

By mid-2002 more than half of the countries targeted for help were still suffering from unsustainable debt levels. The debt situation has been made worse by falling prices for primary products, the exports on which many of these countries depend. Some poor indebted countries are also being pursued by other creditors. Iraq is suing Uganda for failing to honour its debts. A private military company is suing Sierra Leone for unpaid debts.

Jubilee 2000, and NGOs such as Oxfam, Cafod and Christian Aid, are lobbying for the debt relief scheme to be deepened. Some countries, including the UK, are pressing for the IMF/World Bank scheme to be slightly modified to help poor indebted countries. There is opposition to wider debt relief forgiveness from the World Bank's governing body and from countries such as the USA and Japan.

The World Bank's comprehensive development framework

It is possible to identify a number of key strands in present-day World Bank thinking. The World Bank is attempting to draw on what economists have learned about growth and development over the last half-century, and apply this knowledge in a comprehensive development framework.

The framework underscores the growing realisation that the many elements that make up the development process must be planned together and co-ordinated in order to obtain the best results . . .

The complementarities between projects and processes are vital to success . . . A comprehensive framework makes these complementarities explicit by emphasising the relationship among the human, physical, sectoral, and structural aspects of development. (World Bank, *World Development Report*, 2000, p. 3)

● A comprehensive development strategy requires *partnership*. It is too demanding for any one level of government. National governments are to be encouraged to seek agreement with NGOs, international organisations and multinational companies, *and* with regions and cities, on appropriate development policies.
● Localisation is as important as globalisation. Localisation highlights the importance of grass-roots opinions and the local aspirations of groups and communities for growth and development. Localisation is to be promoted alongside globalisation.
● Development in the modern world economy means urbanisation. The provision of an appropriate urban infrastructure is essential: water, sewerage, transport. These are the services which affect the poor. They can often be managed best at local levels, responding to local needs.
● Development challenges are principally *poverty, hunger, ill-health, lack of housing* and *illiteracy*. International trade and capital flows can be harnessed to meet these challenges through integrated strategies which focus on the different aspects of development.

The United Nations and human development

The United Nations has long had a commitment to the reduction of poverty in the world economy. In particular the United Nations Development Programme (UNDP) produces annual Human Development Reports, which rank countries according to their success in meeting human needs.

Development as human development

The UNDP has pointed out that although the economists are now trying to work within a broader definition of development than is encompassed simply by economic growth, they are still using a *goods-orientated* view of development. When development is defined as human development, people come first. It is a *people-orientated* view of development.

Human development is about much more than the rise or fall of national incomes. It is about creating an environment in which people can develop their full potential and lead productive, creative lives in accord with their needs and interests. People are the real wealth of nations. (UNDP, *Human Development Report*, 2001)

How can human development be promoted? It is not appropriate to view human development simply in terms of increased spending on health, education and related activities. The United Nations calls for a change in the philosophy of development policy to reflect the human dimension.

● People must be free to exercise choice, and to participate in decision-making, especially if it affects their own lives. Human development and human rights are interdependent.

● There is a need to focus on what Amartya Sen, the Nobel prizewinning economist, has called capabilities. The question should be, what are people capable of doing or being? For example, can people read or write? Not, how much are we spending on education? Ask whether people are living longer, rather than asking what we are spending on health.

● People are not the problem which economists and economic policy aim to 'solve'. Human development requires that economists do not see people as 'targets' to be 'impacted' by policy. They should be regarded as *beneficiaries* of development.

● Human development requires that policy-makers should be culturally sensitive. Often traditional values are surprisingly positive for human development. And if economists ignore the cultural mores of a society, and treat it in a culturally insensitive way, it can provoke resistance to change and hinder human development.

● Human development highlights the *role of women*. They play a vital role both in productive activities and in maintaining their families. In many societies women bear a disproportionate share of the burden of poverty and hunger.

New challenges to human development

The United Nations Development Programme has also drawn attention to four very worrying setbacks to human development which emerged in the 1990s. First, there is HIV/AIDS. At the end of 2000, 36 million people were living with HIV/AIDS. Seventy per cent of these people are in Sub-Saharan Africa, and 95 per cent in developing countries. Mainly because of HIV/AIDS, life expectancy in six African countries – Botswana, Burundi, Namibia, Rwanda, Zambia and Zimbabwe – has declined by seven years since the early 1990s. Thirteen million children in the world are AIDS orphans.

Second, globalisation has created many opportunities for cross-border crimes. The illegal drugs trade is worth over $500 billion. An estimated 2 million women and children are the victims of illegal trafficking.

Third, transition in central and eastern Europe and in the countries of the former Soviet Union has had adverse effects on incomes, employment, health, life expectancy and school enrolment ratios (Chapter 13).

Finally, although there has been a marked movement towards democracy in developing and transition economies, it is still very fragile in a large number of countries. Elected governments are frequently toppled, bringing economic and social dislocation. There are 12 million refugees, who are victims of conflict, and 5 million people internally displaced.

Measuring human development, the human development index (HDI)

Since 1990 the United Nations has provided an index (HDI) which measures a country's level of human development. The HDI considers three basic dimensions of human development: longevity, knowledge and a decent standard of living. It is measured by life expectancy, educational attainment (adult literacy and school enrolment ratios) and per capita income. Countries rank high on a human development index if people live relatively long lives, are mostly literate, and have sufficient income to rise above poverty.

Australia, for example, is by no means the richest country in the world. But it ranks high on the HDI (second, after Norway) because of its high ranking in terms of life expectancy and education (Table 14.3). At the other end of the scale are some of the poorest Sub-Saharan African countries, with life expectancy under 50 years and very low literacy and school enrolment ratios.

The Millennium Declaration

The United Nations General Assembly (2000) made a Millennium Declaration setting out specific, quantifiable and monitorable goals for development and poverty alleviation by 2015 (Table 14.4), for the 85% of the world's population that lives in the developing world.

Table 14.3 The human development index 2000, selected countries

Country	Life expectancy at birth	Adult literacy ratio (%)	School enrolment ratio (%)	GDP per capitax capita (ppp US$)	Human development index
Norway	78.4	99	97	28 433	0.939
Australia	78.8	99	100	24 574	0.936
Canada	78.7	99	97	26 251	0.936
Sweden	79.6	99	100	22 636	0.936
Belgium	78.2	99	100	25 443	0.935
Bulgaria	70.8	98.3	72	5 071	0.772
Brazil	67.5	84.9	80	7 037	0.750
Ukraine	68.1	99	77	3 458	0.742
Turkey	69.5	84.6	62	6 380	0.735
China	70.2	83.5	73	3 617	0.714
Ethiopia	44.1	37.4	27	628	0.321
Burkina Faso	46.1	23	23	965	0.320
Burundi	40.6	46.9	19	578	0.309
Niger	44.8	15.3	16	753	0.274
Sierra Leone	38.3	32	27	448	0.258

Source: Based on data from UNDP *Human Development Report* (2001).

Table 14.4 United Nations Millennium Declaration goals as a percentage of world population in the developing world

Goal (for 2015)	% achieved or on track	% lagging	% no data available
Gender equality			
Eliminate disparity in primary education	58	5	22
Eliminate disparity in secondary education	42	22	21
Infant and child mortality			
Reduce infant mortality rates by two-thirds	23	62	–
Reduce under-five mortality rates by two-thirds	23	62	–
Maternal mortality			
Reduce maternal mortality ratios by three-quarters	37	48	–
Basic amenities			
Halve the proportion of people without access to safe water	12	70	3
Hunger			
Halve the proportion of people suffering from hunger	62	11	12
Universal education			
Enrol all children in primary school	34	5	46
Achieve universal completion of primary schooling	26	13	46
Extreme income poverty			
Halve the proportion of people living in extreme poverty:			
Business as usual growth pattern	43	34	8
Pro-poor growth pattern	54	23	8

Source: UNDP *Human Development Report* (2001) p. 23.

What are the prospects for achieving these goals?

The UN reports that many countries are already on track to achieve universal primary education and gender equality in education. Also, in 43 countries, where 60 per cent of the world's population live, there is good progress towards the goal of halving the numbers who are hungry. But there are serious problems with all the other goals. Sixty-two per cent of the world's population is in countries where progress on under-five mortality rates is lagging. Seventy per cent of the world's population is in countries where progress on access to safe water is also lagging.

Summary

- This chapter examines the institutions which have governed the world economy since World War II: the International Monetary Fund, the World Bank and the specialised agencies of the United Nations.

- The Bretton Woods institutions did not support an unfettered market mechanism. Under the influence of Keynes, the planners believed that markets do not always work well, and interventions might sometimes be necessary.

- The IMF as originally constituted was responsible for convertibility, exchange rates, balance of payments adjustment, and reserve assets payments adjustment. After 1978 the IMF had a much reduced role, i.e. holding reserve assets and providing the machinery for collaboration and consultation.

- IMF consultation and collaboration is mainly through two major groups, the G-7 and the G-20. The G-7 comprises the leading industrial countries. The G-20 includes other key countries in the developing world.

- There have been many calls for reform of the IMF, focusing in recent times on the Washington consensus which requires countries wishing to access funds from the IMF and the World Bank, to adopt 'market-friendly' economic policies.

- The World Bank provides long-term development finance for developing and transition economies. It is under pressure to take the lead in debt relief initiatives in poor and middle-income countries.

- The United Nations Development Programme has taken the lead in refocusing the development agenda on people-centred human development. The human development index measures a country's level of human development in terms of life expectancy, educational attainment and per capita income.

Key concepts

- Bretton Woods agreement
- International Monetary Fund (IMF)
- International Bank for Reconstruction and Development (World Bank)
- Quota system
- Reserve assets
- Collaboration and consultation
- Conditionality
- Group of Seven (G-7)
- Group of Twenty (G-20)
- Washington consensus
- Structural adjustment lending
- Debt relief
- Comprehensive development framework
- Human development
- Millennium Declaration

Questions for discussion

1 What were the original purposes of the IMF and the World Bank? Have they changed significantly over time?

2 Joseph Stiglitz has strongly criticised the IMF. Why?

3 'Saying that the IMF causes austerity is like saying doctors cause plagues because you find them near sick people' (Kenneth Rogoff, chief economist at the IMF). Do you agree?

4 Why might the IMF's status as a major creditor in the world economy lead to a conflict of interest when it has to deal with financial crises?

5 Do IMF and World Bank policies neglect human development?

6 'Unless societies recognise that their real wealth is their people, an excessive obsession with the creation of material wealth can obscure the ultimate objective of enriching human lives' (UNDP). Do you agree?

7 'The idealists of today often turn out to be the realists of tomorrow' (J. Tinbergen). Would this statement apply to global activists?

Suggested reading

Eichengreen, B., Masson, P. *et al* (1999) *Towards a New Financial Architecture*, Washington, DC: Institute for International Economics.

Mosley, P. (1987) 'Conditionality as a bargaining process: structural adjustment lending, 1980–1986', *Essays in International Finance*, The Princeton Papers, No. 168, Princeton: Princeton University Press.

Stiglitz, J. (2002) *Globalisation and its Discontents*, London: Allen Lane.

Taylor, L. (1997) 'The revival of the liberal creed – the IMF and the World Bank in a globalized economy', *World Development*, vol. 25, no. 2, pp. 145–52.

Tobin, J. (1978) 'A Proposal for international monetary reform', *Eastern Economic Journal*, no. 4, pp. 153–9.

United Nations, *Human Development Reports*, published for the United Nations Development Programme (UNDP), New York and Oxford: UNDP.

Williamson, J. (1989) 'What Washington means by policy reform', in John Williamson (ed.), *Latin American Adjustment: How Much Has Happened?*, Washington, DC: Institute for International Economics.

Websites

- International Monetary Fund: **www.imf.org**
- United Nations: **www.un.org**
- World Bank: **www.worldbank.org**
- World Trade Organisation: **www.wto.org**

Chapter 15

Challenges in the global economy: trade, finance and technology

Introduction

Qualitative and quantitative shifts have come about in trade, finance and technology over the past three decades. World trade continues to grow at a faster rate than world output. There can now be very few communities in the world untouched by foreign trade, where external factors are still only marginal to their well-being. Goods, services, financial capital and people cross national boundaries at an unprecedented rate.

Financial markets have also transformed the global economy. The private capital which circulates between the world's financial centres is so extensive that it dwarfs many national economies. Across the world's regions, stock market prices, interest rates and exchange rates interact, sometimes in a highly volatile way. There have also been fundamental technological breakthroughs over the past thirty years. First there has been the revolution in information and communications. This has the potential to spell the end of 'distance' and permit borderless trade. Second, there have been massive advances in our understanding of genetics. These and other innovations have the potential for substantially increasing material welfare.

Economic liberalisation and technological change is the context in which the world's population is becoming increasingly urban. Eighty-five per cent of the world's population now lives in the developing world. Fifty per cent of the population of the developing world lives in cities. Of the world's hundred largest cities, 70 are in the developing world. People are also crossing national borders in record numbers: 130 million people now live outside the countries of their birth, a figure which is rising by 2 per cent per year.

There are, of course, huge implications of the Iraq war for the international economy. The terrorist attacks of 11 September 2001 directed attention to international terrorism. Other concerns are the threat of bio-terrorism and the vulnerability of the infrastructure.

Out of this background, new issues emerge to challenge and confront economics. Chapter 15 explains some of these issues. They range from global electronic commerce through to money laundering and banking supervision. Each economist is likely to have his or her own personal list of what constitute the most important challenges and opportunities on the international agenda. The ones discussed in this chapter incorporate a long-term vision of the world economy with important interrelationships between trade, financial flows and technological innovations.

Objectives

When you have completed this chapter, you should be able to:

● comment on the likely static and dynamic gains from *electronic commerce*;

● discuss the implications of e-commerce for *commercial security*;

● understand why digitised goods and services pose particular problems for *intellectual property rights* (IPR);

● discuss the role of TRIPS and WIPO in international trade;

● understand the negative effects of the *digital divide*, and the steps which can be taken to reverse them;

● appreciate the scale of *money laundering and illicit trafficking* in the world economy;

● discuss the implications of the new *biotechnology* for world trade.

Global electronic commerce

Electronic commerce refers to commercial transactions which are based on the electronic storage, processing and transmission of data over communications networks such as the internet and the world wide web. Global electronic commerce has been made possible by rapid advances in technology. Digital technologies permit the storage and processing of vast amounts of information. Satellites and optical fibres have dramatically quickened the handling and distribution of this information.

To an economist, in principle, electronic commerce offers the possibility of 'trade without borders'. In practice there is evidence that information and communications technologies may be polarising the world economy into 'online' and 'offline' segments, what is sometimes referred to as the digital divide.

Electronic commerce has risen from the 'grass-roots' without the national or supra-national planning, management or co-ordination that one might have expected. The internet was originally an academic and research network which took off in the 1970s. The world wide web (www) was a runaway success following its creation in the early 1990s. There was no government or business input, yet its growth was phenomenal. The number of internet users has climbed sharply (Figure 15.1), the number of websites now exceeds 20 million (Figure 15.2), and the costs of data transfer have fallen dramatically (Figure 15.3).

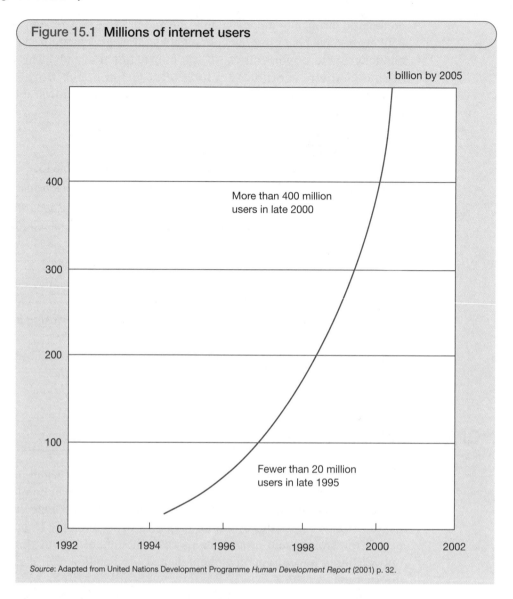

Figure 15.1 Millions of internet users

1 billion by 2005

More than 400 million
users in late 2000

Fewer than 20 million
users in late 1995

Source: Adapted from United Nations Development Programme *Human Development Report* (2001) p. 32.

Static and dynamic gains from electronic commerce

Although electronic transfers of money have been a feature of the international economy for decades, used by banks, credit card agencies, stock brokers and so on, the 'electronic marketplace' which deals in products and services is something new. Estimates of the growth of electronic commerce have been very speculative and optimistic. However, it has undoubtedly grown very fast from its starting point of zero in 1995. Consumer e-commerce reached $28 billion in 2000. Business to business e-commerce is estimated to reach $1.2 trillion by 2003.

Figure 15.2 **Number of websites**

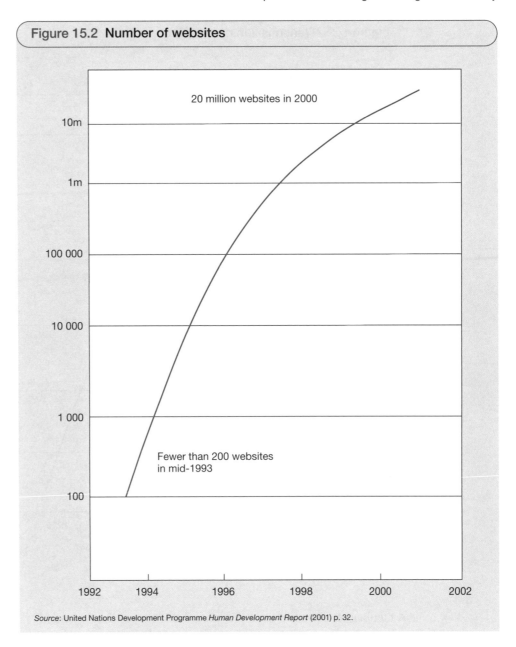

20 million websites in 2000

Fewer than 200 websites
in mid-1993

Source: United Nations Development Programme *Human Development Report* (2001) p. 32.

There is no shortage of comment in the literature on the likely role of electronic commerce in the world economy over the next few decades. The growth of electronic commerce is generally agreed to have enormous potential which can be understood in part in the context of trade theory. There are the static gains from trade which come about via specialisation and exchange, and there are dynamic gains, measurable as productivity increases. For example, between 1975 and 1995, US productivity growth averaged 1 per cent per annum. Between 1995 and 2000, it rose to 5 per cent per annum.

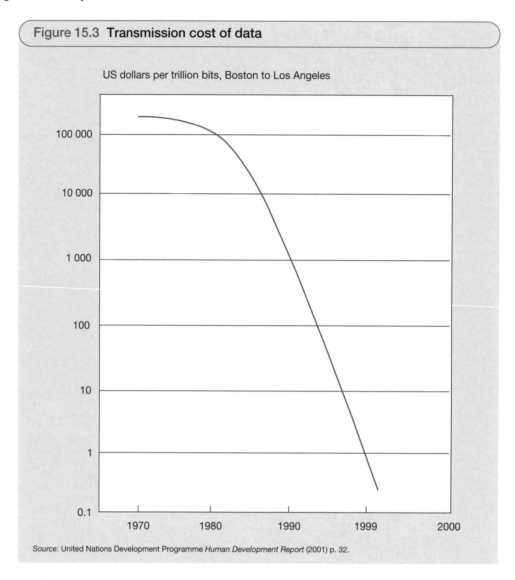

Figure 15.3 Transmission cost of data

US dollars per trillion bits, Boston to Los Angeles

Source: United Nations Development Programme *Human Development Report* (2001) p. 32.

A number of observers have interpreted this rise as the dynamic benefits of electronic commerce. The UNDP *Human Development Report* of 2001 argues that in spite of the poor performance of technology stocks since 2000, and the collapse of many dot-coms, there is still enormous potential in electronic commerce for the international economy.

Many of the dot-coms which failed so miserably in the late 1990s were set up in the belief that it was easy to make money 'online'. Such companies often lacked credible fundamentals and a clear purpose. But online transactions have huge potential for firms which already have a stable base and are looking for expansion. Over the next decade there is likely to be more constructive uses of the potential of e-commerce. Information and communication technologies (ICT) are to be found in the most dynamic sectors of the global economy. They offer great potential for countries to diversify their economies and create worthwhile employment opportunities for people. Industries related to ICT tend to have low start-up costs. They attract young and dynamic entrepreneurs. They are also relatively labour-intensive industries, employing large numbers of well-educated people. In India it is estimated that if present trends continue 30 per cent of India's exports and 8 per cent of its GDP could be derived from ICT-related activities by 2010. These activities now include significant outsourced activities: credit card administration, insurance claims, business payrolls and customer relations. Of the Fortune Top 500 companies, 185 outsource their ICT to India. The global outsourcing market alone is worth more than $100 billion. India also has 1250 companies exporting related software.

Commercial security

Business-to-business transactions dominate electronic commerce. About 80 per cent of the electronic trade in products and services is represented by business-to-business transactions, which is the fastest-growing area of electronic communication. Multinational enterprises use electronic commerce as the basis of their global networks. Companies providing professional services in insurance, finance, engineering, design and architecture, for example, use the internet to sell their services to other businesses. Physical barriers between countries and markets are meaningless in this context.

Economists can readily appreciate the cost savings likely to be associated with business-to-business electronic commerce – the impact on inventories, for example – as firms find it less and less necessary to carry stocks. But again there is a downside. Electronic commerce has implications for commercial security. When firms engage in electronic commerce, they open up their electronic systems to suppliers and customers. This can cover such things as websites, customer software, search engines, manufacturing processes, recipes and so on.

Business-to-business electronic commerce which takes place across national boundaries has highlighted differences between the laws governing such data in different countries. The international law protecting data, patents, copyrights, trade secrets and so on only provides protection at the minimum level. Firms tend to rely on much stronger national laws to protect their interests. But electronic commerce throws up all sorts of anomalies. What appears at first sight to economists to be straightforward and highly efficient 'trade without borders' turns out to be no such thing. One example relates to data collections. In the US a collection of data – for example, a list of names and addresses – cannot be protected under copyright law unless it has enough 'creativity' to qualify as intellectual property. But in the EU data as simple as a list of names and addresses is protected. All kinds of issues are affected by these anomalies. They impact on the relationship between multinational companies and their local suppliers, as well as between companies and their competitors.

Digitised products and intellectual property protection

Digital products are very diverse, ranging from music (singles, albums and compilations) through to books, scholarly articles and films. Sometimes the digital product is very highly priced. In other cases it is inexpensive. The stakeholders in each case will also be different. So there is unlikely to be a single global solution to the problem of digital material and intellectual property rights. It is increasingly being seen as a major challenge to the international trading regime.

Digitised goods and services can now be replicated perfectly at minimum cost, appearing in huge quantities on world markets. They include audio and video material, library works, computer software, computer games, databases and so on. As digitised goods and services grow in importance, firms become increasingly concerned about protecting their innovations. Products can be replicated and distributed widely on world markets, sometimes before the official launch of the product, and always without the knowledge and consent of rights holders.

Intellectual property

The reason why intellectual property has emerged so strongly in the international agenda at the present time is the *leap in technology* represented by digitised products. A detailed report from the US National Research Council puts the problem of digital products into context.

- Natural barriers to copyright infringement have virtually disappeared with digitisation: reproduction is cheap; quality can be maintained, as many copies are made; and the average computer owner can do the copying. In the recent past such copying required significant investment.
- The economics of distribution have changed. Products can be sent worldwide cheaply and instantaneously. It is cheap for the copyright holder to distribute digitised goods. It is just as cheap for individuals and pirates to copy and distribute digitised goods.
- Current intellectual property law is unclear. Individuals do not know what is legal. They can access and copy large amounts of digital information but do not always know whether this violates intellectual property.
- Different people have different expectations and concerns. Authors and musicians may be happy to give away products to build up a reputation. Creators may wish to provide a service free to the community. A good example of open source software is the Linux system. Book publishers and software companies which need to show profit may have very different motivations.
- The legal terms 'international' and 'national' may be irrelevant to an information infrastructure. It is usually impossible to determine the physical location of someone reading electronic information.
- The economics of intellectual property protection is unclear. On the one hand, intellectual property rights are assumed to encourage innovation and creativity. On the other hand, protecting intellectual property rights is a costly exercise. There are the costs of enforcement and broader losses of knowledge and information.

TRIPS and WIPO

In 1994, at the conclusion of the Uruguay Round of trade negotiations (Chapter 5), an agreement was reached on *trade-related aspects of intellectual property rights* (TRIPS). It is binding on WTO members. Disputes between WTO members over TRIPS obligations are subject to the same dispute settlement procedures as other traded goods and services.

Developing countries were allowed a longer period to adjust to the TRIPS agreement than developed countries. The least-developed countries, for example, are not expected to comply fully with TRIPS until 2006. The transition period represented a compromise between the desire of firms in developed countries to invest in research and development of new products and the need for the knowledge embodied in intellectual property.

The UN argues that a desirable IPR regime is one that balances out the costs and benefits for all those involved. In the case of IPRs it was argued in relation to TRIPS that IPRs can disadvantage developing countries. They increase the knowledge gap and shift bargaining power towards the producers of knowledge, most of whom reside in the richer countries.

The need to strike a balance between private interests (rewarding those who research and develop goods and services) and the public need to access information and acquire increased knowledge has clearly been present in international property law for many years. The private interest has required patents and copyrights to be granted, with safeguards in terms of time limits and in terms of the preservation of the cultural heritage, promotion of education and so on.

Intellectual property rights are based on national law. They apply only in that jurisdiction. So a US multinational will not own a single copyright to a film which it distributes overseas. There will be a copyright in each country of the world: a UK copyright, a French copyright and so on. To establish a global IPR regime has required a great deal of global co-operation.

International treaties to provide co-ordination on IPR are administered by WIPO, the World Intellectual Property Organisation, an agency of the UN. WIPO negotiated two international treaties which extend basic copyright to digitised products and services. They are the WIPO Copyright Treaty (1996), and the WIPO Performances and Phonograms Treaty (1996), which together cover data, images, music and software on the internet.

Balancing the concerns of all parties

The issue of digital file-sharing on the internet has been fiercely debated for a number of years. The legal arguments are complex and, in many cases, unclear. Some musicians see the internet as an opportunity to be heard; others see it as very damaging to their living. Whatever the view of the various interested parties, the music fan desires music at the lowest possible cost. Sharing on the internet is only as expensive as the cost of a local phone call. The sharing of digital files is almost impossible to police and is virtually unstoppable. Since the closure of Napster, the most famous file-sharing server, many others have emerged. The music industry has been the first to suffer, but as internet connections become faster the software and film industries will also be hit hard.

The reality is very complex, as Case Study 15.1 illustrates. Musicians in the developing world suffer just as much from counterfeiting and downloading of digital material as musicians in richer countries. It is a global problem. In 1998, Barbados, Jamaica and Trinidad and Tobago, supported by African countries, asked WIPO to devise an international scheme to protect their musicians from piracy and counterfeiting. The programme within WIPO is ongoing. A list of interested parties (stakeholders) has been drawn up by WIPO for the music industry. Identifying the list of interested groups demonstrates the scale of the problem. The identified stakeholders are:

● national copyright offices
● the police force
● revenue and customs
● the audio-visual industry
● the musicians' unions
● producers' associations
● culture and arts ministries
● national broadcasting industries.

Trying to 'balance the concerns of all parties' will not be easy. Meanwhile the music fan continues to download music from the internet.

CASE STUDY 15.1

An anti-piracy program for Africa's music industry

Piracy and counterfeiting is a multi-billion dollar business and a problem around the world. In the United Kingdom alone it is estimated that counterfeiting costs industry some £8.5 billion a year. Counterfeiting also costs in the loss of jobs and incomes and by putting poor quality – sometimes dangerous – goods into the market place. Many countries have devoted significant efforts to building awareness that copying or possessing illegally-copied materials is a crime. However, every year millions of dollars' worth of counterfeit material is seized at border crossings around the world.

The music industry is especially plagued by this problem. Modern technology has provided the means to make low-cost, quality copies at an ever-accelerating speed. Markets are often flooded with counterfeit CDs and tapes within days – if not hours – of new releases becoming available. The loss of revenue is felt throughout the industry, but hits up-and-coming musicians hardest, as it becomes increasingly difficult for them to make a living from their talent. The situation can be particularly severe in developing countries.

'My first cassette was counterfeited, my twelfth, all of them', said Ami Korta, a singer from Mali. 'They are killing us. We also have to pay our bills, our taxes. All we are asking is that they pay for the real copies'.

Companies are affected as well. 'We had to shut down for a while because of counterfeiters', said record producer Djibril Kane of Mali K7. 'One year in the first trimester we sold almost 200 000 cassettes; by the fourth we were down to 40 000. We only had two days to sell new releases before the illegal copies flooded the market.'

The problem affects legitimate distribution of foreign music as well, hampering trade and cultural exchange. 'We used to sign distribution agreements with foreign artists, promote their music and sell them nationally, but we pay millions of francs for those rights', said Fouseni Traore of Seydoni Productions in Burkina Faso. 'While the counterfeiters just buy one of our cassettes, or not even that, they buy it in a neighbouring country, make copies without paying for the rights, and sell them very cheaply. Then we cannot sell our cassettes.'

A number of developing countries have turned to WIPO in search of a solutions, as counterfeiting is quickly eroding local talent and industry. A means to safeguard the market and give creators the recompense they deserve, and thus stimulate them to keep creating, is urgently needed.

Source: WIPO Magazine, July–September 2002, page 10.

Comment on case study 15.1

Musicians suffer greatly from piracy and counterfeiting. It is a worldwide problem, affecting musicians in the developing world as well as in richer countries. Indeed, musicians in developing countries are particularly hard hit because they have so few opportunities for earning a living at home. The singer from Mali is heavily dependent on sales of CDs and tapes. Now the music can be available within hours of its release, in counterfeit CDs and tapes, or through downloading from the internet.

There are music companies in the developing world who are also adversely affected. The companies have to pay for promotion and distribution rights, only to find their incomes undermined by piracy and counterfeiting.

There is an upside to this, however. Some musicians are using the internet exclusively to promote their music: for example, the US hip hop group, Public Enemy. Many musicians see the internet as a way of bypassing the expense of intermediaries like record companies. They then expect to make a living through live appearances and other music-related activities.

The world economy offline and online

International economics provides a basis for understanding the flows of goods and services, factors of production and financial capital in the 'spaces' which make up the world economy. New technology is modifying these spaces, and in the process is shaping both the physical and the social environment. Information and communication technologies are determining a significant part of global economic flows, but can easily bypass its poorer regions and communities unless the problem is recognised and steps are taken to overcome it.

The digital divide

There is, of course, a downside to the picture of the static and dynamic gains from e-commerce. Familiarity with the internet and the web is still restricted to a minority of the world's population. More than three-quarters of internet users

Table 15.1 Internet users as a percentage of the population

	1998	2000
United States	26.3	54.3
High income OECD (exc. US)	6.9	28.2
Latin America and the Caribbean	0.8	3.2
East Asia and the Pacific	0.5	2.3
Eastern Europe and CIS	0.8	3.9
Arab states	0.2	0.6
Sub-Saharan Africa	0.1	0.4
South Asia	0.04	0.4
World	2.4	6.7

Source: Adapted from UNDP *Human Development Report* (2001) p. 40.

live in *high income countries* which contain only 14 per cent of the world's population (Table 15.1).

There are also significant digital divides within countries. In developing countries, internet use is largely restricted to *urban populations*. It can also be concentrated in certain cities and regions. In India there are 1.4 million internet connections, 1.3 million of which are in the five states of Delhi, Karnataka, Maharashtra, Tamil Nadu and Mumbai.

In all countries, developed and developing, internet use tends to be heavily concentrated among the *better-off* and *educated*. At the extreme, 70 per cent of internet users in China, for example, are those with tertiary-level education. In all countries the *young* are more familiar with electronic commerce than the old. Globally, those under 35 are five times more likely to be online than those over 55. In many countries, too, there is a *gender gap* but this is narrowing. In the US, women made up less than 40 per cent of internet users in 1996. Now they account for just over half of internet users.

Without the necessary infrastructure, mobile phones and/or personal computers, and without the human skills necessary to access electronic commerce, not all countries or groups within countries will be able to take advantage of new global business models, which widen employment opportunities for the fortunate minority. Additionally, e-commerce has the potential to lower the costs of goods and services and widen the choices of products and services available, but again only for those who can access the technology. The issue is one of *distribution of benefits*. How can the poorer and less-educated majority of the world's population be enabled to take advantage of the new opportunities?

The United Nations Centre for Human Settlements in its 2001 Report (*Cities in a Globalizing World*) gives fuller reasons why new technologies can, in reality, increase polarisation in the world economy. It is a thought-provoking interpretation of the relationship between trade, technology and space, which merits closer analysis from the standpoint of international economics.

- Certain urban centres in the world economy are emerging as 'powerhouses' of digitised goods and services. These urban centres are based on advertising, publishing, computing communications, design, music, multimedia and so on.
- New technologies enable multinational firms to separate out various functions (manufacturing, finance, marketing) to different locations across the world, to take advantage of different costs, labour laws, tax regimes and so on.
- Decentralised call centres and e-commerce management centres are being located in newly emerging enclaves throughout the world in India, Scotland, the Caribbean and the Philippines.
- Cities are becoming 'mosaics' of growing inequality. Upper-income areas emerge with high computer ownership. Marketing is targeted at these groups. The 'top third' of the market is offered 'baskets' of digitised goods and services: cellular, internet and entertainment. The remaining two-thirds of the population is ignored.
- Networks are limited to demand-rich parts of the world and bypass the poor areas in cities which suffer underinvestment and deteriorating public services. Poor people without online access become even more marginalised as they have to depend on a fast-reducing paper-based system of banks and benefit offices.
- Societies begin to separate into the 'online' and 'offline'. The poor who are 'offline' lack the skills, knowledge and equipment to access ICT. Services are increasingly delivered 'online'. People without internet access can face extra costs and barriers.
- At the extreme, the poor can be denied physical access, as some roads in cities become accessible only to those who have paid for the necessary electronic devices within their cars. Fragmentation is intensified by gated communities: online 'privatopias' from which all others are excluded.

This is a perspective on the effects of technology on spatial dimensions in the world economy, which contrasts with the widely held view that new technologies are making traditional geographical barriers meaningless, bringing the 'death of distance' or the 'end of geography'. 'Cyberspace' is popularly believed to be reducing the familiar physical and economic fragmentation of the world economy, but there is an alternative logic which suggests that in reality new technologies may be increasing polarisation in the world economy. This has both economic and social implications.

Not all is negative, however, and policy-makers will need to take this into account. There are forces which can be harnessed to build on the positive aspects of new technologies. International institutions have become aware of the possible negative effects of the digital divide, and are taking steps to open up new possibilities for poorer countries, and for the poor within those countries. New technologies have the potential to create jobs, improve access to basic services, and increase the effectiveness of governments. Even people living in the remotest areas of the globe can be brought in if they have the necessary resources.

Current initiatives

These are three of the current initiatives being developed within the World Bank, IMF and UNDP. They have websites which can be accessed for further information.

- The netaid.org community. Under the sponsorship of the UNDP, this is an internet-based interactive constituency for development. It was set up in 1999 in partnership with Cisco Systems. At present it has a membership of 2500 NGOs, 400 corporate, and 25 000 individual members.
- The Digital Opportunities Task Force is a partnership between G-8 countries, NGOs, the private sector and developing countries. It was set up in 2000 after the G-8 summit in Okinawa, Japan. It sets out specifically to reduce the digital divide by lowering costs and improving access in the developing world, and encouraging developing and transition economies to participate in business-to-business electronic commerce.
- The WIDE initiative. The UNDP launched the Web of Information for Development (2001). It provides online databases, a discussion forum, and supports partnerships in exporting new technologies. It can be accessed on **www.undp.org/tcdc**.

Money laundering and illicit trafficking

At the G-7 summit in Paris in 1989, the Financial Action Task Force (FATF) was set up to examine measures which could reduce or eliminate terrorist and criminal money moving across national boundaries. The task force comprises delegates from 29 national governments, the European Union and the Gulf Co-operation Council. After the events of 11 September 2001, an extraordinary meeting of the FATF was held, and agreed a new plan of action directed in particular at terrorist financing.

FATF members, who are mainly western and southern hemisphere industrialised countries, plus China, Hong Kong and Singapore, have agreed:

- to make laundering the proceeds of drug trafficking and other serious international crimes a criminal offence;
- to make it mandatory for financial institutions to identify their customers and report unusual or suspicious transactions. The focus is large currency exchanges involving domestic and foreign currency.

Illicit financial transactions have the potential to destabilise the international financial system. By definition, there are no reliable estimates of the scale, sources and destinations of such flows, but the impact of money laundering on the 'real' economy can be extensive. In Colombia in the 1980s, the influx of money from the drugs trade contributed to inflationary pressures, especially in the construction sector of the economy. In Mexico, it is known that money from the drugs trade has financed important construction projects. There have been dramatic increases in the prices of land in certain cities in Latin America, in consequence of money laundering.

Financial liberalisation in the world economy has undoubtedly given a boost to money laundering, aided by the growth of electronic commerce. Private banking appears to be particularly vulnerable to money laundering. Financial assets can easily be transferred from one individual to another, and the identity of the owner concealed. It can be difficult to specify an owner when the owner's identity is concealed by a company or trust, or by an intermediary such as a lawyer or accountant. Even well-established banks do not know on whose behalf they are carrying out financial transactions. Connections between beneficial owners and certain legal entities are easily obscured.

FATF members are expected to exercise control over non-bank financial intermediaries such as stockbrokers, insurance companies, bureaux de change and money transfer companies. It is at this level that member countries have found the greatest degree of difficulty in implementing regulations against money laundering.

The main problems of money laundering, however, lie not with FATF members, but with countries outside FATF which refuse to co-operate in measures to reduce money laundering. In July 2000, FATF issued a blacklist of non-co-operating countries. There were 23 countries on the list. The action proved remarkably effective, as the FATF members threatened countermeasures against blacklisted countries. Russia and the Philippines, still blacklisted, enacted significant anti-money-laundering legislation and avoided the countermeasures. Hungary, Israel, Lebanon and St Kitts and Nevis were also removed from the list after taking appropriate action. But two new countries were added to the list: Grenada and Ukraine. The blacklist as of 21 June 2002 is shown in Table 15.2.

The FATF blacklist has been so effective that it is perhaps surprising that under IMF and World Bank pressure, the blacklist of 'dirty money' havens was temporarily suspended in 2002. No new countries are to be added to the 15 non-complying countries already on the list. One reason for the suspension of the list is that important OECD-based hedge funds and offshore banking centres operate in these countries and it has been argued that greater transparency would destroy business. The US Treasury has tended to support the offshore banking lobby, though perspectives have changed since 11 September 2001. The IMF and the World Bank have also argued that a softer 'co-operative' approach to blacklisted countries could be underpinned by making regulations against money laundering a condition for access to IMF/World Bank lending.

Table 15.2 FATF non-co-operating countries (21 June 2002)

In alphabetical order

1 Cook Islands	6 Indonesia	11 Niue
2 Dominica	7 Marshall Islands	12 The Philippines
3 Egypt	8 Myanmar	13 Russia
4 Grenada	9 Nauru	14 St Vincent and the Grenadines
5 Guatemala	10 Nigeria	15 Ukraine

New biotechnology and trade

Biotechnology is the application of science and technology to any living organism. Included in trade are such things as vaccines, cultures, hormones and bio-technological processes. It is the fastest-growing area of scientific innovation in the world economy, covering pharmaceuticals, cloning and xenotransplantation, diagnostics, testing, genetically modified seeds and GM foods.

The big breakthrough, 'new' biotechnology has come about through DNA coding. Techniques are now available to genetically modify food and crops. This is likely to have a significant impact on agriculture worldwide because genes can be used to help food crops tolerate drought. The yield of crops can be increased through gene manipulation. Genetic controls can be placed on plants and on animals. We are all familiar with the cloning of Dolly the sheep at the Roslin Institute in Edinburgh. DNA vaccines are being developed for a variety of livestock diseases.

DNA technology also has great potential for pharmaceuticals worldwide. Information provided by the human genome is helping in the design and development of drugs. Vaccines for AIDS, malaria and heart disease depend crucially on DNA technology. Biotechnology may also be used to modify those organisms which spread diseases such as mosquitos, parasites and vermin.

Public fear and commercial interests

The new biotechnology has proved to be a very sensitive social and political issue. Concerns which have dominated the headlines include biodiversity, the labelling of GM foods, the use of genetic information and the ethics of cloning. These concerns have spilled over into international trade. For example, in 1996 US exports of soya to the EU for the first time contained genetically modified soybeans. GM soybeans have already been criticised for their possible environmental consequences. There followed an acrimonious public debate in EU countries on the pros and cons of GM foods, with policy on the marketing of GM soya being left to the discretion of individual countries. EU countries as a whole do not offer strong support for GM crops and GM foods as compared with the US (Figure 15.4). 'When highly mobilised and vociferous communities promote their views and values world-wide, the local roots of their preferences can end up having global reach, influencing communities that may face very different trade-offs' (United Nations, 2001).

The UNDP sums up the present dilemma over biotechnology in the world economy by saying that the views of certain countries may not be in the best interests of other countries. The UNDP report quotes the Nigerian Minister of Agriculture who argues that DNA technology and its ability to provide herbicide tolerance, or resistance to insects and disease, holds great promise for Africa: 'We don't want to be denied this technology because of a misguided notion that we don't understand its future consequences.'

The implications of new biotechnology for world trade are as yet unclear. It appears that the international economy must be prepared for the possibility that

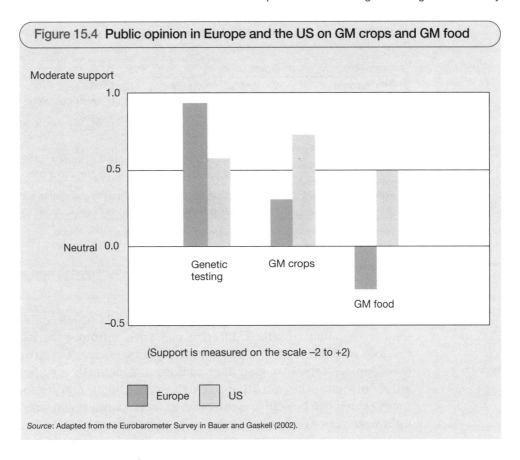

Figure 15.4 Public opinion in Europe and the US on GM crops and GM food

(Support is measured on the scale –2 to +2)

Europe   US

Source: Adapted from the Eurobarometer Survey in Bauer and Gaskell (2002).

countries will make different choices in relation to DNA technology. Countries weigh costs and benefits very differently. People have different attitudes to taking risks, and differ, of course, in their capability for dealing with unintended negative outcomes.

Developed country populations on the whole tend to have a more sceptical attitude to emerging biotechnology because:

● public confidence in developed countries has been undermined by well-publicised disasters such as 'mad cow disease' in the UK and there is little trust in health and environmental regulations;

● the public in developed countries is aware that commercial interests have often overstated the benefits of genetically modified organisms;

● some lobbies in developed countries use public fear of genetically modified products to protect domestic markets. Farmers in continental Europe have used the possibility of genes invading non-targeted crops to lobby for trade protection.

The possibility that countries will make different choices about biotechnology, based on differing assessments of risk and return, is something which is likely to feature strongly on the international agenda in the future.

Table 15.3 Approaches to GM crops in international trade

Approach	Trade policy
Promotional	No restrictions on imports of modified seeds or plant materials. Genetically modified crops used to lower costs and boost exports.
Permissive	Imports and exports follow WTO rules, whether modified or unmodified.
Precautionary	Imports of modified seeds and plant materials restricted. Careful labelling required for modified foods and other commodities.
Preventative	Imports of genetically modified seeds and plants prohibited. Non-modified exports sold at a premium to niche markets.

Source: Adapted from UNDP *Human Development Report* (2001) p. 71, based on Paarlberg (2000).

Table 15.3 presents a useful typology of the way in which countries could tailor their trade policy to reflect different countries' attitudes to risk and return. At the foot of Table 15.3 is a preventative policy stance. Countries which adopt this approach refuse to open their markets to genetically modified crops. Seizing an opportunity, they also perceive an export niche market for non-modified foods, which can be sold at a premium to more cautious consumers. Preventative policy stances are likely to prevail in richer countries. In a poll conducted in 1997, when Europeans were asked who they trusted to provide information about new technologies, the majority favoured the environmental agencies. Public authorities and industry were not trusted to tell the truth about GM crops.

The other end of the spectrum in Table 15.3 represents countries which adopt a promotional stance towards GM crops. Not only are they happy to admit imports of genetically modified foods, but they also see the technology as paving the way for cost reductions which can be translated into exports. Two countries which come into this category are Argentina and Egypt. Argentina has been exporting GM products since the mid-1990s. Egypt has now moved from research to producing commercial GM crops.

Table 15.3 has the merit of showing intermediate policy stances which countries can adopt towards GM technologies. The permissive and precautionary policies are typical of the way many countries are obliged to make choices, weighing up relative costs and benefits. Following WTO standards is only one of the options available. Countries, particularly in the developed world, place a great deal of faith in guidelines drawn up by their own national agencies. It is generally believed that they have greater awareness of local agricultural and environmental conditions. National regulatory systems have the disadvantage, of course, of being able to operate in restraint of trade. Are the safeguards they insist upon justified

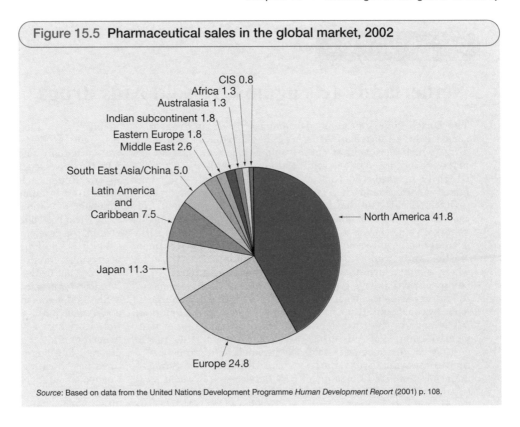

Figure 15.5 Pharmaceutical sales in the global market, 2002

Source: Based on data from the United Nations Development Programme *Human Development Report* (2001) p. 108.

in terms of biosafety or food safety, or is their true intention to restrict trade from foreign producers?

Biotechnology applications in healthcare are also wide-ranging, from vaccines and medicines through to diagnostics and gene therapy. The debates here are dominated by the interests of richer countries. Few developing countries have the research capacity to make an independent contribution, or the income to enter the market as a purchaser of goods and services. Pharmaceutical sales which follow on from research and development are highly concentrated in rich countries (Figure 15.5).

The problem which biotechnology represents for the international community is that it does not address the needs of the majority of the world's population who live in poor countries. This is because research and development is driven by the need for firms to gain a competitive advantage in the world economy. Why should an international pharmaceutical company research a product – AIDS drugs, for instance – which can only be sold in quantities to governments who are spending less than a dollar a month per head of the population on healthcare? One way round this problem is for the international pharmaceutical companies to sell their drugs more cheaply in poor countries than in the US and Europe, but as Case Study 15.2 indicates, this strategy is not without its problems.

CASE STUDY 15.2

Netherlands acts against re-sold Aids drugs

The Dutch government is to recall a large batch of Aids drugs which were sold at cut-price rates in Africa and illegally re-exported to the lucrative European market.

Dutch officials said that more than 35 000 packets of pills with a market value of close to €15m (£9.5m) had been re-sold in the Netherlands and Germany, where a similar investigation is being conducted. Two types of Aids drugs were involved, both made by GlaxoSmithKline.

The case is the first documented example of Aids drugs destined for Africa being re-sold in Europe and threatens to undermine efforts to establish two different price levels for the developed and developing worlds for Aids drugs.

In the face of huge popular and political pressure, pharmaceutical companies have substantially cut the prices of Aids drugs in developing countries over the last two years.

The companies have protested that, if the profitability of their Aids drugs in wealthy markets such as the US and Europe was damaged by cheap drugs flowing back from Africa, they would reduce research into new therapies for Aids.

GSK, the Anglo-American pharmaceuticals group which is the leading producer of Aids drugs, said: 'We are appalled to see that this is occuring illegally and depriving treatment for the people in Africa for whom they were intended.'

The company said it remained committed to its scheme of lower priced Aids drugs in Africa and was co-operating with the authorities in the Netherlands and Germany.

The Dutch Health Supervisory Service said it would recall 3,600 packets of GSK's Combivir and 2,400 packets of Epivir, both of which sell for about €400 per 60-pill packet.

The bulk of the drugs had originally been sold in Senegal, Congo Brazzaville and Ivory Coast. Germany and the Netherlands are two of the highest-priced drugs markets in Europe.

A spokesman said that the Dutch judicial authorities were to prosecute the individuals involved. It is illegal to import drugs into an EU country which were originally sold outside the EU. It is believed the discovery of the drugs, which can be identified by checking batch numbers, followed a tip-off.

Jo Nickolls, policy adviser at Oxfam, the development charity, said: 'It is shocking that people are trying to profit from reduced priced Aids drugs which were intended for people in Africa.'

She said it was important that a system be put in place to allow tiered pricing of Aids drugs to function. This would include different labelling for drugs destined for Africa and more rigorous implementation by developed country governments of laws on illegal reimporting.

According to a United Nations report published earlier this year, there are 28.5m people in sub-Saharan Africa with HIV/Aids. However, only 30 000 of them – about 0.1 per cent – receive the anti-retroviral drugs that have made Aids a treatable disease in western countries.

Source: Geoff Dyer, Financial Times, 3 October 2002. Reprinted with permission.

Comment on case study 15.2

New anti-retroviral drugs provide a treatment for AIDS, but very few receive drug treatment because of the high cost of drugs. Pharmaceutical companies have been under pressure to cut the price of drugs which they sell in developing countries. Tiered pricing allows this to take place. High prices in developing country markets provide the profits out of which pharmaceutical companies can finance research and development. The drugs are supplied to poor countries at a significantly lower price.

The system is undermined if drugs originally sold at cut-price rates in Africa are re-exported to Europe. This has happened with types of AIDS drugs exported by GlaxoSmithKline (GSK). Drugs originally supplied to Senegal, Congo Brazzaville and Ivory Coast have been smuggled back to the Netherlands and Germany.

The UN has argued that educating consumers and purchasing agencies on the reasons for different prices in the developing world could build understanding and acceptance of the tiered system.

Summary

- There have been important shifts in trade, finance and technology, with important implications for the international economy.

- Global electronic commerce offers the possibility of 'trade without borders'. There are static gains via specialisation and exchange, and dynamic gains measurable as productivity increases. But there are enhanced risks in terms of commercial security.

- Digitised goods and services can be easily copied and distributed. This gives rise to problems associated with intellectual property. There is the requirement to balance the private interest, rewarding those who research and develop new goods and services, with the public need for knowledge and information.

- The downside of new digital technologies is the digital divide. New technologies can increase polarisation in the world economy. Societies can separate, with communities being 'online' and 'offline'.

- There are initiatives in the World Bank and UNDP to narrow the digital divide. They are based on the view that new technologies have the potential to increase jobs, improve education and training, and even increase the effectiveness of governments in poor countries.

- Money laundering and illicit trafficking have the potential to destabilise the international financial system. Countries outside the FATF system, which refuse to co-operate in measures to reduce money laundering, have been blacklisted since July 2000.

- The new biotechnology, based on DNA coding, is likely to have significant implications for world trade. For example, EU countries, as a whole, do not support the import of GM crops and GM foods. Countries are likely to tailor their trade policies to reflect different attitudes to risk and return.

Key concepts

- Electronic commerce
- Digital divide
- Digitised goods and services
- Intellectual property
- TRIPS and WIPO

- 'Balancing the concerns of all parties'
- Money laundering
- Illicit trafficking
- 'New' biotechnology

Questions for discussion

1 Three-quarters of internet users live in OECD countries, which contain only 14 per cent of the world's population. What are the implications of this statistic for electronic commerce?

2 How significant is the digital divide in the world economy? Have new technologies increased polarisation?

3 Technology is a tool for development, but is also a source of competitive advantage in the global economy. Can the two functions ever be reconciled?

4 Why are measures to reduce money laundering so difficult to implement?

5 It has been reported that 30 per cent of EU consumers oppose GM foods. What are the implications for international trade?

6 Pharmaceutical companies fear cut-price drugs could be re-imported into their primary markets. Why are they worried? Should we be worried? What, if anything, can be done to reduce re-imports?

Suggested reading

Bauer, M. W. and Gaskell, G. (2002) *Biotechnology: The Making of a Global Controversy*, Cambridge: Cambridge University Press.

Financial Action Task Force on Money Laundering (2002) *Annual Report 2001–2002*, Paris: FATF.

Organisation for Economic Co-operation and Development (2002) *The Economic Consequences of Terrorism*, Paris: OECD.

Paarlberg, R.L. (2000) 'Governing the GM Crop Revolution: Policy Choices for Developing Countries', in *Food, Agriculture and Environment*, Discussion Paper 33, Washington, DC: International Food Policy Research Institute.

Smarzynska, B. K. (2002) *Composition of Foreign Direct Investment and Protection of Intellectual Property Rights: Evidence from Transition Economies*, World Bank Working Paper, Washington: World Bank.

National Research Council (2002) *The Digital Dilemma: Intellectual Property in the Information Age*, at **www.nap.edu/html/digital_dilemma**, accessed November.

United Nations (2002) *Human Development Report 2001: Making New Technologies Work for Human Development*, published for the United Nations Development Programme (UNDP) New York and Oxford: UNDP.

Websites

- OECD: **www.oecd.org**
- WIPO: **www.wipo.org**

The geometry of trade

Chapter 2 (Figure 2.1) used a simple geometric exposition to demonstrate the gains from trade. It was based on two goods (wheat and cloth) produced in country A, and employed the concepts of the community indifference curve, the production possibility frontier, and the terms of trade between wheat and cloth. It showed how the gains from specialisation and exchange in a post-trade situation could put country A on a new indifference curve where it was able to enjoy a higher level of real income.

The advantage of using that particular geometric technique is that the building blocks are usually very familiar to students who have taken an introductory course in economics. The geometric devices of indifference curves, production possibility curves, and domestic and international price lines form part of the tool-box of elementary economics. There are, however, other simple geometric devices which provide students of international economics with scope for stating and developing the pure theory of trade. These techniques form the subject matter of this appendix. The advantages which geometry has over words are principally those of providing clarity and precision to abstract thought. But the pure theory of trade, whether expressed in an algebraic form (system of equations) or by geometry, is not a branch of mathematics. It is the underlying economic ideas which are important.

The offer curve

Figure 2.1 showing the gains from trade illustrated how country A specialised in and exchanged cloth with country B, in response to changes in the relative prices of wheat and cloth brought about by the opening up of the two countries to international trade. Both countries were able to take advantage of the more favourable international price ratio, as compared with domestic prices in the autarky (no-trade) equilibrium. The analysis was underpinned by the theory of comparative advantage.

An alternative geometric way of setting out the free trade equilibrium is to use 'offer curves' for country A and country B. This is a technique with a long history in economics, going back to the 'reciprocal demand and supply curves' in Alfred Marshall's *Pure Theory of Foreign Trade*, published in 1879. The novelty of the offer curve approach is the way in which relative prices are expressed as rays from the origin. In principle, there is an infinite number of possible rays (combinations of relative prices). Three sets of relative prices are illustrated in Figure A.1, Op^1, Op^2, and Op^3. They represent the 'terms of trade', showing how much of its export good a country needs to supply for any given amount of imports.

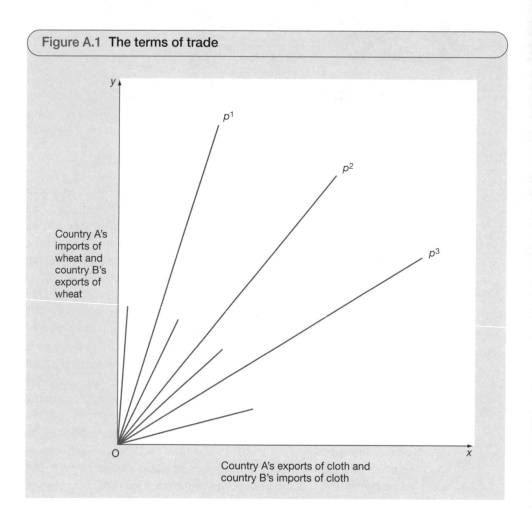

Figure A.1 The terms of trade

The pure trade model assumes, for simplicity, only two countries and two commodities being traded. In Figure A.1, country A, on the basis of comparative advantage, exports cloth. Country B exports wheat. A's export good, cloth, is measured on the horizontal axis, Ox. B's export good, wheat, is measured on the vertical axis, Oy. Axis Oy also shows country A's imports of wheat, which are identical to country B's exports of wheat. Likewise axis Ox shows country A's exports of cloth as being identical to country B's imports of cloth.

Assume now that the terms of trade for country A, which exports cloth, improve. The terms of trade become steeper. They move from Op^3 to Op^2. More wheat is obtained by country A for a given quantity of cloth exports. Of course, this means that country B's terms of trade deteriorate. Country B would gain from a change in the terms of trade from Op^1 to Op^2, giving up less wheat in exchange for a given amount of cloth.

Into the discussion we can now introduce the offer curve (Figure A.2). Country A's offer curve represents the quantity of export goods (cloth) which it is willing

Figure A.2 The offer curve

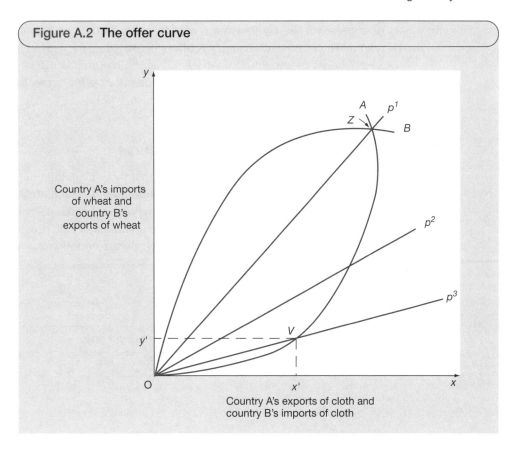

to exchange for import goods (wheat) at the various terms of trade. OA is the offer curve for country A. Each point on the offer curve represents the quantity of cloth which A is willing to exchange for imports of wheat. At point V, A's offer curve indicates that country A is willing to exchange Ox^1 of cloth for Oy^1 of wheat. Its willingness to trade cloth for wheat is a function of the terms of trade. At V, the terms of trade are measured by the slope of Op^3.

If A's terms of trade improve, i.e. if the relative price line becomes steeper, then A will be willing to offer more cloth for a larger quantity of imports. But note that as A gets more and more wheat, it becomes less and less willing to give up cloth for wheat. The offer curve starts to bend upwards because of the decline (relatively speaking) in the marginal utility of wheat. Wheat becomes relatively less desirable as its availability in relation to cloth increases.

The same analysis can be applied to country B, whose offer curve is represented by OB. The post-trade equilibrium can only be the point where the amount of cloth which country A offers in exchange for a given quantity of wheat is equal to the quantity of cloth which country B is willing to accept in exchange for the given quantity of wheat. Only where the two offer curves intersect at point Z in Figure A.2 is this condition fulfilled.

Op^1 represents the equilibrium terms of trade. At the equilibrium terms of trade the amount of cloth which country A offers in exchange for a given quantity of wheat is exactly equal to the amount of wheat which country B offers in exchange for a given amount of cloth. At any other point, on either offer curve, the terms of trade will fail to clear the market. This clearly is the case at V.

The box diagram and the contract curve

What are the reasons for differences in comparative advantage between countries? Chapter 2 pp. 22–5 set out the Heckscher–Ohlin model, which attributes differences in comparative advantage cost to different factor endowments between countries. The box diagram is another simple geometric technique which provides a convenient and precise way of depicting the role which factor endowments play in the pure theory of trade.

Figure A.3 The isoquant curve and the iso-cost line

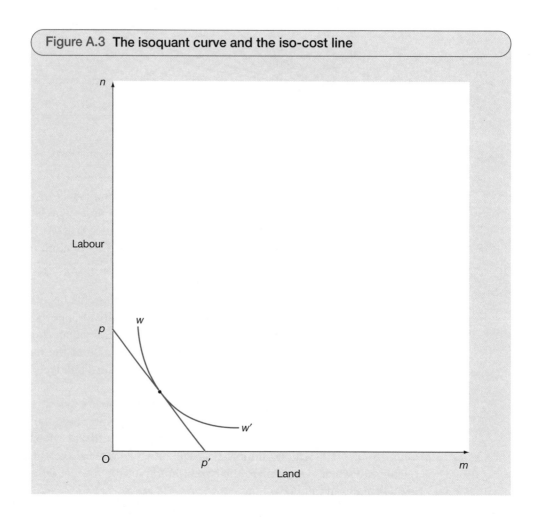

The starting point is the concept of the isoquant (Figure A.3). On represents labour inputs, Om represents land or natural resources inputs. The curve ww' is the isoquant for wheat production, showing the inputs of labour and land needed to produce a given output of wheat. The least cost combination of factor inputs for wheat production is at the point of tangency between a given iso-cost line, pp', and the isoquant. At this point, for wheat production, the relative cost of land and labour inputs, the slope of pp', equals the ratio of marginal physical product of land and labour, the slope of ww'. Similar isoquants and iso-cost lines can be derived for cloth production.

Turning now to the box diagram (Figure A.4), the dimensions of the box $OMO'N$ represent amounts of labour and land in country B. The vertical sides of the box measure the labour endowment of country B, and the horizontal sides of the box the land endowment of country B. The diagonal OO' indicates the relative factor intensity of country B. Any point inside the box represents a given combination of labour and land inputs.

We begin by assuming that country B is in a no-trade situation, producing cloth and wheat from a combination of its labour and land endowments. Cloth output is measured from the origin at O'. Wheat output is measured from the origin at O. Any point within the box represents a given combination of wheat and cloth.

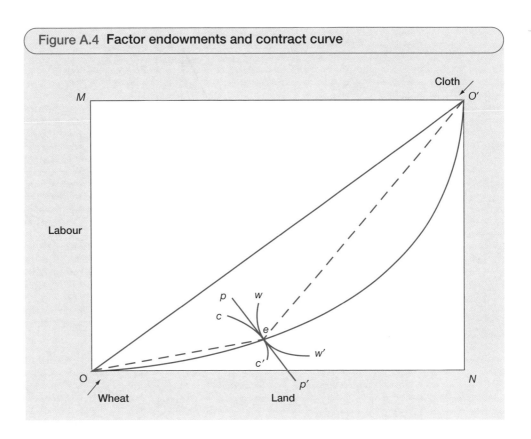

Figure A.4 **Factor endowments and contract curve**

A curve is drawn up, the contract curve (drawn as a solid line), which represents all the efficient combinations of outputs and inputs. In principle there is an infinite number of combinations of inputs of labour and land, and outputs of cloth and wheat. Only two are drawn: cc' represents the isoquant for cloth, ww' represents the isoquant for wheat. Point e is the highest achievable combination of wheat and cloth. The precise combination of wheat and cloth is dictated by consumers, i.e. as indicated by their preferences. At e the factor price ratio is pp'. The dotted line $O'e$ represents the factor intensity of cloth production, and the dotted line Oe represents the factor intensity of wheat production. The different slopes of the dotted lines indicate that wheat is the land-intensive product, cloth is the labour-intensive product.

We can now reintroduce country A into the analysis, assuming that country B, as a potential trading partner, has different factor endowments from country A (Figure A.5).

Superimpose country A's box on that of country B, giving it different horizontal and vertical dimensions. Assume country A has a greater endowment of labour relative to land than country B. This means that country A's box can be represented by the box $OHO''M$. The diagonal OO'' is steeper than B's diagonal OO'. A's contract

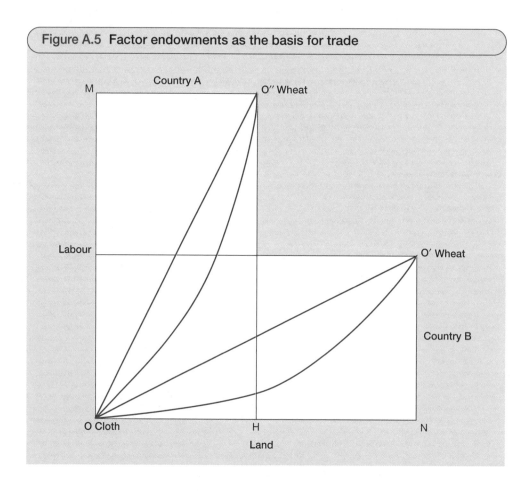

Figure A.5 Factor endowments as the basis for trade

curve is also steeper than B's. This is because country A's producers use more labour inputs relative to land inputs than country B at the least-cost equilibria on their isoquant curves. This is the source of country A's comparative advantage in cloth which is the labour-intensive good. By the same reasoning, B is a country with relatively abundant supplies of land. This is the source of country B's comparative advantage in wheat which is the land-intensive good. In the post-trade situation, A exports cloth in exchange for wheat.

Different factor endowments have provided the basis for trade between country A and country B.

Remember, it is the assumption of the H–O model that country A and country B have identical production functions (same shaped isoquants) for the same commodity, cloth or wheat. It is factor endowments which differ between country A and country B and provide the basis for trade.

Making use of the internet

Getting started

There is a large amount of very useful material on the internet, but the student might find the task of trying to locate it a daunting one.

The first step is to go to a search engine. These include **www.google.com**, **www.lycos.co.uk**, **www.ask.co.uk**, **www.yahoo.com**, and many more. Type in phrases such as *balance of payments* or *transition economies* and you will be given links to a number of useful sites.

PDF file format

PDF is a file format that allows entire publications to be compressed into very small downloadable files that can be read and printed in the 'Adobe Acrobat Reader' program available at **www.adobe.com**. When looking on the internet for economics-related information, much of what you will find is in this file format, especially statistical publications and working papers.

Some useful sites

This range of sites is small in relation to the huge number that are available. Here are the sites which are most useful, along with a comment on their contents.

- **www.wto.org** – The World Trade Organisation website is an important location for information on international trade agreements and the WTO agenda.
- **www.imf.org** – The International Monetary Fund website is one of the most useful, with important economic data. It also gives access to the IMF Staff Papers in PDF format, which are the working papers most frequently cited in this book.
- **www.worldbank.org** – The World Bank site provides news and views as well as a selection of working papers and research conducted by their acclaimed economists.
- **www.un.org** – The United Nations site provides development indicators and other material (see particularly the United Nations Development Programme site).
- **www.oecd.org** – The OECD site provides economic data on OECD countries, along with a very wide range of materials on topics which range from agriculture to money laundering and biotechnology.

- **www.ezb.de** – The European Central Bank site provides European Union statistics, and keeps us informed about interest rates in the euroarea, the value of the euro, and EU balance of payments figures.
- **www.statistics.gov.uk** – This site is not specifically related to economics but has many statistics about the UK economy, particularly public sector spending and UK balance of payments figures.
- **econpapers.hhs.se** – A selection of online economic journals and working papers. Some articles and journals are free to download, some are available on subscription or free only in developing or transition economies. The site has a search facility, or there is the option of browsing through the available publications.
- **www.economy.com/free lunch** – Free access to over 900 000 economic and financial data series.
- **www.sosig.ac.uk/eurostudies** – Free searchable and browsable database of European Studies resources.

Finding economic information and data on the internet need not be difficult. Most of the information is free and available for use. There is also the option of subscribing to online electronic journals, which are also available online in university libraries. The internet is most useful as a source of information on all aspects of the world economy, so make use of it!

Bibliography

At the end of each chapter can be found a list of further reading appropriate to the particular subject matter of that chapter. The references listed in this section are divided into three groups.

- *General reading* comprises a selection of books and articles which take the discipline of international economics forward in some important respects.
- *Research* lists some theoretical and empirical articles from the IMF and World Bank. These articles are at the 'frontier' of the discipline and are likely to be of interest to students thinking about studying international economics at a higher level. They can be downloaded from the web.
- Under *Publications of international organisations* are listed major official publications which appear on a quarterly or annual basis.

Web references are listed separately in Appendix B.

General reading

Baldwin, R. E. (1987) 'The political economy of trade policy', *Journal of Economic Perspectives*, vol. 3, no. 4, pp. 119–35.

Barbone, L. and Zalduendo, J. (1996) *EU Accession and Economic Growth: The Challenge for Central and Eastern European Countries*, Washington, DC: World Bank.

Bauer, M. W. and Gaskell, G. (2002) *Biotechnology: The Making of a Global Controversy*, Cambridge: Cambridge University Press.

Bhagwati, J. N. (1981) *International Trade: Selected Readings*, Cambridge, MA: MIT Press.

Bhagwati, J. N. (1988) 'Export promoting trade strategy', *World Bank Research Observer*, vol. 3, no. 1, pp. 27–57.

Bhagwati, J. N. (1997) 'The global age: from a sceptical south to a fearful north', *The World Economy*, vol. 20, no. 3, pp. 259–83.

Brander, J. and Spencer, B. (1981) 'Tariffs and the extraction of foreign monopoly rents under potential entry', *Canadian Journal of Economics*, vol. 14, no. 3, pp. 371–89.

Burenstam Linder, S. (1961) *An Essay on Trade and Transformation*, New York: John Wiley.

Cassel, G. (1928) *Post-War Monetary Stabilisation*, New York: Colombia University Press.

Claessens, S., Dooley, M. P. and Warner, A. (1995) 'Portfolio capital flows: hot or cold?' *World Bank Economic Review*, vol. 9, no. 1, pp. 153–74.

Corden, W. M. (1971) *The Theory of Protection*, Oxford: Clarendon Press.

Corden, W. M. (1974) *Trade Policy and Economic Welfare*, Oxford: Clarendon Press.

De Melo, J. and Panagariya, A. (1992) 'The new regionalism', *Finance and Development*, December, pp. 37–40.

Deardorff, A. V. (1984) 'Testing trade theories and predicting trade flows', in R. W. Jones and P. B. Kenen, eds, *Handbook of International Economics*, vol. 1, Chapter 10, Amsterdam: North Holland.

Dollar, D. (1992) 'Outward-orientated developing economies really do grow more rapidly', *Economic Development and Cultural Change*, pp. 523–43, Chicago: University of Chicago Press.

Dornbusch, R. (1976) 'Expectations and exchange rate dynamics', *Journal of Political Economy*, vol. 84, pp. 1161–76.

Dornbusch, R. (1992) 'The case for trade liberalization in developing countries', *Journal of Economic Perspectives*, vol. 6, no. 1, pp. 69–85.

Dunning, J. H. (1981) *International Production and the Multinational Enterprise*, London: George Allen and Unwin.

Eichengreen, B., Masson, P. *et al.* (1999) 'Transition strategies and nominal anchors on the road to greater exchange-rate flexibility', *Essays in International Finance* 213, Princeton: Princeton University Printing Services.

Findlay, R. and Lundahl, M. (1994) 'Natural resources, "vent for surplus", and the staples theory', in G. Meier, ed., *From Classical Economics to Development Economics*, Aldershot: Edward Elgar Publishers.

Fischer, S. (2001) 'Ten years of transition: looking back and looking forward', *IMF Staff Papers*, vol. 48 (special edition).

Foreman-Peck, J. (1983) *A History of the World Economy: International Economic Relations Since 1850*, Brighton: Wheatsheaf.

Gardner, R. N. (1956) *Sterling-dollar diplomacy in current perspective*, Oxford: Oxford University Press, expanded edition with revised introduction (1980) New York: Columbia University Press.

Grossman, G. M. and Rogoff, K. (1995) *Handbook of International Economics*, vol. 3, Amsterdam: Elsevier Science.

Gurley, J. G. and Shaw, E. S. (1995) 'Financial aspects of economic development', *American Economic Review*, vol. XLV, no. 4, pp. 515–38.

Haberler, G. (1936) *The Theory of International Trade*, revised English translation, London: Hodge & Co. Ltd.

Helpman, E. and Krugman, P. (1985) *Market Structure and Foreign Trade: Increasing Returns, Imperfect Competition, and the International Economy*, Cambridge, MA: MIT Press.

Hoekman, B., English, P. and Mattoo, A. (eds) (2002) *Development, Trade, and the WTO, a Handbook*, Washington, DC: World Bank Publications.

Jones, R. W. and Kenen, P. B. (1984) *Handbook of International Economics*, vol. 1, Amsterdam: Elsevier Science.

Joshi, V. (1990) 'Exchange rate regimes in developing countries', in '*Public Policy and Economic Development' Essays in Honour of Ian Little*, Oxford: Clarendon Press.

Kindleburger, C. P. (1973) *International Economics* (5th edn), Homewood, Ill: Irwin.

Krugman, P. (1979) 'Increasing returns, monopolistic competition, and international trade', *Journal of International Economics*, vol. 9, no. 4, pp. 469–79.

Krugman, P. R. (1984) 'Import Protection and Export Promotion: International Competition in the Presence of Oligopoly and Economies of Scale', *Monopolistic Competition and International Trade*, Oxford: Clarendon Press.

Krugman, P. (1995) *Strategic Trade Policy and the New International Economics*, Cambridge, MA: MIT Press.

Lange, O. (1938) *On the Economic Theory of Socialism*, Minneapolis: University of Minnesota.

Leamer, E. and Levinsohn, J. (1995) 'International trade theory: the evidence', in *Handbook of International Economics*, vol. 3, pp. 1339–95, Amsterdam: Elsevier Science.

Leontief, W. W. (1969) 'Domestic production and foreign trade: the American capital position re-examined', in *International Trade: Selected Readings*, Harmondsworth: Penguin Books.

Lewis, W. (1978) *Growth and Fluctuations, 1870–1913*, London: George Allen and Unwin.

List, F. (1856) *National System of Political Economy*, trans. G. A. Matile, Philadelphia: J. B. Lippincott & Co.

Meier, G. M. (1990) 'Trade policy and development', in *'Public Policy and Economic Development': Essays in Honour of Ian Little*, Oxford: Clarendon Press.

Mosley, P. (1987) 'Conditionality as a bargaining process: structural adjustment lending, 1980–1986', *Essays in International Finance*, The Princeton Papers, no. 168, Princeton: Princeton University Press.

Mundell, R. A. (1961) 'The theory of optimum currency areas', *American Economic Review*, no. 51, pp. 717–25.

Myint, H. (1958) 'The classical theory of trade and the underdeveloped countries', *Economic Journal*, vol. LXVIII, pp. 317–37.

Myrdal, G. (1957) *Economic Theory and the Underdeveloped Regions*, London: Gerald Duckworth.

Nurkse, R. (1954) 'International investment today in the light of nineteenth century experience', *Economic Journal*, no. 64, pp. 744–58.

Rodrik, D. (1992) 'Conceptual issues in the design of trade policy for industrialization', *World Development*, vol. 20, no. 3, pp. 309–20.

Rodrik, D. (1992) 'The limits of trade policy reform in developing countries', *Journal of Economic Perspectives*, vol. 6, no. 1, pp. 87–105.

Rodrik, D. (1995) 'Political economy of trade policy', in *Handbook of International Economics*, vol. 3, ch. 28, Amsterdam: Elsevier Science.

Rodrik, D. (1997) *Has Globalization Gone Too Far?*, Washington, DC: Institute for International Economics.

Rogoff, K. S. (2002) 'Why are G-3 exchange rates so fickle?', *Finance and Development*, vol. 39, no. 2, Washington, DC: IMF.

Romer, P. M. (1986) 'Increasing returns and long-run growth', *Journal of Political Economy*, vol. 5, pp. 1002–37.

Rostow, W. W. (1971) *Politics and the Stages of Growth*, Cambridge: Cambridge University Press.

Schuler, K. (1996) *Should Developing Countries Have Central Banks?*, London: Institute of Economic Affairs.

Schwartz, A. J. (1993) *Currency Boards: Their Past, Present, and Possible Future Role*, Carnegie-Rochester Conference Series on Public Policy 39, pp. 147–87, North-Holland: Elsevier Science.

Smith, A. (1976) *The Wealth of Nations*, E. Cannan (ed.) with new preface by George J. Stigler, Chicago: University of Chicago Press.

Srinivasan, T. N. (1999) 'Developing countries in the world trading system: from GATT, 1947, to the third ministerial meeting of WTO, 1999', *World Economy*, vol. 22, no. 8, pp. 1017–65.

Stiglitz, J. E. (1999) *Whither Reform? Ten Years of the Transition*, World Bank Annual Conference on Development Economics, Washington: World Bank.

Stiglitz, J. E. (2002) *Globalization and its Discontents*, London: Allen Lane.

Streeten, P. (1989) 'Interests, ideology and institutions: a review of Bhagwati on protectionism', *World Development*, vol. 17, no. 2, pp. 293–8, Washington, DC: Pergamon.

Taylor, L. (1997) 'The revival of the liberal creed – the IMF and the World Bank in a globalized economy', *World Development*, vol. 25, no. 2, pp. 145–52, Washington DC: Pergamon.

Tobin, J. (1978) 'A proposal for international monetary reform', *Eastern Economic Journal*, no. 4, pp. 153–9.

Vernon, R. (1966) 'International investment and international trade in the product cycle', *Quarterly Journal of Economics*, vol. 80, pp. 190–207.

Wilcox, C. (1947) 'International trade organization: the London draft of a charter for an international trade organization', *American Economic Review*, vol. 37, pp. 529–59.

Williams, J. H. (1929) 'The theory of international trade reconsidered', *Economic Journal*, June, pp. 195–209.

Williamson, J. (1989) 'What Washington means by policy reform', in John Williamson, ed., *Latin American Adjustment: How Much Has Happened?*, Washington, DC: Institute for International Economics.

Winham, G. R. (1998) 'The World Trade Organisation: institution-building in the multilateral trade system', *World Economy*, vol. 21, no. 3, pp. 349–68.

World Bank (2001) *Globalisation, Growth, and Poverty: Building an Inclusive World Economy*, World Bank Policy Report, Oxford: co-publication of the World Bank and Oxford University Press.

World Bank (2001) *Making Trade Work for the World's Poor*, Global Economic Prospects for 2002, Washington: World Bank.

Young, A. (1928) 'Increasing returns and economic progress', *Economic Journal*, December, pp. 527–42.

◯ Research from the World Bank and IMF

Allen, M. and Haas, R. (2001) 'The transition in central and eastern Europe: the experience of two resident representatives', *IMF Staff Papers*, vol. 48 (special edition), pp. 9–28.

Bayoumi, T. and Macdonald, R. (1999) 'Deviations of exchange rates from purchasing power parity: a story featuring two monetary unions', *IMF Staff Papers*, vol. 46, no. 1, pp. 89–102.

Berg, A. and Pattillo, C. (1999) 'Are currency crises predictable? A test', *IMF Staff Papers*, vol. 46, no. 2, pp. 107–38.

Bikhandani, S. and Sharma, S. (2001) 'Herd behaviour in financial markets', *IMF Staff Papers*, vol. 47, no. 3, pp. 279–310.

Bleaney, M. (2001) 'Exchange rate regimes and inflation persistence', *IMF Staff Papers*, vol. 47, no. 3, pp. 387–402.

Choudhri, E. U. and Hakura, D. S. (2000) 'International trade and productivity growth: exploring the sectoral effects for developing countries', *IMF Staff Papers*, vol. 47, no. 1, pp. 30–53.

Dell'Ariccia, G. (1999) 'Exchange rate fluctuations and trade flows: evidence from the European Union', *IMF Staff Papers*, vol. 46, no. 3, pp. 315–34.

Hamman, J. (2001) 'Exchange-rate-based stabilization: a critical look at the stylized facts', *IMF Staff Papers*, vol. 48, no. 1, pp. 111–38.

Havrylyshyn, O. (2001) 'Recovery and growth in transition: a decade of evidence', *IMF Staff Papers*, vol. 48 (special edition), pp. 53–87.

Hoekman, B. (1998) 'Using international institutions to improve public procurement', *World Bank Research Observer*, vol. 13, no. 2, pp. 249–69.

Jonsson, G. and Subramanian, A. (2001) 'Dynamic gains from trade: evidence from South Africa', *IMF Staff Papers*, vol. 48, no. 1, pp. 197–224.

Klugman, J. and Braithwaite, J. (1998) 'Poverty in Russia during the transition: an overview', *World Bank Research Observer*, vol. 13, no. 1, pp. 37–58.

Macdonald, R. and Taylor, M. P. (1992) 'Exchange rate economics: a survey', *IMF Staff Papers*, vol. 39, no. 1, pp. 1–57.

Montiel, P. J. and Ostry, J. D. (1991) 'Macroeconomic implications of real exchange rate targeting in developing countries', *IMF Staff Papers*, vol. 38, no. 4.

Nash, J. and Thomas, V. (1991) 'Reform of trade policy: recent evidence from theory and practice', *World Bank Research Observer*, vol. 6, no. 2, pp. 219–40.

Osband, K. and Van Rijckeghem, C. (2000) 'Safety from currency crashes', *IMF Staff Papers*, vol. 47, no. 2, pp. 238–58.

Roland, G. (2001) 'Ten years after . . . transition and economics', *IMF Staff Papers*, vol. 48 (special edition), pp. 29–52.

Schinasi, G. J. and Todd Smith, R. (2000) 'Portfolio diversification, leverage, and financial contagion', *IMF Staff Papers*, vol. 47, no. 2, pp. 159–76.

Semenick Alam, I. M. and Morrison, A. R. (2000) 'Trade reform dynamics and technical efficiency: the Peruvian experience', *World Bank Economic Review*, vol. 14, no. 2, pp. 309–30.

Smarzynska, B. K. (2002) *Composition of Foreign Direct Investment and Protection of Intellectual property Rights: Evidence from Transition Economies*, World Bank Working Paper, Washington: World Bank.

Steinberg, R. H. (1997) 'Trade-environment negotiations in the EU, NAFTA, and WTO: regional trajectories of rule development', *American Journal of International Law*, vol. 91, pp. 231–67.

Tamirisa, N. T. (1999) 'Exchange and capital controls as barriers to trade', *IMF Staff Papers*, vol. 46, no. 1, pp. 69–88.

Taylor, A. M. and Williamson, J. G. (1994) 'Capital flows to the new world as an intergenerational transfer', *Journal of Political Economy*, vol. 102, no. 2, pp. 95–371.

Vamvakidis, A. (1999) 'Regional trade agreements or broad liberalization: which path leads to faster growth?', *IMF Staff Papers*, vol. 46, no. 1, pp. 42–68.

Publications of international organisations

European Central Bank, *Annual Reports and Monthly Bulletins*, Frankfurt.

International Monetary Fund (IMF), *Finance and Development* (quarterly), Washington, DC.

International Monetary Fund (IMF), *International Financial Statistics Yearbook* (annual), Washington, DC.

Organisation for Economic Co-operation and Development (OECD), *Economic Outlook* (annual), Paris.

Organisation for Economic Co-operation and Development (OECD), *OECD Indicators* (annual), Paris.

United Nations, United Nations Development Programme (UNDP), *Human Development Report* (annual), New York.

World Bank, *Global Development Finance* (annual).

World Bank, *Global Economic Prospects* (annual).

World Bank, *World Development Indicators* (annual).

World Bank, *World Development Report* (annual), (co-publication of the World Bank and Oxford University Press).

Index